Relational Ar Ecologies

Examining the complex social and material relationships between architecture and ecology which constitute modern cultures, this collection responds to the need to extend architectural thinking about ecology beyond current design literatures. This book shows how the 'habitats', 'natural milieus', 'places' or 'shelters' that construct architectural ecologies are composed of complex and dynamic material, spatial, social, political, economic and ecological concerns.

With contributions from a range of leading international experts and academics in architecture, art, anthropology, philosophy, feminist theory, law, medicine and political science, this volume offers professionals and researchers engaged in the social and cultural biodiversity of built environments, new inter-disciplinary perspectives on the relational and architectural ecologies which are required for dealing with the complex issues of sustainable human habitation and environmental action. The book provides:

- sixteen essays, including two visual essays, by leading international experts and academics from the UK, USA, Australia, New Zealand and Europe, including Rosi Braidotti, Lorraine Code, Verena Andermatt Conley and Elizabeth Grosz;
- a clear structure: divided into five parts addressing biopolitical ecologies and architectures; uncertain, anxious and damaged ecologies; economics, land and consumption; biological and medical architectural ecologies; relational ecological practices and architectures;
- an exploration of the relations between human and political life;
- an examination of issues such as climate change, social and environmental wellbeing, land and consumption, economically damaging global approaches to design, community ecologies and future architectural practice.

Peg Rawes is Senior Lecturer at the Bartlett School of Architecture, UCL, London. Her teaching and research focus on interdisciplinary links between architectural design, philosophy, technology and the visual arts. Publications include: *Space, Geometry and Aesthetics* (2008) and *Irigaray for Architects* (2007).

Relational Architectural Ecologies

Architecture, nature and subjectivity

Edited by Peg Rawes

Routledge
Taylor & Francis Group

LONDON AND NEW YORK

First published 2013
by Routledge
2 Park Square, Milton Park, Abingdon, Oxon OX14 4RN

Simultaneously published in the USA and Canada
by Routledge
711 Third Avenue, New York, NY 10017

Routledge is an imprint of the Taylor & Francis Group, an informa business

Cover image credit for paperback edition: Agnes Denes, *Wheatfield – A Confrontation*: Battery Park landfill, Downtown Manhattan – with Agnes Denes standing in the field, 1982. Two acres of wheat planted and harvested by the artist on a landfill in Manhattan's financial district, a block from Wall Street and the World Trade Center, Summer 1982. Commissioned by the Public Art Fund, New York City.

British Library Cataloguing in Publication Data
A catalogue record for this book is available from the British Library

Library of Congress Cataloging in Publication Data
Relational architectural ecologies : architecture, nature and subjectivity / [edited by] Peg Rawes.
pages cm
Includes bibliographical references and index.

1. Architecture–Environmental aspects. 2. Architecture and society. 3. Human ecology. I. Rawes, Peg, editor of compilation.
NA2542.35.R45 2013
720.1'08–dc23

2012049735

ISBN: 978-0-415-50857-5 (hbk)
ISBN: 978-0-415-50858-2 (pbk)
ISBN: 978-0-203-77028-3 (ebk)

Typeset in Univers
by Fakenham Prepress Solutions, Fakenham, Norfolk NR21 8NN

MIX
Paper from
responsible sources
FSC
www.fsc.org   FSC® C013056

Printed and bound in Great Britain by
TJ International Ltd, Padstow, Cornwall

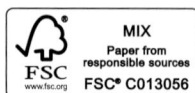

Contents

Contents

Contributors

Anita Berlin has been an inner city GP for over twenty years. She is a Senior Clinical Lecturer at University College London. Her academic interests are medical education, and quality and governance of educational and clinical institutions. Her work focuses on doctor–patient and student–patient relationships, and leadership for learning exploring the practical application of theoretical models to address educational challenges. She is lead for the Social Determinants of Health theme in the curriculum and has worked on international educational development projects principally in Spain and Latin America.

Rosi Braidotti is Distinguished University Professor at Utrecht University and founding Director of the University's Centre for the Humanities. She is the leading feminist poststructuralist and interdisciplinary thinker in Europe whose work examines issues including: new materialisms (including info- and bio-technologies), ecology, nomadic thought, subjectivity and ethics. Her publications include: *Patterns of Dissonance* (Polity Press 1991); *Nomadic Subjects: Embodiment and Sexual Difference in Contemporary Feminist Theory* (Columbia University Press 1994 and 2011); *Metamorphoses: Towards a Materialist Theory of Becoming* (Polity Press 2002); *Transpositions: On Nomadic Ethics* (Polity Press 2006); *Nomadic Theory: The Portable Rosi Braidotti* (Columbia University Press 2011), and *The Posthuman* (Polity Press 2013).

Lorraine Code is Distinguished Research Professor Emerita in Philosophy at York University in Toronto, and a Fellow of the Royal Society of Canada. She is the author of *Epistemic Responsibility* (Brown University Press 1987) and *What Can She Know? Feminist Theory and the Construction of Knowledge* (Cornell University Press 1991). In *Rhetorical Spaces: Essays on Gendered Locations* (Routledge 1995), she addresses incredulity, empathy, relativism and the epistemic power of gossip. *Ecological Thinking: The Politics of Epistemic Location* (Oxford University Press 2006) develops an 'ecological naturalism', which looks to ecological science as a place – literal and metaphorical – where knowledge is 'naturally' made. She is currently working on issues of testimony, ignorance and vulnerability, especially as these pertain to climate-change scepticism. In 2011 she was a Visiting Research Fellow at the Institute for Advanced Study in the Humanities at Edinburgh University.

Verena Andermatt Conley teaches in the Departments of Comparative Literature, and Romance Languages and Literature at Harvard University, Massachusetts. Her recent work deals with critical and cultural theories and their intersections with ecology. Publications include *Rethinking Technologies* (University of Minnesota Press 1993); *Ecopolitics: the Environment in Poststructuralist Thought* (Routledge 1997); *The War against the Beavers: Learning to be Wild in the North Woods* (University of Minnesota Press 2003); and *Spatial Ecologies: Urban Sites, State and World-Space in French Cultural Theory* (Liverpool University Press 2012).

David Cross is an artist and Reader at the University of the Arts, London. Informing his research, practice and teaching is a critical engagement with the relationship between visual culture and the contested ideal of 'sustainable development'. David has given lectures internationally, and chaired events including at the South London Gallery, Tate and Whitechapel. As an artist, he has collaborated with Matthew Cornford since they studied at St Martins School of Art, London, in 1987. David graduated from the Royal College of Art in 1991. The book *Cornford & Cross* (Black Dog Publishing 2009) includes critical essays by John Roberts and Rachel Withers, and sets out a chronology of the artists' projects as a basis for examining the aesthetic and ethical concerns of their practice. Cornford and Cross respond to the intrinsic problems of particular contexts and situations as a way to stimulate discussion on issues of public concern, including environment, development and social justice. (See www.cornfordandcross.com)

Rebecca Empson is a Lecturer in Social Anthropology at UCL, London. She has carried out fieldwork for the past fifteen years among the Buriad in Mongolia. Her recent monograph, *Harnessing Fortune* (OUP 2011), was concerned with the morality of wealth accumulation among nomadic pastoralists along the Mongolian–Russian border. She is currently working on a new project concerned with forms of subjectivity emerging in relation to predicted economic growth in Mongolia as an outcome of recent mineral extraction in the country.

Elizabeth Grosz teaches feminist theory at Duke University, North Carolina, in the Women's Studies Program. She is the author of *Architecture from the Outside* (The MIT Press 2001) and *Chaos, Territory, Art* (Columbia University Press 2008) which both address architecture's relations with philosophy. Her most recent publication on life, politics and art is *Becoming Undone* (Duke 2011).

Bronwyn Hayward is a Senior Lecturer in Political Science at the University of Canterbury NZ. Bronwyn is also a trustee of the Foundation for Democracy and Sustainable Development (London) and visiting fellow of the RESOLVE Research

Group on sustainable lifestyles, values and environment and the Sustainable Lifestyles Research Group, both based at the University of Surrey. Bronwyn is also a co-lead researcher for the Norwegian government funded Voices of the Future about children in a changing climate. Outside her academic work, Bronwyn has worked in children's media, film, television and radio production and served as a member of the New Zealand Broadcasting Standards Authority and is trustee for Life in Vacant Spaces, a trust to develop community, arts and green space in the aftermath of the Christchurch city earthquakes.

Rachel Jones is Assistant Professor in Philosophy at George Mason University, Virginia. She is the author of *Luce Irigaray: Towards a Sexuate Philosophy* (Polity Press 2011) and co-editor of *The Matter of Critique: Readings in Kant's Philosophy* (with Andrea Rehberg, Clinamen Press 2000). She has published articles on Irigaray, Kant, Lyotard and aesthetics, including: 'Adventures in the abyss: Kant, Irigaray and earthquakes' in *Symposium: Canadian Journal of Continental Philosophy* (forthcoming 2013); 'Irigaray and Lyotard: birth, infancy, and metaphysics', in *Hypatia* (2012); and 'Lyotard, Chadwick and the logic of dissimulation' in *Gender after Lyotard* (SUNY 2007).

Katie Lloyd Thomas trained as an architect and is a Lecturer in Architecture at Newcastle University where she has set up a new Masters programme in Architectural Theory and Criticism. She is the editor of *Material Matters: Architecture and Material Practice* (Routledge 2007) and completed her PhD on concepts of materials and the architectural specification at the CRMEP, Middlesex University in 2010. Katie is also a founder member of *taking place*, a group of artists and architects concerned with feminist spatial practice, whose most recent project is a series of artworks 'The other side of waiting' for the Mother and Baby unit at Homerton Hospital, Hackney (see www. takingplace.org.uk). 'The excessive materiality of Stock Orchard Street: towards a feminist material practice' in *Around and About Stock Orchard Street*, edited by Sarah Wigglesworth (Routledge 2011) brings together Katie's main research interests in materiality, the production of building and feminist theory and practice.

Nathan Moore completed a PhD in 2006, at Birkbeck College, School of Law, London, where he is now employed as a law lecturer. In 2012 he began a second PhD at the Bartlett School of Architecture, UCL, London. He has published a number of law related articles under his own name, and in co-authorship with Anne Bottomley of Kent Law School.

Michelle Murphy is a feminist technoscience scholar and historian of the recent past. She is the author of *Sick Building Syndrome and the Problem of Uncertainty* (2006) and *Seizing the Means of Reproduction* (2012), both from Duke University Press. Her current project is called the Economization of Life.

She is Associate Professor of History and Women and Gender Studies at the University of Toronto.

Doina Petrescu is Professor of Architecture and Design Activism at the School of Architecture, University of Sheffield. Her research focuses on three main strands: 'gender', 'resilience' and 'participation' in architecture, all with a strong international dimension. She is also co-founder of *atelier d'architecture autogérée* (aaa), an award winning collective practice conducting research-actions in Paris, which engage citizens in processes of reclaiming and resilient transformation of the city. Her edited publications include: *Trans – Local – Act: Cultural practices within and across* (co-ed., aaa-peprav 2010); *Agency: Working with Uncertain Architectures* (co-ed., Routledge 2009); *Altering Practices: Feminist Politics & Poetics of Space* (Routledge 2007); *Urban Act: handbook for alternative practice* (aaa-peprav 2007); *Architecture and Participation* (co-ed., Spon Press 2005). She is currently working on a book titled *Micropolitics of Architecture*.

Peg Rawes is Senior Lecturer at the Bartlett School of Architecture, UCL, London. Her research has focused on spatiotemporality and embodiment; 'minor' traditions in geometric and spatial thinking; aesthetic and material practices. Publications include: *Space, Geometry and Aesthetics: Through Kant and Towards Deleuze* (Palgrave Macmillan 2008); *Irigaray for Architects* (Routledge 2007); 'Spinoza's Geometric Ecology', *Interstices: Journal of Architecture and Related Arts* (December 2012); 'Spinoza's architectural passages and geometric comportments', in B. Lord (ed.) *Spinoza Beyond Philosophy* (University of Edinburgh 2012); 'Sonic Envelopes', *The Senses and Society*, 3, 1 (2008).

Gail Schwab is Professor of French at Hofstra University, New York, where she also serves as Senior Associate Dean for Curriculum and Personnel in the Hofstra College of Liberal Arts and Sciences. Recent articles on Irigaray include: 'Mothers, sisters, and daughters: Luce Irigaray and the female genealogical line in the stories of the Greeks', in E. Tzelepis and A. Athanasiou (eds) *Rewriting Difference: Luce Irigaray and "the Greeks"* (SUNY Press 2008); and 'Beyond the vertical and the horizontal: spirituality, space, and alterity in the work of Luce Irigaray', in M.C. Rawlinson, S.L. Hom and S.J. Khader (eds) *Thinking with Irigaray* (SUNY Press 2011). She has also translated the major Irigaray collection, *To Speak is Never Neutral* (Continuum 2002). Gail is collaborating on an edited anthology of articles on Irigaray and pursuing her new-found research interest in sustainability and food studies.

Kate Soper is Emerita Professor of Philosophy attached to the Institute for the Study of European Transformations at London Metropolitan University, and a Visiting Humanities Professor at Brighton University. She has published widely on environmental philosophy, aesthetics of nature, theory of needs and consumption, and cultural theory. Her more recent writings include *What is*

Nature? Culture, Politics and the Non-Human (Blackwell 1995), *To Relish the Sublime: Culture and Self-Realisation in Postmodern Times* (with Martin Ryle, Verso 2002); *Citizenship and Consumption* (co-ed., Palgrave 2007) and *The Politics and Pleasures of Consuming Differently* (co-ed., Palgrave 2008). Her study on 'Alternative hedonism and the theory and politics of consumption' was funded in the ESRC/AHRC 'Cultures of Consumption' programme (www. consume.bbk.ac.uk). She has been a member of the editorial collectives of *Radical Philosophy* and *New Left Review* and a regular columnist for the US journal, *Capitalism, Nature, Socialism*.

Acknowledgements

This book has developed over the past three years through exciting and stimulating conversations with each of the contributors, and with the support of my colleagues and students at the Bartlett School of Architecture UCL. Lorraine Code, Elizabeth Grosz, Bronwyn Hayward, Doina Petrescu, Gail Schwab and Katie Lloyd Thomas contributed earlier thought-provoking versions of their chapters at the UCL Conference *Sexuate Subjects* (2010). Jane Rendell, Luis Rego, Mary Rawlinson, and Katie and Gail's collaboration in organising this conference with me also made sure of its success, and the Bartlett School of Architecture's Research Fund provided invaluable financial support, together with generous funding from UCL, KTH Stockholm, Hofstra University and Stony Brook University. I also very warmly thank all the other contributors for their generous, and enthusiastic, participation and time in this project. Thank you also to Laura Williamson at Routledge for her careful and patient responses to my questions during the process. Finally, more than thanks to Tom, whose own critical art ecology has helped make this project live.

The publishers and I also acknowledge permission to reproduce material from the following:

Renata Tyszczuk and Stephen Walker, University of Sheffield and *field Journal*: David Cross, 'Bonjour tristesse: study for an art project. Cerdagne, France 2010', *field*, 4, 1 (January 2011): 135–47.

Women, Gender and Research: Kate Soper, 'Beyond consumerism: reflections on gender politics, pleasure and sustainable consumption', in special issue, 'Gendering Climate Change', *Women, Gender and Research*, 3–4, 2009: 92–100.

Metaphilosophy: Gail Schwab's reviews of *Sharing the World*, *Teaching*, and *Conversations* by Luce Irigaray, *Metaphilosophy*, 42, 3 (April 2011): 328–40.

Duke University Press: 'Sexual difference as sexual selection: Irigarayan reflections on Darwin', in Elizabeth Grosz, *Becoming Undone*, 143–68. Copyright 2011, Duke University Press. All rights reserved. Reprinted by permission of the publisher: www.dukeupress.edu

Routledge: Bronwyn Hayward (2012) Chapter 8: 'The social handprint', in *Children, Citizenship and Environment*, London: Earthscan/Routledge: 139–58.

RESOLVE: Bronwyn Hayward (2010) 'Decentring sustainability and the new consumer politics of UK Uncut', *RESOLVE Working Paper Series* 06-10, Guildford: University of Surrey.

Multitudes: Doina Petrescu, 'Jardinieres du commun', *Multitudes* 42, Paris: Exils, 126–33.

Introduction

Peg Rawes

Relational Architectural Ecologies examines the complex architectural and ecological relationships which constitute modern human cultures and environments. The collection responds to the Greek etymology of the word 'eco' (*oikos*) that Ernst Haeckel's 1866 term 'ecology' defines as the science of 'the household of nature'.[1] It shows how the 'habitats', 'natural milieus', 'places' or 'shelters' that construct architectural ecologies are composed of complex material, spatial, social, political and economic concerns. Its emphasis on these more sociopolitical understandings of ecological thinking and practice therefore contrast with the architectural profession's leading interpretations of *oikos* as the basis for building designs, technologies and material typologies that achieve environmental efficiency; for example, by reducing CO_2 emissions or repurposing renewable energies (e.g. Steele 2005; van Uffelen 2009).

The book has three key aims: first, to extend architectural thinking about ecology beyond current professional sustainable architectural design practices that have developed over the past thirty years, and are defined variously as; 'green building design', 'sustainable architecture', 'sustainable building design technologies' or 'environmentally responsive design'. Second, it explores architectural ecologies by interdisciplinary scholarship from inside architectural practice and theory, and outside the discipline in the visual arts, humanities, social sciences, medicine and in law. Third, it examines how these ecologies are *relational* because they are *co-constituted* by spatiotemporal and sociopolitical values and, importantly, by sex difference. It argues that these relations are essential for enabling communities engaged in producing our built environment (including the architectural and built environment professions) to tackle the environmental and human-related crises that affect our cities, towns and homes today; for example, to address overconsumption, resource depletion and pollution, and the environmental rights of communities. Thus, the definition of architecture presented here is not directed exclusively towards the professionals who design our built environments: instead, the term 'architecture' encapsulates a broader set of environmentally focused questions about the value of the social and material formation of our 'built' environments *for all*.

The essays show that a legacy of ecological thinking and practice since the 1960s environmental movement by women, environmental campaigners, scientists, philosophers and activists is required by architecture, especially because these are not sex-neutral or value-free forms of ecological knowledge. Given the failure of global technocratic and market-led approaches to deal with the issues, the book suggests that such *interdisciplinary* architectural, ecological and relational approaches may be even more urgently required for dealing with the complexities in protecting and creating biodiversity in our architectures and environments.

Importantly, the book's title is not just intended as a poetic trans-position of the term 'ecology' from one place to another, or a simplistic appropriation of it. Rather, it shows that critical and environmentally directed 'architectural' thinking and practice is already a 'living' field of practices shared between communities within and outside formal professional architectural boundaries. Again, in this respect, the book does not employ the more familiar discourses and terminology that the profession tends to use (which, since the 1987 UN Brundtland Report, have been led primarily by technological impera-tives and markets). Instead, its aim is to rethink these boundaries so that new understandings of built, material and immaterial architectures can be explored. By drawing attention to the reflexivity between material and cultural 'biodi-versity' in our built environments, the relationship between architecture and ecology is shown to extend well beyond traditional definitions of environmen-tally responsive architectural design. Relational architectural ecologies therefore highlight important political, poetic and material differences that constitute our biological and environmental relations, especially, sexed difference or the biopolitical structures of power that construct our biological and cultural differences.

Sexed difference – or sexed biodiversity – is a central matter for this collection and reflects the ongoing innovations in feminist thinking and practice for questioning the social justice and ecological health of our societies, and our built and natural environments. The book has two strands that underpin its approach: first, it brings together contributors who took part in the conference *Sexuate Subjects: Politics, Poetics and Ethics* at UCL in London, December 2010 (www.ucl.ac.uk/sexuate-subjects). Second, it reflects feminist philosophy's critical 'sexual' and 'sexuate' difference discourses (Irigaray 1985, 1993, 2004), which have productively shown that subjectivity is biologically and culturally produced. Thinkers, such as Luce Irigaray, have shown that positive physical and psychic expressions of sexed identity difference for women and men, are essential for ecological thinking if serious changes are to be developed for conserving depleted resources, and for reducing pollution and unfettered consumption by developed and rapidly developing nations. The benefits of sexual and sexuate difference are firmly identified here with the value of real political difference for *all members of a society* (i.e. not just those who have access to improved ecological wellbeing via the market), and with the politics of difference that ecological research and activism since the 1960s has established. Relational architectural ecologies are therefore the 'places' that form the built environment in modern global cultures *and* the specific 'lives' that construct these places, reflecting the complex biodiversity of our social and material environments. Moreover, the essays underscore the need for cultivating and protecting ecological biodiversity in human and non-human cultures, versus the pernicious consumption, pollution and waste that unethical forms of advanced capitalism perpetuate, despite significant recent scientific and cultural evidence that these are disastrous on a global scale.

Nature, technology and sustainability in the modern built environment

Contemporary ecological debates in the built environment sectors reflect environmental awareness of human–nature relations following the 1960s environmentalist movements, but discourses about the relationship between human-designed environments and nature are also present in historical analyses of premodern and vernacular architecture (e.g. Zeiher 1996).

Modern architectural discussions about nature have also inherited seventeenth- and eighteenth-century Romantic ideas of the tension between the natural world's positive, aesthetic powers and its destructive, sublime powers, together with Enlightenment desires that nature's beneficial physical powers of progress can be controlled by human design (e.g. Soper 1995). Since the late nineteenth century, these dialectical anthropocentric (human-centred) and non-anthropocentric (non-human) characteristics of nature have been focused in architectural discourses; beginning with 'landscape', and leading to the use of the term, 'environment', from the 1880s, and to 'environmental' discourses in the 1920s (Hawkes 2008: xv). More recently, since the 1980s, this dynamic human–nature relationship has developed into 'sustainable' and 'green' architecture.

Frank Lloyd Wright's term 'organic architecture' coined a modern formulation for employing nature's physical, spatial and aesthetic capacities in the design of modernist buildings (e.g. *The Natural House* 1954; *The Living City* 1958). A series of 'organic' or 'environmental' traditions also evolved during the late nineteenth and twentieth centuries, including designs by Louis Sullivan, Frei Otto, Antoni Gaudi and Buckminster Fuller, which were based on nature's complex geometries, and Hans Scharoun, Alvar Aalto and Carlo Scarpa's use of natural lighting and materials (e.g. Steadman 2008; Gans and Kuz 2003). Again, more recently, organic architecture has evolved into 'biomimetic' computational approaches, which take biological principles of genetic evolution as the basis

3

for morphological, digital and materials-based design (e.g. Hensel and Menges 2006).

Architects have also sought to situate technological approaches to sustainability within the aesthetic and poetic aims of the discipline, in particular, post-war architects including Gunnar Asplund and Sverre Fehn, and contemporary international architects, such as Peter Zumthor, Steven Holl, Elizabeth Diller and Ricardo Scofidio, and Tadao Ando (Hawkes 2008: xvii). However, the phenomenological basis of many of these approaches has not always distinguished their sustainable or ecological aims strongly enough from the professional architectural design literature that co-opts these buildings back into market-led definitions of development: for example, Steele's *Ecological Architecture* (2005) which, while acknowledging the 'murky' use of ecology in the profession, nevertheless firmly endorses its principal understanding of environmental sustainability as that defined by the Brundtland report, where economic and technological modes of sustainable design are *the* central criteria. Also, while he discusses key innovations in sustainably designed buildings by Wright, Fuller, Ando, and McHarg's bioregional landscape design, Steele overlooks the importance of social relations in the production and use of the buildings. This 'murkiness' has been upheld by publications like van Uffelen's *Ecological Architecture* (2009), which uncritically focuses on the seductive aesthetic and commercial appeal of advanced technological and environmentally responsive modern building design. More recently, however, Lee's *Aesthetics of Sustainable Architecture* (2011) has critically appraised the socioeconomic basis of sustainable aesthetic and technological approaches in architectural design, and includes contributions from environmental designers, historians and an anthropologist.

The relationship between nature and technology in modern architecture is also substantial and complex. Over the past forty years, it has largely been characterized by the profession's focus on energy efficiency and recycling, and environmentally responsive building and material technologies: for example, low-energy buildings, material recycling, local sustainable resources, the recovery of vernacular building techniques and the invention of innovative advanced architectural technologies, such as photovoltaic cells and zero-carbon emission technologies (e.g. Zeiher 1996; Roaf *et al.* 2001; Berge 2009). Previously, in the mid twentieth century, although highly utopian, Fuller's Dymaxion architectural projects and 'planetary' writings on sustainable networked architectures (1928–79) combined technological, cybernetic and geometric approaches for designing sustainable systems, operating from the small to the large scale. Reyner Banham's *The Architecture of the Well-Tempered Environment* (1969) established the contemporary profession's early understandings of 'environmental design' as the management of environmental technologies for designing 'habitable' buildings. However, his commitment to advanced architectural technology also firmly situates Banham's thinking within approaches that tend to instrumentalize natural processes to architectural ends (Hawkes 2008: xv).

Since the UN's 1987 Brundtland Report's 'three pillars' of global sustainable development – human, environmental *and* economic sustainability – the profession has developed substantial markets of good practice literature and 'manuals' of sustainable design technology. However, while these publications may acknowledge cultural wellbeing they also focus more strongly on the physical science, technical and vernacular understandings of building structures, reinforcing the profession's commercial commodification and dissemination of ecological knowledge, and with limited attention given to the complex cultural, social and economic questions which underpin the issues (e.g. Roaf *et al.* 2001; Berge 2009; McLennan 2004).

Attempts to increase the quality of environmental and sustainable architecture through national standards of assessment (e.g. the US's Leadership in Energy and Environmental Design standards [LEED], and the UK's Building Research Establishment Environmental Assessment [BREEAM] standards) has resulted in some mainstream professional improvements in energy-efficient buildings that use technologies such as passive ventilation, recycling, low-energy and non-toxic materials. However, these technologically oriented assessment mechanisms have done little to reflect the value of social relations in the design and inhabitation of buildings (cf. Lee 2011). Firmly tied to the profession's commercial interests, such mechanisms are slow to address the status quo at the risk of undermining their constituency's economic stability. A more challenging materials-based attempt to address these questions is found in architect William McDonough and chemist Michael Braungart's *Cradle to Cradle* (2002), which is now a patented certification (C2C) for non-toxic 'life cycle' design, in which all matter is categorized as organic or 'technical' and reused or 'down-cycled' (also see Lee 2011: 8).

Twentieth-century environmental discussions about the modern city also show the dynamic relationship between human-constructed environments and nature's 'organic' resources. Architects and urban planners designing modern industrial and post-industrial cities have attempted to design out, or ameliorate against, nature's forces (e.g. flooding or extreme heat and cold), while also harnessing its energy resources (e.g. hydrology and solar heat) for servicing the needs of densely inhabited modern and global urbanization. In 1902 British urban planner, Ebenezer Howard, published *Garden Cities of To-morrow*, which formulated the utopian 'Three Magnets'· diagram to identify the benefits of the economic and social characteristics of 'town' together with the health and 'nature' of the 'country' in the design of a 'town-country', and leading to the design of small towns such as Letchworth and Welwyn Garden City. Jane Jacobs's post-war *The Death and Life of Great American Cities* (1961) continued this human–nature analysis in her critique of rationalist forms of urbanism (which attacked Le Corbusier's 1920s European Radiant City plans and Burnham's 1950s City Beautiful plans for Chicago; Jacobs 1961: 23–5), arguing that the diversity and health of the modern city is also constructed through its social and economic systems. Published ten years later, Banham's *Los Angeles: The Architecture of Four Ecologies* (1971) also promoted a dynamic systems-based – and avowedly technological – analysis in his utopian examination of the social and urban interactions of the city's beaches, highways, plains and foothills. But his silence about the contemporaneous environmental political awareness means that his progressive vision of a utopic technological built environment is now hard to reconcile with the serious need that planners, urbanists and architects more actively undertake designing for the survival of biodiverse human–nature relations, rather than reverting back to Banham's use of the term as a metaphor for unfettered westernized urban development. More recently, Mike Davis's *Ecology of Fear* (1998) has revisited Los Angeles' anthropocentric and non-anthropocentric environmental relations through the logic of the sublime, this time focusing on the city's environmental, social, political, designed and imaginary identities as sites of ecological disasters and modern-day terror. In contrast, landscape architect Ian McHarg's analysis of complex regional ecosystems and microclimates in *Design with Nature* (1969) provided a more politically and environmentally responsible approach for the built environment sectors that has grounded the profession's commitment to tackling the design of the built environment informed by environmental and physical sciences.

In the years following the Brundtland Report, the architectural profession's focus on the city's complexity as a constructed natural-human organism shifted focus to examining cities as 'sustainable ecosystems', including: Richard Rogers's *Cities for a Small Planet* (Rogers and Gumuchdjian 1997) and Herbert Girardet's *Creating Sustainable Cities* (1999), which examined the global task of dealing with population growth and sustainable design, especially in respect to the intensive growth of cities in China and India. Girardet's vitalist approach calls cities 'superorganisms', which have a metabolism that can be ecologically managed, and points to the value of existing strategies such as peripheral-urban farming in the US or the UK's allotment tradition. This emphasis on the productivity of green spaces for increasing the biodiversity of environmental scales – from the non-human organism, to the human, up to the building and master-planned city-scale – signals a key element of formal and informal sustainable design in developed cities throughout the modern built environment tradition; for example, from the public parks, long-held as 'the lungs' of the city, allotments, roof top and urban-farming schemes, to more recent modes of activist 'guerrilla' or communal edible-garden schemes.

Over the past fifteen years, the need to address the relations between human and natural systems in sustainable and ecological design of the built environment (and the concomitant relations of 'active' technology versus 'passive' natural solutions) has been taken up more explicitly by environmental planners, architects and landscape architects. Australian environmental planners Peter Newman and Isabella Jennings, for example, have argued for a city-planning approach that models cities on natural systems: 'an inclusive one that sees humans as part of local socioecological systems, from bioregions to biosphere, in which the focus is on relationships and processes that support life in its myriad forms, especially partnerships and cooperation' (Newman and Jennings 2008: 4). Drawing from the environmental landscape architect Robert Thayer's 'bioregionalist' research into 'life-places',[2] their ten-step method, 'The Melbourne Principle', links the economic, social, biological and phenomenological spheres with cooperative, participatory, sustainable and well-governanced public and private responsibilities (4).

Developed out of a symposium and exhibition in 1997 in Chicago, Charles Waldheim and James Corner's 'landscape urbanism' has signalled the reconfiguration of the debate between the architectural design, landscape design and urban design disciplines. Corner situates this discourse under the spectrums of 'nature' in landscapes, the constructed 'scapes' of the city, suburb and land, and recent environmentalist awareness of late capitalist cities which reframes celebrated urban parks, such as *Parc de la Villette* in Paris, or Koolhaas's vitalist urbanism. Seeking to rework the urban grid as a new 'field' for multidisciplinary land-based operations, landscape urbanism considers itself at odds with 'sustainable' landscape, and architectural, planning and urbanism, which idealize nature as primary over the complexity of a modern city's functioning. Such approaches, Corner argues, are unsatisfactory for the needs of contemporary designers and planners in dealing with the increased complexity and growth of cities within twenty-first century capitalist structures (Waldheim 2006: 24–6). Corner also presents the new 'field' as a 'space-time ecology', which 'treats all forces and agents working in the urban field and considers them as continuous networks of inter-relationships' (30). He distinguishes it from landscape architecture, environmental urban design and planning, which have evolved from McHarg's work because these have failed to sufficiently address social, cultural and political 'environments'. Thus, although architectural and ecological relations are central to landscape urbanism, its authors retain disciplinary boundaries that protect the authority of urban and architectural design professions; also, by identifying power with the professional design disciplines, the complex non-human alterity of nature remains subsumed to urbanist principles and practices.

In the most recent recasting of this tradition, Corner and Waldheim are included in the Harvard Design School's ambitious 655-page discipline-defining publication, *Ecological Urbanism* (Mostafavi and Doherty 2010).[3] Here, the evolution of the debates into the territory of the ecological is framed as a response to the failure of Kyoto and Copenhagen climate summits (12). In addition, its editors seek to distinguish innovative design research by leading global universities and architectural professionals from the now-conservative value of sustainable and environmental architecture. First, they reject the 'renunciation' of pleasure that is associated with the 'simple technologies' advocated by sustainable architecture (e.g. low-energy and waste recycling). Second, they question the mainstream credentials of nationally approved sustainability LEED and BREEAMS standards. Third, they view sustainable design's small-scale legacy as having failed to address the increasing large-scale complexity and urgency of global urban relations (12–13). Also, notably, underpinning this realignment, Bateson's cybernetic ecology, and the poststructuralist political philosophies of Guattari, Rancière, Agamben, Mouffe and Žižek are cited to underline ecological urbanism's 'capacity to incorporate and accommodate the inherent conflictual conditions between ecology and urbanism' (17).

Political nature and ecology in the humanities and social sciences since the 1960s

The catalytic 1960s and 1970s research by environmental and development studies, social anthropology, and women's studies into the politics of human–nature relations continue to provide significant material and political insights into human and ecological biodiversity. Rachel Carson's *Silent Spring* (1962); Arne Naess's *Deep Ecology* (1973); Gregory Bateson's cybernetic and social anthropological theory of 'ecology of mind' (2000); and Murray Bookchin's 1980s 'social ecology' (1994), exposed the links between cultural and biological approaches to concepts of nature. Physical scientists James Lovelock and Lynn Margulis's 1974 proposal of the Gaia theory, the biosphere's self-regulating physical and biochemical feedback mechanism, also questioned anthropocentric human–nature theories (Lovelock and Margulis 1974). Such thinking and practice showed the extent to which environmental thinking needs to take into account nature's absolute non-anthropocentric status, and to question the benefits of utopian belief in the technological instrumentalization of natural systems.

Also importantly, ecofeminists identified the link between the ethical rights of non-human nature and the politics of sexual difference, further exposing how western culture relied upon damaging instrumental human–nature relations and values (e.g. d'Eaubonne 1974; Daly 1979; Shiva 1991; Plumwood 1993). Carolyn Merchant's anthology *Ecology: Key Concepts in Critical Theory* (1999) situated these new environmentalist politics after Marx and Engel's nineteenth-century dialectical analyses of industrialized capitalism's human–nature power relations (and developed afterwards by Horkheimer, Adorno and Marcuse of the Frankfurt School), providing important social science critiques of advanced global environmental damage (Merchant 2008: 15–42). However, while this anthology considered the built environment in specific sites of negative environmental conflict, it focused on protecting the natural environment for minority groups, such as First Nations populations, rather than broader built environment habitats. Karen Warren's *Ecofeminism: Women, Culture, Nature* (1994) brought together feminist philosophers, ecologists, activists and anthropologists to explore the particularly close relationships between ecology and feminist critiques of contemporary western culture, but again did not explicitly focus on architectural or spatial concepts of interdisciplinary critique and action. Thus, while this scholarship and activism interrogated the political and sexed nature of the environment, and the social rights of women and minority groups in the developed and developing world, it has tended not to foreground the architectural or architectonic characteristics of the issues.

In the visual arts, ecological thinking over the past three decades has reconfigured the 1960s' and 70s' critical and conceptual, environmental and land art practices of artists such as Robert Smithson, Nancy Holt, Agnes Denes, Mierle Laderman Ukeles, and Helen Mayer and Newton Harrison (e.g. Matilsky's *Fragile Ecologies* 1992, and the Barbican Gallery's *Radical Nature*, Manacorda and Yedgar 2009). Recent art historical theory and fine arts practices have also shown how political and poetic spatializations intersect with new aesthetic and poetic definitions of architecture, generating new opportunities for ecological dialogue and exchange between the disciplines (e.g. The Arts Catalyst www.artscatalyst.org; Demos 2012; Marsching and Polli 2012).

In continental and political philosophy critical theories of ecology and relationality construct social, ethical and material analyses, including Félix Guattari's theories of 'ecosophy' (1995, 2000); and his 'geophilosophical' collaboration with Gilles Deleuze which also draws upon the vitalist traditions of nature in Spinoza and Bergson, and from von Uexküll's 'biosemiotic' environmental theory of 'umwelt' (1986; also see Herzogenrath 2009 for discussions of ecology in Deleuze and Guattari). Kate Soper's *What is Nature?* (1995) and Verena Andermatt Conley's *Ecopolitics* (1997) have been significant political philosophical analyses of non-human nature and human–nature relations. Conley's *Spatial Ecologies* (2012) revisits these ecology relations, highlighting their particularly spatial characteristics in modern urban habitats. The necessity of expanding aesthetic, biological and philosophical concepts of subjectivity and nature beyond restricted humanist definitions of the autonomous or 'existential' subject have been explored in Jane Bennett's *Vibrant Matter* (2010), Diana Coole and Samantha Frost's *New Materialisms* (2010), and Tim Morton's *Ecology Without Nature* (2007) and *The Ecological Thought* (2010). Tim Hayward's *Ecological Thought* (1995), Greg Garrard's *Ecocriticism* (2004) and Ursula Heise's *Sense of Place and Sense of Planet* (2008) have also critiqued the reliance on weak theories of subjectivity that do not properly situate these debates at a scale of planetary survival and impact.

Feminist philosophy has also provided significant theorizations of nature, relationality and subjectivity: for example, Lorraine Code's important *Ecological Thinking* (2006) critiques biological sex, cultural difference, nature and scientific thinking, in order to show the positive social and cultural value of *other* sexuate ecological 'architectonics' in lived social, mental and political inhabitations. Feminist philosophy has also shown, very acutely, how subsuming nature to technocratic logics is seriously limited and damaging for our mental and physical environmental health. Philosophers, such as Donna Haraway (2008), Rosi Braidotti (2006) and Elizabeth Grosz (2011), have shown that sex difference already provides an-*other* valuable non-anthropocentric or 'posthuman' humanism which has a far greater capacity to engage with these issues than sex-neutral logics which refuse to acknowledge nature's alterity. Feminist understandings of biological difference therefore positively enable developing new biodiverse architectures and relational powers *for all*.

Like colleagues working in the humanities and social sciences, feminist and Marxist architectural researchers and practitioners have shown that 'architecture' is composed from complex and reflexive relationships between the material, cultural, social and political relationships in ways which could be called 'ecological': for example, showing how the physical and psychological relationships that construct our built and social architectures are complex relational and material ecologies.[4] Feminist architectural researchers have therefore shown that our architectural relations are always sexed, and understanding this can enable positive transformations of the built environment and of the social relations within it (e.g. Kossak *et al.* 2009; Lloyd Thomas 2006; Rendell *et al.* 2000; Rendell 2010; Petrescu 2007; Wigglesworth 2011 and www.swarch.co.uk). Here, then, *relational architectural ecologies* are the poetic, political, social and psychic relationships through which modern subjectivity, and our habits, habitats and modes of inhabitations, are co-constituted (also see Tyszczuk and Walker 2011, and Conley 2012: 6). And, given the disastrous escalation in fragile or damaged cultural and environmental ecologies across local and global scales, architectures which embody such biodiversity are now essential. But these ecologies are not restricted to limited interpretations of *oikos* as home or households. Rather, architecture is comprised of complex sexuate fields, practices, inhabitations, topologies and milieus.

Relational architectural ecologies therefore attempts to contribute to understanding the relationship between expanded notions of architecture and ecology, in conjunction with ecological critiques from feminist and continental philosophy, the arts, humanities and social sciences, towards creating new ethical, poetic and political architectural ecologies. Interdisciplinary ecological and architectural thinking/practices are mutually enhancing relational approaches that offer important ways through which to understand and create enduring ethical, material and social architectures for contemporary and future societies' needs: although the volume also reflects some of the tensions between 'ecofeminist' conceptualizations of nature, feminism and technology, and more recent 'posthuman' philosophies of nature, thereby showing the continuing heterogeneity of the debates.

Relational architectural ecologies are heterogeneous and complex, and operate at all levels of society, on a built environment and urban scale, *and* on the human, corporeal or biological scale of sexed identity difference. They are the spaces in which architecture and ecology meet in the built environments of the hospital, supermarket, urban public space, street or home. They are the diverse concrete and ephemeral spatiotemporal habits, patterns and rhythms of daily life which individuals, communities and societies develop within their cultural contexts and milieus. They are the critical, poetic, political and ethical strategies and imaginaries through which new spaces and places of occupation and inhabitation can be constructed. They are the economic, technological and material constructions of western culture, of digital and global organization, and in this respect they are not always necessarily positive relations. Reflecting ecological thinking from the 1960s, in particular, Rachel Carson's groundbreaking research into the long-term toxic effects of DDT on multiple biodiversities (human and non-human), Gregory Bateson's work on 'ecologies of mind', together with more recent empirical and theoretical materials research by ecofeminists and feminist philosophers, the volume shows that new ecologies also need to be invented to resist dominant 'bad' forms of ecology. In particular, this issue applies to architecture that perpetuates 'bad' ecologies such as uncritical, unethical and damaging short-term, market-led technocratic methods, which continue to deplete the planet of its resources.

Ecological thinking, then, has already travelled far beyond its nineteenth-century scientific 'home' to establish diverse modes of intellectual milieus and disciplinary encounters, critiques, bodies, poetics, methods and actions. In these milieus, architecture is reconfigured from traditions in which difference is present (but considered value-free or neutral) into relational poetic, political and ethical ecologies, for example, as sexuate eco-houses, habitats or ecological 'fieldwork'. As such, architectural ecologies exist across the micro and macro scales, in the 'self-built' habitats, intimacies, dwellings and relationships between people's bodies, spatiotemporalities and psychophysical embodiments (cf. Braidotti's theory of 'care'; 2006).

Part I: Biopolitical ecologies and architectures. Three chapters explore how the modern subject and the built environment comprise biopolitical ecologies. Following philosopher Michel Foucault's theory of biopolitics (2008), our sites of daily inhabitation are understood to be both positively and negatively constituted at a macro and micro scale of social and biological governance or 'design', in conjunction with the individual's aesthetic and psychophysical expressions. **Rosi Braidotti** (Chapter 1) examines how 'nomadic feminism' provides a much-needed affirmative politics for developing sustainable futures and '*zoe*' (life). She considers the way in which advanced capitalism accords or withholds these rights to vulnerable communities and subjects, both at human and planetary scales of existence. When 'human' or 'non-human' subjects are determined through 'governance by fear' ('necro-politics'), the right to positive habitats, social relations and patterns of daily life are seriously disrupted; for example, affecting vulnerable communities' access to energy resources, adequate housing or citizen rights. Faced with these 'matter realisms', however, collective feminist praxis has successfully generated new post-anthropocentric, affirmative *(potentia)* politics, and hence social relations. Equipped with these 'enduring' political imaginaries we can demystify the political, material and temporal relations that have caused our age to be defined as 'anthropocene' (i.e. the geological era that is marked by the impact of our interference on the planet's ecosystems), and to construct new hopeful and sustainable futures. In Chapter 2 **Peg Rawes** examines the need for understanding ecology in architecture as integrated sexed and aesthetic relations. Drawing from artist Agnes Denes's 'geometric' environmental site-specific artworks that repurpose waste-ground, Bateson's theory of 'pattern-difference' in South East Asian art and Guattari's examination of positive aesthetico-political subjects, she explores the need for mental and physical architectures of care for sustaining society's wellbeing, especially in urban environments. **Nathan Moore** (Chapter 3) examines the biopolitics of spatial control and self-control in a London street where *ad hoc* architectural design features produce dysfunctional ecologies of prohibition, and which reflect normalizing economic management of the self. Moore argues that these ecologies of control, or diagrams, are examples of biopolitical relations which Foucault, Esposito and Deleuze have explored, at work in designing exclusion of subjectivities within the urban public environment.

Part II: Uncertain, anxious and damaged ecologies. Three chapters consider the fraught 'architectural' ecologies of climate change, social and environmental wellbeing, and economically damaging global approaches to the design of our environment. **Lorraine Code** (Chapter 4) examines how critiques of climate-change scepticism (*agnotology*), including the influential *Merchants of Doubt* (2010), remain constrained by their lack of situated and sexed ecological knowledge. Code shows feminist ecological thinking's value for politically effective resistance to damaging cultures of consumption in the work of feminist environmental scientists, philosophers and activists such as Rachel Carson, Vananda Shiva, and in her own scholarship. Feminist epistemology and its related practices, she argues, 'requires people to *know*, not just to act, differently: to think ecologically' (Code 2006). In Chapter 5 **Rachel Jones** explores how Irigaray's sexuate environmental rethinking of nature and matter addresses Kant's philosophy of fear and the sublime, and contemporary issues of environmental disaster. Irigaray conceptualizes matter as an originary site of relations for differentiated subjectivities, recasting Kant's negative 'abyss' into a material ecology through which the subject and nature are situated without hierarchy; thereby offering a helpful framework for finding better, non-instrumental approaches to inhabiting and living with our planetary resources. Artist **David Cross**'s visual essay (Chapter 6) examines the increased environmental and relational responsibility now required in the modern subject and arts practitioner, set against the marginalization of low-energy technologies by the French government, in favour of nuclear power. Focusing on France's now-overlooked 1950s solar furnace technology at Mont Louis, Cross suggests that these solar mirror images encapsulate a 'critical' aesthetic reflection of the politics needed to address the pressing issues of climate change and resource depletion.

Part III: Economics, land and consumption. Three chapters examine architectures of consumption, damaging approaches to human and environmental 'productivity', and the underlying economic definitions applied to commonplace daily habits and social rights. In Chapter 7 **Kate Soper** argues that our dependence on excessive consumption betrays any serious political attempt to tackle issues of environmental action. Rather, she argues that feminist epistemologies of difference have been co-opted into designing new sites of expenditure, which are damaging both to the environment and our social relations, especially for women and girls. Such ecologies of consumption are also distributed through unsustainable forms of retail architecture, in particular, the shopping mall. Soper argues that until political and public governance encourage the formation of 'new aesthetics of pleasure', these negative gender identities and environmental relations will persist. In Chapter 8, **Michelle Murphy** explores how population growth and health technologies are evidence of the economic relations that construct modern and developing nations. She argues that western neoliberalism has developed particularly direct forms of economic technology for controlling the modern population's wellbeing, especially women's reproductive health, and girls' economic productivity, in a process that she calls the 'economization of life'. By understanding how economics is a key 'environmental milieu' on a population and biological scale, new political imaginaries can be developed that address how capital and sex organize modern 'life'. **Gail Schwab** addresses how the North American agricultural and food monocultures operate through damaging logics of rational efficiency (Chapter 9). The industrial scale of these economics are shown to be significant sites of damaging political, environmental and ethical relations; for example, by maximizing the productivity of land use, the reliance on biotechnologies in animal husbandry and crop management, and in the mass production of food commodities for the modern supermarket culture.

Part IV: Biological and medical architectural ecologies. Three chapters examine the material, corporeal and technological structures that constitute modern architectures of 'life', health and biological difference.

Elizabeth Grosz re-examines the separation between human and non-human natures in feminist theory to argue that Irigaray's feminist philosophy and Darwin's analysis of biological nature share a concern with biodiverse ecologies that are premised upon sexual difference (Chapter 10). From this unlikely alliance, Grosz shows that productive poetic and sexed biodiverse relations are co-constituted that have value for both human and non-human social and material modes of inhabitation. In Chapter 11, architect, Katie Lloyd Thomas considers the relationality of human and non-human technologies in the context of the neonatal hospital unit. Drawing from responses by mothers whose children require intensive assisted starts to life, Lloyd Thomas examines how neo-natal technology provides a vital ecology between the child, parent and carers. Simondon's relational technical ontology underpins how these sexed neo-natal 'architectures' are new forms of human and non-human maternal relations and networks of care. Anita Berlin (Chapter 12) presents a triadic ecology, or biome, of the complexities of integrated global healthcare provisions. Drawing from Guattari's ecological thinking, and from her own practice as a GP and teaching student doctors, she shows that complex global ecologies of healthcare exist at a series of scales of political imaginary and social relation; for example, connecting the regional National Health hospital bed in the UK to a family's rental payments in the Philippines; from the ethics of the doctor–patient relationship in the GP's surgery to the social and medical benefits of terminally ill patient-led teaching for student doctors.

Part V: Communal ecologies and architectures. In the final part, four chapters examine specific local practices in which social, material and physical architectures or ecologies are constructed, and their scope for future architectural practices and communities. Political scientist and geographer, Bronwyn Hayward, reflects on the difficulties facing New Zealand's Christchurch communities tackling the continuing uncertainty and destruction of the city's infrastructure, resulting from the 2010 and 2011 earthquakes (Chapter 13). Taking this living post-disaster ecology as evidence of limited national and regional governance to integrate and respond to local needs, she questions the idealized promotion of carbon footprints, in contrast to the 'hands-on' activism of the local youth using social media to generate a decentred, collective response. In Chapter 14 social anthropologist Rebecca Empson's visual essay draws from long-term fieldwork among pastoral herding households who live along the Northeast Mongolian-Russian border. These households comprise an ethnic minority called the Buriad, who migrated from Siberia to Mongolia in the early 1900s. She presents the 'material ecologies' of their culture, their domestic lives, homes and craft, such as embroidery, which reflect the evolution of their specific historical relationship to the land, trading routes, cultural rituals and their diasporic memory. Architect, Doina Petrescu (Chapter 15) explores how the 'common' is a political architectural project that is central to feminist strategies for reconstructing our social, political, affective and cognitive agency. She shows how projects developed with Parisian residents – whose 'agents are *mostly women*' – and her collaborative practice, *atelier d'architecture autogérée*, are collective processes of sexed, spatial and ecological invention, which produce new social relations of and for the common. In the closing chapter, **Verena Andermatt Conley** examines how Félix Guattari's 'ecosophy' is a still-valuable exposure of the depletion of biodiversity in the natural and built environment, as well as in our aesthetic and political modes of subjectivity, resulting from advanced capitalist technocracies. Yet Guattari also considers that our and nature's future alterity requires advanced technology to be redirected through aesthetic and ethical 'transversal' practices. Ecological approaches to urban design, for example, require architects, planners and urban designers to actively adopt these transformative approaches to re-cultivate the diversity of our built environments.

Notes

1   Haeckel develops the term in *Generelle Morphologie der Organismen* (1866): also see Pindar and Sutton's note (Guattari 2000: 95). For an outline of the development of ecology as a science from Haeckel, see Kingsland in Real and Brown (2001: 1–13).
2   Thayer credits Peter Berg and Gary Snyder for coining the term 'life-place' in the 1980s. See Thayer (2003: 3, 273).
3   The publication has a global and multidisciplinary reach that includes architects, philosophers, sociologists, planners, urbanists, such as Doina Petrescu, Verena Conley, Homi Bhabha, Bruno Latour and Rem Koolhaas.
4   Also see *Weather Architecture* (2012) by architect Jonathan Hill, in which he considers cultural and historical examples of the influence of weather on architectural design, in light of contemporary understandings of climate change.

Bibliography

Banham, R. (1969) *The Architecture of the Well-Tempered Environment*, London: Architectural Press.
— ([1971] 2001) *Los Angeles: The Architecture of Four Ecologies*, Berkeley: University of California Press.
Bateson, G. (2000) *Steps to an Ecology of Mind*, Chicago: University of Chicago Press.
Bennett, J. (2010) *Vibrant Matter: A Political Ecology of Things*, Durham, NC: Duke University Press.
Berge, B. (2009) *The Ecology of Building Materials*, trans. C. Butters and F. Henley, Oxford: Architectural Press.
Bookchin, M. (1994) *Which Way for the Ecology Movement? Essays by Murray Bookchin*, Edinburgh: AK Press.
Braidotti, R. (2006) *Transpositions. On Nomadic Ethics*, Cambridge: Polity Press.
Brundtland, O. (1987) *Our Common Future*. Online: http://www.un-documents.net/our-common-future.pdf (accessed 5 May 2011).

Carson, R. ([1962] 1965) *Silent Spring*, London: Readers Union.

Code, L. (2006) *Ecological Thinking. The Politics of Epistemic Location*, Oxford: Oxford University Press.

Conley, V.A. (1997) *Ecopolitics: The Environment in Poststructuralist Thought*, New York: Routledge.

— (2012) *Spatial Ecologies: Urban Sites, State and World-Space in French Cultural Theory*, Liverpool: Liverpool University Press.

Coole, D. and Frost S. (eds) (2010) *New Materialisms: Ontology, Agency and Politics*, Durham, NC: Duke University Press.

Daly, M. (1979) *Gyn/ecology: The Metaethics of Radical Feminism*, London: Women's Press.

Davis, M. (1998) *Ecology of Fear: Los Angeles and the Imagination of Disaster*, New York: Metropolitan Books; Henry Holt.

d'Eaubonne, F. (1974) 'The time for ecofeminism', in E. Marks and I. de Courtivron (eds) (1980), *New French Feminisms: An Anthology*, Amherst: University of Massachusetts Press.

Deleuze, G. and Guattari, F. ([1986] 1988) *A Thousand Plateaus: Capitalism and Schizophrenia*, trans. B. Massumi, London: Athlone Press.

Demos, T.J. (2012) 'Art after nature: the post-natural condition', *Artforum*, April 2012: 191–7.

Foucault, M. (2008) *The Birth of Biopolitics: Lectures at the Collège de France, 1978–1979*, trans. G. Burchell, Basingstoke: Palgrave Macmillan.

Gans, D. and Kuz, D. (eds) (2003) *The Organic Approach to Architecture*, Chichester: John Wiley and Sons.

Garrard, G. (2004) *Ecocriticism: The New Critical Idiom*, London: Routledge.

Giardet, H. ([1999] 2009) *Creating Sustainable Cities*, Totnes, Devon: Green Books.

Grosz, E. (2011) *Becoming Undone: Darwinian Reflections on Life, Politics and Art*, Durham, NC: Duke University Press.

Guattari, F. (1995) *Chaosmosis: An Ethico-Aesthetic Paradigm*, trans. P. Bains and J. Pefanis, Bloomington: Indiana University Press.

— (2000) *The Three Ecologies*, trans. I. Pindar and P. Sutton, London: Athlone Press.

Haraway, D.J. (2008) *When Species Meet*, Minneapolis: University of Minnesota Press.

Hawkes, D. (2008) *The Environmental Imagination: Technics and Poetics of the Architectural Environment*, Abingdon: Routledge.

Hayward, T. (1995) *Ecological Thought: An Introduction*, Cambridge: Polity Press.

Heise, U. (2008) *Sense of Place and Sense of Planet: The Environmental Imagination of the Global*, Oxford: Oxford University Press.

Hensel, M. and Menges, A. (eds) (2006) *Morpho-Ecologies*, London: Architectural Association.

Herzogenrath, B. (ed.) (2009) *Deleuze/Guattari and Ecology*, Basingstoke: Palgrave Macmillan.

Hill, J. (2012) *Weather Architecture*, London: Routledge.

Howard, E. ([1902] 1965) *Garden Cities of To-morrow*, London: Faber and Faber.

Irigaray, L. ([1989] 1993) *Thinking the Difference: for a Peaceful Revolution*, trans. K. Montin, London; New York: Continuum; Routledge.

— (1985) *Speculum of the Other Woman*, trans. G.C. Gill, Ithaca, NY: Cornell University Press.

— (2004) *Key Writings*, London: Continuum.

Jacobs, J. (1961) *The Death and Life of Great American Cities*, New York: Random House.

Kingsland, S.E. (2001) 'Defining ecology as a science', in L.A. Real and J.H. Brown (eds) *Foundations of Ecology: Classic Papers with Commentaries*, Chicago: Chicago University Press.

Kossak, F., Petrescu, D., Schneider, T., Tyszczuk, R. and Walker, S. (eds) (2009) *Agency: Working with Uncertain Architectures*, London: Routledge.

Lee, S. (ed.) (2011) *Aesthetics of Sustainable Architecture*, Rotterdam: 010 Publishers.

Lloyd Thomas, K. (ed.) (2006) *Material Matters: Architecture and Material Practice*, Abingdon: Routledge.

Lovelock, J.E. and Margulis, L. (1974) 'Atmospheric homeostasis by and for the biosphere: the Gaia hypothesis', *Tellus*, 26, 1–2: 1–10.

Manacorda, F. and Yedgar, A. (eds) (2009) *Radical Nature: Art and Architecture for a Changing Planet 1969–2009*, London: Barbican Art Gallery and Koenig Books.

Marsching, J. and Polli, A. (eds) (2012) *Far Field: Digital Culture, Climate Change, and the Poles*, Bristol: Intellect.

Matilsky, B.C. (ed.) (1992) *Fragile Ecologies: Contemporary Artists' Interpretations and Solutions*, New York: Rizzoli International.

McDonough, W. and Braungart, M. (2002) *Cradle to Cradle: Remaking the Way We Make Things*, New York: North Point Press.

McHarg, I.L. (1969) *Design With Nature*, Garden City, NY: American Museum of Natural History, Natural History Press.

McLennan, J.F. (2004) *The Philosophy of Sustainable Design: the Future of Architecture*, Kansas City, MO: Ecotone.

Merchant, C. (ed.) ([1999] 2008) *Ecology: Key Concepts in Critical Theory*, Amherst, MA: Humanity Books.

Morton, T. (2007) *Ecology Without Nature*, Cambridge, MA: Harvard University Press.

— (2010) *The Ecological Thought*, Cambridge, MA: Harvard University Press.

Mostafavi, M. and Doherty, G. (eds) (2010) *Ecological Urbanism*, Baden, Switzerland: Lars Muller and Harvard University, Graduate School of Design.

Naess, A. (1973) 'The shallow and the deep, long-range ecology movement: a summary', *Inquiry*, 16, 1–4: 95–100.

Newman, P. and Jennings, I. (2008) *Cities as Sustainable Ecosystems: Principles and Practices*, Washington, DC: Island Press.

Oreskes, N. and Conway, E.M. (2010) *Merchants of Doubt: How a Handful of Scientists Obscured the Truth on Issues from Tobacco Smoke to Global Warming*, New York: Bloomsbury Press.

Petrescu, D. (ed.) (2007) *Altering Practices: Feminist Politics and Poetics of Space*, London: Routledge.

Plumwood, V. (1993) *Feminism and the Mastery of Nature*, London: Routledge.

Rendell, J. (2010) *Site-writing: The Architecture of Art Criticism*, London: I.B. Tauris.

Rendell, J., Penner, B. and Borden, I. (eds) (2000) *Gender Space Architecture: An Interdisciplinary Introduction*, London: Routledge.

Roaf, S., Fuentes, M. and Thomas, S. (2001) *Ecohouse: A Design Guide*, Oxford: Architectural Press.

Rogers, R. and Gumuchdjian, P. (1997) *Cities for a Small Planet*, London: Faber and Faber.

Shiva, V. (1991) *Ecology and the Politics of Survival: Conflicts over Natural Resources in India*, Thousand Oaks, CA: Sage Publications.

Soper, K. (1995) *What is Nature? Culture, Politics and the Non-Human*, Oxford: Blackwell.

Steadman, P. (2008) *The Evolution of Designs: Biological Analogy in Architecture and the Applied Arts*, New York: Routledge.

Steele, J. (2005) *Ecological Architecture: A Critical History*, London: Thames and Hudson.

Thayer, R. (2003) *Life Place: Bioregional Thought and Practice*, Berkeley: University of California Press.

Tyszczuk, R. and Walker, S. (eds) (2011) *Ecology, field*, 4, 1.

Uffelen, C. van (2009) *Ecological Architecture*, Berlin: Braun.

Waldheim, C. (ed.) (2006) *The Landscape Urbanism Reader*, New York: Princeton Architectural Press.

Warren, K. (ed.) (1994) *Ecofeminism: Women, Culture, Nature*, London: Routledge.

Wigglesworth, S. (ed.) (2011) *Around and about Stock Orchard Street*, Abingdon: Routledge.

Wright, F.L. ([1954] 1971) *The Natural House*, London: Pitman.

— ([1958] 1970) *The Living City*, New York: Horizon Press.

Zeiher, L.C. (1996) *The Ecology of Architecture: A Complete Guide to Creating Environmentally Conscious Building*, New York: Whitney Library of Design, Watson-Guptill Publications.

Part I

Biopolitical ecologies and architectures

Chapter 1

Posthuman relational subjectivity and the politics of affirmation

Rosi Braidotti

This chapter deals with the discursive and analytic conditions that frame contemporary subjectivity which, I will argue, is both posthuman and relational. At the core of new subject formations there is a double shift from the anti-humanism of the post-structuralist generation, to a post-anthropocentric approach. This shift takes place within globalized advanced capitalism that is marked by high levels of technological mediation, internally contradictory temporalities and necro-political governmentality, or governance by fear. The posthuman indicates the shifting locations of the human in the era that is also known as the anthropocene. Throughout the chapter I will take feminist theory and praxis as the main point of reference, stressing the transformative and affirmative character of feminist politics.

Posthumanism

The critique of humanism by post-structuralists, including the feminists, is a fundamental starting assumption. Their dynamic brand of social constructivism combines the analysis of techniques of subjectivation with the creation of empowering new ontologies of the self, and of self–other relations. Post-structuralists' vital materialism emphasizes the sexualized nature of human embodiment and inscribes relationality as the ontological feature of the human. By the same token, it positions the radical immanence of power relations at the core of the debate. In a Foucauldian perspective, for instance, power is not only negative or confining *(potestas)*, but also affirmative *(potentia)* or productive of alternative subject positions and social relations.

Theoretically, this embodied and embedded brand of materialist philosophy of the subject introduces a break from the pillars on which the classical Cartesian vision of the rationalist subject rested, namely: universalism and dualism. The generation of Foucault, Derrida, Irigaray and Deleuze rejected universalist claims to a subject position that allegedly transcends spatio-temporal and geopolitical specificities and therefore is abstract in the sense of disembodied and dis-embedded. For feminists, the mindset of universalism, best exemplified in the notion of 'transcendent reason' (Lloyd 1985), 'abstract masculinity' (Hartsock 1987) and 'triumphant whiteness' (Ware 1992), is objectionable not only on epistemological, but also on ethical grounds. Situated feminist perspectives lay the preconditions for ethical accountability for one's own implications with the very structures one is analysing and opposing politically.

Post-structuralism marks the switch from Cartesian dualism to a Spinozist monistic philosophy that stresses the unity and self-organizing vitality of matter, and redefines the binary relationship between self and other. Post-structuralists point out that the notion of 'otherness' functions through dualistic oppositions that confirm the dominant vision of 'sameness' by positing subcategories of difference and distributing them along asymmetrical power relations. In other words, the dominant apparatus of subjectivity is organized along a hierarchical scale that rewards the sovereign subject as the zero-degree of difference. Deleuze and Guattari call it 'the Majority subject' or the Molar centre of being (1980). Irigaray calls it 'the Same', or the hyper-inflated, falsely universal 'He' (Irigaray 1974, 1977), whereas Hill Collins calls to account the white and Eurocentric bias of the subject of humanistic knowledge (Hill Collins 1991).

Furthermore, this insight counts not only for individuals, but also for their cultures. Thus, in European philosophy, this 'difference' has been predicated on relations of domination and exclusion: to be 'different from' came to mean to be 'less than'. In the dualistic scheme of thought, difference or otherness is a constitutive axis which marks off the sexualized other (woman), the racialized other (the native) and the naturalized other (animals, the environment or earth). These others, however, are constitutive in that they are expected to confirm the same in His superior position and thus they are crucial to the assertion of the power of sameness.

To say that the structural Others of the modern subject re-emerge in postmodernity amounts to making them into a paradoxical and polyvalent site. They are simultaneously the symptom of the crisis of the subject, and for conservatives even its 'cause', but they also express positive, that is non-reactive, alternatives. It is a historical fact that the great emancipatory movements of postmodernity are driven and fuelled by the resurgent 'others': the women's and gay rights movements; the anti-racism and decolonization movements; the anti-nuclear and pro-environment movements are the voices of the structural Others of modernity. They also inevitably mark the crisis of the former 'centre' or dominant subject-position. In the language of philosophical nomadology, they express both the crisis of the majority and the patterns of becoming of the minorities. The aim of critical theory consists in providing both the methodological navigational tools and an ethical compass to allow us to tell the difference between these different flows of mutation.

According to the deeply seated anti-humanism of these philosophies, the fact that the dominant axes of definition of the humanistic subject of knowledge contribute to fixing the axes of difference or of otherness, has another important implication. Post-structuralist anti-humanism undoes from within the unitary identities indexed on phallocentric, Eurocentric and normative standardized views of what constitutes the humanist ideal of 'Man'. It engenders, simultaneously, the processes of sexualization, racialization and naturalization of those who are marginalized or excluded, but also the active production of half-truths, or forms of partial knowledge about these others. Power produces through exclusion: the others are included in this script as the necessary outside of the dominant vision of what it means to be human. Now, however, more specifically, we need normative distinctions between reactive, profit-oriented differences on the one hand and affirmative empowerment of alternative differences on the other. The criterion by which such difference can be established is ethical, and its implications, political.

Post-anthropocentrism

The insights of the posthumanist generations are currently developing in the direction of post-anthropocentrism. Spectacular developments, notably in neural sciences, the study of the earth and ecological systems and bio-genomics, as well as information digital technologies, have altered our shared understanding of what counts as the basic unit of reference for the human. The extent to which competing views about the human are central to contemporary scientific enquiry cannot fail to affect feminist practice, notably the terms and theoretical framework that shape our shared understanding of a feminist political subject. In the geological era that is already known as 'anthropocene' – that is to say a chronological time in which human activity is having a significant impact on the Earth's ecosystem and on our collective capacity to survive – we have moved towards a more complex relationship to our planetary destiny. This shift also affects the status of theory: is the anthropocene the era in which critical theorists, including feminists, need to re-examine received ideas about the political subject? Doing this means taking some critical distance from the method of social constructivism, which has been endemic to European and North Atlantic feminist politics since Mary Wollstonecraft's passionate refutation of J.J. Rousseau's naturalization of inequalities between the sexes.

To advance the argument further, we need to consider the perverse multiple temporalities of globalized advanced capitalism. This system is a 'difference engine' that promotes the marketing of pluralistic differences and the commodification of the existence, the culture, the discourses of 'others', for the purpose of consumerism. As a consequence, the global system of the post-industrial world produces scattered and poly-centred, profit-oriented power relations. In our post-Cold War era, power functions not so much by binary oppositions, but in a fragmented and all-pervasive manner. This rhizomatic or web-like structure of contemporary power and its change of scale, however, do not alter fundamentally its terms of application. If anything, power relations in globalization are more ruthless than ever.

Late post-industrial societies have proved far more flexible and adaptable towards the proliferation of differences than the classical Left expected. These 'differences' have been however, turned into and constructed as marketable, consumable and often disposable 'others'. Popular culture – from music to cinema, new media, fashion and gastronomy – is a reliable indicator of this trend, which sells 'world music', or a savvy mixture of the exotic and the domestic, often in the mode of neocolonial appropriation of multicultural others.

In other words, advanced capitalism functions as the great nomad, the organizer of the mobility of commodified products. A generalized practice of 'free circulation' pertains, however, almost exclusively to the domain of goods and commodities, regardless of their place of origin, provided they guarantee maximum profit. But people do not circulate nearly as freely (Virno 2004; Lazzarato 1996). It is therefore crucial to expose the perverse nomadism of a logic of economic exploitation that equates capitalist flows and flux with profit-minded circulation of commodities. Given that technologies – more specifically the convergence of information and bio-technologies – are intrinsic to the social and discursive structures of post-industrial societies, they deserve special attention. The most critical aspect of the technological apparatus is the issue of access and participation. Considering the inequalities in the availability of electricity supplies, let alone telephone lines and modems, well may one wonder about the 'democratic' or 'revolutionary' potential of the new electronic and biogenetic frontiers. Thus, access and participation to the new high-tech world is unevenly distributed worldwide, with gender, age and ethnicity acting as major axes of negative differentiation (Eisenstein 1998).

In his political analysis of the historical condition of postmodernity, Brian Massumi (1998) describes global capitalism as a profit-oriented mix-and-match system that vampirizes everything. His system rests on the paradox of the simultaneous occurrence of contradictory trends. On the one hand the globalization of the economic and cultural processes engenders increasing conformism in life-style, tele-communication and consumerism. On the other hand, the fragmentation of these processes, with the concomitant effects of increased structural injustices, the marginalization of large sections of the population, and the resurgence of regional, local, ethnic and cultural differences not only between the geo-political blocks, but also within them (Eisenstein 1998).

Given that the political economy of global capitalism consists in multiplying and distributing differences for the sake of profit, it produces ever-shifting waves of genderization and sexualization, racialization and naturalization of multiple 'others'. It has thus effectively disrupted the traditional dialectical relationship between the empirical referents of Otherness – women, natives and animal or earth others – and the processes of discursive formation of genderization/racialization/naturalization.

The spasmodic concurrence of these phenomena is the distinctive trait of our age. The commodification of differences turned the 'others' into objects of consumption, granting them alternatively a familiar and a threatening quality that bypasses the doors of the dialectics. We have entered into a zigzagging pattern of dissonant nomadic subjects. How to overcome the dualistic mode that has become so entrenched to our way of thinking remains the main challenge.

The posthuman turn pushes this dislocation further. It can also be described as a sort of 'anthropological exodus' from the dominant configurations of the human (Hardt and Negri 2000: 215) – a massive hybridization of the species which topples the anthropocentric Human from the sovereign position it has enjoyed for so long. This sovereign position was represented in a universal mode as Man, but this pseudo-universal has been widely criticized (Lloyd 1985) precisely because of its partiality. Universal Man, in fact, is implicitly assumed to be masculine, white, urbanized, speaking a standard language, heterosexually inscribed in a reproductive unit and a full citizen of a recognized polity: hardly a universal position.

Massumi refers to the posthuman as 'Ex-Man', 'a genetic matrix embedded in the materiality of the human' and undergoing significant mutations: 'species integrity is lost in a bio-chemical mode expressing the mutability of human matter' – bodily materialism dis-gregating (Massumi 1998: 60). Haraway puts it like this: 'this is Man the taxonomic type become Man the brand' (1997: 74). What emerges from this is the vital politics of life, as non-human energy and self-organizing matter.

Feminist theory looks carefully at the dislocation of the dialectical relationships between the traditional axes of difference (sexualization/racialization/

naturalization) and attempts to come to terms with this challenge. A methodo-logical challenge arises as a result: the advanced, bio-genetic structure of capitalism as a schizophrenic global economy does not function in a linear manner, but is web-like, scattered and poly-centred. It is not monolithic, but an internally contradictory process, the effects of which are differentiated geopolitically and along gender and ethnicity lines, to name only the main ones. This creates a few methodological difficulties for the social critic, because it translates into a heteroglossia of data. We need to adopt *non-linearity* as a major principle and to develop cartographies of power that account for the paradoxes and contradic-tions of the era of globalization, and which do not take shortcuts through its complexities.

Considering the extent to which contemporary capitalist economies depend on the commodification of life itself, there is an opportunistic form of posthuman condition emerging from the very post-anthropocentric opportunism of advanced capitalism. The bio-genetic structure of advanced capitalism is such that it is not only geno-centric (Fausto-Sterling 2000: 235), but also ruthlessly and structurally unjust. The epistemological analysis intersects with the political one: because the self-replicating vitality of living matter is targeted for consumption and commercial exploitation of bio-genetic culture, environmentally based political struggles have evolved into a new global alliance for sustainable futures. Haraway recognizes this trend and pays tribute to the martyrized body of onco-mouse (Haraway 1997), as the farming ground for the new genetic revolution and manufacturer of spare parts for other species. Vandana Shiva (1997) also stresses the extent to which the bodies of the empirical subjects who signify difference (woman/native/earth or natural others) have become the disposable bodies of the global economy. Contemporary capitalism is 'bio-political' in that it aims at controlling all that lives: it has already turned into a form of biopiracy in that it aims at exploiting the generative powers of women, animals, plants, genes and cells. This means that human and anthropomorphic others are relocated in a continuum with non-anthropomorphic or 'earth' others. The categorical distinction that separated the Human from his naturalized others has shifted, taking the humanist assumptions about what constitutes the basic unit of reference for the 'human' into a spin.

Let's take, for example, Dolly the sheep as the main figuration for the perverse temporalities and contradictions that structure our technological culture. Dolly is that sex which is not one – a collective entity repackaged as a bounded self. She/it is simultaneously the last specimen of her species – descended from the lineage of sheep that were conceived and reproduced as such – and the first specimen of a new species: the electronic and bio-genetic sheep that Phillip Dick dreamed of, the forerunner of the android society of *Blade Runner*. Cloned, not conceived sexually, heterogeneous mix of organism and machine, Dolly simply changes the name of the game. Severed from reproduction and hence divorced from descent, Dolly is no daughter of any member of her/its old species – simultaneously orphan and mother of her/itself.

Copy made in the absence of one single original, Dolly pushes the logic of the postmodern simulacrum to its ultimate perversion. She/it brings Immaculate Conception into a bio-genetic third-century version. The irony reaches a convulsive peak when we remember that Dolly died of a banal and all too familiar disease: rheumatism. After which, to add insult to injury, she/it suffered a last indignity: taxidermy. She/it was embalmed and exhibited in a science museum as a scientific rarity (shades of the nineteenth century) and a media celebrity (very twentieth century!). Dolly is simultaneously archaic and hyper-modern, she/it is a compound of multiple anachronisms, situated across different chronological axes, she/it inhabits different and self-contradictory time zones. Like other contemporary techno-teratological animals or entities (onco-mouse comes to mind), Dolly shatters the linearity of time and exists in a continuous present. This techno-electronic timeless time is saturated with a-synchronicity, that is to say, it is structurally unhinged.

Thinking about Dolly blurs the categories of thought we have inherited from the past – she/it stretches the longitude and latitude of thought itself, adding depth, intensity and contradiction. Because she/it embodies complexity, this entity which is no longer an animal but not yet fully a machine, is THE philosophical problem of today.

I refer to these bio-mediated practices of bodily materialism as 'matter-realism', radical neo-materialism or posthuman nomadic feminism. Central to them is the changing conceptual structure of matter itself, under the impact of contemporary bio-genetics and information technologies. I believe that a monistic political ontology that stresses processes, vital politics and non-deterministic evolutionary theories, is helpful in coming to terms with these new scientific developments. Politically, the emphasis falls on the micro politics of relations, and on posthumanist ethics that traces transversal connections among human and non-human agents. This high degree of transversality actualizes an ethics based on the primacy of the relation, of interdependence, which values non-human or a-personal Life. This is what I call *zoe* itself (Braidotti 2006).

Necro-political governmentality

If insights about the possibility of ending life on earth were a common nightmare in the nuclear era, the post-nuclear condition extends the horizon of extinction to most species and is now able to set a date to it. This inaugurates a negative or reactive form of pan-human planetary thinking, which recomposes humanity around a commonly shared threat. We are all humans, though some are definitely more mortal than others, and we share this vulnerability with animals and plants. Thanatology or necro-politics is central to our political economy. Michel Foucault's essential insight into bio-power remains valid in so far as it also concerns the necro-political aspects. Bio-power is as much about letting some die as it is about actively working towards the survival of others.

The emphasis on the politics of life itself and especially the shifting boundaries between life and death add a necro-political dimension to contemporary debates on power, with emphasis on the destructive consequences of bio-genetic capitalism (Foucault 1976, 1984a, 1984b), in terms of species extinction and environmental disasters. 'Life' can be a threatening force, as evidenced by new epidemics and environmental catastrophes that blur the distinction between the natural and the cultural dimensions. 'The politics of life itself' makes technologically mediated 'life' into a contested political field (Rose 2001). Living matter itself becomes the subject and not the object of enquiry. These concerns have both the neo-liberal (Fukuyama 2002) and the neo-Kantian thinkers struck by high levels of anxiety about the sheer thinkability of human future (Habermas 2003).

The main field of necro-political research concentrates on the brutality of the new wars, the governance by fear, and the renewed expressions of violence which refers not only to the government of the living, but also to multiple practices of dying. Bio-power and necro-politics are two sides of the same coin, as Mbembe (2003) brilliantly argues. The post-Cold War world has seen not only a dramatic increase in warfare, but also a profound transformation of the war instance as such in the direction of a more complex management of survival and of extinction. 'Necro-politics' defines power essentially as the administration of death: 'the generalized instrumentalization of human existence and the material destruction of human bodies and population' (Membe 2003: 19). And *not* only human.

The implications of this approach to bio/necro-power are radical: it is not up to the rationality of the Law and the universalism of moral values to structure the exercise of power, but rather the unleashing of the unrestricted sovereign right to kill, maim, rape and destroy the life of others. This same power, following Agamben (1998), structures the attribution of different degrees of 'humanity' according to hierarchies that are disengaged from the old dialectics and unhinged from any political rationality. They fulfil instead a more instrumental, narrow logic of opportunistic exploitation of the life in you, which is generic and not only individual. The colonial plantation as the prototype of this political economy of detention, confinement and ultimate destruction turns the slave into the prototype of 'homo sacer'.

Contemporary necro-politics has taken the form of the politics of death on a global and regional scale. The new forms of industrial-scale warfare rest upon the commercial privatization of the army and the global reach of conflicts, which de-territorialize the use of and the rationale for armed service.

Reduced to 'infrastructural warfare' (Mbembe 2003), and to a large-scale logistical operation (Virilio 2002), war aims at the destruction of all the services that allow civil society to function: roads, electricity lines, airports, hospitals and other necessities. It also aims at protecting mineral extraction and other essential geo-physical resources needed by the global economy. In this respect, the 'new' wars look more like guerrilla warfare and terrorist attacks than the traditional confrontation of enlisted and nationally indexed armies. One thinks specifically of the case of suicide bombers in the war on terror.

As a result, the 'population', as a political category, has also become disaggregated into 'rebels, child soldiers, victims or refugees, or civilians incapacitated by mutilation or massacred on the model of ancient sacrifices, while the "survivors", after a horrific exodus, are confined to camps and zones of exception' (Mbembe, 2003: 34). Arjun Appadurai (1998) has also provided incisive analyses of the new 'ethnocidal violence' of the new forms of warfare which involve friends, kinsmen and neighbours. He is appalled by the violence of these conflicts: 'the focus here is on bodily brutality perpetrated by ordinary persons against other persons with whom they may have – or could have – previously lived in relative amity' (Appadurai 1998: 907). Clearly, this exercise of violence cannot be adequately described in terms of disciplining the body, or even as the society of control – we have rather entered the era of orchestrated and instrumental massacres, a new 'semiosis of killing', leading to the creation of multiple and parallel 'death-worlds' (Mbembe 2003: 37).

The social reality of refugees and asylum seekers also becomes an emblem of the contemporary necro-power. Diken (2004) argues that refugees are the perfect instantiation of the disposable humanity of 'homo sacer' and thus constitute the ultimate necro-political subject. The proliferation of detention and high-security camps and prisons within the once civic-mended space of the European City is a further example of the loss of credibility of the rational bio-political order. The camps – 'sterilized, monofunctional enclosures' (Diken 2004: 91) – stand as the symbol of the indictment of liberal Western democracies. The link to colonialism is clear: de-colonization created nation-states whose people, once enslaved, are now free to circulate globally. These people constitute the bulk of the unwanted immigrants, refugees and asylum seekers who are contained and locked up across the developed world. In a twist not deprived of ironical force, world migration is perceived as a particular threat in Europe precisely because it endangers Europe's main infrastructure: the welfare state.

How does the necro-political dimension intervene in the discussion about feminist politics of affirmation? What are its implications for the practice of critical theory? Bio-power since Foucault led to a more sophisticated understanding of practices that latch onto 'life' as the main target. But death as a concept remains simultaneously central to political theory – in the form of the horizon of mortality and the concern for human vulnerability – and unspoken. Death as a concept remains unitary and undifferentiated, while the bios–zoe horizon proliferates and diversifies.

My point is that the new necro-political practices mobilize not only generative forces, but also new and subtler degrees of extinction. This type of vitality, unconcerned by clear-cut distinctions between living and dying, composes the notion of 'zoe' as a non-human yet paradoxically affirmative life force. This vitalist materialism rests solidly on a neo-Spinozist political ontology of monism and radical immanence. Nomadic theory's main contribution to this debate rests on the concepts of radical immanence and non-deterministic vitalism, which unfold onto an affirmative ethics of bio-egalitarianism. Bio-centred egalitarianism is a philosophy of radical immanence and affirmative becoming, which activates a nomadic subject into sustainable processes of transformation. The *zoe*-centred embodied subject is shot through with relational linkages of the symbiotic, contaminating/viral kind which interconnect it to a variety of others, starting from the environmental or eco-others.

The transformative and affirmative character of feminist politics

How can we engage in affirmative politics, which entails the creation of sustainable alternatives geared to the construction of social horizons of hope, while at the same time doing critical theory, which implies resistance to the present? This is one of the issues Deleuze and Guattari discuss at length, notably in *What is Philosophy?* (1991), in the relationship between creation and critique. It is however a problem that has confronted all activists and critical theorists: how to balance the creative potential of critical thought with the dose of negative criticism and oppositional consciousness that such a stance neces-sarily entails.

Central to this debate is the question of how to resist the present, more specifically the injustice, violence and vulgarity of the times, while being worthy of our times, so as to engage with them in a productive, albeit opposi-tional and affirmative manner. I shall return to this issue in the final section of this chapter. There is a contextual and a conceptual side to this problem and I will discuss each one of these and then examine some of their implications.

This engagement with the present – and the spirit of the times – sets the political agenda in a variety of realms, ranging from sexuality and kinship systems to religious and discursive practices. The analyses of these themes are transmitted through narratives – mythologies or fictions – which I have renamed as 'figurations' (Braidotti 2002, 2006), or cartographies of the present. A cartog-raphy is a politically informed map of one's historical and social locations, to enable the analysis of situated formations of power and hence the elaboration of adequate forms of resistance. Michel Foucault (1975) worked extensively on the notion of genealogy or counter-memories as a tool to draw the 'diagrams of the present' in his analysis of the microphysics of power in post-industrial societies. Gilles Deleuze and Félix Guattari (1980) also stressed the importance of immanent analyses of the singular actualizations of concrete power formations.

Feminism also pioneered the practice of the politics of locations (Rich 1985) as a method for grounding activism. It also perfected the strategy of positive renaming and re-signification of the subject. A location is an embedded and embodied memory: it is a set of counter-memories, which are activated by the resisting thinkers against the grain of the dominant social representations of subjectivity. A location is a materialist temporal and spatial site of co-production of the subjects in their diversity. Accounting for this complexity is therefore anything but an instance of relativism. Locations provide the ground for political and ethical accountability. Remembrance, cartographies of locations, political (dis-)identifications and strategic reconfigurations are the tools for consciousness-raising which were devised by transformative epistemologies such as feminism and race theory (Passerini 1988; Haraway 1990; West 1994).

Both my practice and my concept of the political therefore pay tribute to this tradition of radical politics at a point in history where the general tendency is to dismiss it or deride it as a failed historical experiment. The main thesis I want to defend is that one of the most significant theoretical innovations it introduced is what later became known as 'radical immanence' (Deleuze and Guattari 1980). This includes the notions of political passions, affirmative ethics and the rigorous vision of affectivity, which they entail.

Oppositional consciousness

The conceptual case of my argument rests on the rejection of the traditional equation between political subjectivity and critical oppositional consciousness, and the reduction of both to negativity. There is an implicit assumption that political subjectivity or agency is about resistance, and that resistance means the negation of the negativity of the present. A positive is supposed to be engendered by this double negative. Being against implies a belligerent act of negation, the erasure of present conditions.

This assumption shares in a long-constituted history of thought, which in Continental philosophy is best exemplified by Hegel. The legacy of Hegelian-Marxist dialectics of consciousness is such that it positions negativity as a necessary structural element of thought. This means that the rejection of conditions or premises that are considered unsatisfactory, unfair or offensive – on either ethical or political grounds – is the necessary pre-condition for their critique. A paradoxical concomitance is thus posited between the conditions which one rejects and the discursive practice of critical philosophy and subsequent actions. This paradox results in establishing negativity as a productive moment in the dialectical scheme which fundamentally aims at overturning the conditions that produced it in the first place. Thus, critical theory banks on negativity and, in a perverse way, even requires it. The corollary of this assumption is that the same material and discursive conditions that create the negative moment – the experience of oppression, marginality, injury or trauma – are also the condition of their overturning. The material that damages is also that which engenders positive resistance, counteraction or transcendence (Foucault 1975). The process of consciousness-raising is crucial to the process of overturning or over-coding the negative instance. What triggers and at the same time is engendered by the process of resistance is collective oppositional consciousness. There is consequently a political necessity to elaborate adequate understandings and suitable representations of our real-life conditions. The negative experience can be turned into the matter that critical theory has to engage with. In this process, it turns into the productive source of counter-truths and values, which aim at over-coding the original negative instance. Epistemology therefore clears the ground for the ethical transformation that sustains political action.

This process is too often rendered in purely functional terms as the equation of political creativity/agency with negativity, or unhappy consciousness. I want to suggest, however, that much is to be gained by adopting a non-Hegelian analysis that foregrounds instead the creative or affirmative elements of this process. This shift of perspective assumes philosophical monism and the recognition of an ethical and affective component of subjectivity; it is thus both an anti-dualistic and an anti-rationalist position. A subject's ethical core is not his/her moral intentionality, as much as the effects of power (as repressive – *potestas* – and positive – *potentia*) his/her actions are likely to have upon the world. It is a process of engendering modes of becoming (Deleuze 1968). Given that in this neo-vitalist view the ethical good is equated with radical relationality aiming at affirmative empowerment, the ethical ideal is to increase one's ability to enter into modes of relation with multiple others. The oppositional consciousness and the political subjectivity or agency it engenders are processes or assemblages that actualize this ethical urge. This position is affirmative in the sense that it actively works towards the creation of alternatives by working through the negative instance, and by cultivating the relations that are conducive to the ethical transmutation of values.

What this means practically, is that the conditions for political and ethical agency are not dependent on the current state of the terrain. They are not oppositional and thus not tied to the present by negation; instead they are affirmative and geared to creating possible futures. Ethical and political relations create possible worlds by mobilizing resources that have been left untapped, including our desires and imagination. The work of critique must focus on creating the conditions for the overturning of negativity precisely because they are not immediately available in the present. Moving beyond the dialectical scheme of thought means abandoning oppositional thinking, so as to index activity in the present upon the task of sustainable possible futures. The sustainability of the future rests on our ability to mobilize, actualize and deploy cognitive, affective and ethical forces that had not been activated so far. These driving forces concretize in actual, material relations and can thus constitute a network, web or rhizome of interconnection with others. We have to learn to think differently about ourselves. To think means to create new conceptual tools that may enable us to both come to terms and actively interact with empowering others. The ethical gesture is the actualization of our increased ability to act and interact in the world.

To disengage the process of subject formation from negativity, and to attach it to affirmative otherness means that reciprocity is redefined not as mutual recognition, but rather as mutual definition or specification. We are in *this* together in a vital political economy of becoming that is both trans-subjective in structure and trans-human in force. Such a nomadic vision of the subject, moreover, does not restrict the ethical instance within the limits of human otherness, but also opens it up to interrelations with non-human, posthuman and inhuman forces. The emphasis on non-human ethical relations can also be described as a geo-politics or an eco-philosophy, in that it values one's reliance on the environment in the broadest sense of the term. Félix Guattari's idea of the three ecologies, the social, the psychic and the environmental, is very relevant to this discussion. Considering the extent of our technological development, my emphasis on the eco-philosophical aspects is not to be mistaken for biological determinism. It rather posits a nature–culture continuum (Haraway 1997; Guattari 1995, 2000) within which subjects cultivate and construct multiple ethical relations. The concepts of immanence, multiple ecologies and of neo-vital politics become relevant here.

I have argued so far that oppositional consciousness is central to political subjectivity, but it is not the same as negativity so that, as a consequence, critical theory is about strategies and relations of affirmation. Political subjectivity or agency therefore consists of multiple micro-political practices of daily activism or interventions in and on the world we inhabit for ourselves and for future generations. As Rich put it in her recent essays, the political activist has to think 'in spite of the times' and hence 'out of my time', thus creating the analytics – the conditions of possibility – of the future (Rich 2001: 159). Critical theory occurs somewhere between the no longer and the not yet, not looking for easy reassurances but for evidence that others are struggling with the same questions. Consequently, 'we' are in *this* together indeed.

Rosi Braidotti

Affirmative politics

What is positive in the ethics of affirmation is the fact that it activates the relational powers of the subject and indexes them to the transformation of negative into affirmative affects. This implies a dynamic view of all affects, even those that freeze us in pain, horror or mourning. The slightly depersonalizing effect of the negative or traumatic event involves a loss of ego-indexes perception, which allows for energetic forms of reaction. Clinical psychological research on trauma testifies to this, but I cannot pursue this angle here today. Diasporic subjects of all kinds express the same insight. Multi-locality is the affirmative translation of this negative sense of loss. Following Glissant (1990), the becoming-nomadic marks the process of positive transformation of the pain of loss into the active production of multiple forms of belonging and complex allegiances. Every event contains within it the potential for being overcome and overtaken – its negative charge can be transposed. The moment of the actualization is also the moment of its neutralization. The ethical subject is the one with the ability to grasp the freedom to depersonalize the event and transform its negative charge. Affirmative ethics puts the motion back into e-motion and the active back into activism, introducing movement, process, becoming. This shift makes all the difference to the patterns of repetition of negative emotions. It also reopens the debate on secularity, in that it actually promotes an act of faith in our collective capacity to endure and to transform.

What is negative about negative affects is not a normative value judgement but rather the effect of arrest, blockage, rigidification, that comes as a result of a blow, a shock, an act of violence, betrayal, a trauma or just intense boredom. Negative passions do not merely destroy the self, but also harm the self's capacity to relate to others – both human and non-human others, and thus to grow in and through others. Negative affects diminish our capacity to express the high levels of interdependence, the vital reliance on others that is the key to both a non-unitary vision of the subject and to affirmative ethics. Again, the vitalist notion of Life as 'zoe' is important here, because it stresses that the Life I inhabit is not mine, it does not bear my name: it is a generative force of becoming, of individuation and differentiation; a-personal, indifferent and generative. What is negated by negative passions is the power of life itself – its *potentia* – as the dynamic force, vital flows of connections and becoming. And this is why they should neither be encouraged nor should we be rewarded for lingering around them too long. Negative passions are black holes.

In affirmative ethics, the harm you do to others is immediately reflected in the harm you do to yourself, in terms of loss of *potentia*, positivity, capacity to relate and hence freedom. Affirmative ethics is not about the avoidance of pain, but rather about transcending the resignation and passivity that ensue from being hurt, lost and dispossessed. One has to become ethical, as opposed to applying moral rules and protocols as a form of self-protection: one has to endure.

Endurance is the Spinozist code word for this process. Endurance has a spatial side to do with the space of the body as an enfleshed field of actualization of passions or forces. It evolves affectivity and joy, as in the capacity for being affected by these forces, to the point of pain or extreme pleasure. Endurance points to the struggle to sustain the pain without being annihilated by it. Endurance has also a temporal dimension, about duration in time.

Being worthy of what happens to us

One of the reasons why the negative associations linked to pain, especially in relation to political processes of change, is ideologically laden. It has to do with the force of habit. Starting from the assumption that a subject is a molar aggregate, that is to say, a sedimentation of established habits, these can be seen as patterns of repetitions that consolidate modes of relation and forces of interaction. Habits are the frame within which non-unitary or complex subjects get re-territorialized, albeit temporarily. One of the established habits in our culture is to frame 'pain' within a discourse and social practice of suffering which requires rightful compensation. Equally strong is the urge to understand and empathize with pain. People go to great lengths in order to ease all pain. Great distress follows from not knowing or not being able to articulate the source of one's suffering, or from knowing it all too well, all the time. The yearning for solace, closure and justice is understandable and worthy of respect.

This ethical dilemma was already posed by J.F. Lyotard (1983) and, much earlier, by Primo Levi about the survivors of Nazi concentration camps. Namely that the kind of vulnerability we humans experience in face of events on the scale of small or high horror is something for which no adequate compensation is even thinkable. It is just incommensurable: a hurt, or wound, beyond repair. This means that the notion of justice in the sense of a logic of rights and reparation is not applicable. For the post-structuralist Lyotard, ethics consists in accepting the impossibility of adequate compensation – and living with the open wound.

This is the road to an ethics of affirmation, which respects the pain but suspends the quest for both claims and compensation and resists the logic of retribution of rights. This is achieved through *a sort of depersonalization of the event*, which is the ultimate ethical challenge. The displacement of the 'zoe'-indexed reaction reveals the fundamental meaninglessness of the hurt, the injustice or injury one has suffered. 'Why me?' is the refrain most commonly heard in situations of extreme distress. This expresses rage as well as anguish at one's ill fate. The answer is plain: actually, for no reason at all. Examples of this are the banality of evil in large-scale genocides like the Holocaust (Arendt 1963), the randomness of surviving them. There is something intrinsically senseless about the pain, hurt or injustice: lives are lost or saved for all and no reason at all. Why did some go to work in the WTC on 9/11 while others missed the train? Why did Frida Kahlo take that tram which crashed so that she was impaled by a metal rod, and not the next one? For no reason at all. Reason has nothing to do with it. That's precisely the point. We need to delink pain from the epistemological obsession that results in the quest for meaning and move beyond, to the next stage. That is the path to transformation of negative into positive passions.

This is not fatalism, and even less resignation, but rather a Nietzschean ethics of overturning the negative. Let us call it *amor fati*: we have to be worthy of what happens to us and rework it within an ethics of relation. Of course repugnant and unbearable events do happen. Ethics consists, however, in reworking these events in the direction of positive relations. This is not carelessness or lack of compassion, but rather a form of lucidity that acknowledges the meaning-lessness of pain and the futility of compensation. It also reasserts that the ethical instance is not that of retaliation or compensation, but it rather rests on active transformation of the negative.

In other words, the 'worthiness' of an event – that which ethically compels us to engage with it, is not its intrinsic or explicit value according to given standards of moral or political evaluation, but rather the extent to which it contributes to conditions of becoming. It is a vital force to move beyond the negative.

This requires a double shift. First, the affect itself moves from the frozen or reactive effect of pain to proactive affirmation of its generative potential. Second, the line of questioning also shifts from the quest for the origin or source, to a process of elaboration of the questions that express and enhance a subject's capacity to achieve freedom through the understanding of its limits. Affirmative ethics assumes, following Nietzsche, that humanity does not stem from freedom, but rather that freedom is extracted out of the awareness of limitations. Affirmation is about freedom from the burden of negativity, freedom through the understanding of our bondage.

Conclusion

The real issue about the ontological relationality of the posthuman subject is conceptual: how do we develop a new post-unitary vision of the subject, of ourselves, and how do we adopt a social imaginary that does justice to the complexity? Shifting an imaginary is not like casting away a used garment, but more like shedding an old skin. How do changes of this magnitude take place? It happens often enough at the molecular level, but in the social it is a painful experience, given that identifications constitute an inner scaffolding that supports one's sense of identity. Part of the answer lies in the formulation of the statement: 'we' are in *this* together. This is a collective activity, a group project that connects active, conscious and desiring citizens. It points towards a virtual destination: post-unitary nomadic identities, floating foundations and so on, but it is not utopian. As a project it is historically grounded, socially embedded and already partly actualized in the joint endeavour, that is, the community, of those who are actively working toward it. If this be utopian it is only in the sense of the positive affects that are mobilized in the process: the necessary dose of imagi-nation, dreamlike vision and bonding without which no social project can take off.

The ethical process of transforming negative into positive passions engenders a politics of affirmation, in the sense of creating the conditions for endurance and hence for a sustainable future. Virtual futures grow out of sustainable presents and vice versa. Transformative politics takes on the future as the shared collective imagining that endures in processes of becoming. The ethical-political concept here is the necessity to think with the times and in spite of the times, not in a belligerent mode of oppositional consciousness, but as a humble and empowering gesture of co-construction of social horizons of hope.

The final aspect of affirmative politics I want to spell out is that of the generational timelines, in the sense of the construction of social horizons of hope, that is, of sustainable futures.

The future today is no longer the self-projection of the modernist subject or the gloom of the postmodern one. It is a rather humble act of faith in the possibility of endurance (as duration or continuity) that honours our obligation to the generations to come. It involves the virtual unfolding of the affirmative aspect of what we manage to actualize in the here and now. Virtual futures grow out of sustainable presents and vice-versa. This is how qualitative transformations can be actualized and transmitted along the genetic/time line. Posthuman relational ethics takes on the future affirmatively, as the collectively shared project of becoming. Futurity is non-linear evolution: an ethics that moves away from the paradigm of reciprocity and the logic of recognition, and that installs a rhizomatic relation of mutual affirmation.

Sustainability expresses the desire to endure, in both space and time. In Spinozist-Deleuzian political terms, this sustainable idea of endurance is linked to the construction of possible futures, in so far as the future is the virtual unfolding of the affirmative aspect of the present. An equation is therefore drawn between the radical politics of dis-identification, the formation of alternative subject positions and the construction of social hope in the future. This equation rests on the strategy of transformation of negative passions into affirmative and empowering modes of relation to the conditions of our historicity.

In order to appreciate the full impact of this idea, we need to think back to the perverse temporality of advanced capitalism, with which I started this chapter. In so far as the axiomatic of capitalism destroys sustainable futures, resistance to it entails the collective endeavour to construct social horizons of endurance, which is to say of hope and sustainability. It is a political practice of resistance to the present, which activates the past into producing the hope of change and the energy to actualize it. Doing so processes negative forces and enlists them to the empowering task of engaging with possible futures. Hope is an anticipatory virtue that activates powerful motivating forces: counter-memories, imagination, dreamwork, religion, desire and art. Hope constructs the future by opening up the spaces to project active desires onto; it gives us the force to process the negativity and emancipate ourselves from the inertia of everyday routines. It is a qualitative leap that carves out active trajectories of becoming and thus can respond to anxieties and uncertainties in a productive manner and negotiate transitions to sustainable futures.

Bibliography

Agamben, G. (1998) *Homo Sacer: Sovereign Power and Bare Life*, trans. D. Heller-Roazen, Stanford, CT: Stanford University Press.

Appadurai, A. (1998) 'Dead certainty: ethnic violence in the era of globalization', *Development and Change*, 29: 905–25.

Arendt, H. (1963) *Eichmann in Jerusalem*, New York: Viking Press.

Braidotti, R. (2002) *Metamorphoses: Towards a Materialist Theory of Becoming*, Cambridge Polity Press; Blackwell.

—— (2006) *Transpositions: On Nomadic Ethics*, Cambridge: Polity Press.

Deleuze, G. ([1968] 1990) *Expressionism in Philosophy: Spinoza*, trans. M. Joughin, New York: Zone Books.

Deleuze, G. and Guattari, F. ([1980] 1987) *A Thousand Plateaus: Capitalism and Schizophrenia*, trans. B. Massumi, Minneapolis: University of Minnesota Press.

—— ([1991] 1994) *What is Philosophy?* trans. H. Tomlinson and G. Burchill, New York: Columbia University Press.

Diken, B. (2004) 'From refugee camps to gated communities: biopolitics and the end of the city', *Citizenship Studies*, 8, 1: 83–106.

Eisenstein, Z. (1998) *Global Obscenities: Patriarchy, Capitalism and the Lure Of Cyberfantasy*, New York: New York University Press.

Fausto-Sterling, A. (2000) *Sexing the Body: Gender Politics and the Construction of Sexuality*, New York: Basic Books.

Foucault, M. ([1975] 1977) *Discipline and Punish*, trans. A. Sheridan, New York: Pantheon Books.

—— ([1976] 1978) *The History of Sexuality. Vol. I.*, trans. R. Hurley, New York: Pantheon Books.

—— ([1984a] 1985) *History of Sexuality, Vol. II: The Use of Pleasure*, trans. R. Hurley, New York: Pantheon Books.

—— ([1984b] 1986) *History of Sexuality, Vol. III: The Care of the Self*, trans. R. Hurley, New York: Pantheon Books.

Fukuyama, F. (2002) *Our Posthuman Future: Consequences of the Biotechnological Revolution*, London: Profile Books.

Glissant, E. ([1990] 1997) *Poetics of Relation*, trans. B. Wing, Ann Arbor: University of Michigan Press.

Guattari, F. (1995) *Chaosmosis: An Ethico-Aesthetic Paradigm*, trans. P. Baine and J. Pefanis, Sydney: Power Publications.

— (2000) *The Three Ecologies*, trans. I. Pindar and P. Sutton, London: Athlone.

Habermas, J. (2003) *The Future of Human Nature*, Cambridge: Polity Press.

Haraway, D. (1990) *Simians, Cyborgs and Women*, London: Free Association Press.

— (1997) *Modest Witness*, London: Routledge.

Hardt, M. and Negri, A. (2000) *Empire*, Cambridge, MA: Harvard University Press.

Hartsock, N. (1987) 'The feminist standpoint: developing the ground for a specifically feminist historical materialism' in S. Harding (ed.) *Feminism and Methodology*, London: Open University Press.

Hill Collins, P. (1991) *Black Feminist Thought: Knowledge, Consciousness and the Politics of Empowerment*, New York: Routledge.

Irigaray, L. ([1974] 1985a) *Speculum of the Other Woman*, trans. G.C. Gill, Ithaca, NY: Cornell University Press.

— ([1977] 1985b) *This Sex Which Is Not One*, trans. C. Porter and C. Burke, Ithaca, NY: Cornell University Press.

Lazzarato, M. (1996) 'Immaterial labour', in M. Hardt and P. Virno (eds) *Radical Thought in Italy: A Potential Politics*, Minneapolis: University of Minnesota Press.

Lloyd, G. (1985) *The Man of Reason: Male and Female in Western Philosophy*, London: Methuen.

Lyotard, J.F. ([1983] 1989) *The Differend: Phrases in Dispute*, Minneapolis: University of Minnesota Press.

Massumi, B. (1998) 'Requiem for our prospective dead! (toward a participatory critique of capitalist power)', in E. Kaufman and K.J. Heller (eds) *Deleuze and Guattari: New Mappings in Politics, Philosophy and Culture*, Minneapolis: University of Minnesota Press.

Mbembe, A. (2003) 'Necropolitics', *Public Culture*, 15, 1: 11–40.

Passerini, L. (ed.) (1998) *Identità Culturale Europea: Idee, Sentimenti, Relazioni*, Florence: La Nuova Italia Editrice.

Rich, A. (1985) *Blood, Bread and Poetry*, New York: W.W. Norton.

— (2001) *Arts of the Possible*, New York: W.W. Norton.

Rose, N. (2001) 'The politics of life itself', *Theory, Culture and Society*, 18, 6: 1–30.

Shiva, V. (1997) *Biopiracy: The Plunder of Nature and Knowledge*, Boston, MA: South End Press.

Virilio, P. (2002) *Desert Screen: War at the Speed of Light*, London: Continuum.

Virno, P. (2004) *A Grammar of the Multitude*, New York: Semiotext(e).

Ware, V. (1992) *Beyond the Pale: White Women, Racism and History*, London: Verso.

West, C. (1994) *Prophetic Thought in Postmodern Times*, Monroe, ME: Common Courage Press.

Chapter 2

Architectural ecologies of care

Peg Rawes

'Amber Field'

On 1 May 1982 the conceptual and environmental artist, Agnes Denes, began planting the first furrow of a field of wheat, in a two-acre landfill site in Battery Park, Manhattan (Denes 1993: 387–95). Over the next two months, together with two assistants and a small group of volunteers, Denes cultivated and harvested a crop of wheat that has continued to resonate over the past thirty years as a potent image of the complex relationship between environmental resources, urbanism, architectural and spatial practices. Denes's writing about this site-specific environmental artwork highlights the fragile artifice required to produce its temporary ecology: the clearance of industrial waste metal, domestic rubbish and building rubble that had to be undertaken before the mere one inch of topsoil, brought onto site by eighty lorries to allow sufficient growth, could be spread. This labour, together with the irrigation system and fertilizers used by Denes and her team, formed part of the 'care' required to enable the crop's growth (Denes 1993: 390).

Defined by Denes as a 'symbol, a universal concept', *Wheatfield – A Confrontation* (1982), and its now-iconic globally disseminated image of the artist on site in front of the then-intact Twin Towers (figure 2.1), highlights the complex imbrication of built, social and environmental relations that form modern twenty-first-century globalized relations and the planet's increasingly urbanized environments.[1] In particular, Denes's spatiotemporal ecology sought to raise questions about these global trading, economic, food and waste

2.1
Agnes Denes,
*Wheatfield – A
Confrontation*:
Battery Park
landfill,
downtown
Manhattan – with
Agnes Denes
standing in the
field, 1982. Two
acres of wheat
planted and
harvested by the
artist on a landfill
in Manhattan's
financial district,
a block from
Wall Street
and the World
Trade Center,
Summer 1982.
Commissioned
by the Public Art
Fund, New York
City.

relations; issues which are even more at stake today given the recent collapses in global finance and regulations, the impact of climate-based and tectonic disasters in developed and newly developing urban regions, and rising social and political tensions over access to energy resources.

While Denes has not been naïve about the idealism housed in her intervention, she has also insisted upon its critique of New York as one of the leading sites of integrated globalized technology and economics. For Denes, the project's aim was to 'waste valuable real estate' and 'obstruct the machinery' so as to highlight the 'mismanagement, waste, world hunger and ecological concerns' that are designed into modern regimes of 'food, energy, commerce, world trade, economics' (389). Thus, while producing a self-consciously 'golden' moment of horizontal ecology at the foot of the vertical field of Manhattan's financial district, *Wheatfield* still inhabits a multivalent currency in ecological discourses, employing an environmental critique of the pathology housed in advanced capitalist urbanism, together with a positive, alternative political imaginary or ecology (cf. Bateson). This chapter explores these 'ecological' relations with the aim of examining how professional architecture's under-standing of sustainable design needs to be rethought, particularly when it is led by financial and technocratic markets. Together with Denes's conceptual artworks, I examine how Gregory Bateson's discussion of 'aesthetic' ecology in the visual arts, and Félix Guattari's critique of 'biopolitical regimes', embed ecological thinking and practice into social, material and technological relations which may enable architects to develop more enduring and collective 'architec-tures of care'.

'Sustainable' urban development

Manhattan's intensive urbanism has been extensively mapped out by cultural and architectural critics, including Fredric Jameson (1998) and Carol Willis (1995), who have drawn attention to the financial profit accrued by key economic partners who have stood to gain from commercially-driven urban and architectural design protocols, property speculation, and *laissez-faire* planning. Denes's critique of the relations between financial capital, high-tech urbanism and the environment also figures here, not only because of her concern with the consequences of damaging land use by market-led spatial relations in the city, but because of her attention to the environmental and social relations that advanced capitalist urbanism also generates. Looking back, her critique about the 'shallowness' of these unsustainable forms of economic development and their related architectural markets is all the more poignant given that the project took place five years prior to the consolidation of just this kind of formulation in the UN's 1987 Brundtland Report, *Our Common Future*, and if one also keeps in mind that the UN's own 'home' (*oikos*), the Secretariat Building, is situated just a few kilometres away on the east side of Manhattan. Affirming the logic of advanced capitalism in its three 'pillars' of economic, social and environmental sustainability, *Our Common Future* effectively established the ground upon which technological approaches to sustainability have been tied to global financial and legal frameworks, including, of course, in the built environment sector:[2] for example, the report has sanctioned the built environment professions' development of 'sustainable' advanced urban and building technology markets over the past twenty-five years, under the rubric of a range of environmental terms including 'green', 'responsive' or 'environmental' design (Brundtland 1987: Chapter 2; Drexhage and Murphy 2010: 12).

In a recent revision to UN environmental policies, the International Institute for Sustainable Development's (IISD) 2010 report for the 2012 United Nations Conference on Environment and Development in Rio de Janeiro looked back at the effectiveness of the mandate and progress in sustainable urbanism. Its authors noted the successful development of 'ecocities' (such as Abu Dhabi's Masdar City), new renewable energy sources, low-energy building technologies, 'smart media grids', water conservation and the increased pedestrianization of urban environments, and observed the political and ideological shift towards climate change as the leading term of reference, rather than earlier references to 'sustainability' (Drexhage and Murphy 2010: 14–15). But they also admitted that progress 'has not moved beyond slow incremental steps to transformative action … Efforts to implement sustainable development have taken place in an environment of mainstream economic planning and market-based investment, *in a manner that will not disrupt overall growth*' (12; my italics). And yet, despite this caveat, their primary solution remains focused on the development of mechanisms to achieve a new global 'green economy' by: the 'integration' between sustainable economic growth and environmental protection; the development of 'new metrics' for measuring these relations and resources and for 'implementation, transparency and accountability'; increasing public–private partnerships, and improving the communication of successful strategies (20).

Tim Jackson's recent commentary on the actual outcome of Rio 2012 is more depressing, concluding that there was an outright failure by world leaders to even address excessive consumption in 'sustained' growth:

> There are 15 mentions of [the] term ['sustained'], occasionally with 'inclusive' and once or twice with 'equitable' added as a qualifier. ... This is hidebound recidivism at its very best. We're no longer even using the terminology of green growth or sustainable growth. Instead of accepting the responsibility of the richest to develop a new economic model, this language has set back by a decade any attempt to question the model that led us to the brink of financial disaster, perpetuates huge consumption inequalities and is driving us towards ecological collapse. ...
>
> All these economists coming late to the table talking about better measures, without questioning the underlying model isn't really advancing things. It may even be holding them up, particularly if the same economists then spend years arguing that it's impossible to agree on the right measure.
>
> (Confino 2012)

Wheatfield's aesthetic ecological image of 'Integrated World Capitalism' (Guattari's term for post-industrial capitalism; Guattari 2000: 32) highlights the damaging nature of these relations under such weak definitions of sustainable development, even when applied to one of the most utopic sites of successful advanced capitalism. Also, unsurprisingly, the value of 'other' modes of environmental technologies are overlooked in the first UN report's discussion of the built environment, in favour of technologies which contribute towards the development of large-scale global economic markets. This pursuit of advanced technologies contrasts with Denes's image of an-'other' technology represented in the form of the female conceptual land-artist with a pre-modern technology in hand (it is unclear exactly what kind of 'tool' it is). Depressingly, this continuing focus on the large-scale global impact of high-tech commercial architectural and urban markets, and their related advanced building technologies is still lacking in the 2010 recommendations, indicating that more nuanced discussions about technologies which do not only perform to capitalist protocols remain invisible. Denes's image is also worth noting in contrast to these familiar reinforcements that the most effective way to maintain and develop human and environmental 'life-places' (Thayer 2003) is achieved by increasing market-led technologies, rather than tackling the exclusionary, and yet supposedly 'value-free', cultures that result in unhealthy, homogeneous commercial urban development. So, while the impermanent artifice of her work may not meet the criteria required by current ecological practices,[3] Denes's desire to 'dig deep' (390) in the shallow instrumental ground[4] of modern globalization has nevertheless been an exceptionally strong political and material imaginary for a considerable number of artists, environmentalists and activists, and now, more recently, for architects, planners and urbanists who are engaging in questions of 'landscape' and 'ecological urbanism'.

The network of relations that constitute *Wheatfield*'s enduring 'aesthetic ecology' is a diverse series of inhabitations, although some of these affiliations are clearly more instrumental than others. Take some of its restagings which highlight how the project's ecology of sexed aesthetic relations has developed over the past thirty years: ranging from Denes's profile as one of the founding practitioners of women's environmental art in environmental and ecological websites (e.g. Women Environmental Art Directory: www.weadartists.org/artist/denes), to her inclusion in one of the earliest and one of the recent survey exhibitions of conceptual environmental art, *Fragile Ecologies* (Matilsky 1992) and *Radical Nature* (Manacorda and Yedgar at the Barbican Art Gallery 2009). In the latter, photographs of the work were shown, and it was also restaged as *The Dalston Mill* (2009) in the plot for the new Dalston Junction underground station in East London by EXZYT, a French architect-collective from Paris. This particular resiting of the work included a working bread-mill with ovens, which extended the communal 'ecology' from Denes's agricultural scale of cultivation into a more localized set of food relations (Manacorda and Yedgar 2009; Spatial Agency 2012).

In the built environment professions, Denes's conceptual and environmental practice has been appropriated by 'ecological urbanism', the latest generation of architectural, landscape, urban and planning discourses to emerge out of the North American architectural academy and profession. This new 'territory' repositions the built environment professions' concern with the design and interaction between 'ecological' human and natural relations in the production of the city, prefigured in the 1990s by the architect Charles Waldheim in his term 'landscape urbanism', and promoted by the landscape architect James Corner's thinking and practice (Waldheim 2006; Corner 1999). Occupying a two-page full-colour spread in the introduction to the Harvard Design School's publication *Ecological Urbanism* (2010), *Wheatfield* is 'retrofitted' (Mostafavi and Doherty 2010: 26) into the rubric of a reinvigorated ecological architectural discourse that also maintains the profession's global ambition and reach. In addition, this volume neatly situates the symbolism of Denes (but *without* actually discussing the precise terms of her practice) in relation to Guattari and Bateson's thinking, thereby appearing to endorse not only the heterogeneity of 'ecological urbanism' as its new 'home' (*oikos*), but also its capacity for theoretical, political and aesthetic interdisciplinarity.[5]

This recent evolutionary 'turn' from landscape to ecological thinking is also firmly situated in relation to the continued modernist fascination with its capitals: evident, for example, in claims for James Corner's practice Field Operations and architects Diller Scofidio + Renfro's New York *High Line* (www. thehighline.org), which recently celebrated the opening of its second section. This conceptualization of the park as an elevated walkway is taken as a demonstration of landscape urbanism's successful reinvention of the long-held close relationship between natural and designed landscapes, parks or fields for the wellbeing of the city and its occupants. On the periphery of New York, Corner is now also reprogramming the 2,200-acre site of the world's largest landfill on Staten Island into a masterplan for Fresh Kills Park (2001–40). In the UK, his global practice has opened an office in London, and has been responsible for the design of the south Olympic Park, and reconditioning Everton Park for the Liverpool 2012 Biennale, further showing how this formation of ecological relations and the 'improvement' of environmental, social and mental relations are branded through national and international private and public-institution interests. Unsurprisingly, back in *Wheatfield*'s locale, Battery Park City Authority now promotes itself as a premier site of environmental architecture in the city. Its Green Guidelines highlight the 'diversity' of its public, private, commercial and institutional spaces which have transformed its early days of landfill riverfront into a functioning and productive mixed-use financial area of the city (Battery Park City Authority 2008).

More broadly across the profession, the increased promotion of environmentally responsive architecture over the past two decades has included design approaches that range from innovative approaches to recycling materials, local low-carbon energy resources and passive ventilation; from highly utopian and purely technocratic approaches to socially aware forms that involve urban gardening, green walls, vertical farming or urban agriculture, as the discipline rethinks its traditions and methods for environmental urbanism (e.g. see Zeiher 1996; McLennan 2004; Roaf *et al.* 2003; Steele 2005). However, if these 'good practice' guides are situated in relation to the UN's formulation of largely 'instrumental' sustainability there is still some considerable distance between protecting the interests of commercially driven architectural design and the critique of global relations that Denes set out to expose. *Wheatfield*'s value, then, lies not only in its prescient political imaginary of the current crisis in global international relations across all its scales of capitalism and advanced technology, which it embodied so aptly in 1982, but also in the tension between these political, economic and social differences post-2001, and in ways not yet materialized at the time of the work's physical manifestation. Though temporary, *Wheatfield*'s ecological duration therefore well exceeds its actual material manifestation, and is evidence that aesthetic ecologies are oscillating social, environmental and mental relations. As such, it reminds us of the 'bio-powers' (cf. Foucault 2008) that co-constitute aesthetic and ecological relations in the contemporary city at all scales – through markets, professions, communities, microeconomics and environmental activism – and which are also comprised of both the highly damaging ecologies of advanced capitalism as well as 'other' ecologies of care.

Pattern difference

Denes's aim to create a specifically aesthetic 'language of perception that allows the flow of information among alien systems and disciplines' to make 'new associations and valid analogies possible' (387) shares a cybernetic approach with Gregory Bateson's 'ecology of mind'. For Bateson, verbal and non-verbal aesthetic relations – that is ecologies – operate throughout all modes of psychic expression, as well as in biodiverse physical forms. Any ecology is constituted by the 'difference' or 'pattern' of information that organizes its material and immaterial relations, but I also turn to him because of his attempts to generate an understanding of ecology in the 'non-verbal arts', and to define difference through the aesthetic and geometric patterns of psycho-physical information. In the following section of this chapter I show that Guattari also shares Bateson's concern with the mental health of society, as an essential ecological mode required for protecting and enabling human health and the planet's survival, and for demystifying the structures of pathological ecologies.

Bateson's 1967 essay, 'Style, Grace, and Information in Primitive Art', attempts to consider culture and the 'non-verbal arts' by showing how psychic information or 'pattern' constitutes a primary kind of aesthetic ecology.[6] Bateson argues that relational forms of communication, such as the production of an artwork or a design, are constituted out of patterns of 'information' or 'difference', generating an ecology of relations that exist simultaneously on psychic, social and material levels. He argues that the visual arts are specific modes of coded information which 'integrate' these modes through unconscious or non-verbal pattern relations (Bateson 2000: 131). Drawing upon Freud's conceptualization of primary and secondary consciousness, which attempted to deal with the 'problem of integration' (and what Bateson also calls 'grace'), Bateson observes that while Freud recognizes the absolute difference between conscious and unconscious meaning, his schema mistakenly attributes non-verbal content to a repressed secondary order. Instead, Bateson redefines this unconscious non-verbal information as primary process, 'as continually active, necessary, and all-embracing' (136). Bateson then goes on to examine how primary process operates in the relationship of the self to the other, and their respective habits and habitats, by way of 'patterns of relationship' that we call 'feelings – love, hate, fear, confidence, anxiety, hostility etc.', noting also that these are often taken more as quantitative relations, 'rather than by precise pattern' (140).

For Bateson, then, the visual arts are inherently concerned with the production of difference. In addition, the unity of a visual work is always constructed out of the relationship between its distinct singular parts so that, in the final part of the essay, his examination of a 1937 painting of a cremation ceremony by a renowned Balinese artist, Ida Bagus Djati Sura, leads him to observe that: 'If the picture were *only* about sex or *only* about social organization, it would be trivial. It is nontrivial or profound precisely because it is about sex and social organization and cremation, and other things. In a word, it is only about relationship and not about any identifiable relata' (151).

However, not all of Bateson's thinking about ecology is to be accommodated into my discussion, since his terms of reference for 'grace' and 'style' here link back to problematic early twentieth-century discussions of identity formation in genetics and religion. In addition, Bateson also considers the production of meaning within a given ecology to be contingent, rather than the insistence upon the absolute difference, including sexual difference, which feminist thinkers, including Donna Haraway, Rosi Braidotti, Lorraine Code and Elizabeth Grosz (and others in this volume) require. His thinking also contrasts with Denes's and Guattari's insistence upon the biopolitical construction of 'integrated' global relations (and, which I will show below, also underpins Spinoza's 'absolute' divine and non-anthropocentric substance). But I refer to this essay because it outlines a process ecology that is nevertheless constitutive of psychic and biological sex difference, together with an aesthetic technical 'patterning' of difference in the communal habits of life and death within a 'built' environment. In this respect, Bateson is committed to recognizing the social, environmental and psychic differences for men and women, and for the collective sexed community, towards an aesthetic ethics of care required for the wellbeing of the individual, her/his society, and for environmental survival. This commitment to an ecological architectonics of care is underscored by his warning that without these aesthetic relations, 'pathological' ecologies and short-circuit modes of integrated technology will persist – such as antibiotics that have made 'parasites immune', the 'relationship between mother and neonate [that] has been almost destroyed', or the toxic impact of DDT that Rachel Carson's ground-breaking study exposed in modern large-scale agricultural methods (145–6). Such failings, Bateson observes, fully demonstrate that 'purposive rationality unaided by such phenomena as art, religion, dream, and the like, is necessarily pathogenic and destructive of life' (146).

Biopolitical ecologies

Denes's 1968 'eco-logic' demand to 'think globally and act independently' (Denes 1993: 387), and Bateson's ethico-aesthetic responsibility of a society to nurture the sexed psycho-social diversity of its community are concerns that Guattari echoes in his 'eco-logical praxis' (Guattari 2000: 33) of *The Three Ecologies*: 'Here we are talking about a reconstruction of social and individual practices which I shall classify under three complementary headings, all of which come under the ethico-aesthetic aegis of an ecosophy: social ecology, mental ecology and environmental ecology' (28).

Originally published three years after the 1986 Chernobyl disaster, which has resonated again more recently in light of the meltdown of the Fukushima nuclear plant reactors after the tsunami hit the east coast of Japan in March 2011, Guattari's deliberately 'ethico-political' ecological inquiry examines the consequences of advanced capitalism – and what he calls Integrated World Capitalism – for the future survival of biodiverse *l'altérité* across the mental, physical, technical, aesthetic and biological spheres. Starved of properly differentiated and differentiating ecological relations that tackle these issues in an integrated way, Guattari observes the real decline in mental, social and environmental health (19); for example, in the rampant property speculation and urban development of New York, or in the toxic growth of algae and acidification that has led to the destruction of the ecosystem in Venice's lagoon (29), which has been traced back to the overuse of fertilizers, and build up of industrial sewage and human waste.

Following Foucault's analysis of biopolitical relations (Foucault 2008) Guattari analyses how Integrated World Capitalism's regimes of power extend through the economic, juridical, techno-scientific and 'subjectification' semiotic regimes (Guattari 2000: 32), and which clearly also play out in commercial architectural, urban and planning relations. He warns that the homogenizing force of these combined bio-powers are toxic to subjectivity's biodiversity in all its forms, from the macro to micro levels of 'life'; from our access to housing, education, health or food resources; the flourishing of our mental health, aesthetic or sexuate expressions; to our rights to enfranchized agency and social justice. Furthermore, because these regimes operate at all levels of society and organization, it is no longer possible to take up positions 'outside': 'It is equally imperative to confront capitalism's effects in the domain of mental ecology in everyday life: individual, domestic, material, neighbourly, creative or one's personal ethics' (33). However, while Guattari's biopolitics shares with Foucault the understanding that these powers extend through from the top to the bottom, his outlook on this 'inconcluded middle' (36), in which 'good' ecologies exists with 'bad', also has affinity with Bateson's analysis of primary difference in mental ecologies from which new heterogeneous 'ethico-aesthetic' social and individual agencies are possible.

Guattari's 'transversal thinking' (29) therefore departs from Foucault's biopolitics to promote the 'resingularization' of 'heterogenic' collectives in a society that is 'more united and increasingly different' (45). In the closing paragraphs of the text he returns to Walter Benjamin's discussion of the 'double process' in the production of aesthetic life that brings 'information' and 'sensation' together into a multivalent ecology: 'It sinks the thing into the life of the storyteller, in order to bring it out of him again. Thus traces of the storyteller cling to the story the way the handprints of the potter cling to the clay vessel' (44). Guattari's call for new singularities and subjectivities operates through the necessary ethical re-integration of repressed other natures (both anthropocentric and non-anthropocentric) into traditional and advanced technological and scientific realms. However, his commitment to wholly new subjectivities means that while the three ecologies 'originate from a common ethico-aesthetic discipline, they are also distinct from the practices that characterize them' (45). Transversal thinking and practices therefore also reconfigure sexed difference beyond 1980s feminism: but given recent feminist theories by Braidotti, Code, Conley or Grosz, who have shown that sexuate difference is necessary for building new social, mental and environmental ecologies *for all*, we might now say there is a closer correspondence here with Guattari's 'transversal' subjectivities. Also, insofar as his ecologies take the production of modern subjectivity as a co-constitutive physical and mental process in aesthetic and technological modes, there are significant points of contact with the collective 'ethico-aesthetic' practices of Agnes Denes and, I suggest below, Donna Haraway.[7]

Geometric ecologies

Funded by the Finnish Government as its contribution to World Environment Day at the 1992 Summit in Rio, *Tree Mountain* is a forest of silver fir trees planted in a spiralling geometric pattern in a disused quarry site outside Ylöjärvi, Finland (see figures 2.2 and 2.3). Denes asked each participant to sign a 'Certificate of Preservation' that commits them and their descendants to be 'custodians' of their respective tree, ensuring that the lifespan of the forest exceeds each single human life and is protected by collective ownership. Denes has described how she intended that the spiralling growth of this protected aesthetic ecosystem will also register the change in ecological and artistic 'climates' during its anthropomorphic and non-anthropomorphic lifespans (Denes 1993: 390–1).

Both the mathematical geometry[8] used to cultivate this ecological habitat and the material 'substance' of the work – that is, the trees and the land – have recognizably anthropocentric and non-anthropocentric qualities. But the

2.2
Agnes Denes, *Tree Mountain – A Living Time Capsule – 11,000 Trees, 11,000 People, 400 Years*, 1992–96. Winter view, 2001 (detail of forest). 420 x 270 x 28 metres, Ylöjärvi, Finland. Eleven thousand trees were planted in a complex mathematical pattern by eleven thousand people from around the world, to be maintained for 400 years. One of the largest reclamation sites in the world, *Tree Mountain*, created from refuse material of a mine for this project, was declared a national monument to serve future generations with a meaningful legacy. Dedicated by the President of Finland, dignitaries and participants from around the world, 1996. *Tree Mountain* is to be surrounded by two rows of white birches at a later date.

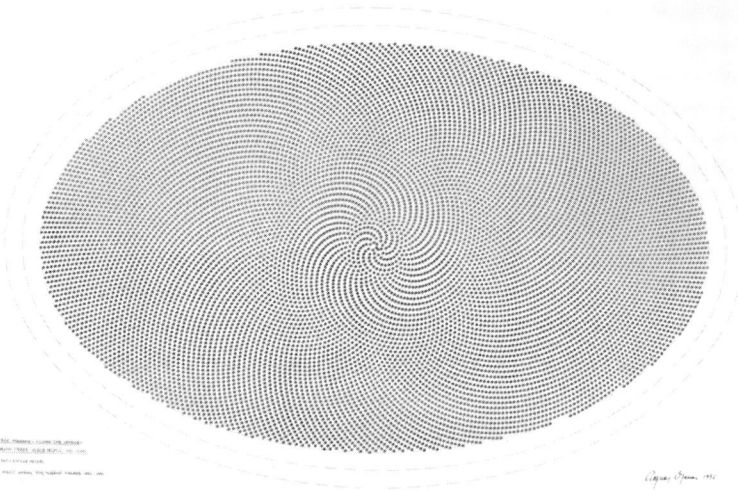

2.3
Agnes Denes, *Tree Mountain – A Living Time Capsule – 11,000 Trees, 11,000 People, 400 Years*, 1992–96. Ariel view of mathematical pattern into which the trees were planted.

value placed on the non-human qualities of the project recall Spinoza's complex seventeenth-century 'geometric ecology' which he develops in the *Ethics* (1677). Here, Spinoza shows that a wholly non-anthropocentric 'Substance' expresses both organic and non-human modes of life, as well as physical and psychic human habits, such as our emotions. Nature, or substance, and consequently all entities, always exist because of 'constructing' processes *(natura naturans)*, and 'construction' processes *(natura naturata)*. As such, geometric substance, human substance and non-human substance are always situated in relation to other processual entities in what might be called a 'natural geometry'. We can therefore suggest that this natural geometry of the silver fir, the landfill site, the participants and the geometric configuration of *Tree Mountain* constitute a durational ecology.

Second, this 'natural geometry' also incorporates an aesthetics of care or wellbeing that is promoted by Spinoza in his account of the 'common' durational and shared pattern of human relations. These durational habits are expressed as our passions or emotions of joy, sadness, melancholy or delight. Understanding how we inhabit these emotions – what Spinoza calls, 'affects' – enables the individual to reach a self-awareness, joy or agency, particularly in the form of the 'common notions' (also, interestingly, the common notions are then the third 'level' in Spinoza's tripartite ecology). In addition, the common experience of inhabiting these affects highlights how attaining a sense of wellbeing is not just a matter for the single individual, but is a matter of concern for the multitude (cf. Negri 2004).[9] Third, like Spinoza's analysis of an ecology of multimodal relations between human and non-human modes of life (and inorganic entities), Denes's geometric 'ethics of care' (cf. Braidotti, 2006b) reflects this multi-durational organization, in which the individual artist, participant communities, and the site itself are constructed as non-contingent 'singularities' or subjects with agency. Geometric thinking and practice is therefore shifted from being perceived as an instrumental technology that generates short-term economic or aesthetic gain, into an 'in-process' ecology that cultivates human and non-human relations of care.

Denes's geometric ecology – her *technical* ethics of care – also inhabits a companion space with the 'critical intelligence' of Donna Haraway, whose engaged questioning of advanced technologies provides an important feminist critique for discussing built and biological ecologies. As Braidotti notes, '*Critical intelligence for Haraway is a form of sympathy*' (Braidotti 2006a: 200; italics in original), rerouting the role of technology away from claims for autonomous scientific objectivity into a situated ethics of sexed responsibility for, and by, all. But I also want to draw correspondence between the two women in order to note the aesthetic 'technicity' (Loo 2011) of their approaches. Haraway's political imaginaries operate at the scale of biological ontologies and extend up through to the scale of non-human species filiation, survival or extinction.

Her figurations of the Cyborg and 'companion species' critique the construction of 'life' by neutral value-free advanced technologies. Instead, she argues that the individual's, the community's and society's habits and respective habitats can only be ethical and non-exclusionary if advanced technology is 'situated' and sexed (Haraway 1991, 2003). Denes's geometric figurations are also evidence of a critical sympathy, even though the technologies that she employs (such as Euclidian-derived geometries and pre-modern agricultural technology) are not advanced forms, and her familial custodianship is more conservative than Haraway's approach to cross-species cooperation and filiation between biodiverse subjects and communities. Nevertheless, there is a technicity in Denes's 'natural' and planetary geometric ecologies: for example, her concern with disrupting the technocratic 'machinery' of advanced capitalism, protecting a depleting population of silver fir, or drawing attention to the environmental damage of industrial and domestic waste landfills (a critical sensibility that is also present in her isometric map projections of 1974–6). In each practice, then, there is critique of advanced globalized and technological human–nature relations, but with the suggestion that *other* critical, sympathetic and, consequently, aesthetic technicities also exist.

Such difference-relations are also present in Bateson's aesthetic and Guattari's biopolitical ecologies, helping to examine how technological and aesthetic relations are integrated in the built environment. These earlier examples of 'architectures of care' are also visible in the work of contemporary architects whose ecological practices employ 'sympathetic' critiques about the profession's techniques and technologies. Such aesthetic architectural ecologies include: Doina Petrescu's collaborative practice, *atelier d'architecture autogérée* (aaa), who have worked with Parisian communities to develop a communal 'ECObox' economy, and the ecological design of housing and public space in their local neighbourhood (see Chapter 15); and UK architect, Sarah Wigglesworth's sustainable school and community designs in which non-specialist client design preferences are prioritized, rather than profit-driven commercial design protocols (see www.swarch.co.uk). Also, recently, the affordable housing crisis in the UK that has resulted from three decades of the 'dysfunctional' market-led mortgage economy (Barnett 2012), has converged with the urgent need to improve living-space standards in new home design (previously protected during the 1960–70s). Architects, including Wigglesworth, the Royal Institute of British Architects (RIBA) (e.g. its *Case for Space* report 2011), the Commission for Architecture and the Built Environment (CABE), and the Homes and Communities' Agency (HCA), have addressed how to construct better affordable, environmental and high-quality living space for diverse needs across the age ranges (Barnett 2012).

These architectural design approaches for improving social wellbeing and affordable housing, as part of the social and ecological biodiversity that a modern city clearly should provide, contrast with the large-scale 'shallow' built environment sectors where technocratic markets are still seen as the means to develop 'sustainable' solutions. Instead, in developing the 'architectures of care' that are now even more urgently required by today's complex cities, integrated sexed and ethical aesthetic ecological methods are essential 'technologies'. With these criteria, architects, urban designers and spatial practitioners may be more enabled to cultivate and protect today's and future generations' social wellbeing and biodiversity.

Notes

1 Thanks to Katie Lloyd Thomas for her helpful comments on this chapter.
2 The Brundtland Report defined sustainable development as that which

> meets the needs of the present without compromising the ability of future generations to meet their own needs. It contains within it two key concepts: the concept of 'needs', in particular the essential needs of the world's poor, to which overriding priority should be given; and the idea of limitations imposed by the state of technology and social organization on the environment's ability to meet present and future needs.
>
> (Brundtland 1987: Chapter 2)

3 David Cross has questioned if the agricultural techniques ('agri-business techniques', Guattari 2000: 21) used to create *Wheatfield* can really be called 'ecological' in today's terms.
4 Fritjof Capra defines Deep Ecology thus:

> Shallow ecology is anthropocentric. It views humans as above or outside of nature, as the source of all value and ascribes only instrumental or use value to nature. Deep ecology does not separate humans from the natural environment, nor does it separate anything else from it. It does not see the world as a collection of isolated objects but rather as a network of phenomena that are fundamentally interconnected and interdependent. Deep ecology recognizes the intrinsic values of all living beings and views humans as just one particular strand in the web.
>
> (Sessions 1995: 20)

5

> The prevailing conventions of design practice have demonstrated a limited capacity both to respond to the scale of the ecological crisis and to adapt their established ways of thinking. In this context, ecological urbanism can be seen as a means of providing a set of sensibilities and practices that can help enhance our approaches to urban development. This is not to imply that ecological urbanism is a totally new and singular mode of design practice. Rather, it utilizes a multiplicity of old and new methods, tools, and techniques in a cross-disciplinary and collaborative approach toward urbanism developed through the lens of ecology. These practices must address the retrofitting of existing urban conditions as well as our plans for the cities of the future.
>
> (Mostafavi and Doherty 2010: 26)

6 Architect Christopher Alexander developed a universal language of 'pattern' in his co-written book *A Pattern Language: Towns, Buildings, Construction* (1977), which is now being reconsidered by architects seeking to find mathematical 'grammars' for parametric and morphological design.

7 This sensibility is also voiced by many of the contributors in this volume.
8 This classical geometry contrasts with claims for 'organic' and non-anthropocentric geometric topologies in much contemporary digital architectural design discourse (see Rawes 2012).
9 Naess also generated an 'equation' of wellbeing in the mid-1960s, preceding the current biopolitical interest in calibration of happiness by some forty years (Naess 1995: 81).

Bibliography

Alexander, C., Ishikawa, S., Silverstein, M. with Jacobson, M. Fiksdahl-King, I. and Angel, S. (1977) *A Pattern Language: Towns, Buildings, Construction*, Oxford: Oxford University Press.

Barnett, L. (2012) 'Home truths: architects tackle the housing crisis', the *Guardian*, Wednesday 11 July. Online: http://www.guardian.co.uk/artanddesign/2012/jul/11/housing-crisis-affordable-living-architecture (accessed 20 July 2012).

Bateson, G. (2000) *Steps to an Ecology of Mind*, Chicago: University of Chicago Press.

Battery Park City Authority (2008) 'Green Guidelines: Growing a Green Community'. Online: http://www.batteryparkcity.org/page/page23.html (accessed 5 June 2012).

Braidotti, R. (2006a) 'Posthuman, all too human: towards a new process ontology', *Theory, Culture and Society*, 23, 7–8: 197–208.

— (2006b) *Transpositions: On Nomadic Ethics*, Cambridge: Polity Press.

Brundtland, O. (1987) *Our Common Future*. Online: http://www.un-documents.net/our-common-future.pdf (accessed 5 May 2011).

Confino, J. (2012) 'Rio+20: Tim Jackson on how fear led world leaders to betray green economy', the *Guardian*, Monday 25 June. Online: http://www.guardian.co.uk/sustainable-business/rio-20-tim-jackson-leaders-green-economy?INTCMP=SRCH – Rio+20 (accessed 14 July 2012).

Corner, J. (ed.) (1999) *Recovering Landscape: Essays in Contemporary Landscape Architecture*, New York: Princeton Architectural Press.

Denes, A. (1993) 'Notes on eco-logic: environmental artwork, visual philosophy and global perspective', in special issue: 'Art and Social Consciousness', *Leonardo*, 26, 5: 387–95.

Drexhage, J. and Murphy, D. (2010) 'Sustainable development: from Brundtland to Rio 2012'. Background paper prepared for consideration by the *High Level Panel on Global Sustainability* at its first meeting, 19 September. Online: http://www.un.org/wcm/webdav/site/climatechange/shared/gsp/docs/GSP1-6_Background%20on%20Sustainable%20Devt.pdf (accessed 4 April 2012).

Foucault, M. (2008) *The Birth Of Biopolitics: Lectures at the Collège de France, 1978–1979*, trans. G. Burchell, Basingstoke: Palgrave Macmillan.

Guattari, F. (2000) *The Three Ecologies*, trans. I. Pindar and P. Sutton, London: Athlone Press.

Haraway, D.J. (1991) *Simians, Cyborgs and Women: the Reinvention of Nature*, London: Free Association Press.

— (2003) *The Companion Species Manifesto: dogs, people, and significant otherness*, Chicago: Prickly Paradigm Press.

Jameson, F. (1998) 'The brick and the balloon: architecture, idealism and land speculation', *New Left Review*, 228, March–April. Online: http://newleftreview.org/I/228/fredric-jameson-the-brick-and-the-balloon-architecture-idealism-and-land-speculation (accessed 30 September 2010).

Loo, S. (ed.) (2011) *Technics, Memory and the Architecture of History*, Symposium for *Interstices 13*, Launceston: University of Tasmania.

Manacorda, F. and Yedgar, A. (eds) (2009) *Radical Nature: Art and Architecture for a Changing Planet 1969–2009*, London: Barbican Art Gallery and Koenig Books.

Matilsky, B.C. (1992) *Fragile Ecologies: Contemporary Artists' Interpretations and Solutions*, New York: Rizzoli International.

McLennan, J.F. (2004) *The Philosophy of Sustainable Design: The Future of Architecture*, Kansas City, MO: Ecotone.

Mostafavi, M. and Doherty, G. (eds) (2010) *Ecological Urbanism*, Baden, Switzerland: Lars Muller and Harvard University, Graduate School of Design.

Naess, A. (1995) *Ecology, Community and Lifestyle*, trans. D. Rothenberg, Gateshead, Tyne and Wear: Athenaeum Press.

Negri, A. (2004) *Subversive Spinoza: (Un)contemporary Variations*, trans. T.S. Murphy, M. Hardt, T. Stolze and C.T. Wolfe, Manchester: Manchester University Press.

Rawes, P. (2008) *Space, Geometry and Aesthetics: Through Kant and Towards Deleuze*, Basingstoke: Palgrave Macmillan.

— (2012) 'Spinoza's geometric ecologies', *Interstices: Journal of Architecture and Related Arts*, 'Under Construction: Technics, Memory and the Architecture of History', 13: 60–9.

RIBA (2011) *The Case for Space: The Size of England's New Homes*, London: Royal Institute of British Architects.

Roaf, S., Fuentes, M. and Thomas, S. (2003) *Ecohouse 2: A Design Guide*, Oxford: Architectural Press.

Sessions, G. (ed.) (1995) *Deep Ecology for the Twenty-first Century*, Boston, MA: Shambhala Publications.

Spatial Agency (2012) Online: http://www.spatialagency.net/database/why/political/exyzt (accessed 5 June 2012).

Spinoza, B. ([1677] 1992) *Ethics: Treatise on the Emendation of the Intellect and Selected Letters*, S. Feldman (ed.), Indianapolis: Hackett Publishing.

Steele, J. (2005) *Ecological Architecture: A Critical History*, London: Thames and Hudson.

Thayer, R. (2003) *Life Place: Bioregional Thought and Practice*, Berkeley: University of California Press.

Waldheim, C. (ed.) (2006) *The Landscape Urbanism Reader*, New York: Princeton Architectural Press.

Willis, C. (1995) *Form Follows Finance: Skyscrapers and Skylines in New York and Chicago*, New York: Princeton Architectural Press.

Zeiher, L.C. (1996) *The Ecology of Architecture: A Complete Guide to Creating Environmentally Conscious Building*, New York: Whitney Library of Design, Watson-Guptill Publications.

Chapter 3

Diagramming control

Nathan Moore

3.1
Device at the
Britannia Building
Society, Euston
Road.

Introduction

Being employed by Birkbeck College School of Law in London, while also
attending the postgraduate programme at the Bartlett School of Architecture, I
had occasion to walk around the Bloomsbury area of London quite a bit. Doing
so, I began to notice one or two peculiar 'architectural' features that set me
thinking. I put 'architectural' in quotes, because to refer to these features as

architectural is actually a bit of a stretch: they don't derive from, or aspire to, the tradition of architectural craft that seeks, at its best, to combine aesthetic possibility with the potentials of social and political life. Rather, these features seemed to be afterthoughts, *ad hoc* additions that, in an extremely rough and ready manner, sought to answer an apparent problem that, at the time of the architectural plan, had not been foreseen. Being improvised, these features have no common factor in the usual sense of architectural design or form, making it difficult to group them within a particular category or genre. What they do share is an intent, or particular relation to the world. Consequently, their commonality is more virtual than actual (but nonetheless real), and it was this in particular that forced me to start thinking about them.

Perhaps the clearest example of the type of feature I am referring to is the one (pictured) to be found at the Britannia Building Society, on Euston Road. The fire escape, set back from the pedestrian pavement, and sheltered in a fairly large alcove, has had added to it, at some later date, a contraption fashioned as a grid of vertical iron bars, of differing heights, and connected by horizontal brackets. The device has been bolted into the floor in one corner of the space. Attached to the wall outside the alcove is a stationary CCTV camera, trained at the corner opposite the iron grid. What caught my attention about this grid, initially, is its ugliness. No thought had been given to the way this apparatus looks. However, two things quickly followed: first, that this grid had been added to prevent people from sitting or standing in the corner of the alcove that it covered; and, second, that the area covered by the CCTV camera did not have a similar device to prevent occupation of the opposite corner.

Having a law background, the second point was particularly suggestive: the use of surveillance obviously recalled the work of Michel Foucault. However, at the same time, something about this space, and the use of the grid, seemed to escape the concept of the panopticon, going beyond the function of the gaze as a disciplinary mechanism. The grid, in the arrangement outside the building society, served as an alternative or substitute for a CCTV camera. On the other side, not being covered by a camera, occupation of the space has been prevented by the grid as a physical object. Is it, then, that the grid is simply a brute expression of force, achieving the same function as the CCTV but, presumably, on the cheap? On one level, this would seem a fair conclusion. However, I was not convinced that this described the main function of the device. This hunch grew as, walking further afield in Camden, I began to find other examples of such architectural devices. By no means were these features uniform, nor were they necessarily added later. However, they were suggestive of a logic that went beyond mere equivalence with CCTV cameras, and the economy of the gaze.

From economy to ecology

The phrase 'economy of the gaze' is useful because it reminds us that, for Foucault, the 'gaze' is of interest only to the extent that it is a mode of power, a mode which, in particular, is to be understood as a matter of economy (Foucault, 1977, 2001). Economy here refers to an efficient arrangement, not necessarily limited to efficient *acts*, but including, more expansively, a *preparedness* or even stockpiling of the ability to act, seemingly as and when necessary. However, this does not lead to the conclusion that, at some point, action will occur; economy is not a means to an end, but an end in its own right, and consequently, what is important is to stockpile, to hold in reserve, *and to continue holding in reserve*.

Foucault's work demonstrates that the modes and articulations of what is considered to be economic do not remain fixed. In this chapter, I will stick to Deleuze's distinction between discipline and control as two different economic regimes (Deleuze 1995). With discipline, the confining gaze ideally serves to encourage the prisoner (and those like him or her) to hold him or herself in check, thereby making him or herself available for the requirements of discipline, *by excluding alternative modes of behaviour*. Control withdraws the apparent normative guarantee at the heart of the disciplinary regime, so that the individual is no longer available, *but exposed*. Here, it is less a matter of excluding, in advance, what is undesirable, as it is to economise this very power of exclusion, so that the individual is called upon, again and again, to transform itself – not to negatively become 'normal' through the exclusion of 'abnormality', but to exercise exclusion as a formal operation, where what is excluded ceases to be important, or even have significance. Today's abnormality is tomorrow's normality, such that the two terms cease to have any real distinction – or, at least, no longer operate as if they were distinct. What is crucial for control is their *relation*, and the possibility of constantly re-mobilising relations irrespective of the terms related, a process Deleuze and Guattari call 'axiomatizing' (1984: 248).

This is not to say that, today, there are no panoptic effects, but that *the* panopticon, as a diagram of power, has been displaced. As Deleuze writes, the contemporary situation does not operate by confining bodies, by holding them in *a* gaze, through which a natural inclination for self-ordering might be revealed; no, today bodies are set in motion, and it is in the condition of movement that what is economic – what can be captured and stored up – is to be realised, even if such realisation is continuously suspended.[1] We can even consider this geometrically, inasmuch as the panoptic gaze suggests a *line* of sight, a line determined by its two ends, watcher and watched. This brings its own difficulties, as I have suggested elsewhere (Moore 2012–13), but in any case, once it is no longer a matter of fixing a proper place and distance, then the line no longer holds; or at least, it begins to take on a life of its own. If the emphasis shifts to putting bodies into movement, to making watcher and watched circulate (what Foucault, 1980, called *malveillance*) then we become more interested in points on the line, of, in effect, being able to divide the line up. However, this has the curious effect of indeterminacy, inasmuch as a line is *infinitely* divisible. So too with contemporary economic efficiency: one is required to manage a sort of brink or edge, that draws close, yet is never close enough to be crossed. As Deleuze and Guattari describe it, one reaches a limit, but draws back from the threshold (Deleuze and Guattari, 1988: 440).

To have shifted from a line of holding confinement, most noticeably exercised through the line of sight, to an infinitely divisible line, means that a certain spatialisation – or at least, a spatial shift – has occurred. However, this space is a curious one: less a space contained within a boundary line, and much more a line that, by being infinitely divisible, seems to contain within it an infinite space, even when the line in question is of a very definite length or circumference.[2] In short, the line implicates space, not the common sense space of everyday experience, but a space of virtuality, a space that rather than act as a background to be moved in or across, is itself *in* movement – a space that moves in place, without going anywhere.

This space could be called all sorts of things, but it is difficult to imagine a better word than 'ecology', not taken from the various green movements, but from the work of Gregory Bateson. Bateson presents ecology as a cybernetic system, meaning that it operates informationally. Information, in Bateson's sense, is the difference which makes a difference (Bateson 1972: 315). An ecology is then an information relay that responds to differences, such that these differences produce an altered function or auto-intervention within the ecological system itself. The system responds to a stimulus or difference by making the necessary adjustments, so that it might carry on performing in its usual or habitual pattern. Consequently, what is apparently the repeated and constant behaviour of a system is in fact the result of a continuous process of intervention (responding to difference), so that continuity might be produced. Continuity is, then, the result of discontinuity: it is produced from discontinuities, but also, if it successfully produces its own continuity, it neutralises, or renders unconscious, those discontinuities.

In which case, what tends to dominate is the perception of a system as an isolated, or unitary, entity. This is of concern for Bateson. Such a limited perception encourages a potentially disastrous imbalance in the system: the broader ecology appears divorced from the actors 'within' it, such that the former becomes merely a context within which the latter's purposeful activity is pursued (Bateson 1972: 432–45). However, if we understand ecology as a system generated from discontinuity and difference, then it is not possible to finally seal any system off from any other. Like an infinitely divisible line, any particular ecology depends upon a singular virtual space, the border of which cannot be clearly defined; or rather, an ecology has an essentially vague border which 'contains within it' an infinite relation to all other ecologies.

For Bateson, difference is not a physical feature of some entity: a difference is only such relative to that which it is different from (Bateson 1972: 412). Consequently, the existence of difference is a matter of perception: a difference can only be perceived to be such as *between* two objects or features, as a divergence from pre-established *patterns* of operation (413). A pattern depends, for its success as a continuing system, upon its reinforcement by other patterns: for example, an English speaker will know that the missing letter from the word-pattern 'q_iet' is 'u', because of the more general pattern that dictates that the letter 'q' must be followed by the letter 'u'. The operation of ecology, informationally, is then negative, in Bateson's view, because it operates by restricting probabilities: we know that 'u' is the missing letter because the 25 alternative letters are precluded by the patterns of the English alphabet (Bateson 1972: 408).

Implicit in this is that the difference that makes a difference must only be different enough – it has to be something to which an ecology is capable of responding, and so can't be so different as to be overwhelming or disruptive (noise). The difference that makes a difference is then to be found at that vague limit point where an ecology becomes virtual space, where other ecologies or systems are perceived not as external or separate, but as more or less implicated in the ecology to hand. To follow Deleuze, rather than a border, we find a fold. What is clear for Bateson, however, is that this vague implication of ecologies (which is nevertheless specific, so that *an* ecology is singular) is first and foremost evident only to an ecological *mind*. It is for this reason above all others that the term 'ecology' is appropriate: it is the science of the home or environment, a rigorous diagramming of the possibilities of an ecology opening out onto other ecological systems.

As such, we should consider *economy* as dependent upon *ecology*, with the latter serving not only as a resource for economic innovation, but also as providing an 'outside' or line of flight to be captured and excluded. The relation between the two is complicated under control, inasmuch as economy increasingly takes, as its conscious purpose, the subsumption of ecology within economy: no longer a disciplinary island in an ecological sea, control economy seeks both to become the entire territory, while (and this is crucial) recognising the impossibility of such an endeavour (hence, the schizophrenia of capital). Economy begins to prioritise its own outside as a way to destabilise fixed relations: to continuously re-expose, to deny the shelter of a border. To borrow from the sociology of risk, we might say that control ceases to use risk calculation as a way to bracket out uncertainty, and instead harnesses uncertainty as a method for destabilising provisional risk assessments. Consequently, the probable and the improbable (one might say, the normal and the abnormal), are increasingly difficult to distinguish, leading to an increase in (and utilisation of) fear (Massumi 1993; Wilkinson 2001).

Norms

To further understand the difference between discipline and control, it is useful to turn to the comments of François Ewald (1991) on normative systems. In his view, a system articulates power at specific points, through the formation of a particular normative framework, but without being able to close itself off as a definitive site of power. This touches upon the core of the issue, inasmuch as power is no longer understood as being exercised and delegated from a source, in a top-down manner, but is understood, normatively, as a horizontal network. However, within this network, sites and practices coalesce in singular configurations that nevertheless produce hierarchical relations. The point is that these hierarchies are stand-alone affairs, which depend upon their effectiveness and operationability for their authority, rather than their place within a relatively stable pyramid of power. Power is not so much delegated to these points, than it is captured by them through *the efficient dispositions of men and things* that they are able to render (Foucault 2001). This means that the 'source' of power is in the very circulation of power, its mobility. We would then need to think of power as being *innovated* rather than delegated, inasmuch as the retention of power increasingly depends upon an intensified focus on its mobility, and, crucially, the expression of that mobility as constant adaptability and innovation.

Within the logic of discipline, the norm takes on the characteristic of being a measure. More to the point, it is a self-referential measure that creates information by applying an average standard to a collection of data. We should note that the phrase 'collection of data' is crucial, because this serves to create a locality of power through which the latter can be actualised. To borrow an example from Ewald, if we are interested in being informed about the height of French men aged 20–65 then we have immediately created a locality, a *space for power*, through the collection of French men within that age range. However, this group still lacks sense inasmuch as it is simply a collection of actual living beings that are more noticeable for their differences than their similarities; but once we record their heights, and derive from this an average, then we at once have a measure by which to order (and hence unify) the members of the group: each member of the group, in terms of height, is understood *by reference to* the average height of the group as a whole, which now serves as a common standard. The average height is thus the norm of the group. Obviously, this notion can be applied to anything, including behaviour – in this sense, the panopticon is an attempt to make the individuals within it conform to the average of the group to which they have been deemed to belong. However, this average cannot be cut off from the divergences which actually constitute it. In other words, the norm, as the measure of average behaviour, cannot be separated out from what is abnormal – the former is extracted from the latter. As such, right and wrong, good and bad are no longer polar opposites, but points on a continuum that shade into each other (Ewald 1991: 157). Consequently, normativity is an informational system that produces continuity from discontinuities.

Control

The shift from discipline to control is sufficiently fundamental that we can consider the latter to be a new regime of power, yet the normative characteristics of both are similar. If we accept Ewald's description of normativity, then it is still the case that control extracts averages – that is, norms – from a range of differences. However, these averages no longer function as standards of convergence – they are no longer the proper condition to which bodies should try to conform, through the exclusion of alternatives. Rather, the norm exists only negatively, in a ghostly fashion, to mark the divergence of every body from it. If the norm is necessarily an abstraction, then it is not incarnated in any actual body. That there might be bodies more or less close to it, in terms of its measurements, is irrelevant, because the norm exists only as an expression of the qualities of a particular group, smoothed out into an average that, while applicable to members of a group *because they are members of that group*, is not capable of being occupied, as the space of the average, by any one of them as individuals. Being average says little about the characteristics of the individual in question, but everything about the character of the group. Consequently, even with discipline, we must consider the norm to be a sort of ghostly projection that is never embodied but, instead, makes sensible, as divergences, those that are embodied *relative* to it. The point about this is that, essentially, to be embodied marks one as being *not* average. At the core of the normative system is the surprising presumption that to be specifically embodied is already to depart from the norm. We cannot then say that to not exist is then what is most average, but more subtly that the average is a sort of suspension of existence: an exclusion of incorporation, as if the latter were simply noise (Terranova 2004: 10–20).

Control is conscious of the fact that not only do bodies diverge from the norm, they do so necessarily, because they are bodies. In that light, trying to make bodies conform to the norm, simply because it is the norm, appears untenable. Indeed, the norm is the demonstration of the impossibility of making bodies conform. For this reason, control tends toward a celebration of difference (that is, abnormality) and the promotion of divergence. Rather than discipline's conscious purpose of excluding the abnormal, control's conscious purpose is to ramify it. In other words, it innovates, encouraging abnormality as the vector of adaptability. Here, we should recall the phrase Foucault adopts, regarding the efficient disposition of men and things. What control operates is not a specificity as regards a particular disposition – it does not promote this or that arrangement as more or less desirable – but rather the *processes* of disposing. Control is concerned with the arrang*ing* of men and things, of the constant movement of bodies without end, regardless of what they are moving to or from: it is the mobilisation that control seeks, a sort of perpetual relative nomadism, where economy pursues a becoming-ecological.

However, control plays a double game. The promotion of the other, of the abnormal, must be understood as an entirely cynical and ironic gesture by control, and the (ab)normality it promotes is akin to the axiomatic functioning of capital, as described by Deleuze and Guattari (1984: 248–9), inasmuch as control does not posit a particular set of qualities as desirable or proper, but rather points to *the impossibility of achieving anything desirable or proper* as its sole justification, and as the 'basis' for its right of intervention.[3] In all cases, it cracks open the specificity of things so as to mobilise them as abstract processes: it disembodies. In this, the disposition of men and things, and the related point of economic efficiency, takes on a particular hue: the correct disposition of things requires paradoxically that things be, now, where they will be in the future. To be efficient is to be ahead of oneself, so that the present becomes that *which will have been*. This is why the current specificity of any embodiment must be decoded, and re-arranged axiomatically, in order to make live today what will come to pass tomorrow. The irony of control corresponds to the remark of Keynes that in the long run we are all dead, its priority then being to achieve, as a sort of superior health, the immediate transformation of all into a living death. To make the future live now means making the present die in its place. Co-extensively, potential is then maximised by paradoxically excluding all specific actualisations on the basis that *all actualisations are equally probable* (and thus completely uncertain).

Dividuality and design

The individual is, from a Foucauldian perspective, unthinkable outside the regime of discipline. Discipline produces individuals (Ewald 1991). Control produces something else, which Deleuze calls *dividuality* to refer to entities that, from the perspective of the individual at least, appear to be something less, or a breaking down of the unity of the individual. Dividuality is the measure of the tendencies and potentials of bodies, not as organised unities, but rather as an array or assemblage of faculties and abilities. As such, human biography no longer pertains to the marshalling of resources so as to produce a 'finished' or normal individual, but rather to a never-ending set of processes that are managed distinctly in terms of one's work, leisure, loves, health, finances and so on, so as to produce efficient movements in specific contexts. In other words, dividuality is a question of constantly innovating oneself, but also of accounting for such innovations (Power 1994).

What are the implications of this for architecture? We must consider architecture as economo-logies of control, as spaces of pre-emption that are concerned to dividualise through ongoing articulations of corrective, and accountable, ergonomics. A good example of this can be found in the work of the Design Against Crime Research Centre, at Central Saint Martin's College of Art and Design in London (DAC). DAC is interested in the design of urban space, and how such design impacts upon the incidence of criminal (or undesirable) behaviour. In a number of articles available via the Design Against Crime website, an ostensible link between crime and design is repeatedly set out. As Gamman and Thorpe sum up:

> Crime is a voracious form of premature obsolescence. Replacement of insured stolen items increases levels of product consumption that are unsustainable. Additional to the ecological cost of crime are the social and economic impacts linked to 'courts, cops and corrections' – money better spent on building social innovation and sustainability.
>
> (Gamman and Thorpe 2008: 2)

The first sentence of this quote sums up the logic of control accurately: the true problem, the real threat of crime and undesirable behaviour, is that the wrong type of future will be rendered now – a future-present of 'premature obsolescence' that is then understood as a failure of efficiency and an affront to good economy. It is also noticeable that the more disciplinary response to this problem – 'courts, cops and corrections' – is singled out as no longer being the most efficient one, not simply because it is not as cost effective in combatting premature obsolescence, but because it is *reactive*, responding to crime only after the event. Against this, it is necessary for design to combat crime before it has even happened, being less concerned with the specificity of the designed object and more with the social relations passing through that object, necessitating ever more design innovation addressed to the very *forging* of those social relations:

> [design] work is never 'finished', but always in the stage of 'becoming', [and] is linked to ideas about improvement and radical social innovation but also to monitoring the behaviour of adaptive criminals, competitive rivals and changing market requirements. This notion that [Design Against Crime]

products must evolve or become obsolete intrinsically links DAC products with a consumer and market led model of the design process.

(Gamman and Thorpe 2006: 10).

It is not a question of designing a finished object, or even an institutional practice, but rather of developing an ongoing modulatory process, that seeks to both intervene in, and pre-emptively discourage, certain types of behaviour.

DAC presents itself as 'unique because it extends the concept of "user driven innovation" to that of "user/mis-user and abuser driven innovation"', summed up as a process of 'thinking thief' when designing (Gamman and Thorpe, 2007). Similarly, quoting another associate of DAC, Paul Ekblom, Gamman and Thorpe write, '[o]ur research projects attempt to "... help designers keep up with the adaptive criminal in a changing world"' (Gamman and Thorpe, 2008: 9). Significantly, rather than seek to try to exclude what might be called the 'bad other' (criminal, vandal, graffiti writer, etc.), DAC's design process actually seeks to *incorporate* him/her as part of the overall project, as an ongoing point of modulatory intervention. The abnormal is not to be confined or rehabilitated but rather incorporated within the design norm itself and, crucially, this cannot happen once and for all, but must be a continuous, never-ending process, because the abnormal is, necessarily, mobile: it adapts and transforms. The adaptive design abuser is a vector for both decoding design *and* axiomatising it, and this tends toward a sort of doubling of the designed object or space. This is because such design should not only be, in advance, resistant to abuse, but also, and even more importantly, it must *signal* this resistance: the perfected form of dissuasion is one where the abuser assesses, *without needing to carry out the design-abusive act*, that he or she will not be successful in criminalising the design.

(Ab)normal architecture

The articulation of the indistinctness of the normal and the abnormal, under control, therefore requires a new ergonomic, one that addresses less the contours of a formed, moulded body, and more the arranging of dividual tendencies and their constant modulation. In a sense, modulation occurs always at a boundary, inasmuch as it involves reassessing oneself, of adapting oneself as one moves from one zone to another. This boundary effect is well encapsulated in Borden's description of the 'go-between' screens at Broadgate:

What the ... gates do is less prevent the horizontal movement of the body and more challenge the self-perception of visitors, at the moment they

pass through the gate, as to whether they are allowed on to the site. ...
[T]he combination of hard architecture, soft gates and other boundaries ...
works not so much to physically exclude the unwanted, but to provoke in
their own mind, as they momentarily pass through the thickness of the
edge, the questions, 'Should I be here, and now? Do I have the right of
passage?'

(Borden 2000: 232–3)

The significance of the boundary is less to do with the demarcation between
two differing zones or spaces, and much more a matter of the boundary being,
in a sense, purified of its hinterland so that, under control, all space can potentially be an infinitely divisible boundary. Just as Design Against Crime must
be taken as aiming towards spaces of safety by necessarily transforming the
designed environment into a *signifier of safety*, so too (ab)normal space is a
sort of smooth space, without the character of the border, achieved not by
removing boundaries, but rather by making them highly mobile, virtual, and
discriminating: borders that can actualise potentially anywhere, depending upon
the body to be modulated. For this reason, if we understand disciplinary space
to be a space of confinement and emplacement, control space is something
of an opposite: open (Wallenstein 2009), transparent spaces that re-mobilise
points of access. Where one crosses from and to is less significant than the
act of crossing itself.

Control space then revives a particular meaning of the term *nomos*,
which is otherwise usually translated as 'order' or 'law'. In his etymology of the
word *nomos*, jurist Carl Schmitt detects a significant spatial aspect in its Greek
origins, with references to appropriation, division, and production, no single
one of which, within *nomos*, can be prioritised over the other (Schmitt 2006:
Chapter Four). However, Deleuze and Guattari link *nomos* to pasturage, thereby
emphasising *distribution in an open space*, rather than the pre-given divisions
of a bounded space that, for them, can only arise subsequent to a process of
intensive distribution (1988: 557, note 51). Space does not come pre-packaged
into distinct areas or zones, but rather is formed as such. This aspect of distribution is evident in Borden's analysis, when he writes that 'boundaries are not
finite, but zones of negotiation' (2000). That is, boundaries are (ab)normalising
zones of interaction which impose and encourage *efficient conducts*. Foucault
describes governmentality as the 'conduct of conducts', and the French *conduit*
also indicates a sort of channelling or shaping of behaviour, of encouraging, and
managing, flows. This intensive negotiation is not with another party, but only
with oneself, a calling into doubt of one's right so that one is subtly encouraged
to monitor and police oneself: one is induced to consider that one's presence
requires some manner of justification, that, even before being there, a debt is
owed. To be (ab)normal means, to borrow from Derrida, that *one fails to arrive.*

Conduits of arrival

Rather than conceptualise space as necessarily bounded, of being divisible into discrete parts, it is more fruitful to consider it as an infinitely divisible arrangement of conduits. The walls of the conduit are not boundaries so much as they are slick, imperceptible chutes that can open at any point to give access to other chutes. It is a question of dividualised movement, such that non-arrival comes to be seen as the consciously purposeful, and most proper. In the two lectures translated as *Aporias*, Derrida deconstructs the Heideggerian distinction between the human and the animal, which assigns proper being only to the former on the basis that the human both speaks and dies. This latter is particularly significant: the animal does not die, it can only perish, simply stop or end. The animal has no relationship to its own death, no relation to the thing that, from a human perspective (understood as *dasein*), is its most *proper* thing. Derrida critiques this distinction by pushing it even further, arguing that the difference between animal and human is, in fact, always blurred. *Dasein* exceeds itself by awaiting its own death and so is, in a sense, projected forward, beyond itself. For Heidegger, animals lack this excess, having no relationship to their own death, but Derrida points out that any decision as to the character of *dasein* (i.e. that it awaits its own death) must occur here, on this side of the border between life and death *without waiting* (Derrida 1993: 52–4). Consequently, the decision about the difference between humans and animals is *im*proper because it contains within it the projection forward of *dasein*, foreclosing that which is awaited, so putting the human on the same level as the animal. It could be said that, finally, it is impossible for the human to have a *proper* relation to death, because there remains, in the decision as to what is proper, a sort of animal-like recoiling from death, in favour of an overdetermined assertion that one is, now, that which properly is.

Hence the significance of arriving. Projecting forward means that one is, now, waiting. What is awaited? Derrida's answer to this is the *arrivant*, who is always unexpected. One awaits without realising that one is waiting, and will only become aware of this (that one *was* waiting) after the arrivant has arrived. This arrival will redraw the boundary by making it apparent (making visible the line between 'here' and 'there', where the arrivant has come from) and, in so doing, make those who have awaited aware that the boundary was not where they thought it to be (1993: 33). The flip side of this is the impossibility of receiving the arrivant anywhere which has been predetermined. By arriving unexpectedly, from there, the arrivant reconfigures where it arrives (33). From this perspective, the arrivant is an ecological persona, (non)arriving in that space where an ecology opens to all other ecologies. Its arrival does not transform the present into an empty future (it will have been awaited), but rather transforms the past relative to a new present (it was awaited).

Nevertheless, it seems that the arrivant is close to the design abuser as imagined in DAC's 'thinking thief', because, just as the arrivant rearticulates boundaries, causing *eco-nomos* to be redistributed, so too DAC aspires to create an environment undergoing constant transformation, constant modulation, in response to the arrival of the adaptive design abuser. However, a fundamental difference exists, separating the design abuser from the arrivant: the latter calls the presumed boundaries into question by arriving, while the former requires a proliferation of mobile boundaries that are to prevent the design abuser from arriving: *he or she is to be deflected in advance*. In this sense, DAC awaits the design abuser because this is, in fact, all that it can do – all space, all environment, all design, is to prioritise waiting for the design abuser, through the production of objects and spaces that are to be constantly mobilised in order to ensure his or her non-arrival. The fate of control is to wait without end, warding off what it waits for by always beginning the awaiting anew – yet another modulation as a new axiom of arrival is added, and conduits re-arranged.

This logic is apparent in the sorts of device I came across in Camden. Rather than holding and confining, they seek to deflect bodies, to decode them into so many processes of dividuality by ensuring that, in the seemingly small and insignificant spaces they cover, bodies do not arrive, that they are kept on the move, conducting themselves away. Clearly, a decision has been made: only an animal body would want to arrive in such spaces, only an animal body would want to come to rest there. To stop moving is inefficient and uneconomic. Consequently, I would suggest that, if the panopticon served as a diagram of discipline, these small devices should be considered as diagramming a new regime, that of control. Such a diagram would have to include at least four vectors:

1   Modulatory (ab)normality: control adopts a cynical attitude towards the indiscernibility of the normal and the abnormal, through which it fosters a constant mobility that should not allow bodies to come to rest anywhere. Spatially, this means that the specificity of place is decoded in order to render space formally as simply 'here' and 'there'. As such, a new boundary, conduit, or axiom is added that can be crossed by bodies but, at the same time, does not allow a body to arrive anywhere. Consequently, control space is an open, non-differentiated space that constantly modulates the formality of 'here' and 'there', so that a new boundary can always be added.

2   Cynical irony: control makes the indiscernibility of proper and improper, design user and abuser, citizen and criminal, the very basis of its operation. Thus, bodies are caught up in a double-bind (that is, captured) (Bottomley and Moore 2012) which demands both that they arrive, in the limited sense of crossing a boundary, and don't arrive, by being deflected by a boundary.

Like 'here' and 'there', access and refusal are purely formal, and operate irrespective of any content or quality to be accessed. Indeed, such content is only permissible to the extent that it can be decoded, meaning, in this sense, rendered formal. In this process of making formal, the double-bind of arrival/non-arrival, of human/animal, can be made *efficient* – a source of economy.

3   If discipline seeks to separate economy and ecology, control attempts to subject ecology to economy. It does this by becoming informatic, such that the indeterminiablity of its own border becomes the site, and motor, of an infinite debt or accounting (often rooted in, and as, fear). As such, it seeks to assign to itself the implication of ecologies, not to control the selection of possibilities for actualisation, but to claim for itself *all* possibilities as facets of itself. It achieves this by seeking to suspend the actualisation of potential by making all things equally possible. Consequently, economology appears co-extensive with the whole of the possible: the apparent ecology of all ecologies, or 'nature'.

4   Efficient displacement: it is desirable for a body to be, now, where it will be in the future. Ultimately, this means that all bodies should be reduced to a sort of near-death experience, which seeks to neutralise, in advance, the unforeseeable dimensions and capabilities that bodies might otherwise develop. Control positively does not want to know what a body can do; or rather, it only wishes to know so that it might neutralise it pre-emptively. Through an enforced relative nomadism, control makes any body that arrives an animal or pest: an efficiency failure. On this basis, the biopolitical basis of control is revealed to be less an outright extermination, as it is an allowing to die, so long as this dying occurs elsewhere. Bodies removing themselves is more economic than mass extermination.

Notes

1   Deleuze uses the word 'modulation' to refer to such processes (Deleuze 1995).
2   See Rawes (2008: Chapter Four), and Berlinski (1996: Chapter Seven).
3   If we accept that discipline relies upon a sort of repressed mobility, we can understand the processes of coding and overcoding to be concerned to fix movements as a first requirement for knowing them, and utilising them: hence the processes of confining and holding central to discipline. Control, though, is concerned to decode, fostering movement itself, irrespective of any quality or specificity it might have – change for change's sake, or innovation. The counterbalance, as it were, to decoding is axiomatisation, which provides a set of parameters for harnessing movement in movement, rather than, as with coding, attempting to fix or hold it. Control is a logic of fluids, rather than solids, and for this reason, rather than holding and confining, we should understand it to be a process of modulatory capture (Bottomley and Moore 2012).

Bibliography

Bateson, G. (1972) *Steps to an Ecology of Mind*, London: University of Chicago Press.

Berlinski, D. (1996) *A Tour of the Calculus: The Philosophy of Mathematics*, London: Heinemann.

Borden, I. (2000) 'Thick edge: architectural boundaries in the postmodern metropolis', in I. Borden and J. Rendell (eds) *Intersections: Architectural Histories and Critical Theories*, London: Routledge.

Bottomley, A. and Moore, N. (2012) 'Law, diagram, film: critique exhausted', *Law & Critique*, 23, 2: 163–82.

Deleuze, G. (1995) 'Postscript on control societies', in *Negotiations*, M. Joughin (trans.), New York: Columbia University Press.

Deleuze, G. and Guattari, F. (1984) *Anti-Oedipus: Capitalism and Schizophrenia*. R. Hurley M. Seem, and H. R. Lane (trans.), London: The Athlone Press.

— (1988) *A Thousand Plateaus: Capitalism and Schizophrenia*, B. Massumi (trans.), London: The Athlone Press.

Derrida, J. (1993) *Aporias*, T. Dutoit (trans.), Stanford, CT: Stanford University Press.

Ewald, F. (1991) 'Norms, discipline and the law', in R. Post (ed.) *Law and the Order of Culture*, Berkeley: University of California Press.

Foucault, M. (1977) *Discipline and Punish: The Birth of the Prison*, A. Sheridan (trans.), London: Penguin Books.

— (1980) 'The eye of power', in C. Gordon, L. Marshall, J. Mepham and K. Soper (eds), *Power/ Knowledge*, Harlow: Longman.

— (2001) 'Governmentality', in *The Essential Works of Foucault 1954–1984 Volume 3: Power*, R. Hurley and others (trans.), London: Penguin Books.

Gamman, L. and Thorpe, A. (2006) 'What is socially responsive design – a theory and practice review'. Online: http://www.designagainstcrime.com/files/what_is_srvd_theory_practice_lisbon06.pdf (accessed 1 August 2010).

— (2007) 'Design methodology'. Online: http://www.designagainstcrime.com/index.php?q= designmethodology (accessed 1 August 2010).

— (2008) 'Less is more: what design against crime can contribute to sustainability'. Online: http://www.designagainstcrime.com/files/Changing_the_Change_Less_is_More.doc (accessed 1 August 2010).

Massumi, B. (1993) *The Politics of Everyday Fear*, Minneapolis: University of Minnesota Press.

Moore, N. (2012–13) 'Image and affect: between neo-Baroque sadism and masochism', *New York Law School Law Review*, 57: 97–113.

Power, M. (1994) *The Audit Explosion*, London: Demos.

Rawes, P. (2008) *Space, Geometry and Aesthetics: Through Kant and Towards Deleuze*, Basingstoke: Palgrave Macmillan.

Schmitt, C. (2006) *The Nomos of the Earth*, G. Ulmen (trans.), New York: Telos Press.

Terranova, T. (2004) *Network Culture: Politics for the Information Age*, London: Pluto Press.

Wallenstein, S-O. (2009) *Bio-Politics and the Emergence of Modern Architecture*, New York: Forum.

Wilkinson, I. (2001) *Anxiety in a Risk Society*, London: Routledge.

Part II

Uncertain, anxious and damaged ecologies

Chapter 4

'Manufactured uncertainty'

Epistemologies of mastery and the ecological imaginary[1]

Lorraine Code

When Virginia Woolf, in *A Room of One's Own*, deplores her exclusion from the carefully manicured grounds and hallowed halls of an Oxbridge college and its library, she has no illusions about the reasons why. She is a woman. 'Only the Fellows and Scholars are allowed here [on the turf]: the gravel is the place for me' she writes. Small wonder that she comments of her fictional, authorial self: '"I" is only a convenient term for somebody who has no real being' (Woolf 1929: 6–8), for its effects extend beyond the putatively anonymous authorship of this text. The exclusionary issue here is Woolf's sexed/sexuate being. No doubt had she been otherwise other – not middle class, not white – she would have been doubly, triply excluded. But being a woman was enough. No such multiple identities were at issue, for in the actions and policies that kept her out, sexual difference overrides and sustains other differences even in their multiple modalities, affirming the outrageousness, the unthinkable invasion of a woman in the halls of academe. Equally compelling is the idea that the gravel is the place for her, which is literally and metaphorically far-reaching in its implications. This reference to place, to a lowly place at that, presages the ideas germane to the issues I will discuss here, where place, situations, spaces are ecologically, epistemologically, and ontologically significant in ways that their merely background taken-for-grantedness effectively obscures.

      The minimal significance mainstream Anglo-American theories of knowledge and ethics accord to place, in which they are supported by and support a picture of knowers and/or 'moral agents' as mere place-holders in/on unspecified and putatively irrelevant places, upholds long-standing assumptions about the interchangeability of knowers and the known in properly objective acts of knowing, doing, and being. The very idea that knowing could be constitutive of place and place of knowing in ongoing reciprocal practices appears, in the post-positivist legacy, to threaten epistemic anarchy or to initiate a descent into the chaos of relativistic unknowing. Let us think, then, about the gravel: the gravel as 'the place for me'. In the scenario Woolf constructs, the gravel would not be the place for 'him' or for his *semblables*, whose rightful place need not be specified because it is everywhere and anywhere: that the turf with its well-tended comfort is his, is presupposed in institutional and social structures so firmly in place that they need neither be noticed nor spoken. In such unmarked places, hegemonic knowing and doing occur, and work to determine the structures and demographic hierarchies enacted on/with those relegated to the gravel.

As a way into thinking about how understanding the effects of sexual differences can contribute to present-day understandings of the impact and expressions of social justice and citizenship I will propose some links between Luce Irigaray's observation that 'To construct only in order to construct never-theless does not suffice for dwelling' (Irigaray 2004: 144), and my claim that 'ecological thinking is about imagining, crafting, articulating, endeavouring to enact principles of ideal cohabitation' (Code 2006: 24). In tracing some lines of thought which bear, if obliquely, on the resources of ecological thinking for enacting a viable conception of *sexuate* subjectivity, I am indebted to Alison Stone's reading of Irigaray who, she says, uses 'sexuate' in three main senses: 1. of law and rights; 2. of a culture insofar as it recognizes sexual difference; and 3. of our nature *qua* sexed (Stone 2006: 16). I draw, sometimes tacitly, on the second and third senses, attempting to make good the promise implicit in the quotation from *Ecological Thinking* by considering some implications for sexuate subjects of thinking ecologically, and for ecological thinking of addressing the sexuate being of ecological subjects. These ideas bear on my larger quarrel with climate change scepticism and the mockery it performs, in the name of abstract instrumental reason, of such nuanced idea(l)s as 'dwelling' and 'ideal cohabitation'.

Formidable among the obstacles to effecting a shift away from a hegemonic epistemic imaginary of mastery and control is the climate-change scepticism whose effects inform much of what follows. A powerful force of resistance to acknowledging the ecological implications of climate change is a stubborn commitment in late twentieth and early twenty-first century western/ northern capitalist societies and mainstream Anglo-American philosophy to a sovereign individualism: a commitment manifested by knowers and doers who, it seems, have no sex, no place, and no personal allegiances in any ontological, self-constituting or self-sustaining way. The 'god trick' Donna Haraway deplores continues to exert a strong, if elusive, appeal (Haraway 1991: 189). As I note in *Ecological Thinking*, ethical self-mastery, political mastery over unruly and aberrant Others, and epistemic mastery over the external world persist as the goals of the Enlightenment legacy, in philosophy and in the social-political imaginaries of (mostly white) capitalist societies. These discourses shape and are shaped by a reductivism for which epistemic and moral agents are undifferentiated subjects, isolated units on an indifferent landscape, to which their relation is one of disengaged indifference. They enlist ready-made, easily applied categories to control and contain the personal, social, and physical-natural world within a neatly manageable array of 'kinds', obliterating differences in projects of assembling the confusion of those worlds into maximally homogeneous units. Such taxonomies sustain the *instituted* social imaginary (Castoriadis 1994) for which instrumental rationality is the epitome of human reason, while the *instituting* ecological imaginary I have endeavoured to configure and promote seeks to disrupt these assumptions, all the way down. Ecological subjectivity, sexuate subjectivity animates these contestations, struggling to dislodge the intransigent, overweening power of mastery and domination. Here, then, a focus on sexuate subjectivity works to uncover, to demonstrate how sexual difference has played into – has, in effect, been in many respects constitutive of – these oppressive and damaging structures; and how bringing it into central focus could perform a version of consciousness-raising at a deeply theoretical level, where the effects of sexual differences might be exposed and re-evaluated on a slate wiped relatively clean of the residual baggage they always carry and the detritus they leave in their wake. The hope – perhaps the impossible dream – is that ecological thinking could reconfigure subjectivity, sociality, knowledge, and moral-political thinking by enlisting the potential of sexuate epistemic and ethico-political practices to produce *habitats* where people can live well together, and respectfully with and within the physical/natural world.

These grand gestures of contestation cannot be undertaken only as a large, overarching project, even though they have large and grand goals. They need to be addressed and analysed locally, not just in being located in specific places, although this matters too; but also in their diverse particularities, in which even when the principal focus is on sexual difference and sexuate subjectivities, these will be enacted and weighted differently in ecologically specific situations where the detail of situation and place will be as significant as will the connections and differences between them. Hence, this line of thought involves a cautious, even ambivalent turn toward particularity/particularities: knowing, acting, thinking ecologically involves intelligently mapping particularities while guarding against initiating a descent into pure particularism (Code 2010). It thus requires a delicate balancing, thinking by analogy from place to place, maintaining an openness to learning from disanalogy when analogies fail to go through, or prove unstable.

'Manufactured uncertainty' – *Merchants of Doubt*

Climate-change scepticism and its advocates stand in a starkly antithetical relationship to ecological thinking with its implicit commitment to sustainable practices, and equally to the assumptions about sexuate subjectivities and the politics and ethics of knowledge that (sometimes tacitly) inform it. Climate-change scepticism with the *agnotology* it generates trades on a certain cynicism about knowledge (Procter and Schiebinger 2008),[2] about human (anonymous but instrumental) subjectivity, and about the earth/the world (in Hannah Arendt's sense) and people's lives, all in the name of a profit-driven and curiously conceived freedom-promoting and preserving instrumentalism. It is animated by and animates a starkly atomistic, resolutely neutral conception of subjectivity, in practices and rhetoric that oppose sustainable ecological regulatory measures from a conviction that they tamper with, and indeed jeopardize, said freedom.

Among many possible resources, I am focusing here on Naomi Oreskes's and Erik M. Conway's 2010 book *Merchants of Doubt* for its clear exemplification of some of the major obstacles in the way of fulfilling 'our responsibilities for nurturing the sustainable ecologies of our local and global communities, environments, and interactions', thereby fostering social justice. I take this book as my point of entry because of how clearly it depicts the quintessentially neutral stance adopted by science – intentionally homogenized and reified – in dispassionately sustaining a level of doubt, and indeed ignorance, in a dominant, and still predominately white western society and population. It is a populace for whom the very idea that 'science has shown' carries a cachet enhanced by this presumed neutrality, which suggests that the facts alone are so compelling that reason – anyone's reason – must assent to their validity. Behind this veil of scientific neutrality there need be no suggestion that specifically sexed, gendered, raced, situated, and not disinterested human subjectivities have produced the science invoked. The veil likewise screens out any suggestion that the effects of what science has shown will be enacted in specifically sexed/gendered, situated, and thence not disinterested or homogeneously implicated, lives. This simple assumption pales before a still more contestable, if characteristic, absence of any explicitly articulated conception of epistemic subjectivity, thus by default exposing the morally-politically egregious measures climate-change deniers are prepared to engage, by omission as much as by commission. No idea of promoting ideal cohabitation, of imagining environments and interactions where people can live well together – can *dwell*, in the richest sense of that word – is in evidence. The way of thinking the authors depict is coldly inhospitable to thoughts about how sexuate subjectivities are differentially constituted in this bleak picture of a social-ecological order where it is hard to see how anyone could be 'at home'.

The idea that climate-change deniers are motivated by financial gain will not be a surprise. More startling, perhaps, and germane to my thinking here, are their fears about the loss of *freedom*, generically conceived, that ecologically inspired regulatory measures would entail. Such fears, according to this account, override financial issues in significance and urgency, at least in the USA, and quite probably elsewhere in the affluent western world. Yet by reading this putative threat to freedom against the grain, an opening can be found for critically imagining beyond the instituted imaginary that informs the politics of research central to the analysis: a space for reimagining ways of bringing sexuate eco-subjectivity into the practices that must follow if sustainable 'dwelling' is to be the goal of such ecological thinking as must be enlisted to displace this promulgation of doubt.

For the deniers, the issue, baldly put, is that if threats to the environment require regulatory measures, then they interfere intolerably with human freedom – with Liberty – and thus cannot be contemplated. This idea of freedom is at the core of the autonomous self-contained and self-sustaining individualism that informs the liberal democracies of the white capitalist western-northern world, whose masculinist-patriarchal enactments and effects – its demeanour of neutrality notwithstanding – have long been the subject of feminist critique. In a free society, the argument goes, 'we' (whoever we are) will – *ex hypothesi*, so to speak – refuse to be constrained in our freedom to smoke, to pollute, to use pesticides, when and as we will. Germane to bringing the issue of sexuate subjectivity into this hostile framework is to reaffirm how this operative ideal attests to a governing conception of subjectivity/subjectivities for whom, generically and neutrally, there can be no contestation of the freedom at issue, no question about its attainability, its everyday observance, and its viability as a sacrosanct human value. In this framework, as it is reinforced by the preoccupations and fears of the climate sceptics, there is no shred of interest in who these perfectly free subjects are, or in how sexual or any other differences from a white sex/gender neutral human norm could play into the local and global communities, environments and interactions where such freedom is staunchly defended, yet where so many women, and other Others, are still free to walk only upon the gravel. This operative conception of freedom is sloganized, fetishized in a curiously repellent, non-affiliative way. It is an unsustainable, sharply individualistic freedom – the freedom of the 'buffered self', in Genevieve Lloyd's apt term, (Lloyd 2008: 322) of masculinist modernity – born perhaps of the imagined self-sufficiency integral to a frontier mentality, and nourished not by an imaginary of dwelling and mutuality, but of acquisition, shopping, and immediate gratification. It is unsustainable in itself in looming crises of scarcity and, more to the point, it is a freedom without the resources to sustain in/as viable subjectivity the subject who adamantly affirms it as his.

Oreskes and Conway record how seamlessly the conviction has prevailed in post-1970s America, with variations still today, that there could be 'no freedom without capitalism and no capitalism without freedom' (Oreskes and Conway 2010: 64–5). As it has become increasingly obvious that industrial emissions were damaging human and ecosystem health, and has likewise become clear that 'regulation' – which 'flew in the face of the capitalist ideal' – was the inevitable and only responsible response, the struggle has turned into a battle of science against science. Thus for example against the (US) Environmental Protection Agency's efforts to improve indoor air quality by exposing the harms produced by tobacco smoke, sceptics charged that such proposals relied on 'bad science' as an excuse for interfering with individual liberty: 'It wasn't just money at stake; it was individual *liberty*. Today, smoking, tomorrow ... who knew? By protecting smoking, we protected freedom' (Oreskes and Conway 2010: 145). In the controversy over pollution – to which, as I will show, Rachel Carson's reputation continues to be sacrificed – the argument was that if science was working against 'the blessings of liberty' and challenging the freedom of free enterprise then 'they would fight it as they would fight any enemy'. For indeed, Oreskes and Conway observe, 'science *was* showing that certain liberties are not sustainable – like the liberty to pollute' (239). Such is the animating spirit of the climate of resistance within which new sexed/sexuate models of ecology and sustainability have to be conceived.

Ecological thinking

Why, then, would people – ourselves included – whose lives are constructed around the illusions unsustainable practices install, relinquish the privileges that, in consequence of those illusions, have been theirs. This is the question. Such resistance, encapsulated in charges that climate change scientists are promulgating irrational fears, attests to the intensity of the struggle between those who think and act within the (instituted) hegemonic imaginary of mastery and entitlement, and those who are committed to interrogating and unsettling it. At one level, the issue seems to be about puerile projects of fighting science with science, where 'good science' and 'bad science' are often thus categorized less according to the quality of the knowledge they produce, more according to the interests they serve. Questions about epistemic responsibility seem not to figure at all in the struggles (Code 1987).

To cite just one example: into the 1990s debates over risks posed by ETS (Environmental Tobacco Smoke) in North America, a publication, *Bad Science: A Resource Book* (1993), was inserted (described by Oreskes and Conway as 'a how-to handbook for fact fighters').[3] Its intent was to challenge the authority and integrity of the US Environmental Protection Agency's (EPA's) research into the effects of second-hand smoke. Clearly, the issue is about two lines of enquiry, each driven by a specific agenda, about which most members of even a well-educated lay public are not qualified to pronounce judgement. Yet contrasting the evidence from both sides does seem to confirm the dispassionate, if not disinterested approach and agenda driving the EPA scientists' research, while the *Bad Science* text (at least in the extensive excerpts and analyses the authors provide) relies on cautionary quips and throwaway lines about betrayal of public trust, and policy decisions that will be costly for everyone. One noteworthy 'MESSAGE' (sic) to which I have alluded earlier reads: '*Proposals that seek to improve indoor air quality by singling out tobacco smoke only enable bad science to become a poor excuse for enacting new laws and jeopardizing individual liberties*' (Oreskes and Conway 2010: 144–5, italics in original). As the authors note, *Bad Science* does quote 'experts', many of whom were paid consultants to industry. At other times it follows 'a more sophisticated strategy: reminding readers of the fallibility of science' (146). A similar strategy runs through the *agnotology* literature.[4]

It is difficult to do justice to the sexed/gendered implications of these assumptions while the conviction persists that these are generically *human* issues, to which neither sex nor any other specificity – race, class, ethnicity, disability – is relevant. In mainstream Anglo-American inquiry, the *Merchants of Doubt* text is not unusually at fault in this regard: its political motivations are laudable for various modalities of ecological thinking, and for these reasons I am discussing it. But these commitments and allegiances make the 'liquidation of the subject' (Alcoff 2007: 53–4) from much of the text all the more striking. For all its impressiveness, Oreskes's and Conway's inquiry is limited for ecological-sexuate-gendered purposes by the almost-but-not-quite erasure of the subjectivities of those on whom challenge and change depend. Perhaps owing to the residual power of an unreconstructed image of science with its tacit presumption of impersonal objectivity, the subject – even the subject seeking to defend *his* freedom – makes few explicit appearances, although the scientists on both 'sides' are named and credentialled. Yet the extent to which these concerns about freedom recur in the story exposes the constitutive effects of a tacit conception of subjectivity which merits further analysis. The human generically conceived is only obliquely present in this text, stripped of its subjectivity and, *a fortiori*, of its *gendered* and other specificities. Hence, the question 'Whose *freedom* are we talking about?' has to move into focus in charting the uptake which realizing the transformative-disruptive potential of Oreskes's and Conway's investigations requires. The freedoms abstractly invoked, yet zealously defended, are not equally distributed across the sex/ gender – or any other – order in western societies. Recall Val Plumwood's classic reminder (following Irigaray) that women 'provide the environment and conditions against which male "achievement" takes place, but what they do is not itself counted as achievement' (Plumwood 1993: 22). Reading 'freedom' for 'achievement' here underscores my point.

Because the investigations Oreskes and Conway report take place behind a mask of impersonal epistemic replicability, appeals to specifically sexuate, situated, ecologically imagined subjects and practices have to negotiate through fixed assumptions about human sameness and the enhanced epistemic reliability of dislocated research. Such appeals are not easy to insert into an individualist-masculinist yet putatively gender-neutral frame of reference; nor is the issue just about individual reform, but about communal-collaborative-collective social change that requires destabilizing an entrenched imaginary of individualistic mastery and control, all the way down. Thus, revisiting a simple but persistent sexed-gendered connection, such disruptions will begin by recognizing that 'mastery' has to be read in light of the historically presumptive *maleness* of the masters who, when/if they make space for women on the turf they have jealously staked out as theirs, still more than a full decade into the twenty-first century, do so on their own terms, relegating such women to the margins: the gravel. Recall Margaret Whitford:

> to speak or write like a man is to assert mastery, to claim truth, objectivity, knowledge, whereas to speak like a woman is to refuse mastery, to allow meaning to be elusive or shifting, not to be in control, or in possession of truth or knowledge. So to be assertive, to make claims, to be 'dogmatic', which means to have a thesis, a meaning, a political position, is to take up a 'male' stance, whatever one's sex.
>
> (Whitford 1991: 50)

An urgent point on which feminists and other Others from the white patriarchal norm have insisted is that all freedom is someone's freedom, all knowing is someone's knowing, where someone can be singular or plural – or singular because plural, but either way, it matters. Even if 'freedom' is declared as though it were clear, unambiguous, and univocal in its meaning, representing it thus could claim plausibility only after its sexed-gendered and other enactments were deconstructed and evaluated each in its place and situation. Evidently, the freedom the merchants of doubt want to protect is a freedom principally available to propertied white men. Hence, 'taking subjectivity into account' (which I have advocated elsewhere: Code 1995) requires taking *sexed/sexuate* subjectivities into account, in the specificities of their time and place; seeking to understand how the doing, knowing, being, dwelling at issue are enacted, there. As Plumwood long ago reminded us, integral to the social imaginary that sustains mainstream Anglo-American philosophy is an assumption that the human is implicitly masculine, not just conceptually but in its effects, 'while the feminine is seen as a derivation from it' (Plumwood 1993: 23). Likewise, the contestable ideal of autonomy underlying the pleas for freedom Oreskes and Conway report has, throughout the history of western liberal political thought, derived from and celebrated the possibilities afforded by and to affluent white male/masculine lives. Freedom to find himself at home on the turf is an emblematic affirmation of the maleness of this ideal, available only to those who need not notice the mundane tedium of *allgemeine Alltäglichkeit* (ordinary everydayness), with its routine disdain for things female: for the repetitious reproductive labour of quotidian domesticity (Code 2000). Even after decades of feminist theory and practice these issues remain urgently under-addressed.

From an ecologically informed stance, Mick Smith, in *An Ethics of Place* (2001) offers an analysis of the situation that confirms my own view:

> As modernity's offspring we ... tend to understand our own identities and social relations ... [as] concrete and isolable individuals each on their own disparate trajectories, each with *particular* identities derived from ... certain essential, quantifiable, and indefeasible properties. We are born under the sign(s) of one-dimensional *man*; *Homo economicus*, that self-contained and self-serving caricature of modern humanity, a parodic recapitulation of the instrumental order of capitalism and phallocracy. ... Only 'man' is intrinsically valuable. Women and nature are made subject to reason's cold calculations, their reality recognized only insofar as they become hard currency to be valued and traded according to their use.
>
> (Smith 2001: 171)

By these standards, recalling Woolf, women have 'no real being'; and although such thoughts are old news to feminist theorists and activists and to ecological thinkers, they persist. At once ethical-political and epistemological, they call for critical-creative re-enactments of subjectivity at a social, collective level, distantly analogous to older consciousness-raising practices. They require rethinking/re-enacting *who we are*, in ways sufficiently powerful to dislodge, to unsettle, these deeply sedimented convictions. This is the hardest and the most urgent demand: somehow it is easier, more imaginable, to think and engage in renewed, revisionary ways of doing, thinking, knowing. But to practise a philosophy which requires – which *must* require – rethinking and re-enacting *who we are* is ontologically and epistemologically radical, upheld as those assumptions are by the instituted social-political-epistemic imaginary in which as inhabitants of the affluent west we live and think and have our being, however obliquely or contrarily. Nor is the issue quite as Smith puts it in urging an '*alternative* conception of subjectivity' (Smith 2001: 173, my italics) because the language of alternatives is misleading in its suggestion that both or all ways are up for grabs: *we* can opt for one or another, interchangeably and intermittently, as we would select from a smorgasbord of edibles. It is, rather, about an activism that works singly and collectively to unmask, discredit, and displace that 'caricature of modern humanity', revealing it for the dangerous illusion it is through ongoing, piece-by-piece exposures and deconstructions of its contributions to producing the anti-ecological, unsustainable conditions that prevail in the western/northern world: to undermine its credibility.

The issue is ontological and practical, ethical, political, and episte-mological. Sexuate practices are peculiarly well equipped to animate the engagement such a radical revisioning requires, precisely because they offer a particular line of vision, a way of seeing which, I suggest, evinces certain affin-ities to W.E.B. Du Bois's 'phenomenological concept of double consciousness' (Gordon 2000: 38), which Du Bois himself characterizes as 'a sense of always looking at one's self through the eyes of others, of measuring one's soul by the tape of a world that looks on in amused contempt and pity' (Allen 1997: 51). This imposed incongruity with/in oneself was for Du Bois a product of oppression, and a source of ongoing agony. But Ernest Allen Jr. proposes revisiting the implications of 'double consciousness' in ways that suggest something of the ontological deconstruction and reconstruction feminist women may also have to perform – for we too, albeit with radically different implications – have had to judge ourselves through the eyes of others. In a recommendation that echoes some of the tenets of standpoint epistemology, Allen notes:

> rather than *celebrating* an authentic "dual consciousness" as a tool for achieving enriched cultural or political syntheses, or as a platform for generating multiple levels of understanding – in other words, as a potential solution in whole or in part – Du Bois treated the question of "twoness" chiefly as a (real or imaginary) problem, even as he affirmed the desirability of preserving certain of its (unspecified) forms.
>
> (Allen 1997: 51)

At the risk of proposing helping ourselves to concepts forged in forms of oppression that cannot have been ours, and performing epistemic violence in so doing, I think there is something to be learned by analogy for feminists now, about sexuate being, from Allen's reading of the ontological and epistemological celebratory power implicit in Du Bois's thought, in both its negative and its positive connotations. Indeed, there is a notable precedent to this proposal in Maria Lugones's landmark and poetically rich analysis of 'world-travelling', where she urges feminists and other Others to engage in careful, imaginative-creative practices of attempting to enter another's world as a way of beginning to understand, tentatively, and rarely conclusively, how it is to live in that world, those multiple worlds that enable her to *be*, to play – though not in a mocking or frivolous sense – with the enabling and constraining qualities of that 'world' (Lugones 1987).[5] The implication is that a world-traveller will not – should not – emerge unchanged from the journey. Something akin to these ideas is implied in my remarks about rethinking who we are, and about the resources to be found in conceiving subjectivity ecologically.

Ecological subjectivity

The life and work of Rachel Carson are instructive, indeed inspirational: in *Ecological Thinking*, I represent her as an exemplar of ecological subjectivity. She lives and enacts ecological thinking as a way of inhabiting the world that confers content on the term, the idea, and the practice in ways consonant with Verena Conley's claims for ecological subjectivity as 'relating consciousness of the self to that of being attached to and separated from the world' (Conley 1997: 10).[6] For Conley, the task for ecological thinking is nothing less than that of unmasking 'mass-produced subjectivity in societies of control with their consequences for natural and social ecology' (Conley 1997: 74–5). In all of these thoughts, critical attentiveness to ways of being contests unexamined ontological presumptions of human sameness, and of the liberal unified self.

Carson is not just the ecological but also the sexuate subject, albeit, given the sexual climate of her times, often silently, tacitly, with positive and negative implications. Her scientific practice hovers on the edge of being explicitly sexed female/feminine and discredited accordingly, again given the mores of her time. Some of her best, most ecologically sophisticated work sits just here, in a not-yet-realized sex/gender specific frame and style (also see Hacking 1982). It is she who exemplifies the power and the perils of the informed, careful advocacy that is a crucial piece of sound ecological practice. (It contrasts starkly with the *Bad Science: A Resource Book* agenda.) For a time, she walks away from the gravel onto the turf of scientific and public legitimacy and acclaim, but uneasily and often precariously. She in/as her sexed body – as a sexuate being – dies from breast cancer: from one of the ecologically most powerful and poignant effects of the substances she studies (Sideris 2008). She is a *who* – in Arendt's sense – not a *what*: the only ecological subject in its sexed and pilloried being who claims a fully narrated place in the *Merchants of Doubt* text – who is after the fact castigated as a murderer, and is now again being cast out to the periphery, the rough ground, as the sacrificial subject who embodies the intensity of ecological being and doing, destined it would seem to go on demanding a safe place to dwell on well-tended turf, with a rhetoric that recalls Margaret Whitford's astute comments about mastery. She is not the only scientist identified by name in the text, nor the only one whose qualifications and training are cited: the climate-change defenders and deniers, too, are identified with their credentials. Yet their place-holder status in asserting and performing their mastery, whether for or against, and in claiming 'truth, objectivity, knowledge' (Whitford 1991: 50) is neutrally assumed despite their bitter disagreements.

No one needs to be reminded that there is a peculiar vulnerability to the situation of a woman in science, well into the second decade of the twenty-first century, but dramatically more so for a woman of Carson's time, and one so readily discredited on specifically – if then only tacit – sexuate grounds. These sexed dualities in Carson's work and thought are virtually covered over in her time, and often exposed, overexaggerated, and deplored in ours – indeed, flagrantly deplored by the science deniers: the 'fact fighters'. Although sex-specific charges were only occasionally directed at her or at her work in her lifetime, they were there, if veiled. Accusations of hysteria have been and continue to be a recurrent charge. In the Oreskes and Conway chapter such charges are multiply detailed. They have as much to do with her sex as with careless, epistemically irresponsible accusations of practising bad science – where the irresponsibility adduced often has less to do with the substance of Carson's research and more with the attackers' and discreditors' failure to base their charges on adequate research into the ongoing complexities, for example, of knowing about DDT, which is not a static phenomenon as a rock might be.

Carson clearly understands the scientific allure of mastery and control, but her practices for achieving it require following up narrow and precise local hypotheses that differ for each of species she studies – as in her research on the Japanese beetle, the gypsy moth, Dutch elm disease; as they differ again for investigating the long-term implications for human health of diverse substances and circumstances. She is wary of too-ready translation from one domain or species to another. Yet the hypotheses she works from guide inquiry whose empirical generalizations stand up well against the quick and dirty solutions proposed by the chemical industry and its champions. Catching a central contrast between an ethos of mastery and an ecological ethos, Carson deplores a stubborn corporate resistance to taking a longer view to waiting 'an extra season or two' (Code 2006: 98) when a quick (chemical) fix is ready to hand. Ecologically, and appropriately, thinking as she does requires factoring time, place, and history, into responsible scientific assessments of ecological effects. Thus, for example, taking such requirements very seriously, Oreskes and Conway observe of female reproductive health that to know whether the effects of DDT were significant in the respects that matter, for Carson, it would be necessary to study the cells of women who had been exposed early in life, 'when environmental exposures where high'. Impressively for establishing this claim, just such a study was conducted in 2000–1 on women in their 50s and 60s, who had been exposed to DDT as children or teenagers. 'The results showed a fivefold increase in breast cancer risk among women with high levels of serum DDT or its metabolites' (Oreskes and Conway 2010: 229). Such findings vindicate Carson's approach even as they require a further departure from the spectator epistemology of standard empiricism: a shift toward horizontal as contrasted with vertical, top-down analysis; toward taking a longer view across terrains and timeframes. The recurrent problem is that causal connections often are not immediately apparent to people who are neither informed nor prepared to look ecologically: it is so easy to discount causal claims that extend temporally and geographically away from a chemical application; that require time, imagination, conjecture, and patience to be able to see the links that enable confirmation or falsification. Carson's ecological approach vindicates just such a longer view.

Carson, as Oreskes and Conway note, 'documented at great length both the anecdotal and systematic scientific evidence that DDT and other pesticides were doing great harm' (Oreskes and Conway 2010: 219). Ironically, her respect for the anecdotal, which was integral to her practice, contributed to the fluctuating respect and easy vilification in the condemnatory rhetoric of her detractors. It connects with the rhetorical, conceptual architecture of the epistemological-scientific world where Carson worked, structured as it was by hierarchical divisions between fact and anecdote, truth and narrative, reason and feeling, of which the first item in each pair – which is closely associated with mastery – claims greater public and professional credibility, authority, and reliability than the second. The division locates anecdote, narrative, and feeling on the negative, subjective, feminized side where meaning can be 'elusive or shifting', while for epistemologies of mastery, it is in *facts* alone, dispassionately discovered, that truth is to be found. In her respect for testimony, for down-on-the-ground experiential reports commonly dismissed as merely *anecdotal*, Carson's epistemic practice unsettles these distinctions – and earns her the label 'subversive' in so doing.

Although such discrediting in her time was less often conveyed in sexed/gendered terms than it subsequently has been, the flavour was unmistakable. Now, as Oreskes and Conway show, it is less carefully masked. Thus it can be no coincidence that the most damning website currently devoted to discrediting her, which comes from a 2009 project of the Competitive Enterprise Institute, is called rachelwaswrong.org (Code 2012). Quite apart from the contents of the items on the site, the chastising 'bad little girl' tone of naming it thus is egregiously insulting: a woman too insignificant to be referred to by her full adult name has ventured too far on to territory that should not be hers, and is sternly reprimanded, sent back to the rough ground, or indeed sent home. This is the woman who in her time and still in ours was dismissed as hysterical, scaremongering.

The larger issues are about how credibility plays out in the politics of knowledge; how credibility is tacitly coded masculine, and how thought styles, styles of reasoning tainted with female/feminine associations, or research projects that study the affective, experiential detail of women's workplace vulnerability cannot readily succeed in claiming a place within the scientific world of the credible or the rational except by following its formal, disinterested, dislocated, putatively gender-neutral dictates. Michael Smith, for example, in an article tellingly titled 'Silence, Miss Carson' (which he borrows from an 'unbalanced' review of *Silent Spring*) points to a prevailing attitude according to which she was 'an uninformed woman who was speaking of that which she knew not. Worse, she was speaking in a man's world, the inner sanctum of masculine science in which, like the sanctuary of a strict Calvinist sect, female silence was expected' (Smith 2008: 172). The point is that to understand Carson both as a human being and as a woman struggling to be a scientist in an inhospitable environment is to understand something of the *dis*-ease, the *un*-ease of that position, whose sources are sexed/gendered/sexuate despite these categorizations being less visible in her time and milieu where sexuate thinking had not yet travelled, than in ours. It is to think of her, then, through a doubled consciousness. She is both an exemplary ecological subject, to some extent to her triumph, and a vulnerable yet courageous exemplar of path-breaking sexuate being, if perhaps not in her own eyes.

Reading Carson as a quintessentially ecological subject, whose sexuate being seems both to be an asset that shapes her practice and to be the hardest thing, returns us to sexual difference and even to the possibility of taking essential sexuate being *as* in some sense *real* (admitting but not belabouring its socially constitutive/constructed makeup); to affirm it and see in it a certain power and a perpetually beleaguered promise, not to effect the reversal in gendered values that feminists of the 1980s following Carol Gilligan deplored but to draw on its values in circumstances that are usually local because of the meticulously detailed work knowing them well enough requires on all fronts: for example, research into the smallest minutiae (as Orestes and Conway detail) in order to discredit the detractors/the merchants of doubt; at the theoretical/social level to show in a specifically, often perhaps too particularly local level, how the local can model the larger world and illumine the larger issues, if by analogy.

To keep afloat on a tidal wave of capitalist opposition from those who think they have too much to lose and cannot see how much they have to gain – even of freedom, more intelligently thought through – self-consciously sexuate practices might be enlisted to initiate a renewed kind of cohabitation where no one need be relegated to the gravel: a respectful way of *dwelling* that from their very sexuate being some women have, somehow, been able to animate. This, perhaps, is the utopian dream. It would require sustained advocacy which is also in some of its aspects a feminized practice, and which also meets with curious levels of resistance at places where its combative (masculinist) truth-denying reputation consistently drowns out its emancipatory potential, as if people were too stupid to practise, judge, and evaluate it well. Undoubtedly, people will advocate for what they care about and/or fear to lose. But the response need not be to condemn advocacy as such, but only its blindly aggressive instantiations. As educators we need to learn and teach how to advocate responsibly, knowledgeably, and humbly – paradoxical as this may seem – in a minutely informed and ethically/politically respectful way, analogous, perhaps, to how Oreskes and Conway conduct their investigations piece by piece, in order to show at many different levels how zealously the deniers seek to defend places and putative values that are quite simply unsustainable. Part of the bad press advocacy encounters has to do with an ongoing separation, in philosophy at least, of epistemology and ethics-politics, where no room can be made for the urgency of the epistemic responsibility that must, I contend, come to be recognized as a truly overarching value.

The larger implication is that initiating sustainable being, dwelling, and knowing requires radical contestations of mastery and the arch-masculinity that fosters it, toward a greater respect for the limitations of our knowledge and the need – where the urgency of the situation allows it – to welcome ambiguity both in Simone de Beauvoir's sense (Beauvoir 1948), and in the sense captured by Whitford, and explicitly feminized. Hence I end with an *aporia*, a tension that could be productive, but could also be immobilizing, but which I cannot resolve here. The task for us now – where 'us' is the most contestable of these terms – is to work with this tension toward some of the ends I have noted, treading a narrow line between a reversion to conventional difference stereotypes with their capacity to keep women walking on the gravel, and a celebratory enactment of female sexuate values and their/our capacities to travel mindfully to other worlds that might perform some of the social-political re-energizing the new social movements of the 1960s initiated, that are still available now as more sophisticated, more nuanced resources, as we work to 'cultivate new subjectivities'.

For the merchants of doubt, impersonal putatively gender-neutral facts are marshalled to promote or defend an impersonal, gender-neutral freedom, while the doubled interplay in Carson's story contests neutrality all the way down even, perhaps paradoxically, in her amply demonstrated, scientific expertise. It can perform such contestations only in complexly textured practices where, epistemologically, the task is not only an empirical one, but also and simultaneously phenomenological and hermeneutic. Indeed, it can be effectively empirical only by becoming attuned to the phenomenological and hermeneutic richness of the everyday, which is the primary source of the testimony on which Carson so often relies. The epistemological and ethical-political dimensions of such practices of inquiry cannot responsibly be held apart if sustainable futures are to be promoted in opposition to doubters determined to gainsay them in the name of a freedom that is destructive at the core, even of the subjects who champion it.

Appendix

The Competitive Enterprise Institute describes itself as:

> a non-profit public policy organization dedicated to advancing the principles of limited government, free enterprise, and individual liberty. Our mission is to promote both freedom and fairness by making good policy good politics.

We make the uncompromising case for economic freedom because we believe it is essential for entrepreneurship, innovation, and prosperity to flourish.

(http://cei.org/about-cei)

'Who was Rachel?'

Born in 1907, Rachel Carson grew up on a farm in Pennsylvania and eventually went on to study marine biology, earning her Masters degree in the subject from Johns Hopkins University. Carson taught at the University of Maryland for a few years, but eventually went to work at the Department of Interior, during which she wrote books and articles related to the environment. The first three books focused on the sea and did not provoke much attention, but her third book – *Silent Spring* – became a best seller that changed the way people think about chemicals and the environment.

Silent Spring began as a series of articles published in the *New Yorker* magazine. The book's ostensive purpose was to alert the world about the risks associated with pesticides and other chemicals, which Carson feared could cause widespread problems in the environment and harm public health. But rather than offering her concerns in a measured way, Carson painted an extreme view that chemicals were causing – or would cause – cancers and harming wildlife – essentially producing a world in which no birds sing and one in four people would potentially die from chemically caused cancers.

While many have believed that such strong rhetoric was needed to garner necessary attention to the issue, the book created a culture of fear – which produced extreme anti-chemical policies rather than policies to simply find ways to manage risks. Ironically, some of those policies have contributed much more to public health risks than they have to reducing them. This website documents some of these problems with the hope that better information about Carson's legacy will reverse misguided public policies and prevent the implementation of new ones.

(http://rachelwaswrong.org/who-was-rachel/)

Notes

1 An earlier version of this chapter was presented as the Keynote address for the panel 'Sexuate Sustainable Practices and Ecologies', at the conference, *Sexuate Subjects: Politics, Poetics and Ethics*, UCL, London, December 2010.
2 Loosely defined, *agnotology* is the study of ignorance, of not knowing.

3   Oreskes and Conway observe:

> The phrases 'excessive regulation', 'over-regulation', and 'unnecessary regulation' were liberally sprinkled throughout the book. Many of the quotable quotes came from the Competitive Enterprise Institute (CEI), a think tank promoting 'free enterprise and limited government' and dedicated to the conviction that the 'best solutions come from people making their own choices in a free marketplace, rather than government intervention'.
>
> (*Bad Science: A Resource Book*, BN: 2074144197, Legacy Tobacco Documents Library, and CEI, 'About CEI', http://cei.org/about; cited in Oreskes and Conway 2010: 147)

4   It is worth noting that neither the *agnotology* text I have cited nor other contributions to this line of enquiry represent ignorance only negatively. Indeed, most interesting in this literature are numerous examples of the productive effects of ignorance recognized and interpreted.

5   My thanks to Peta Bowden for reminding me of Lugones's relevance here.

6   The phrase 'a way of inhabiting the world' is also from Conley (1997: 114), citing Michel de Certeau.

References

Alcoff, L.M. (2007) 'Epistemologies of ignorance: three types', in S. Sullivan and N. Tuana (eds) *Race and Epistemologies of Ignorance*, Albany: State University of New York Press.

Allen, E. (1997) 'On the reading of riddles: rethinking Du Boisian "double consciousness"', in L.R. Gordon (ed.) *Existence in Black: An Anthology of Black Existential Philosophy*, New York: Routledge.

Beauvoir, S. de (1948) *The Ethics of Ambiguity*, trans. B. Frechtman, New York: Citadel Press.

Castoriadis, C. (1994) 'Radical imagination and the social instituting imaginary', in G. Robinson and J. Rundell (eds) *Rethinking Imagination: Culture and Creativity*, London: Routledge.

Code, L. (1987) *Epistemic Responsibility*, Hanover, NH: University Press of New England.

— (1995) *Rhetorical Spaces: Essays on (Gendered) Locations*, New York: Routledge.

— (2000) 'The perversion of autonomy and the subjection of women: discourses of social advocacy at century's end', in C. Mackenzie and N. Stoljar (eds) *Relational Autonomy*, New York: Oxford University Press.

— (2006) *Ecological Thinking: The Politics of Epistemic Location*, New York: Oxford University Press.

— (2010) 'Particularity, epistemic responsibility, and the ecological imaginary', in *Philosophy of Education Archive*. Online: http://ojs.ed.uiuc.edu/index.php/pes/article/view/2997/1074 (accessed 30 November 2011).

— (2012) 'Feminism, ecological thinking and the legacy of Rachel Carson', in M. Luxton and M.J. Mossman (eds) *Reconsidering Knowledge: Feminism and the Academy*, Winnipeg, Manitoba: Fernwood Press.

Competitive Enterprise Institute. Online: http://cei.org/about-cei (accessed 30 November 2011).

Conley, V. (1997) *Ecopolitics: The Environment in Poststructuralist Thought*, London: Routledge.

Gordon, L.R. (2000) *Existentia Africana: Understanding Africana Existential Thought*, New York: Routledge.

Hacking, I. (1982) 'Language, truth and reason', in M. Hollis and S. Lukes (eds) *Rationality and Relativism*, Cambridge, MA: MIT Press.

Haraway, D.J. (1991) *Simians, Cyborgs, and Women: The Reinvention of Nature*, New York: Routledge.

Irigaray, L. (2004) *The Way of Love*, New York: Continuum Press.

Lorraine Code

Lloyd, G. (2008) *Providence Lost*, Cambridge, MA: Harvard University Press.

Lugones, M. (1987) 'Playfulness, 'world'-travelling, and loving perception', *Hypatia: A Journal of Feminist Philosophy*, 2, 2: 3–19.

Oreskes, N. and Conway, E.M. (2010) *Merchants of Doubt: How a Handful of Scientists Obscured the Truth on Issues from Tobacco Smoke to Global Warming*, New York: Bloomsbury Press.

Plumwood, V. (1993) *Feminism and the Mastery of Nature*, London: Routledge.

Procter, R.N. and Schiebinger, L. (eds) (2008) *Agnotology: The Making and Unmaking of Ignorance*, Stanford, CT: Stanford University Press.

Rachel Was Wrong. Online: http://rachelwaswrong.org/ (accessed 30 November 2011).

Sideris, L.H. (2008) 'The ecological body: Rachel Carson, *Silent Spring*, and breast cancer', in L.H. Sideris and K. Dean Moore (eds) *Rachel Carson: Legacy and Challenge*, Albany: State University of New York Press.

Smith, Mick (2001) *An Ethics of Place: Radical Ecology, Postmodernity, and Social Theory*, Albany: State University of New York Press.

Smith, M. (2008) '"Silence, Miss Carson!": Science, gender, and the reception of *Silent Spring*', in L.H. Sideris and K. Dean Moore (eds) *Rachel Carson: Legacy and Challenge*, Albany: State University of New York Press.

Stone, A. (2006) *Luce Irigaray and the Philosophy of Sexual Difference*, Cambridge: Cambridge University Press.

Whitford, M. (1991) *Luce Irigaray: Philosophy in the Feminine*, London: Routledge.

Woolf, V. ([1929] 1977) *A Room of One's Own*, London: Granada.

Chapter 5

Fear, the sublime and sheltered difference

Rachel Jones

The earth does not merely subside beneath the hammering of civilizations, it fascinates and converts the structures of experience, it murmurs below and within the demotic of everyday life, speaking not only through our farms and our bestiaries, but through all the surfaces we have pinned down, all the technologies implicating its elemental support, all the materialities that bind the life-world to a particular order of things.

How can we map out and reconnoiter the pregiven world without accounting for the wild body of the earth and the ways it has worked itself into the very hides of everyday phenomena? Our life-worlds are moored to this durable geographical subsoil; their very pregivenness is an effect of its slow-moving history.

(Hachamovitch 1994: 141)

In this chapter, my concern is also with 'the wild body of the earth', though less with the ways in which it has 'worked itself into the very hides of everyday phenomena' and more with the moments in which it shifts and moves in ways that rupture the everyday; less with the 'slow-moving history' of a durable subsoil, and more with the violent eruptions of material forces that shake the ground beneath our feet. Nonetheless, by failing to think in terms of the slow-moving temporalities that often characterise geological and ecological processes, and instead prioritising short-term gains in resources and profit, western modernity has made the 'geographical subsoil' much less durable, and eroded the sustaining powers of the earth on which our life-worlds depend. To the fear that is provoked by 'the wild body of the earth' as it erupts in volcanoes or earthquakes, we can thus add a new, perhaps specifically contemporary fear: the fear that the earth may cease to sustain life, and that this may be, at least in large part, the result of specifically human uses (and abuses) of our earthly home.

In the west, the fear of impending ecological disaster is both causally and conceptually connected to a more long-standing fear of an earth that moves beneath our feet. This fear has a history, becoming particularly acute at that moment in western modernity when human existence became increasing dependent on an instrumental relation to the earth. Such a relation requires that the earth provide a body of resources for the maximisation of non-essential goods – or 'conveniences', as Locke calls them – and profit. It is fundamentally disrupted and disturbed when the earth ceases to lend itself to human manipulation and instead moves of its own accord, in apparently unpredictable and uncontrollable ways. It is thus not by chance that it is in the eighteenth and early nineteenth centuries, as the development of modern capitalism and industrialisation proceed apace, that the unruly movements of a wildly uncontainable nature were theorised under the aesthetic rubric of the sublime.

This material-economic context is certainly not the only reason for the emergence of discourses on the sublime, which mirror the excess they attribute to material nature by combining aesthetic, political, psychological, metaphysical and ethical concerns. Nonetheless, such discourses reflect the ways in which, in western modernity, a nature that exceeds human control, and that disrupts or even destroys man's industriousness, becomes particularly disturbing for a life-world increasingly dependent on managing and extracting the earth's resources (as well as particularly captivating in contrast to a life increasingly conducted in contained urban spaces; see Battersby 1989: 71–80). Among its operations, the sublime allowed the more unruly and disruptive forces of material nature to be re-harnessed – albeit often uneasily – both for a particularly cultivated type of aesthetic pleasure, and for the moral lessons such forces (and pleasures) might afford. The discourses that evolved around the sublime also allowed a historically and culturally specific fear, tied to changing relations to material nature in an increasingly industrialised world, to be naturalised and normalised, by being presented as the result of universal human capacities as well as the survival instincts of the species.

The fear of dynamic nature thematised in the sublime – the fear of an earth that refuses to operate as standing reserve or to be managed into productivity – is thus symptomatic of the very instrumentalising attitude that has bequeathed us a new fear, the fear that as a result of human activity, the earth's resources may have been irrevocably damaged or destroyed. To an Enlightenment fear of wild nature that Kant called an abyss for the imagination

(Kant 1987: 115; V:258), we can add a post-Enlightenment fear that Bonnie Mann has called 'the terror of non-existence, the fear that natural beauty will be forever stamped out, that our own existence, as a species, will end. We are suspended over the abyss of the impending *absence* of nature' (Mann 2006: 163). Bound up in this new fear is the same, instrumentalising attitude that brought us to this fearful point in the first place: the anxiety that the earth may no longer sustain us is at least in part a fear that our ways of life, the life-worlds we are all too invested in, may no longer be provided for; that the 'conveniences' of contemporary western life may not last for ever, or continue to proliferate. Yet harboured within this fear there is also a possibility and a provocation: a call to rethink our relations to the materiality of the earth in ways that might provide for more sustainable futures. In this chapter, I want to take up that provocation, drawing on the work of Luce Irigaray to return to an earth that moves, and to a relationship with that earth which is no longer predicated on a supposedly natural fear of the potency of active matter.

In some ways, Irigaray is not the most obvious choice for reassessing the fears (and promise) of the sublime. Her work does not offer the thorough-going critique and reappropriation of the sublime developed (in very different ways) by other feminist thinkers such as Barbara Freeman (1995), Christine Battersby (2007), and Mann herself (2006). Added to this is the way that Irigaray's work sometimes seems to privilege the category of the beautiful over the sublime, in ways that are problematic given the historical gendering of these categories (whereby the beautiful is linked to distinctly feminine forms and the sublime with masculinised power and authority).

More interesting, however, are the places where her writings blur the very distinction between the beautiful and the sublime, in ways that maintain the significance of the sublime as a site where self and other meet and finite human beings are opened onto the infinite, while displacing the oppositional dynamics and dramatic severings that characterise the traditional (Kantian) sublime, where man is imaginatively pitted against the material forces of nature, or confronted by a threatening excess he must resist and overcome.[1] In particular, Irigaray's writings deliberately appropriate and rework the sublime figure of the abyss, displacing the traditional fears of the 'wild body of the earth' housed within its darkness, and offering possibilities for transforming the relations to material nature that are both framed and perpetuated by the Kantian sublime.[2] Such possibilities, I will suggest, are fostered less by an explicit reworking of the concept of the sublime, than by Irigaray's critical transformation of the underlying conceptual framework that makes the sublime a coherent aesthetic category. Thus, before examining her refiguring of the abyss, I will first outline the underlying patterns of thought that characterise the (primarily Kantian) model of the sublime that Irigaray critiques, followed by the broad strokes of her critical and transformative response.

Kant's sublime and the daring adventure of reason

In Kant's mature aesthetics, as elaborated in the *Critique of Judgment*, sublime feeling is divided into two modes. In the mathematical sublime, an encounter with the apparently unending – the receding horizons of the open sea or vast mountain ranges, for example – triggers the idea of infinity. The imagination strives, yet painfully fails, to provide a representation adequate to this idea, yet its very striving is what makes the subject aware of its own power to *think* that (the infinite) which no sensible image can ever contain. As Irigaray will emphasise, in this version of the sublime, it is only because reason seeks to enframe the infinite within the idea of an unconditioned whole that sensible nature *becomes* 'an abyss in which the imagination is afraid to lose itself' (Kant 1987: 115; V:258), as the (cultured) imagination strives to grasp nature's apparent infinity in a single (impossible) representation (see Irigaray 1985: 209).

However, it is in the dynamic sublime that the subject is more directly confronted by 'the wild body of the earth': by powerful natural forces capable of destroying human beings considered as material, mortal creatures themselves. Providing such encounters occur at a safe enough distance, the sublime arises if the subject counters this reminder of their physical fragility with an awareness of their potential as a moral agent to determine their own will. In such a response:

> we regard nature's might (to which we are indeed subjected in these [natural] concerns) as yet not having such dominance over us, as persons, that we should have to bow to it if our highest principles were at stake and we had to choose between upholding or abandoning them.
>
> (Kant 1987: 121; V:262)

By thus resisting our own (natural) fears of nature's might, we become conscious of 'our superiority to nature within us, and thereby also to nature outside us' (123; V:264).

At first sight, Kant's writings on the sublime might seem to offer at least some acknowledgement of the powers of an active, material world with which human beings are in dynamic relation, as (at least partly) material beings themselves. However, the affordance of something resembling active agency to material nature is closed off in three related ways. First, in the third *Critique*, the sublime is identified with a feeling in the subject rather than a quality or power of objects. Material nature – both as appearance, and as dynamic force – is only a catalyst for sublimity. Describing natural phenomena as 'sublime' is an act of 'subreption' (114; V:257) that involves projecting a feeling generated and registered within the subject onto the external world.

Second, the powers of nature that trigger the sublime are disarmed by an oppositional dynamic which involves resisting, transcending and (in the case of our own fear) even mastering nature's might, reinforcing a split not only between man and nature, but within human beings themselves. It is not so much the abyssal powers of material nature that are the source of sublime feeling as the gulf between the faculties: the productive tension that opens up as the imagination shuttles between reason's power of ideas and the limits of sensibility, and strives to reconcile them. The key relation in the sublime is thus less between man and nature, and more between the rational and moral vocation of human beings on the one hand and the material and physical aspects of their existence on the other.

Third, while Kant's sublime presents nature as full of active material forces – 'thunderclouds piling up in the sky and moving about accompanied by lightning and thunderclaps, volcanoes with all their destructive power, hurricanes with all the devastation they leave behind' (120; V:261) – such activity is in no way indicative of a productive or formative force. On the contrary, the natural forces that provoke sublime feeling appear 'contrapurposive' (99; V:245): by exceeding both human beings' physical limits, and the conceptual forms through which they make sense of the world, such forces resist being grasped as part of nature, understood as a systematic totality of bounded objects. Thus, while Kant's account of the sublime seems at times to displace the first *Critique*'s schematisation of matter as substance (and hence as unchanging permanence; see Kant 1990: B278), replacing this with the unstable eruptions of an animate materiality, in fact, this account reinforces a hylomorphic frame in which form is given to matter by the activity of the subject's faculties. The 'activity' attributed to material nature is unruly and disruptive rather than generative of form: for it is 'in its chaos that nature most arouses our ideas of the sublime, or in its wildest and most ruleless disarray and devastation' (99–100; V:246).

Such a view is reinforced by the second part of the third *Critique* on teleological judgement. Here Kant discusses the way that 'savage, all-powerful forces of a nature working in a state of chaos' may seem to be the cause of the shaping of both land and sea. Although such forms 'may now seem very purposively arranged', they are in fact 'merely the result of eruptions, either of fire or of water, or of upheavals of the ocean'. Kant's 'merely' here underlines his insistence that these movements of material nature contain nothing purposeful, but are the result of 'a wholly unintentional mechanism'; such natural forms only seem purposive because rational human agents judge them *as if* purposively designed (315; V:428).

Similarly, Kant dismisses as a 'daring adventure of reason' the idea that nature was purposively generated by 'mother earth', emerging 'like a large animal … from her state of chaos' and giving birth to creatures with increasingly purposive forms, until 'in the end this womb itself rigidified, ossified, and confined itself to bearing definite species that would no longer degenerate, so that the diversity remained as it had turned out when that fertile formative force ceased to operate' (305; V:429). Although Kant is prepared to entertain such speculations (which at least acknowledge the need for some kind of organic final cause to explain the generation of organic forms), his views on hylozoism make it clear why he thinks that, in the end, they must be rejected: for while we can 'with great caution' entertain the idea of matter imbued with life by something else (and hence becoming organised, 'animal' and organic), 'we cannot even think of living matter … as possible. (The [very] concept of it involves a contradiction, since the essential character of matter is lifelessness, [in Latin] *inertia*.)' (276: V394). Whatever the apparent activity accorded to material nature in the sublime, its dynamism is the result of blind mechanism, and its contra-purposiveness is directly linked to Kant's insistence that matter itself ('mother earth') cannot be thought in terms of an active formative principle – unless this principle is supplied from elsewhere, such as the conceptual categories of human understanding.

The sublime abyss of sexuate difference

One of the reasons Kant gives for rejecting the 'daring' supposition of the earth itself as a great originary mother is that this 'fertile formative force' would have to generate beings different in kind from itself. Thus, while this would still be 'a *generatio univoca* in the most general sense … because anything organic would be produced only from something else that is also organic' – that is, mother earth conceived as a large birthing animal – it would also be a '*generatio heteronyma*' rather than *homonyma* 'where the product shares even the organization of what produced it'. Yet, Kant insists that 'As far as our empirical knowledge of nature goes, we do not find anywhere a *generatio heteronyma*' (305; V:419).

Small wonder then, that in a letter to Schiller, Kant finds himself puzzled by the need for two sexes for reproduction in both flora and fauna, calling this an 'abyss' for thought:[3] while male and female of the same species seem to be a clear example of *generatio homonyma*, the fact that each sex can participate in the generation of offspring whose organisation is different in kind (belonging to a different sex) from its own seems to insert a '*generatio heteronyma*' into the heart of generation, despite Kant's insistence on conceptualising it in terms of sameness (*generatio univoca* and *homonyma*) rather than originary difference. As Irigaray suggests, sexual difference remains an unanalysed remainder in Kant's thought, a paradox generated by the tendency to 'forc[e] into the same representation – the representation of the self/same – that which insists upon its *heterogeneity*, its *otherness*' (Irigaray 1985: 137).

In response, it is just this difference that Irigaray insists upon. If the necessity of two sexes for the propagation of the species operates as a sublime abyss for Kant, where his imagination is indeed 'afraid to lose itself', Irigaray asks us to expand our imaginations to include this sublime thought and to recall sexuate difference as both ontological difference and a sensible transcendental. For her, it is sexuate difference that is the 'fertile formative force' that animates an active matter such that nature is founded on *generatio heteronyma* as its primary organising principle.

The heteronomy of sexuate difference is encapsulated in Irigaray's thought of being (as) two, where the two (sexes) need to be thought in ways that reduce neither to the terms of the other. Given that, in the western tradition, it is the male subject who has typically operated as norm and ideal, while woman has been defined as his 'other', Irigaray argues that finding the terms for a distinctively female subject is a necessary condition for thinking the heteronomy of sexuate difference that articulates our being. While attending to sexual difference thus means acknowledging the way generation begins between two (sexes), it also means attending to the way that each human being is born from a specifically female body, characterised by its capacity to birth. Thus, where Kant shies away from the thought of an originary mother from whose womb the whole of nature springs, Irigaray asks us – more modestly but no less challengingly – to recall the singular relation to the body of the mother through which each of us comes into the world.

More specifically, this means that the primary relation making all other relations possible is that of being borne as an 'other within', rather than the constitutive cut between self and other, subject and object, rational agent and material nature. Here we begin to see why the oppositional relations that structure the Kantian sublime become unsustainable from Irigaray's perspective. The urgency of rethinking our relations to the sensible and material follows from her emphasis on the carnate, sexuate nature of human beings themselves, as well as on our beginnings in birth, and the way that each of us comes into (a fully relational) being thanks to the female body's capacity to sustain otherness within in a negotiated ('placental') economy of differential relations (Irigaray 1993b: 37–45). The recollection and active cultivation of sexuate difference Irigaray proposes thus *necessarily* means re-working our conception of matter. In particular, it involves challenging Kant's claim that 'we cannot even think of living matter', and reconceiving the generative powers of the female body as an active *giving* of forms, the site of a formative activity and of the *generatio heteronyma* of sexuate difference.

On Irigaray's reading of Kant, the threat posed by the 'ruleless disarray' of material nature is far from being contained within the limits of a purely aesthetic experience; on the contrary, this material excess is the implicit spur driving the entire Kantian project, making it necessary to re-secure knowledge (and stabilise nature) by re-grounding it in the subject:

It sometimes happens that the sun causes the earth to shake underfoot, and people fear being turned upside down [*l'angoisse d'un renversement*], or thrown sickeningly down into the abyss, or even flying off into the void. To re-establish the balance that has been so dangerously disturbed, the philosopher decides that from now on nature overall will be put under the control of the human spirit and her origins will be based on her necessary obedience to the law.

(Irigaray, 1985: 203; translation modified)

This passage introduces Irigaray's most explicit and sustained critique of Kant, in the section of *Speculum* entitled 'Paradox A Priori'. Read in conjunction with the earlier chapter, 'Any Theory of the Subject Has Always Been Appropriated by the "Masculine"', this section draws out the multiple ways in which the Kantian subject remains dependent on both the object and materiality, in ways that are both registered and disavowed. Thus Irigaray foregrounds the way that, in Kant's critical philosophy, objects are only constituted as such via the synthesising work of the faculties, yet in turn, the subject can only situate itself as such in relation to the objects it constitutes.[4] Despite Kant's aim of re-grounding knowledge in the constitutive powers of the knowing subject, this means, she suggests, that the object operates as a 'bench mark that is ultimately more crucial than the subject' (Irigaray 1985: 133).

In ways that recall Kant's own division between the matter and form of intuition towards the start of the first *Critique* (Kant 1990: A20/B34), Irigaray foregrounds an even more fundamental dependency by repeatedly drawing attention to the way that the subject must be 'given' the matter of sensation if it is to have anything it can work up (or form) into objective representations in the first place:

If there is no more 'earth' to press down/repress, to work, to represent, but also and always to desire (for one's own), no opaque matter which in theory does not know herself, then what pedestal remains for the ex-sistence of the 'subject'?

(Irigaray 1985: 133)

Yet at the same time, as we have seen in Kant's accounts of aesthetic and teleological judgement, the subject necessarily opposes its own form-giving activities to the chaos of disorganised matter. Irigaray thus emphasises that the subject is dependent on a material 'otherness' from which he must carefully distance himself.

Along with the transcendental schema, which map sensible intuitions in ways that fit the subject's organisational categories (see Irigaray 1985: 204), the structures of the sublime provide some of the scaffolding that makes such a distancing possible. Indeed, it is when the categories *fail* that the sublime is called upon as a necessary supplement: the abyss that sensible nature becomes for the imagination in the sublime operates as a screen, protecting the subject from an excessive materiality that cannot be fully schematised or contained in the unified form of an object. The sublime abyss thus constitutes what Irigaray calls 'the intervention of a spacing in negativity' (209), reinforcing a split between rational (self) and sensible (other); negating the power of the latter to determine the former; and allowing the subject to orient itself instead towards the culti-vation of its moral vocation: 'however negative the world or the imagination may be, the "soul" – still – is enlarged. ... Culture, also, is based upon this *abyss* that reason represents for the imaginary' (209–10). Irigaray presents the subject's imagination as caught between two abyssal chasms that threaten to engulf it: the threatening materiality of chaotic nature, and the unrepresentable ideas of (moral) reason. By resisting the power of the former, it gains the strength to reach towards the distant horizons of the latter; thus the negation of nature's material excess generates a spiritual surplus that feeds the soul.

For Irigaray, this negation is symptomatic of the way the Kantian subject is constituted by cutting himself off from an originary maternal darkness: a materiality that exceeds him, yet through which he was brought into existence as a singular being before being constituted as a subject. The abyssal shadows that haunt the Kantian system simultaneously mask and recall this more originary repression of maternal-material origins. In ways that are fundamentally at odds with the female body's capacity to shelter and sustain an other within, the Kantian subject seeks to invert the original condition of human existence and overcome 'the anguish of being imprisoned *within* the other, of being placed *inside* the other' (1985: 137; my emphasis) by projecting the other *outside* the self, whether as bounded object or chaotic excess. Within this economy, the sublime figure of the abyss both externalises and blacks out the subject's links to maternal matter, repressing man's origins in sexual difference as well as a specifically female body.

Sheltering sexuate difference

Irigaray's analysis exposes the ways in which the autonomy of the Kantian subject is premised on a split from maternal materiality in ways that make the sublime archetypal, rather than exceptional, and that lock the subject into a self-perpetuating dialectic in which material dangers prompt an ever-renewed cultural resistance:

Fear and awe of an all powerful nature forbid man to touch his/the mother and reward his courage in resisting her attractions by granting him the right to judge himself independent, while at the same time encouraging him to prepare himself to continue resisting dangers in the future by developing (his) culture.

(Irigaray 1985: 210)

It is precisely the development of this culture in its modern capitalist form that results in nature being seen as (at worst) a threat to be mastered and (at best) a useful resource to be managed; and that results in fear of the wild body of the earth being supplemented with a fear that we may have so depleted the earth's resources that it may cease to sustain life.

In response, Irigaray calls for nothing short of a transformation of culture, at the heart of which lies a transformation of our understanding of the relation between culture and nature. As indicated above, this transformation is to be effected by recognising sexuate difference as ontological difference in ways that entail, first, acknowledging the active and formative capacities of matter understood as the site of sexuate difference as generative; and second, cultivating a relational model of the self that does justice to the originary sexuate relations through which we are brought into being, and that takes its orientation from the capacity of the female body to bear otherness within without assimilation or negation. Together these starting points entail thinking of ourselves as constituted not by our ability to separate ourselves from material nature, as an 'other' to be mastered or overcome, but through a set of sexuate, embodied relations that bind human beings into the complex web of agentic materiality we might call 'nature', once we cease to see the latter as the totality of objects represented by and for a subject.[5] This does not mean simply collapsing culture into nature, but rethinking culture in terms of processes of cultivation that can be more – or less – attentive to (sexuate) difference and that work across political, linguistic, social and cultural forms in an embodying of thought that is simultaneously spiritual and material, figural and affective.

The resources for such a thoroughgoing cultural transformation would necessarily be manifold. To foreground just two of the figures through which Irigaray seeks to contribute to this project, and which are particularly pertinent here: in the thought of a 'sensible transcendental' (Irigaray 1993a: 32, 115, 129), Irigaray demands we rethink the dominant hylomorphic frame of the western tradition so as to acknowledge the ways in which (spatio-temporal) forms can emerge out of the fluid movements of an active and mobile matter. And in her rethinking of the elements, she seeks to escape a model of the earth based on the alignment of matter with solid, inert substance, and to reawaken us to an active materiality that shapes and forms in the fluid movements of fire, air and water, as well as those of a living earth and flesh (see Irigaray 1992, 1999). This forgotten elemental multiplicity does not obey the laws of solids, but flows between one and another, shaping both in relation: a generative, maternal-materiality.

As long as this fluid, aerial matter remains unthought, then 'in this unthought, the force of mother-nature prevails' (Irigaray 1999: 12).[6] By failing adequately to acknowledge human beings' dependency on mother-nature, active matter becomes a dominating (rather than a generative) force, insofar as its repression silently subtends thinking as its necessary condition. Western metaphysics is thus haunted by abyssal absences that arise from the constitutive erasure of maternal generative power; from the void woman becomes as her formative capacities are forgotten and annulled; and from the 'unthought' remainder of a fluid, elemental matter.

In response, Irigaray seeks to figure what the subject of western metaphysics sees only as absence – or a threatening darkness in which there is nothing to be seen – as a fluid and generative spacing:

> [D]eeper than the greatest depths your daylight could imagine ... Neither permanently fixed nor shifting and fickle. Nothing solid survives, *yet that thickness responding to its own rhythms is not nothing*. Quickening in movements both expected and unexpected. Your space, your time are unable to grasp their regularity or contain their foldings and unfoldings.
>
> (Irigaray 1992: 13, my emphasis)

In the fluid darkness of the pregnant female body, rhythmic movements generate dense patterns of folding and unfolding, holding together a relational space-time without need to demarcate self and other through clear and impermeable boundaries. This maternal fluidity resists both the alignment of woman with inert matter, and the identification of matter with substance that can be divided and contained by fixed forms. Active, but not simply chaotic, maternal-materiality is here figured as replete with fluid movements that are rhythmic, not random: this fluid quickening cannot be reduced to an excessive otherness lacking any determinable form at all:

> This excess is (not) nothing: the vacation of form, the faults in form, the return to another edge where she re-touches herself without anything/ thanks to nothing. Lips of the same form – but of a form that is never simply defined – ripple outwards as they touch and send one another on a course that is never fixed into a single configuration.
>
> (Irigaray 1985: 230; translation modified)

Here we see one of the ways in which Irigaray reclaims and reworks the figure of the abyss, in ways that transform the conjoined figures of woman and matter. That which exceeds the forms of objective unity – that which is no-thing for a subject – is not a simple gap or absence – is not, in fact, nothing – but instead, a spacing *between* lips that allows them to touch on each other, closing without becoming sealed into one, opening without losing all contact, continually taking up different forms without becoming form-less. 'My lips ... accompany the abyss, but do not meet each other there. ... The wall between them is porous. It allows passage' (Irigaray 1992: 65–6). Instead of the 'vacation of form' which temporarily threatens the Kantian subject in the sublime, this pulsing, mobile opening allows (spatial and temporal) forms to emerge relationally, in the fluid movements shared between one (lip) and another.

Such movements produce temporary definition, without allowing form to become fixed or 'simply defined': Irigaray's rhetorical manoeuvres transform the negating void of the abyss into a spacing that preserves the possibility of future relational (and generational) becoming and change. In contrast to the Kantian sublime, where the infinite is projected out, above and beyond the subject – 'Your infinity? An uninterrupted sequence of projected points. With nothing linking them. Emptiness' (Irigaray 1992: 71) – Irigaray attends to the 'in-finite' possibilities for becoming that inhabit the finite, fissuring the already formed, but turning those 'faults in form' into spaces for further becoming.

In refiguring the edges of the abyss as two lips, and the no-thingness between them as the fluid affordance of a relational spacing, Irigaray transforms the abyss that threatens to paralyse the Kantian subject into a shelter for (sexuate) difference. In keeping with her attempt to articulate the possibility of a distinctive female subject who is *neither one nor two*, this sheltering takes at least two, distinct, but mutually supportive forms.

First, by refiguring the abyss as a fluid spacing, and its edges as the lips through which a woman touches herself as they touch on each other, Irigaray realigns the abyss with one of the most developed (and well known) images through which she seeks to articulate a distinctively female subject. The image of the lips not only provides Irigaray with a way of figuring a female morphology in which woman is no longer defined as lack (of the phallus) but in relation to herself; it also offers an alternative model of self-constitution to that in which identity is secured via opposition or negation (as in the Kantian sublime). While each lip is distinct, it is also inseparable from the other, gaining its distinctness only in relation, through movements which shape both together, without making them one and the same.

The abyss is thus transformed from a figure of negativity into a positive image of female difference and specificity, a figure for an autonomy rooted in female auto-affection. However, if one condition of a culture of sexuate difference is to find modes of speaking (as a) woman in ways that no longer reduce her to the 'other' of a male subject, equally, the possibility of articulating a distinctively female subject position depends on maintaining the dis-symmetrical difference between the sexes. Irigaray does not pretend that this difference does not cause anxiety or that attending to it is without risk; nonetheless, she transforms the abyss from an obliterating darkness into a reminder of such irreducible difference:

But this difference creates an abyss. And is there anyone who does not fear the abyss? How can there be attraction between different beings in spite of the abyss? What risk is there in attraction through difference?

Not in me but in our difference lies the abyss. We can never be sure of bridging the gap between us. But that is our adventure.

(Irigaray 1992: 28)

Here the abyss is no longer located in woman as man's 'other'; instead, it shelters a spacing between that belongs to neither, and that – if properly cultivated and sustained – prevents each from appropriating the other.[7] Irigaray's questioning voice calls on us to attend to this spacing – too often foreclosed or blacked out in the history of philosophy. To do so means positioning the other as neither a threat, nor a projection of one's own desires, nor an appropriable resource; but to take the risk of relating to others in and through their differences. Thus approached, the abyss becomes the space of a possible adventure in difference.

Conclusion: *e pur si muove*

If Irigaray reclaims the figure of the abyss and transforms it into a shelter for (sexuate) difference: what else might be sheltered in this figuring of difference? How might such a sheltering of difference afford ways of re-imagining human beings' relation to material nature – to 'the wild body of the earth' with which I began?

As we have seen, Irigaray's approach involves taking the trace of activity left to material nature by Kant in his images of disruptive chaos and ruleless disarray, and restoring it to a mode of activity with the status of formative principle: a *generatio heteronyma*.[8] In so doing, Irigaray realises one of Kant's worst fears: the 'daring adventure of reason' might be closer to the truth than Kant thinks, displacing the subject from his axial position as the source of all purposive form. The figure of the abyss transformed into a pulsing opening asks us to recall this active, (self-)shaping materiality, capable of sculpting space and time in its rhythmic movements. Instead of a cut dividing self from other, this pulsing space-time *between* differentiates without fully separating.

One of the possibilities sheltered by Irigaray's refiguring of the abyss is thus that of regarding human beings as part of a material world that actively cultivates form in manifold ways, rather than as constitutively opposed to nature as 'other': a materiality to be mastered and overcome, managed at a distance, consumed as objects, and generally treated as a resource for human activities (what Heidegger calls the 'standing reserve'). Irigaray's concerns resonate with those of Mann cited earlier, that such an attitude has left us 'suspended over the abyss of the impending *absence* of nature' (Mann 2006: 163). Mann shows how sublime fear of this impending absence can provoke a different ethical response to that valorised by Kant: instead of reasserting moral authority by separating ourselves from nature, we might instead become more deeply aware of our dependencies on and responsibilities towards the material world.

Such a shift allows the centrality of human interests to be displaced in relations to nature whose non-oppositional character involves a blurring of the beautiful and sublime, in ways reminiscent of many of Irigaray's writings:

> If we are reoriented in our relation to the natural world by experiences of beauty that evoke the sublime, then we are oriented toward the preservation of the beauty of nature quite apart from human interest. Here the ecology of place becomes a global ecology.
>
> (Mann 2006: 165)

In turn, Irigaray's insistence on our own corporeal (sexuate) nature on the one hand, and on rethinking matter as active on the other, furthers Mann's aim of shifting our horizons towards those of a global ecology: it is harder to think of nature in terms of purely human interest when human beings themselves are seen as inseparably bound up with, and only emerging within, an active materiality that reaches far beyond themselves.

Irigaray's approach also echoes that of Mann insofar as both thinkers emphasise human beings' dependencies on material nature and the vulnerabilities that thereby arise. As Mann suggests, the vulnerability to which the sublime testifies and which, in its traditional forms, it seeks to overcome, can also be reclaimed as a starting point for rethinking alternative, non-instrumental relations with both human others and material nature:

> relations of dependence are the irrevocable aspect of the human condition that both lends itself to and is disclosed in sublime experience. The ethical and political implications of this vulnerability to others can be temporarily denied or thwarted by the subject who flees dependence, but they must ultimately be affirmed if we are to live these relations in aesthetically, ethically, and politically sustainable ways.
>
> (Mann 2006: 132–3)

Drawing on Butler's *Precarious Life*, Mann argues that dependency and vulnerability are intrinsically bound up with human existence as constitutively bodily and relational; they are not simply to be overcome, but afford an opening onto a reorientation of our modes of sociability, as well as our political and ethical life. Nonetheless, even while Mann draws on Butler to emphasise the relational constitution of the self ('the ties we have to others ... constitute what we are';

Butler 2004: 22; cited in Mann 2006: 133), there is a risk that a trace of the Kantian sublime remains, insofar as dependency and vulnerability are still figured as that by which we are undone, even if this undoing is embraced as an alternative basis for political community ('Let's face it. We're undone by each other. And if we're not, we're missing something'; Butler: 23). It is here that Irigaray's relational ontology is helpful, insofar as our vulnerabilities and dependencies are seen not only as having the potential to undo the subjects we have become, but as an active element within the relations that bring us into being and make us the subjects that we are. On her model, otherness – be it that of other human beings or material nature – does not first come from outside to sustain or undo us, but is always already bound up in the formation of who and what we are, as sexuate, corporeal beings, constituted through generative difference.

Finally, by realising Kantian fears of an active matter, Irigaray also enables us to question the supposed 'naturalness' of the fear of dynamic nature that structures the Kantian sublime. If an active, generative materiality animated by the principle of sexuate difference is restored to ontological primacy, and both human beings and the nature of which they are a part are seen as the product of a *generatio heteronyma*, then it is not clear that our *only* response to an earth that moves in ways beyond our expectations and control need be one of fear. Doubtless, earthquakes, hurricanes and volcanoes still have the power to devastate and destroy (though as recent events in Japan and Haiti remind us, their most destructive effects are often the result of human intervention, whether in the form of technological, political or economic structures); but our response to such material forces might not always be fear – or not simply fear – but could also contain wonder or even joy, if the movement of the earth is seen as a reminder of the life that sustains us and binds us together, as natal and not just mortal beings, born from an active and generative materiality.

Such joy is briefly figured by Isak Dinesen, as she recounts her experience of an earthquake in Kenya. Dinesen traces the broad pattern of the Kantian sublime as she passes from fear of her own destructability ('I am going to die, this is how it feels to die') to awe at the 'tremendous perspective' opened up by the idea of nature's vastness or power. But she also moves to a third stage, in which she is transported in joy by:

> the consciousness that something which you have reckoned to be immovable has got it in it to move on its own. That is probably one of the strongest sensations of joy and hope in the world. The dull globe, the dead mass, the earth itself, rose and stretched under me. It sent me out a message, the slightest touch, but of unbounded significance. It laughed so that the Native huts fell down and cried: *E pur si muove.*
>
> (Dinesen 1985: 208)[9]

It is this possibility of joy in active matter that is sheltered by Irigaray's re-figuring of the abyss, in ways that would allow us to cultivate a different kind of relation to material nature, one based more on wonder at its generative capacities than on the mastery of fear, more on nurturing life than avoiding death.

In an intriguing passage in the third *Critique*, Kant suggests that the feeling of the sublime furthers life via 'a momentary inhibition of the vital forces followed immediately by an outpouring of them that is all the stronger' (Kant 1987: 98; V:245). As his account progresses, this concern with 'vital forces' is displaced by a rational agent who is able 'to regard as small' his natural concerns, including life itself (121; V:262). Irigaray's conceptualisation of active matter returns us to a concern with life, a pulsing, corporeal, generative life of which we are a part. Her work thus makes a valuable contribution to the ways in which we negotiate our relation both to the sublime and to the material world, caught as we are between two historical fears: the abiding fear of nature's might, manifest in the tremors of the earth that continue to reveal the fragility of our technological efforts at mastery; and the fear that the ingenious beings that Sophocles' called the strangest and most wondrous of all might finally have so worn down the earth that they have estranged themselves from their terrestrial home, rendering it terrifyingly inhospitable (Sophocles 1960: 192; I.332–40). By resituating human beings within an active and generative materiality, and allowing us to see an earth that moves as not just a harbinger of death, but a joyful reminder of birth, Irigaray's work provides some of the resources for transforming the oppositional and instrumentalising relations that simultaneously reflect and produce such fears. It is thus not only sexuate difference that is sheltered in her refiguring of the abyss, but with it, possibilities for different futures – futures perhaps no less fearful, but ones in which we might learn to respond to our fears in ways that tend towards the fostering of life and relation.

Notes

1 This way of characterising the sublime is drawn from Battersby's extensive work on the topic; see for example Battersby 2007: 136.
2 See also my article 'Kant, Irigaray and Earthquakes: Adventures in the Abyss' (Jones, forthcoming 2013), in which I draw on the penultimate section of this chapter and in which I explore Irigaray's refiguring of the abyss in relation to Kant's pre-critical writings on the Lisbon earthquake.
3 See Kant's letter to Schiller, 30 March 1795 (Kant 1922: 11); cited in Battersby 1998: 71.
4 This is not only the case at the transcendental level, where the rule-bound function of synthesising intuitions into the unity of an object simultaneously allows those intuitions to be referred to a single subject or consciousness, but also at an empirical level, as the subject can only determine the temporal order of its own consciousness against the benchmark of objects that function as external and permanent reference points.
5 On rethinking nature as capable of agency, see Plumwood 1993 and 2001.
6 While the passage from which this citation is taken could easily be directed at Kant, it appears in the context of Irigaray's critical dialogue with Heidegger, in which she suggests that his

privileging of earth perpetuates a forgetting of air and reveals the extent to which he remains trapped within (traditional western) metaphysics.

7 Kant's alignment of sexual difference with the abyss is continued by Lacan, who uses this image repeatedly to figure the fact that, according to him, there is no such thing as a sexual relationship; for example, 'love is impossible and the sexual relationship drops into the abyss of nonsense' (Lacan 1999: 87). Irigaray's refiguring of the abyss is thus also a critique of Lacan that seeks to reclaim the possibility of a relation between two – differently constituted – sexuate subjects.

8 This does not mean, of course, that material nature cannot act in ways that, from a human perspective, are profoundly destructive, but that such destruction is a side-effect of a primarily formative force, which does not always cohere with human aims and aspirations.

9 Dinesen's reclamation of active materiality is here bound up with another kind of 'othering', reflected in the colonial context of her comment about the 'Native', in ways that need to be subjected to critique (just as the perpetuation of racial 'others' in feminist philosophy generally and Irigaray's work in particular has rightly been critiqued).

Bibliography

Battersby, C. (1989) *Gender and Genius*, Bloomington: Indiana University Press.

— (1998) *The Phenomenal Woman*, Cambridge: Polity.

— (2007) *The Sublime, Terror and Human Difference*, London: Routledge.

Butler, J. (2004) *Precarious Life*, London: Verso.

Dinesen, I. (1985) *Out of Africa, and Shadows on the Grass*, Harmondsworth: Penguin.

Freeman, B. (1995) *The Feminine Sublime*, Berkeley: University of California Press.

Hachamovitch, Y. (1994) 'The earth that does not move', in A.B. Dallery and S.H. Watson (eds) *Transitions in Continental Philosophy*, Albany, NY: SUNY Press.

Irigaray, L. (1985) *Speculum of the Other Woman*, trans. G. Gill, Ithaca, NY: Cornell University Press.

— (1992) *Elemental Passions*, trans. J. Collie and J. Still, London: Athlone.

— (1993a) *An Ethics of Sexual Difference*, trans. C. Burke and G.C. Gill, London: Athlone.

— (1993b) *je, tu, nous: Towards a Culture of Difference*, trans. A. Martin, London: Routledge.

— (1999) *The Forgetting of Air*, trans. M.B. Mader, Austin: University of Texas Press.

Jones, R. (forthcoming 2013) 'Kant, Irigaray, and earthquakes: adventures in the abyss', *Symposium: Canadian Journal for Continental Philosophy*, 17, 1.

Kant, I. (1922) 'Kants Briefwechsel Band III: 1795–1803', in *Kants Gesammelte Schriften*, 29 vols, Königlich Preußischen Akademie der Wissenschaften, Vol. XII, Berlin: Walter Gruyter.

— (1987) *Critique of Judgment*, trans. W. Pluhar, Indianapolis, IN: Hackett.

— (1990) *Critique of Pure Reason*, trans. N. Kemp Smith, London: MacMillan.

Lacan, J. (1999) *Encore, The Seminar of Jacques Lacan, Book XX: On Feminine Sexuality, the Limits of Love and Knowledge*, trans. B. Fink, New York: Norton.

Mann, B. (2006) *Women's Liberation and the Sublime: Feminism, Postmodernism, Environment*, Oxford: Oxford University Press.

Plumwood, V. (1993) *Feminism and the Mastery of Nature*, London: Routledge.

— (2001) *Environmental Culture: The Ecological Crisis of Reason*, London: Routledge.

Sophocles (1960) 'Antigone', in D. Grene and R. Lattimore (eds) *Greek Tragedies: Volume I*, trans. E. Wyckoff, Chicago: University of Chicago Press.

Chapter 6

Bonjour Tristesse

David Cross

In the Pyrenees near the border between France and Spain, three historic solar energy collectors signal a route away from consumer society's dependence on destructive sources of energy, and embody the possibility of retrieving a more coherent, progressive, and sustainable modernity. Yet they have been overshadowed by the nuclear industry in France, and the fossil fuel industry worldwide. With energy depletion and climate damage threatening the bases of society and culture, the marginalization of such technology cannot be seen as purely rational. I aim here to consider how scientific reason relates to hidden phobias and unspoken desires.

A solar furnace applies the optical phenomena of focus, reflection and magnification to intensify the image of the sun (Trombe 1956: 63–72). As with a photographic camera, the result achieved is a function of focal length, aperture and exposure time. My hope is that while optics form the basis for connections between the solar furnace and the photographic camera, so photography and film theory might enhance the understanding of solar furnace technology by situating it within the cultural sphere. In turn, a psychoanalytic approach to the paradigm of scientific objectivity (Figlio 1996) could help relate it to the subjective experience that underlies social trends, such as changing public attitudes to research.

The first double reflection solar furnace was built in 1952 at Mont Louis, France by Professor Félix Trombe, Director of Research at the Centre National de la Recherche Scientifique (National Centre for Scientific Research), Paris, in collaboration with Albert Le Phat Vinh and Marc Foëx (Trombe and Le Phat Vinh 1973: 57–61).

In this photograph, Trombe uses the parabolic mirror from a wartime anti-aircraft searchlight to focus the sun's rays to a burning point. But the mirror also doubles, enlarges and distorts the scientist's image, which the camera renders in perspective as an ellipse, like a cameo. This transformation of his image seems incidental to the scientific research, and if Trombe sees it, he does not acknowledge it. His goggles attract the viewer's attention to his face, which is expressionless, fixated on the point of light where the sun's rays converge. Nor does Trombe acknowledge the camera or photographer; despite the intense heat of his experiment, he seems cool and indifferent to his photographic image.

Similarly, the camera records an image of the optical processes of reflection, focus and exposure, without acknowledging its own relationship to the situation. Yet this photograph is clearly staged, and composed to serve as both factual document and publicity image. Already separated from the mesmerizing scene by the passage of time, the viewer is positioned by the photograph as a detached spectator rather than someone who might affect, or be affected by the event.

A working reconstruction of Félix Trombe's solar furnace was established at Mont Louis in 1980 by Denis Eudeline, an engineer and public advocate of solar technology for international development. The sun's rays are reflected by a flat mirror onto a convex parabolic mirror, which superimposes multiple images of the sun onto a single focal point, instantaneously producing temperatures in excess of 3000 degrees Celsius with near-zero emissions of CO_2 or other pollutants.

Trombe and his colleagues conducted the original high-temperature solar-energy research during the Cold War. With potential applications to space technology and atomic warfare, the research had military importance, so the experimental furnace was installed within the ramparts of the seventeenth-century fort at Mont Louis. The fort was designed for Louis XIV, 'The Sun King', by the military architect Sebastien le Prestre, Marquis de Vauban, to defend the border between France and Spain. Now a UNESCO World Heritage Site, the fort still serves as a military base and is the French National Centre for Commando Training.

The circular 'halo' in this photograph is produced by the intense sunlight reflecting off the lenses inside the camera, making explicit the mechanical nature of the image. Occurring along specific sight lines, this 'lens flare' signals a reciprocal relationship between the camera, the solar device and the fortress, with their shared logic of vision as control.

I love these solar mirrors, while I have to concede that as all technologies are grounded within social relations, none is inherently liberating. Equally, I am still attracted to the notion that the camera has the potential to transform thought; though my own sense of self has been conditioned by countless photographs that have inculcated in me ideological models of individual and social identity.

To combine my attempt at emancipatory self-consciousness with a critical focus on imaging technology, I put myself in the picture. I faced the mirror of Mont Louis, raised the camera, and closed one eye. Through the viewfinder, my frame of vision was filled with the solar reflector.

With the camera obscuring my face, my own image was reduced to a figure, both fragmented and recombined into a mosaic of reflections registered on the electronic sensor of the digital camera, and on my retina. The telephoto lens produced a luminous but flattened image of the giant parabolic mirror, so that its concave form appeared convex, and its reflective surface appeared transparent. The idea that I was inside the image of technology folded ambiguously into the thought that the image was already inside me. I became disoriented, and my narcissistic fantasy of control fused with its counterpart: the fear of failure.

Steadying myself, I remember looking through the aperture at the centre of the reflector to see the fields and trees in the valley beyond.

The success of Trombe's experiments at Mont Louis led in 1968 to the construction of the most powerful solar furnace in the world, the 'Grand Four Solaire' at Odeillo. The ultra-high temperatures produced by the furnace enable the study of the fundamental science of energy and matter, with applications including the development of aerospace ceramics, the production of industrial gems, the destruction of asbestos and clinical waste, and the containment of nuclear waste. The centre's research into photovoltaic cells and the splitting of water molecules to produce hydrogen contributes to the development of transformation, storage and transport of energy (Centre National de la Recherche Scientifique).

The research spans from the nuclear and space programmes of the Cold War to the search for renewable energy following the first Oil Crisis. These give the building a shifting symbolic identity, charged with both aggressive and defensive significance – from anticipation of nuclear warfare to more peaceable efforts to reconcile technology with ecology.

In photographing this building, I was looking to portray it as a proclamation: that science funded by the state and conducted in the public interest (if not directly under democratic control) is not merely a utopian fantasy to be dismissed as part of the demise of Modernism. Yet in the clear mountain light, the bright vision evoked its inverse; I became irritable, and distracted by a mental image of polluted skies reflected in the polished surfaces of corporate architecture in the City of London.

The research at Odeillo led to the construction of a solar power station nearby, at Targassonne. Here, banks of mirrors reflect the sun into a furnace at the top of the tower, registering a multiple exposure of the solar image as thermal energy to drive a turbine. The centre was named Thémis, after the Greek goddess of divine order and justice.

Thémis opened in 1983 to provide sustainable employment generating ultra-low-carbon electricity. But French state subsidies for nuclear energy offered Electricité de France higher profits, and in 1986 the plant was scheduled to be demolished, and the site razed.

Yet just as Thémis concentrates the image of the sun, its mirrors can be realigned to capture starlight and electromagnetic radiation. An international group of astrophysicists and scientists with the Commissariat à l'Energie Atomique and the Conseil Européen pour la Recherche Nucléaire successfully bid to use the apparatus as a space telescope, and so the decision to destroy Thémis was deferred.

In choosing my position to take this photograph, I climbed up the hill as though scouting for a location shot or restaging a film still, perhaps a cinematic image reworking a classical narrative of loss and redemption. Seen from a high viewpoint, the architecture of the installation resembles an amphitheatre, quietly associating the shared infrastructure of power with the public spaces of democracy and culture.

Fredric Jameson developed the work of Ernest Mandel, who identified a series of fundamental breaks or leaps in technology following the original Industrial Revolution: displacing renewable energy, machine-made steam engines were followed by electric and combustion motors, then nuclear-powered and electronic devices (Jameson 1991: 35). Jameson showed that under capitalism, each cultural moment embodies the logic of its technological base.

Just as a globalization dependent on fossil and nuclear fuels produces conflict between internationalism and environmentalism, the geography of a more durable modernity would be constrained to renewable energy. Technology might be seen not as generalized human ingenuity detached from physical reality, but as specific to its material base, and so would have to respond to geology, topography and the 'bioregional' variations of vegetation and climate. A re-localization of energy production might favour a redistribution of political power, but what of cultural influence? Could the paradigm of linearity, centralization and isolation be inflected with reciprocality, contingency and interdependence? If so, maybe the signification of ecology could inform an 'ecology of signification'.

Climate damage caused by fossil fuel use is increasing the levels of water vapour in the atmosphere, with jet aircraft contrails making an additional, disproportionate contribution to 'global dimming', or the loss of sunlight. As I was taking this photograph the sky became obscured by clouds, so I used a polarizing filter to retain definition and contrast.

Bonjour Tristesse (1954) is a novel by Françoise Sagan. Set in a luxurious villa on the French Riviera, the story is told by Cécile, a young woman whose mother died when Cécile was an infant. Cécile lives a life of extravagant socializing with her father Raymond, a suave but vacuous advertising executive with a penchant for young and superficial women.

Although Cécile failed her philosophy exam, she is taking a long summer holiday in the villa with her father and Elsa, his latest girlfriend. But the simple pleasures of days in the sun become complicated when Raymond also invites Anne, whose maturity, creativity and personal integrity give her an authority that Cécile finds both reassuring and oppressive.

Raymond makes a surprise decision to reject Elsa and to marry Anne, who then assumes responsibility for Cécile's moral and intellectual development. Lucid and self-aware, Cécile understands that although the struggle against limitations is a critical aspect of adolescence, the passage to adulthood entails freely chosen responsibility. Torn between enlightened self-interest and self-centred hedonism, she intervenes in the relationships around her. Cécile grasps the psychological dynamics, but underestimates the forces involved. While the ensuing disaster might have been imagined, it could not have been predicted, so it is lifted from a crime to a tragedy.

Acknowledgements

My special thanks go to Denis Eudeline, Directeur Four Solaire Developpement, Mont Louis, France; Emmanuel Guillot, Ingénieur de Recherche, Laboratoire Procédés, Materiaux et Energie Solaire, Odeillo, France; and Dr Jane Rendell, Professor at the Bartlett School of Architecture, London.

A version of this article was previously published in *field* (January 2011). I warmly thank Dr Renata Tyszczuk and Dr Stephen Walker of the University of Sheffield for their permission to reproduce it here.

Bibliography

Centre National de la Recherche Scientifique, Processes, Materials and Energy Laboratory. Online: http://www.promes.cnrs.fr/ (accessed July 2012).

Cross, D. (2011) 'Bonjour Tristesse', *Field*, 4, 1: 135–47.

Figlio, K. (1996) 'Knowing, loving and hating nature – a psychoanalytic view', in *FutureNatural: Nature, Science, Culture*. Edited by George Robertson, Melinda Mash, Lisa Tickner, Jon Bird, Barry Curtis and Tim Putnam, New York: Routledge.

Jameson, F. (1991) *Postmodernism, or, The Cultural Logic of Late Capitalism*, London: Verso.

Trombe, F. (1956) 'High temperature furnaces', in *Proceedings of the World Symposium on Applied Solar Energy, Phoenix, Arizona, 1955*, Stanford, CT: Stanford Research Institute.

Trombe, F. and Le Phat Vinh, A. (1973) 'Thousand KW Solar furnace, built by the National Center of Scientific Research, in Odeillo (France)', *Solar Energy*, 15: 57–61.

Part III

Economics, land and consumption

Chapter 7

Beyond consumerism

Reflections on gender politics, pleasure and
sustainable consumption[1]

Kate Soper

In recent times, movements for gender and sexual emancipation have removed
social oppressions. But they have done little to date to challenge the consumerist
model of the 'good life' that is responsible for global warming, and have even
reinforced its hold in certain respects. Freedom from domesticity and the patriarchal division of labour has not led – as many feminists had hoped it would – to
greener and fairer ways of thinking about human prosperity, but has gone together
with increased commodification and the expansion of the 'shopping mall' culture.
This chapter reflects on these tensions and reviews the aims and achievements
of gender and environmental politics in the light of them. But it also argues that
Western societies are now entering a cultural moment characterised by a more
troubled relationship to unchecked consumption. The upshot is the emergence of
consumption as a site of new forms of political engagement, ethical consideration
and aesthetic representation. The 'alternative hedonism' implicit in these forms of
consumer ambivalence is presented in this context as the impulse behind a new
'political imaginary' that could help to promote a fairer, environmentally sustainable
and more enjoyable future – and thus fulfil some of the more radical aspirations that
have been associated with the movements for gender and sexual emancipation.

Gender politics and market society

Any thinking about gender and climate change needs to address a key tension
at the heart of the globalised economy, namely, that the consumer culture on
which it depends, although closely associated with 'freedom and democracy', is

precipitating ecological collapse. What has helped to advance gender and sexual emancipation has also been the vehicle of unsustainable modes of consumption. The 'cultural revolution' achieved by Western feminism, for example, has been remarkable (Coward 1999), but it has coincided with the huge expansion of the shopping-mall culture. It has not unsettled the presiding structures and institutions of economic power, nor led – as many feminists of my generation had hoped it would – to greener and fairer ways of thinking about human prosperity.

On the contrary, the links between feminism and ecology have been attenuated. Movements for sexual emancipation have been co-opted by the market, with 'Third Wave' feminism and 'girl power' providing the springboard for all sorts of consumer oriented media interventions, brand development and advertising spin.[2] And with the shift from an older-style social movement politics to a focus on 'identity' have come ways of thinking about self-hood, the body, gender 'bending' and 'performance', that have encouraged a culture of 'tribalism' and self-styling rather than the forms of solidarity that had been rooted in an earlier eco-socialist-feminist politics. 'Identity politics' undeniably offered an important counter to the Eurocentric and essentialising conflations of social and sexual differences of an earlier moment on the Left. My point is simply that it went together with a shift of political project, away from any Marxist/socialist agenda and economic critique to an altogether more pluralist and sceptical conception of social change.

In a further twist to this story, we might note that in cultural studies the advance of feminism brought to attention, but did rather little to transform, the long-standing feminisation of consumption – an aspect of the link that Andreas Huyssen first brought to attention in his formula 'mass culture as woman' (Huyssen 1987: 47). Theorists in the academy, although often critical of the implied disparagement of women by their association with shopping as opposed to 'higher' forms of cultural activity, tended on the whole to counter that disdain, not by challenging the elision itself between femininity and consumption, but by recasting it as a form of female empowerment. The tendency in the 1980s–1990s was to celebrate the licence given to self-making, gender performance and the reconstruction of identity by consumer culture rather than to criticise its forms of hedonism, or issue cautions about its social and ecological exploitations (Littler 2009: 171-87; cf. Littler 2008; McRobbie 2008; Bowlby 1985, 1993; de Grazie and Furlough 1996; Nava 1992, 1996; Radner 1995).

In this process, an ongoing history of female counter-consumerist activism was ignored or downplayed, namely, the important role that women have played in various boycotts or buycotts. Or where that activity *was* recognised as speaking to a rather different – and more politically contestatory – female role in consumption, it was criticised for its unreconstructed view of women as mothers and homemakers – in other words, for its reliance upon an essentialist conception of female nature as inherently suited to domestic and nurturing tasks. The emphasis on empowerment also encouraged complacency about what has actually been going on in the world of shopping – where marketing of gender stereotypes, albeit now in a mildly ironised form, has relied on sweatshop labour and continued to bring in massive profits. The fashion industry, for example, through its provision of an endless variety of very cheap clothing has persuaded many women into hyper-consumerist and throwaway dress habits. New fashion lines in shoes and other items are now replaced much more rapidly than before, with the average number of articles of apparel bought by women rising from 34 to 57 per annum in the last decade (Schor 2008). Cosmetics and plastic surgery have also proved a huge growth area. More insidiously, there has been the intensive – and highly gendered – infiltration of the child's world by branding gurus and marketing experts over the same period: a brainwashing and theft of youth that would be regarded as sinisterly totalitarian were it to occur in any other context but that of the market (Boycott 2004; cf. Palmer 2006; McRobbie 2008: 544-49; Schor 2004). 'Third Wave' feminists have been understandably wary of lending themselves to the puritan or sexually repressive element that lurks in some of the critiques of these forms of commercialism. But this reluctance has meant that this feminist cultural theory has been resistant to making the links between consumption and the green agenda, and done little to associate feminism with critique of the growth model of the economy.[3]

It would, however, be silly to imply in any attack on feminism's recent record on consumption, that it is only women and pre-teen girls who have done the consuming, or only feminist cultural theory that can be called to account. Let us not forget that most of the commodities we are talking about owe their production to companies and financial institutions in which men have retained the commanding positions, and that it is feminist theory that has exposed this gender bias in industry and its ramifications. Nor should we overlook the fact that the market in goods and services for both sexes and all age ranges has expanded relentlessly in recent decades. The enticements offered to adults, especially men – notably cars, hi-tech electronic equipment, sports goods and services – are generally much more environmentally destructive than those on offer to children. And they can be just as grotesque.

It is true that the IT revolution and the postmodern economy have had some impact in 'virtualising' and 'miniaturising' commodities. Much faith was placed in the 1980s–1990s in the power of the e-revolution to 'im-materialise' culture. We heard of the new airiness and translucence of objects, of their ceding to images and holograms, of the old space-time frames being overthrown in a new co-presence of everything, of the ways in which the old narratives of flesh and matter would cede to those of cyborg disembodiment. But to read such cultural commentary today is to be struck not only by the undialectical, and often plainly fatuous, quality of much of its vision, but above all by its Promethean abstraction from any environmentalist concerns about resource attrition, global warming and pollution. One designer at the time, while heralding the end of an older materialism, also confidently looks forward to a 'new hedonism of travel' based around spaceships modelled on the Orient Express and having an ambience 'redolent of Ludwig of Bavaria'. 'What, after all,' she asks, 'could be more enticing than the prospect of an elaborate pendulum-clock or a veiled lady in an environment where gravity must be artificially maintained?' (Dona 1988: 154). Today, not even the few remaining avatars of space tourism, such as Richard Branson with his Galactic flights, would be capable of quite such nonchalance.

The economy has also become increasingly dependent for its 'health' on our collective preparedness to spend the money we earn by working too hard and too long on the commodities which help to compensate for the forms of need satisfaction we have increasingly sacrificed through overwork and over-production. This is a dynamic that tends to the elimination of straightforward and inexpensive forms of gratification, only then to profit further through the provision of more expensive compensatory modes of consumption for those who can afford them. The leisure and tourist industry has increasingly tailored its offerings to the over-worked, with holiday breaks that promise to make good the loss in 'quality' time. Then there is the extra you often now have to pay for dealing with a person rather than a machine; the speed dating and Wife Selecting agencies that promise to make up for your loss of the arts of loving and relating; the multiplication of gyms to which people drive in order to do treadmill running in cities where, because there are so many cars on the street, they no longer find it pleasant or safe to walk or run.

Countering responses

But this focus would be misleading if it were taken to mean that there were no opposition mounting to this peculiar scenario. For Western society is now beginning to experience a more troubled relationship to unchecked consumption. Alarms over anthropogenic global warming have, of course, played a major role in this. But there have been other factors at work, many of them fuelled by the latest financial crisis. There is the anger – and anxiety – many now feel about living in a world that has so plainly favoured the greed and ever more conspicuous – and environmentally vandalising – consumption of the already very wealthy, and allowed the gap between richest and poorest to grow to inflammatory proportions. To this we can add the evidence of a growing disquiet over the negative legacy of the consumerist lifestyle for consumers themselves. Today the affluent lifestyle is being brought into question not only because of its environmental consequences, but also because it distrains on both sensual pleasure and more spiritual forms of well-being. We can note in this connection the many laments for what has gone missing from our lives under the relentless pressure from neo-liberal economic policies, where people often say they would prefer less tangible goods such as more free time, less stress, more personal contacts and a slower pace of life. These voicings of discontent – many of which have a gendered narrative – are still fairly low-key, diffuse and politically unfocused. They are the frustrated murmurings of those who are aware of their impotence to take on the corporate giants, and have little coherent idea of what to put in place of the existing order. But their regrets are real enough, and they feed into a sense of the opportunities squandered in recent decades for enjoying more relaxed and less reductive ways of living.

This new climate of disenchantment is reflected in recent media coverage, with its concerns over the ill health, childhood obesity, car congestion, noise, excessive waste and loss of the 'arts of living' that are the unwanted by-products of consumerism (Schor 2004; Levett 2004; Bunting 2004; Hodgkinson 2004; Honore 2005; Shah 2005; Thomas 2008, 2009). It is registered, too, in the concerns of policy makers with the economic and social effects of the high-stress, fast-food lifestyle, and in recent studies that have indicated that buying more does not bring greater happiness, and economic growth has no direct correlation with improved levels of well-being. The world's wealthiest societies have consistently scored rather poorly on the New Economics Foundation 'Happy Planet' measures of the relative environmental efficiency of nations in supporting well-being (New Economics Foundation (2006); cf. Lane 2001; Layard 2005; Frey and Stutzer 2002; Jackson 2004, 2009; Jackson and Marks 1999; Evans and Jackson 2007). Indeed recent research suggests that those people who have woken up to what the Sustainable Development Commission has called the 'inadequate surrogacy' of their consumerist lifestyle, and opted for less materialistic values, have gained in happiness and well-being (Brown and Kasser 2005; Kasser 2002, 2007). This is also suggested in personal reports from the 'Voluntary Simplicity' movement (www.simpleliving.net) and the more recently formed Center for the 'New American Dream' whose mission is 'to help people live the dream, but in a way that ensures a livable planet for current and future generations' (www.newdream.org), and in the continuing expansion of the 'Slow Food' (www.slowfood.net) and 'Slow City' (www.cittaslow.net) networks.

Even those most committed to keeping us in the shopping malls, the corporate giants and their supportive governments, have come close to acknowledging their vulnerability to such 'awakenings' and the vagaries of public spending that might ensue. One already detected a sense of this, for example, in the calls following the Twin Towers attack, for us to commit to 'patriotic shopping' as a way of showing our support for the Western way of life: calls whose interference in our private market choices was at odds with the usual neo-liberal view of consumers as 'sovereign', and which said much about the dependency of corporate power on our continued loyalty to a consumerist way of life. And now today the idea that we have some kind of duty to spend our way out of the 'credit crisis' is being insistently repeated by politicians.

In all these ways and for all these reasons, the consumerist lifestyle is beginning to generate new tensions even within its own 'Western' heartlands, and even as it continues to offer to less wealthy nations a virtually unchallenged model of progress and human prosperity. These developments are reflected in recent academic engagement with 'political consumerism' or 'virtuous' shopping (Micheletti 2003; Micheletti and Peretti 2003; Barnett *et al.* 2005; Harrison *et al.* 2005). They have also prompted new work in feminist cultural studies, notably by Joe Littler, who argues that academics now need to revisit the relations between consumption and feminism and develop a feminist response robust enough to encompass criticism of female co-option in consumer inequality and over-consumption (Littler 2009, 2008). Such arguments bear directly on my own response to the current context, which has come through the development of the concept of 'alternative hedonism', that is, the pursuit and enjoyment of other pleasures (Soper 2007, 2009b). Although I have not given this any overt gender slant, the gender implications are discernible in key aspects of its 'post-consumerist' vision, notably its challenge to a work ethic and culture rooted in the conventional gender division of labour.

'Alternative hedonism'

In contrast to the mainstream responses on global warming that emphasise the technical fixes that might allow us indefinitely to pursue consumerist lifestyles, alternative hedonism dwells on the pleasures to be gained from a less work-driven and acquisitive way of life. It is premised on the idea that even if consumerism were indefinitely sustainable it would not enhance human happiness and well-being, or not beyond a certain point that has already past. And it claims that it is new forms of desire rather than fears of ecological disaster that are most likely to encourage more sustainable modes of consuming. The chances of shifting to a less rapacious consumption are thus presented as dependent on the emergence and embrace of new modes of thinking about human fulfilment and the life–work balance, especially, in the first instance, on the part of the affluent global elites. A counter-consumerist ethic and politics should therefore appeal not only to compassion and environmental concern, but also to the more self-regarding gratifications of working and consuming differently. It should develop and communicate a new erotics of consumption or hedonist 'imaginary'. The burden of ecological argument should in this sense fall on the construction of a

new politics of prosperity rather than on the philosophy of nature. The en
in short, should fall less on the 'right' ways of valuing nature and more on the
conditions of a just and sustainable human fulfillment (cf. Soper 2011).

By focusing on the ways in which emerging forms of disaffection
with consumerism constitute an immanent critique of consumer culture, the
'alternative hedonist' perspective aims to avoid the moralising about 'real' needs
that has often characterised earlier critiques of consumer culture. The concern is
not to prove that consumers 'really' need something quite other than what they
profess to need (or want) – a procedure which is paternalistic and undemocratic
– but to reflect on the hedonist aspirations prompting changes in experienced or
imagined need, and their implications for the development of more sustainable
modes of consumption (cf. Soper 2009b).

This position connects with an earlier left-wing tradition of Marxist
and Frankfurt School critique of commodification and 'commodity aesthetics'. Yet
it differs in the attention paid to the domain of consumption as a potential source
of ethical pressure and political agency. The Critical Theory emphasis was on the
manipulation of consumer 'needs' and wants rather than on the reflexivity of
consumers, and production alone was seen as the site of potential mobilisation
against the capitalist order, through the agency of worker militancy. By contrast,
'alternative hedonism' argues that challenges to the status quo are more likely
to be registered initially at the level of consumption – in calls for a less materially
encumbered and work-driven existence. Such 'agency' would no longer be class
specific, but more diffusely exercised – even if in the first instance many of the
more rebellious consumers would probably be relatively well off.

Re-thinking the 'work–life balance'

I want now, in conclusion, to turn briefly to some key aspects of the new
'political imaginary' I have associated with 'alternative hedonism', and say a
word on its gender implications and how it might gain wider appeal.

What above all has to be challenged by anyone serious about ecology,
in other words about providing for a just and sustainable future for the planet,
is our general subordination to a time economy and work ethic which sees free
time as a threat to prosperity rather than a form in which it can be realised.
For the work-centred society does grave damage not only to the environment
but also to human well-being. An unprecedented productivity that might have
allowed for a more sustainable expansion of leisure, has been swallowed up in
an ever-expanding provision of commodities. Dramatic illustration of the opportunities missed in the US has been provided by Juliet Schor, who has argued
that if Americans had settled for a 1948 standard of living (measured in terms of
marketed goods and services), every worker in the United States could now be

taking every other year off from work – with pay. Instead, free time fell by nearly 40 per cent post-1973 so although the average American by 1990 owned and consumed more than twice as much as he or she did in 1948, he or she also had considerably less leisure (Schor 1991: 2; cf. de Graaf 2003). Similar trends are evident in the UK, where two-fifths of the workforce are now working harder than in the 1980s. The tendency, moreover, has been for the more 'workaholic' elements to set the pace for everyone else, with the threat of loss of work or promotion opportunities being used as a constant discipline against resistance to longer hours. Self-reported stress caused or made worse by work more than doubled between 1990 and 2001/2 (Bunting 2004: 180). Low-paid women are often particularly vulnerable (Huws 2003: 77–84). And it is the less well-off generally who are suffering the most dispiriting routines and practices: couples, for example, so busy they scarcely see each other all week; parents doing back-to-back shifts because childcare is simply proving too expensive.[4] Even in areas, such as teaching, where job satisfaction in the past has to some extent compensated for relative lack of earnings, stress and insecurity have now begun to take their toll. A recent study has found an increase in depression, strain, sleep loss and unhappiness during the 1990s among Britain's six million public service workers, whose job satisfaction has now fallen dramatically. It is also those with university degrees who now report the lowest levels of job satisfaction.[5]

A reduction in the working week or daily workloads, together with provision for more secure part-time employment, would significantly relieve the stress on both nature and ourselves. It would allow everyone to reap the benefits of co-parenting, and open up new ideas about personal well-being and success. A post-materialist culture would also reduce the speed at which people, goods and information had to be delivered or transmitted thus having hugely beneficial effects on resource attrition and carbon emissions. People would commute less and enjoy healthier modes of travel, such as walking, cycling, boating. These moves would make roads safer, transform city and rural living and offer experiences of landscape unavailable to those in cars or planes. It would also bring a return of high street retailers in place of supermarket shopping, boost local economies, help reduce crime and foster new forms of street conviviality.

There are, of course, huge problems confronting any attempt to 'slow down' along these lines because of the integration of national economies in a pace of life determined by the dynamics of globalisation. But we now desperately need another model of development and a beginning has to be made somewhere.[6] The affluent societies of Europe and Scandinavia are well placed to spearhead a new order and to catalyse the political will for change, and were they to take a global lead on this, they could promote an alternative model of prosperity through which the less 'developed' countries might critically reconsider the conventions and goals of 'progress' itself – and thereby better understand the worst consequences of north-west 'over-development' and how to avoid them.

An alternative cultural 'political imaginary' along these lines would involve a profound shift of values foreshadowing the ousting of monetary greed from its central place in our culture. Aesthetically, it implies a fundamental revisioning of the perceived attractions of material culture, a shift of optic and hedonist perception. I have compared this to the 'consciousness raising' brought about through Western feminism and its gradual but profound impact on our way of life. As individuals became alerted to the role of gender in their being, and to its social construction and hence mutability, so they entered into complex – and often painful – processes of self-change. A green economic and cultural renaissance working upon consumer sensibilities over coming years could result in some similar revisioning of self-interest and aesthetic response. The result would be that a lifestyle once seen as compelling comes to seem confining, and previously sought-after commodities come to be viewed as cumbersome and ugly through association with unsustainable resource use, noise, toxicity or their legacy of un-recyclable waste (Soper 2008).

The revisioning in question here is not a case of 'pure' aesthetic judgement in the disinterested Kantian sense, since it is closely aligned with a general re-thinking of pleasure and the good life that would be achieved through a 'green' renaissance. If, for example, you come to know that x does you harm, you tend to perceive it differently. The green renaissance would harness this interdependency of belief and aesthetic experience for its own counter-consumerist purposes, and seek to extend it to the environment at large, such that goods that were unsustainable, even though not responsible for any immediate personal damage to the individual, ceased to exercise their former aesthetic compulsion.

Images of waste in the form of negative sublimes that stifle and overwhelm us with the burden of our own productions, may also have a part to play in these aesthetic shifts, since the junk excreta of consumerist society is so plainly and repellently undesirable. The move to sustainable consumption will also require – though I recognise how controversial this will sound – a more courageous challenge to the 'political incorrectness' of excessive and nonchalant consumers. It is still very difficult to criticise the environmental squandering involved in people's consumption habits – and there is much embarrassment all round if one does. But faced with the oppressive effects of the climatic impact of First World affluence on other, more deprived, areas of the globe, and on all future generations, it is no longer clear why highly wasteful and polluting forms of personal consumption should remain exempt from the kinds of criticism that we now expect to be brought against racist or sexist or blatantly undemocratic attitudes and modes of behaviour. If we have a cosmopolitan care for the well-being of the more deprived people of the world, and a concern about the quality of life of future generations, we need a dramatic change of attitudes to work, consumption, pleasure and self-realisation. Such a change is tantamount to a revolution in our ideas of 'progress' and 'development'. And as such it will surely be comparable in the forms of personal epiphany and transformation it will demand to those brought about through the feminist, anti-racist and anti-colonialist movements of recent history.

Notes

1 An earlier version of this chapter was published in 'Gendering Climate Change', a special issue of *Women, Gender and Research* journal, published by Kilden Information Centre for Gender Research in Norway (Soper 2009a).
2 'Third Wave' is used to refer to the feminism of the 1980s onwards, to distinguish it from the 'second wave' of the 1960–70s (itself distinguished from late nineteenth- and early twentieth-century 'first wave' feminism).
3 This link has, of course, been made by eco-feminists. However, many women, myself included, are troubled by the inclination of eco-feminists to assume that women are by nature carers and have some special responsibility for the environment that men do not have. I would also question the readiness of many eco-feminists to endorse a 'back to nature ethic', rather than to think in terms of the more humanly complex and rewarding life that may be found beyond consumerism.
4 A survey by Dr Roger Henderson for the At Home Society, 2005 covering 1,074 working and cohabiting adults over the age of 18, found that more than a fifth of couples were so busy they could go for a week without seeing each other, often with serious impact on their relationship (the *Independent* 2005).
5 Study from Andrew Oswald and Jonathan Gardner reported in the *Guardian*, 'Job Satisfaction falls for Public Workers' (Elliott 2001).
6 And results from a simulation model of the Canadian economy suggest that it is possible to have full employment, eradicate poverty, reduce greenhouse gas emissions and maintain fiscal balance without economic growth. For further details, see the Low Grow model advocated by Peter Victor (2008) and the papers from the Sustainable Development Commission (2003).

Bibliography

Barnett, C., Cloke, P., Clarke, N. and Malpass, A. (2005) 'Consuming ethics: articulating the subjects and spaces of ethical consumption', *Antipode*, 37, 1: 23–45.
Bowlby, R. (1985) *Just Looking*, London: Methuen.
— (1993) *Shopping with Freud*, London: Routledge.
Boycott, O. (2004) 'Make-up and marketing – welcome to the world of 10 year old girls', the *Guardian*, 8 September.
Brown, K.W. and Kasser, T. (2005) 'Are psychological and ecological well-being compatible? The role of values, mindfulness, and lifestyle', *Social Indicators Research*, 74: 349–68.
Bunting, M. (2004) *Willing Slaves: How the Overwork Culture is Ruling Our Lives*, London: Harper Collins.
Coward, R. (1999) 'Do we need a new feminism?' *Women, A Cultural Review*, 10, 2: 192–205.
Dona, C. (1988) 'Invisible design', in J. Thackera (ed.) *Design After Modernity*, London: Thames and Hudson.
Elliott, L. (2001) 'Job satisfaction falls for public workers', *Guardian*, 22 March.
Evans, D. and Jackson, T. (2007) 'Towards a sociology of sustainable lifestyles', RESOLVE Working Papers 03-07. Online: http://www.surrey.ac.uk/resolve (accessed 8 July 2012).
Frey, B. and Stutzer, A. (2002) *Happiness and Economics*, Princeton, NJ: Princeton University Press.

de Graaf, J. (ed.) (2003) *Take Back Your Time: Fighting Overwork and Time Poverty in America*, San Francisco: Berret-Koehler.

de Grazie, V. and Furlough, E. (eds) (1996) *The Sex of Things: Gender and Consumption in Historical Perspective*, Berkeley: University of California Press.

Harrison, R., Newholm, T. and Shaw, D. (eds) (2005) *The Ethical Consumer*, London: Sage.

Hodgkinson, T. (2004) *How to be Idle*, London: Hamish Hamilton.

Honore, C. (2005) *In Praise of Slowness: Challenging the Cult of Speed*, New York: Harper One.

Huws, U. (2003) *The Making of a Cybertariat: virtual work in a real world*, London: Merlin Press.

Huyssen, A. (1987) *After the Great Divide: Modernism, Mass Culture and Postmodernism*, Bloomington: Indiana University Press.

the *Independent* (2005) 'All work and no play makes love drift away', 28 October.

Jackson, T. (2004) *Chasing Progress: beyond measuring economic growth*, London: New Economics Foundation.

— (2009) *Prosperity without Growth*, London: Earthscan.

Jackson, T. and Marks, N. (1999) 'Consumption, sustainable welfare and human needs', *Ecological Economics*, 28: 421–42.

Kasser, T. (2002) *The High Price of Materialism*, Cambridge, MA: MIT Press.

— (2007) 'Values and Prosperity', paper to Sustainable Development Commission seminar on 'Visions of Prosperity', 26 November. Online: http://www.sd-commission.org.uk/publications (accessed 8 July 2012).

Lane, R. (2001) *The Loss of Happiness in Market Democracies*, New Haven, CT: Yale University Press.

Layard, R. (2005) *Happiness: Lessons from a New Science*, London: Allen Lane.

Levett, R. (2004) *A Better Choice of Choice: Quality of life, consumption and economic growth*, London: Fabian Society.

Littler, J. (2008) *Radical Consumption? Shopping for Change in Contemporary Culture*, Milton Keynes: Open University Press.

— (2009) 'Gendering anti-consumerism: alternative genealogies, consumer whores and the role of *ressentiment*', in K. Soper, M. Ryle and L. Thomas (eds) *The Politics and Pleasures of Consuming Differently*, London: Palgrave.

McRobbie, A. (2008) 'Young women and consumer culture', *Cultural Studies*, 22, 5: 531–50.

Micheletti, M. (2003) *Political Virtue and Shopping*, London: Palgrave.

Micheletti, M. and Peretti, J. (2003) 'The Nike sweatshop email: political consumerism, internet and cultural jamming', in M. Micheletti, A. Follesdal and D. Stolle (eds) *Politics, Products and Markets: Exploring Political Consumerism Past and Present*, New Brunswick, NJ: Transaction Publishers.

Nava, M. (1992) *Changing Cultures: Feminism, Youth and Consumerism*, London: Sage.

— (1996): 'Modernity's disavowal: women, the city and the department store', in M. Nava and A. O'Shea (eds) *Modern Times: Reflections on a Century of English Modernity*, London: Routledge.

New Economics Foundation (2006): 'Happy planet index'. Online: http://www.happyplanetindex.org/reveals.htm (accessed 8 July 2012).

Palmer, S. (2006) *Toxic Childhood*, London: Orion.

Radner, H. (1995) *Shopping Around: Feminine Culture and the Pursuit of Pleasures*, New York: Routledge.

Schor, J. (1991) *The Overworked American: The Unexpected Decline of Leisure*, New York: Harper Collins.

— (2004) *Born to Buy, the Commercialised Child and the New Consumer Culture*, London: Simon and Schuster.

— (2008) Interviewed by J. Littler, in *Cultural Studies*, 22, 5: 588–98.

Shah, H. (2005) 'The politics of well-being', *Soundings*, 30: 33–44.

Soper, K. (2007) 'Re-thinking the "good life": the citizenship dimension of consumer disaffection with consumerism', *Journal of Consumer Culture*, 7, 2: 205–29.

— (2008) 'Alternative hedonism, cultural theory and the role of aesthetic revisioning', *Cultural Studies*, 22, 5: 567–87.

— (2009a) 'Beyond consumerism: reflections on gender politics, pleasure and sustainable consumption', *Women, Gender and Research*, special issue, 'Gendering Climate Change', 3–4: 92–100.

— (2009b) 'Introduction' in K. Soper, M. Ryle and L.Thomas (eds) *The Politics and Pleasures of Consuming Differently*, London: Palgrave.

— (2011) 'Eco-criticism and the politics of prosperity', plenary paper to the *Emergent Critical Environments Conference*, Queen Mary College, London University, 11 September. Online: http://www.youtube.com/watch?v=Xn6LVB3s4dl (accessed 8 July 2012).

Sustainable Development Commission UK (2003) 'Redefining prosperity, resource productivity, economic growth and sustainable development'. Online: http://www.sd-commission.org.uk/publications (accessed 8 July 2012).

Thomas, L. (2008) 'Alternative realities: downshifting narratives in contemporary lifestyle television', *Cultural Studies*, 22, 5: 680–99.

— (2009) 'Ecochic: green echoes and rural retreats in contemporary lifestyle magazines' in K. Soper, M. Ryle and L. Thomas (eds) *The Politics and Pleasures of Consuming Differently*, London: Palgrave.

Victor, P. (2008) *Managing without Growth. Slower by Design, not Disaster*, London: Edward Elgar Publishing.

Chapter 8

Economization of life

Calculative infrastructures of population and economy[1]

Michelle Murphy

A bottle filled with the insect *drosophila* – an organism that is born, reproduces, and dies in a flicker – is photographed at three points in time (Figure 8.1). In the first snapshot, the sparsely populated bottle, rich in food, finds generations of happy fruit flies gradually increasing and living long lives. In the second photo, the happy fruit flies multiply rapidly, sharply increasing their numbers until, in the third image, the fruit flies are so numerous the bottle can no longer support them, a point in time where death rises, birth declines, and population growth crashes.

For Raymond Pearl, the prominent and prolific American biologist who conducted this experimental work in the 1920s, 'population', as a living

8.1
Fruit flies in a bottle, at three points in time. From Raymond Pearl (1930) *The Biology of Population Growth*, New York: Alfred Knopf.

form, was governed by a law of 'how things grow': a law expressed within the walls of a bottle and which further could be graphed as 'the logistic curve', today more commonly called the growth curve or the S curve (Pearl 1927a, 1930) (Figure 8.2). According to Pearl, this curve ordered any crowd of living beings at any scale: drosophila in a bottle and humans too, in a city, a nation, or a planet.

Pearl's work on population growth took place in an era of eugenics, when a pressing question for many biologists, social scientists, politicians, and feminists was how to alter fertility in order to redirect heredity, with aspirations of engineering the evolution of fitter future races. In contrast, for Pearl, at stake in population's temporal shift was not hereditary or evolutionary futures, but *economic futures* – how to balance population with production. Population could be engineered toward future economic progress.

In this translation from flies to human, the physical limits of the glass bottle stood in for the larger unseeable scale of national economic production. For human populations this limit was determined by the so-called 'stage' of economic productivity: agrarian, industrial, and so on. As the stage of economic productivity 'progressed' the upper limit of the growth curve moved higher up the graph; that is, larger populations could be sustained (and hence mass death avoided) at greater levels of economic progress. For Pearl, the proof that the growth curve applied to humans was to be found in the 'natural experiment' of colonized Algeria, where French colonial machinery had kept impeccable records. According to Pearl, the 'civilizing' of Algeria, the purported improvement from primitive living to a more efficient colonial agricultural productivity, caused a new 'swarm of babies,' a growing aggregate of Algerians that then hit a new upper limit, which in turn prompted a 'process akin to natural selection [in which

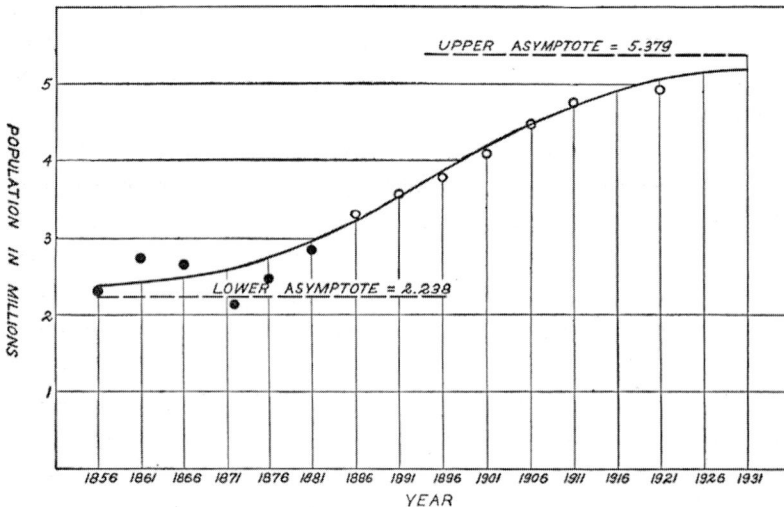

The growth of the indigenous native population of Algeria. The observations from the Column A of Appendix Table 12 are plotted as circles, solid before 1886 and open thereafter. The smooth curve is the graph of equation (xix).

8.2
Pearl's population growth curve for Algeria, depicting how French colonialism produced through birth and death rates his 'law of growth'. From Raymond Pearl (1930) *The Biology of Population Growth*, New York: Alfred Knopf.

a] good many natives had to be eliminated before the survivors were reasonably unanimous in their belief that the old days were gone forever' (Pearl 1930). For Pearl, colonialism in Algeria was evidence of a shift in birth/death relations towards a new economic-population plateau.

Pearl's growth curve exemplifies how historically specific imaginaries produced and problemitized population. Population was and is an unstable conjuration, demarcated variously by scientific and political practices, without a secured ontology. While 'population' is often used casually as a neutral name for human groups, replacing the pernicious use of racial categories, the term is nonetheless a baggage-laden concept with its own histories, aporias, disciplinary matrixes, and power relations. Pearl's work signals how population was reassembled in the early twentieth century with the help of laboratory practices, fruit flies, colonialism, and agricultural statistics, and with the subject figures of biologist, economist, civilized and native.

There are four salient points Pearl's research captures about the changing imaginary for populations in the twentieth century.

First, visualizing change over time by charting a growth curve made population into an experimental object in need of governance. The curve delivered a dynamic target for adjustment, experiment, and manipulation. For example, the curve could be smoothed by controlling fertility, or used to calculate and then encourage the optimum population size for a given level of productivity (East 1927; Fairchild 1927). Unlike Malthus's famous eighteenth-century Law of Population, with Pearl's formulation of a growth curve mass death, famine and overpopulation were entirely avoidable if production progressed or populations were optimized.

Second, Pearl's call for manipulating this curve reached towards the horizon of economic prosperity, not improved racial kinds. The curve not only adjusted itself relative to national production, but was adjustable for the sake of production. In other words, population (and hence reproduction) primarily inhabited economic time, not evolutionary time. Human birth rates shifted relative to economic conditions, such that a harsh, crowded, or more dangerous environment created by poverty led to higher birth rates (Pearl 1927b). For Pearl, shifts in birth rate relative to personal wealth 'are primarily to be regarded … as adaptive regulatory responses – that is biological responses to evolutionary alterations in the environment in which human society lives. In this environment, the economic element is perhaps the most significant biologically' (Pearl 1930). Here, 'economics' becomes human life's most important environmental milieu. The economic environment is the human's primary ecology. Rates of fertility and death were calculable in new ways as *economic effects* in need of governing at macro scales.

Third, population as imagined through a growth curve was not a thing, but a set of *relations*, such as rates of change over time, most importantly rate of growth. In this sense, population was materialized not just as size, but through a host of quantitative measures (birth rates, death rates, infant mortality rates, and so on) understood as snapshots of dynamic temporal associations, and thus shared much with an emerging twentieth-century sense of a national economy measured by gross domestic product (GDP), rates of growth, inflation, unemployment rates, and so on. Such temporalized indexes created calculative infrastructures of interlocking relationships to be governed by the twentieth-century state, as well as colonial, and later postcolonial, institutions. Beyond representations, such measures structured economy and population as dynamic contingent relations that could, and should, be acted upon via those measures.

Fourth, the drosophila bottles offered a scopic scale of quantity and temporality in which individual lives are but a flicker and what comes into view are tendencies, forecasts, and correlations only perceivable and calculated *en masse*, and across generations. Importantly, at this scale where the individual human being recedes from view, what new practices for valuing/devaluing life become allowable?

This final observation expresses the central concern of this chapter: after eugenics (today commonly reviled for its genocidal and racist legacies) what infrastructures were produced in order to render palpable, pliable, and governable this economized version of population? What methods for valuing and devaluing life have become acceptable through the figure of population?

Pearl's research is just one important example in a set of practices that helped to achieve what I am calling the 'economization of life'. The economization of life names a matrix of practices emergent in the twentieth century that attributed quantitative value to human life relative to macroeconomic growth and speculative time instead of ecological or evolutionary logics.

That life and economic value have become entwined is not news. Biobanks, cell lines, *in vitro* fertilization services, and stem cell products are common features of contemporary commodified biopolitical landscapes. The surprise has quickly faded on announcements that molecular and cellular scales of biotechnologized life are harnessed toward economic value. This chapter emphasizes another mode (in addition to commodification) by which life, techno-science, and capitalism have become entangled, a mode that operates at the macro scale of economic relations, and which is not collapsible to commodification. In short, the *economization of life* concerns: 1. aggregate forms of life exemplified by population; and 2. technical infrastructures that connect population to the macro scale of national, regional, or global economy as tracked by the discipline of economics and other social sciences.

It is precisely this conjuncture of economic logics and life that Michel Foucault began to excavate in his lectures on the *Birth of Biopolitics* (Foucault 2008). The sense of the economization of life offered here unfaithfully departs from Foucault to re-situate the history of the codependent politicization of national economy and population as, one, unfolding within cold war and postcolonial geopolitics and, two, crucially achieved through sexed bodies and reproduction. In the same Cold War/postcolonial moment that molecular and cellular scales of reproduction were becoming profoundly alterable in laboratories, the mass-production and global dissemination of cheap birth control technologies offered a means for redirecting the recombinatory futures of population and economy in projects of 'population control' and family planning. During the cold war, The Bomb as a weapon of mass death that allowed survival under deterrence was joined by The Pill as an icon that entangled projections of mass death and promises of future personal and financial prosperity (giving a double entendre to the term nuclear family).

When I use the phrase 'the economy' here, I am naming a historically specific entity of 'the national economy' that is invoked today with phrases like 'it's the economy stupid' or calls to 'stimulate the economy'. While national accounting practices and political economy certainly have a longer history, it was only over the twentieth century that the economy as a figure of national aggregate economic activity was concretized as a phenomenon through infrastructures of data collection, giving rise to a plethora of governable indexes, such as gross national product (GNP), inflation, unemployment rates, and later cost of living, consumer confidence, and so on (Speich 2007; Bergeron 2004; Mitchell 2005). Such measures formed a matrix of relations to be governed. Like population, the economy was not a thing as much as a relational entity conjured through calculative infrastructures of accounting and new branches of economics, particularly Keynesian macro-economics. Regardless of one's political economic ideology, today we all live in a post-Keynesian world where the globe is covered with nations that have 'macro-economies' in need of alteration. The economy was, of course, a site of cold war contestation: should it be planned or 'free'; if free, what role did the state have in fostering it, or setting the conditions for the economy? Monetary policy, inflation rates, tax increases (or decreases), and other stimuli were all methods of adjusting the economy. With mid-century decolonization, the economy became the charge of nation-states, which in turn became the universal unit of governance across the globe, with each nation-state presiding not only over its people, but its economy. Economies were thus to be 'developed' and 'modernized', while building modern national economies was a core aspiration of postcolonial national projects around the world (Gilman 2004; Goswami 2004). Significantly GNP per capita became the global comparative measure of a nation's economy, sorting the world into more or less developed economies, with more or less promising futures. Governing population for the sake of the economy was thus a quintessential feature of postcoloniality.

The calculative infrastructures that made up the economization of life tended to be contrasted with the racist orientations of eugenics, and yet at the same time population reinvigorated temporalized racial logics of modern and backward, giving an economic alibi, and new lease, on old evolutionary temporal hierarchies of human worth. Like eugenics, the economization of life not only offered a way to calibrate human worth, but also forms of human waste, human surplus, unproductive life, and life in excess of economic value.

My claim, then, at its broadest, is that the second half of the twentieth century saw the assembly of large heterogeneous national and trans-national infrastructures for the speculative measure and manipulation of living human aggregates, not in terms of heredity or evolution, but instead for the sake of the economy. Moreover, indexes, curves, rates, and ratios produced economy and population as relational entities brought to life through a recursive tangle of dynamic correlations tracked through quantitative measures – in need of antici-patory governance, adjustment, and stimulus. And further, I will be suggesting that fertility was a pivotal focus of economization, turning sex and reproduction into an experimental milieu for the development of technical infrastructures for governing life and speculating on human value.

I will offer here three chronologically arranged moments – three snapshots – that aspire to historicize the calculative infrastructure that makes up the 'economization of life' since the late twentieth century. These three moments offer a counterpoint to Pearl's three photographs capturing the law of population. To situate my claims, these three moments emphasize how sexed living-being and reproduction in its aggregated population form were stitched to shifting liberal practices of fostering the economy as they were significantly forged in cold war/postcolonial circuits connecting the United States and South Asia (particularly Pakistan and Bangladesh).

Moment one: transition

It is September 1959 and Frank Notestein, an eminent American demog-rapher, is standing at a lectern at the newly founded Institute of Development Economics in Karachi, Pakistan. Notestein's topic – *Abundant Life* – hinges on the play between abundance as quality and quantity. He argues that future economic growth, and hence what he calls 'the good life' of modern production and consumption, is dependent on the quantitative reduction of population growth (Notestein 1960). In short, reductions in future population quantity lead to good economic quality.

A month before Notestein's speech, Eisenhower's Presidential Committee on Military Assistance had concluded that supplying arms and military training to strategic 'front line' cold war nations, though essential, was not sufficient to ward off 'imperial communism' (President's Committee 1959). The report surprised many by calling for economic assistance combined with population control, expanding the Cold War into the realms of sex. According to the report's logic, swelling and decolonizing poor populations threatened to undermine the expansion of capitalism, hence birth control was part of a national security solution. Only with population control could the US extract 'the maximum result out of our [military] expenditure' (*New York Times* 1959). Lyndon Johnson's administration, in turn, would become deeply committed to this cold war problemitization of fertility, especially persuaded by a RAND economist's calculation that money spent for each 'averted birth' was '100 times more effective' in raising GDP per capita than the same amount spent on 'productive investments' such as building industrial infrastructures (Enke 1966).

As a result, by the late 1960s, there was a dramatic US investment in demography as a discipline with its metrics of 'levels of living', 'births averted', 'cost of children', and again 'rates of increase' that collectively called forth population as a relational entity in need of adjustment. Notestein, a demographer (with prominent positions at the UN, Princeton, and the newly minted Population Council), is among the most significant US figures in a transnational effort to craft governable demographic measures. His signal contribution concerned 'the demographic transition,' a promissory exercise that pegged temporal changes in fertility rates and death rates to economic development in the form of a graph (Mackinnon 1995; Sretzer 1993; McCann 2009). Based on records of Europe's past during the Industrial Revolution, the demographic transition was used as a predictive model for recently decolonized countries' entry into so-called modernization.

The demographic transition modeled a staged transformation for the decolonizing world from primitive accumulation through modernization, and into the industrialized future. Echoing Pearl's research, in the first stage primitive humans had high birth and death rates, keeping population size steady. In the second stage cheap public health measures introduced by colonial rulers had reduced death rates, thus leading to an increase in the rate of population growth, which threatened to turn previous colonies away from continuing on the path of modernization. With industrialization, Europe had seen a drop in birth rates, so that again population growth was steady, and thus 'underdeveloped' decolonizing nations also needed to alter their birth rates to achieve full modernization. As such, the demographic transition (still widely used) offered an explicit reframing of Pearl's growth curve along old temporal hierarchies of primitive and modern (Engerman *et al.* 2003). This revival of Pearl's curve pinpointed a window where population growth could ideally be altered to achieve economic modernity.

In 1959, Notestein was thus part of the Cold War, performing as a postcolonial expert, invited by Pakistani state planners working under the military dictatorship of Ayub Khan, a so-called 'military modernizer' who was a strategic US ally. Following the displacements and migrations of partition, demographic data was particularly important to establishing the scope of the new Pakistani state. Efforts built upon the finely articulated colonial bureaucratic infrastructures of national census and accounting. The economists and experts hosting Notestein, in turn, exemplified the rising prominence of South Asian, and especially Pakistani, social scientists and economists in transnational circuits, particularly at the relatively new entities of the World Bank and the International Monetary Fund.

Notestein's particular enactment of expertise at this Karachi seminar was a staged polemic for the need to co-plan aggregate fertility and economy. On cue, Notestein declared Pakistan at a particular stage of modernization: 'in the immediate future ... there is a conflict between qualitative and quantitative abundance of life' (Notestein 1960). The so-called compressed pace of moderni-zation in Pakistan compared to the norm of Europe was interpreted through the demographic transition to indicate population growth had to be purposively reduced to support increased economic productivity (typically measured in GNP per capita) and avoid projected catastrophe, such as famine, but also communism. Here, the fertility rate (as potential future lives) needed proper adjustment to manage the temporal shift into economic modernity. The rubric of 'abundant life' was symptomatic of a broad re-formulation of the deadly racial logic of mid-century eugenics. What Foucault describes as 'some must die so that others might live' was transformed into 'some must not be born so that future others might live more abundantly/consumptively' (Foucault 2003).

Averting births was an investment in future prosperity. Lives 'economically underdeveloped' were correlated to 'lives less worth being born'. Importantly, demography and economy calibrated together the 'differential value' of abundant life crystallized as the changeable metric 'GDP per capita': a 'national accounting' of total monetary value of goods and services produced for (not in) a country, divided by population. GDP per capita became the index by which the value per person was calibrated and compared globally. What I am arguing here is that the correlation of economy and population transitions allowed new explicit measures of lives less abundant in the measure 'lower GDP per capita.'

Importantly, and like Pearl's bottles, the demographic transition offers a distanced and beyond-human temporal and quantitative scale of concern. It offers *measures* (rates of growth and GDP per capita) rather than kinds of people as the target in need of change. Moreover, the demographic transition has a speculative function that designates potential future lives (babies yet unborn) as avertable for the sake of anticipatory economic measure. These three features worked together to make explicit economized calculations of differential life worth palatable as an aspect of governance in the late twentieth century.

It is important to keep in mind that models of the demographic transition articulated a *problemization* of life and economy, but did not prescribe any one governmental approach to its solution. Infrastructures that produced the problem of economized life offered targets in need of governance and investment without themselves legislating any particular style of governance. Thus, the measures of economized life could underwrite violent, coercive, and racist projects, as much as foster voluntary or even feminist ones, or even socialist and communist projects.

Thus, in this first moment, the demographic transition illustrates the entangled directing of economy and population through reproduction as a crucial component of a speculative and promissory postcolonial economic development.

Moment two: affect

A page from a standardized KAP survey circulated by the Population Council in 1970 provides field workers with a flowchart script that asks, 'Do you think there are conditions under which it is all right for married couples to do something to prevent or delay pregnancy?' The question is followed by a list of multiple choice answers: for the health of the mother; for the family economic situation; to help family happiness; a small population is good for the country (Demographic Division of the Population Council 1970). KAP stands for Knowledge, Attitudes, and Practices. By 1970, over 400 KAP surveys had been conducted in some 49 countries. KAP surveys employed a sample survey method most typically used to measure the likely formation of a demand for a commodity. As one demographer explained, 'the most important function of such surveys is similar to any market research project: to demonstrate the existence of a demand for goods and services, in this case for birth control' (Stycos 1964). In those countries without family planning projects, the KAP survey was understood to not just measure but also to *stimulate* interest in family planning, and thus was useful for its persuasive impact (Warwick 1993). KAP surveys recursively hailed desire while measuring desire.

By 1970, a KAP survey would use the 'full market approach,' which highlights socioeconomic measures of consumption, of wage-labor participation, and of propensity to save. More than that, the full market approach was also about drawing out, and measuring 'desire,' the 'impressionability' of that desire to mass media, and the relation between desire and its commodity fulfillment. Should fertility be up to fate? Is prosperity due to luck, or hard work? In short, KAP surveys provoked, altered, and captured aggregate attitudes and desires within market logics.

Once surveyed, a sample might well be surveyed again and again, marking change over time in response to different family planning projects, thereby turning the sample into a longitudinal experimental site. Refracting fertility through attitudes and consumption, KAP surveys were but one genre of a profuse array of social science survey techniques in the 1970s and 1980s that sought to characterize fertility and contraceptive use as quantifiable and governable data. For example, the UN sponsored World Fertility Survey of the 1970s collected data on 350,000 people in over 62 countries. The Matlab demographic surveillance site has continuously studied a region of about 250,000 people in a rural area of Bangladesh from 1965 until the present, collecting often daily data.

Attitudes and sensibilities as qualities of populations were the concern of some of the earliest family planning survey work. For example, Ansley Coale in his landmark 1958 book based on the Khanna Study in India named as a prerequisite for fertility decline the acquisition of a 'calculus of conscious choice' (Coale and Hoover 1958). Coale's work helped to spark the inclusion of questions that sought to simultaneously hail and detect numeracy, consumption, and monetary practices as attributes of the modern subjectivity necessary for family planning programs (Walle 1992). Another frequent measure that surveys sought to prompt was 'unmet need,' defined as the gap between the desire for fewer children and the availability of contraception.

In sum, KAP surveys attempted to both provoke and measure forms of aggregate desire and attitude, identify avenues for their reorganization through advertising or marketing, and finally program the satisfaction of desire through the acceptance of family planning commodities or services. In other words, KAP surveys can be seen as a technique for simultaneously measuring, hailing, and altering *affect* – capacities to feel, think, and desire or, put another way, capacities to respond. KAP surveys encouraged a particular 'affective economy' of nuclear family units managing their intimacy as desiring subjects, and moreover as subjects who desired abundant life, the good life of quality not quantity (Ahmed 2004).

By 1970, the US government, through the agency of USAID, was the world's most important funder of family planning around the world. The notion of 'unmet need' was central to what it called its 'supply-side' strategy to family planning, in which need (or demand) followed supply, not vice-versa (Ravenholt and Gillespie 1976). While KAP surveys measured unmet need as the gap between desire and the availability of contraceptive supply, USAID's supply side approach saw unmet need as desire, and hence demand, stimulated and prompted by supply. In other words, offering contraception triggered new desires for it. Commodities could prompt new affective arrangements. Need and the desire to alter fertility were sentiments stimulated by opportunities for consumption even more so than surveys. Ideally, for USAID, near free contraception would be delivered to each and every household in the developing world. Supply-side methods expressed a new form of governmentality emerging in the 1970s which sought to stimulate consumer desire and choice, not for the sake of profit directly from a sale, but for the sake of altering population and economy.

The KAP survey, joined by supply side methods, might well have been fostering calculation as a means to rearrange affect for the sake of adjusting a chain of contingent relational measures – altering birth rates which in turn enhanced GNP per capita. Circulations of affect were thus crucial to the calculative infrastructure assembling the economization of life. As in the realm of marketing, affect was a malleable feature of populations that could be redirected and prompted (Lury and Lash 2007). Populations could be enticed to 'choose' to manage fertility, and individuals would do what they 'want' to do, but this mass 'want' would be stimulated and then fulfilled. I am not arguing here that attitudes and desires were simply implanted into subjects, but rather that particular kinds of affects were encouraged, evoked, and valued at the scale of population through an infrastructure of social scientific practices. Subjects were encouraged to respond to being governed by making themselves available to and recognizable through those affects imbued in family planning projects as moments of modernity, freedom, abundance, individuality, family, nationalism, and the good life (Cohen 2001).

The KAP survey continues to live today as a tool within the widespread practice of 'social marketing' organizations. Social marketing is a technique used in contemporary public health and economic development campaigns that applies commercial marketing practices to non-commercial goals, such as changing behaviors and attitudes (Bhandari 1976; Davies *et al.* 1987). Moreover, social marketing projects typically see 'the market' as the most efficient way of distributing a social intervention.

Through social science practices from surveys to social marketing, affect and choice became indexed in a 'field site' mobilized not only towards altering birth rates, but as aspects of experiments towards developing new techniques of governing the economy. The KAP survey was a symptom of a metamorphosis in governmentality away from the state planning of population and economy that characterized the 1960s towards the emergence of nonprofit organizations and transnational development projects as organizers of services, data, and affectively charged subjects. The KAP survey was an example of a technique in a calculative infrastructure that conjured, experimentalized, and harnessed subjects to the project of knitting sexed living-being to the economy.

Moment three: investment

It is 1992, the Cold War is over, and Lawrence Summers is not yet an economic advisor to Obama, instead he is chief economist for the World Bank. He is making a keynote lecture. 'Investing in ALL the People', at the Eighth Annual General Meeting of the Pakistan Society of Development Economists in Islamabad. Here, Summers famously argued for the economic benefits of educating girls.

He calculated that each year of schooling pulled down fertility rates by 5 to 10 percent, such that US$30,000 spent on educating 1,000 girls would prevent 500 births. In contrast, a typical family planning program that spent $65 to prevent one birth through contraception would accomplish the same reduction of 500 births for the larger amount of $33,000. Education thus offered a saving of $3,000 (Summers 1992a).

In addition, educating girls was correlated with measures of lower mortality and higher income. Thus for Summers, 'educating girls quite possibly yields a higher rate of return than any other investment available in the developing world' (Summers 1992b). Here, I might observe, first, how fertility prevention is temporally pushed forward in the human life cycle to the pre-childbearing years of girlhood; and, second, how fertility reduction has become so thoroughly correlated with economic productivity that it could now serve as a conduit for further removed interventions – such as education. Altering education alters fertility rates, which in turn alters the economy. By the end of the Cold War, the voluminous social science data produced through decades of family planning, development, and public health projects had built a dense multi-sited archive of measured relationships for adjustment, stimulation, and intervention by national and transnational economic development planners.

Summers' argument about investment and rates of return rests on the notion of 'human capital,' a Nobel Prize winning concept crafted in its neoliberal form in the 1960s by Theodore Schultz and Gary Becker, both of the Chicago School of Economics. Human capital is defined as the embodied knowledge, skills, personality, and health of people that make them economically productive. The notion of human capital is not the same as that of a human commodity – a person who is owned by someone else, bought and sold. Rather, in economics, capital names resources that are used in producing goods or services, but are not themselves commodities for sale (as, for example, a machine in a factory). Hence, the term human capital designates the embodied capacities of a person that can produce future economic benefits for that person, her employer, and even her national economy. For example, paying for someone to become educated is an investment in her human capital correlated with future pay offs in terms of higher wages for her, but also providing a better worker for her employer. Thus, human capital designates people and affect as sites for investment, and considers their embodiment a kind of anticipatory, future-oriented, value.

Becker developed his concept of human capital through theoretical mathematical models of fertility, the sexual division of labor, and family dynamics, research that formed what he called the 'new home economics'(Becker 1974). For Becker all human behavior is already forward-thinking, rational, and engaged in cost/benefit calculi and thus all human behavior, including *within* families, is best understood in economic terms. Becker's model compares the rates of return of investments in the human capital of children – such as education – with the rates of return on the bare cost of children (children without human capital whose economic returns to the family are as unskilled child laborers). This work correlates higher returns on investments into human capital for families with fewer children (Becker and Tomes 1976).

Importantly, the concept of human capital shifts the vision of the iconic economic subject from a worker or consumer to an *entrepreneur*, from a subject who must gain a modern conscious calculus to a subject that already has such a calculus – a reknitting of *homo economicus*. As Shultz explained in his 1979 Nobel Prize lecture, poor farmers and women were, 'within their small, individual, allocative domain' all 'fine-tuning entrepreneurs' (Schultz 1979). With human capital, even the poorest child is an entrepreneur ready to participate in calculative infrastructures. Or as Geeta Patel insightfully suggests, they become 'risky subjects' compelled to calculate their uncertain fates through speculation (Patel 2006).

This focus on human capital helps move the point of intervention from altering fertility directly to education, from distributing contraception to women to investing in girls, a change that has come to dominate World Bank and international development programs in the last decade. According to a 2000 World Bank report around its slogan *The Quality of Growth*, the rates of return on human capital are considered best in open markets, where 'human capital's value depends in part on its owners' ability to deploy it in a competitive market in which the rules of the game reward innovation, entrepreneurship and higher productivity' (Thomas *et al.* 2000). Here, quality shifts yet again, as an entangled attribute of both an economy's growth and the individual's embodied and social development from child to adult. Quality versus quantity is again reworked, with quality manifested as the speculative success of the impoverished girl to become a worthy investment, and quantity as the specter of the uninvested, racialized multitude of the poor. As risky subjects, poor girls become a 'risk pool' worthy of speculation. In the process, the figure of the Third World girl is substituted for the bourgeois knowledge worker as the iconic figure of human capital.

A campaign begun in 2006 on The Girl Effect by the Nike Foundation (with its deep corporate investments into narratives of potential harnessed) and the NoVo Foundation (a project of investment banker Warren Buffet's family) has been one of the most influential projects for promoting 'the girl' as the solution to the 'world's mess'. Following the investment into a girl's education – 'put her in a school uniform' – is a cascade of purported relational effects leading from the increased value of her life to her village to women's rights to national production to world salvation: 'invest in a girl and she will do the rest.' In its promotional video it offers the following equation: 'Girl → School → Cow → \$ → Business → Clean H20 → Social Change → Stronger Economy → Better World,' a phantasmagram in which the weight of the world's economic future rests on the risky subject of the girl-child (www.girleffect.org).

The Girl as human capital produces value because she is *simultaneously* a site of investable potential and a remainder. The Girl as an abstraction has been neglected in census data, without birth registration, ignored by cold war development and patriarchal traditions, and is hence an undervalued stock. She is heralded as an opportunity for the future and as an undervalued leftover. She can be discerned as an investable opportunity precisely because of the archive of calculative infrastructures that decades of the economization of life have created.

Investments into the human capital of the girl child, as yet another practice within the economization of life, help to reveal that implied in designation of value are also devaluations: of the potential children of the adult a girl may someday become; of the adults that uncapitalized girls grow up to be as a future form of underproductive lives, no longer worthy of investment; and of boys who offer lower rates of return. Next to the figure of girled human capital are the less discussed figures of disposable and avertable human life, whose future is expendable: the export zone worker, the migrant, the unruly male.

As an effect of a matrix of measurement, The Girl is a figure of concern precisely because the numbers designate her with high rates of return, raising the question, what if the math hadn't added up, and in fact another object or another human kind or different life form was calculated as the better investment?

Economization of life

The three moments sketched above suggest the tangle of multilayered practices that have accumulated to produce the economization of life. Of course, there are many more genealogies that one could add to this trilogy. What these practices tended to share was a concern more with instrumentality – what could be done to alter fertility rates, affect, and rates of return – than with truth claims, trading in a cosmology of speculative correlations that could be tweaked and stimulated. Tellingly, in 2010, Summer's findings have been replicated in a report on the value of investing in Third World girls by Goldman Sachs, hedged with its standard disclaimer that accompanies all its market forecasts (Lawson 2007).

While the techniques that perform the economization of life were so often co-developed in South Asia as a crucial 'testing site' and as an important node of postcolonial social science production, they have traveled and scattered more broadly, twisting across the globe as malleable and mobile techniques for conjuring value from aggregate life.

The economization of life can be thought of not only as a historically specific experimental mode of making value, but as a mode which was built through an extensive transnational calculative infrastructure, producing reams upon reams of data, circulating enormous flows of funds, distributing millions of commodities in the name of projects to capitalize and modernize dispossession through sexed life in the name of the economy. As such, it was a regime of value in which reproduction and social reproduction – and hence implicitly sex, heteronormativity, and women – far from being ignored, were at the center. It is ironic that the 1970s and 1980s gave rise to Marxist feminist critiques of the unrecognized and unwaged role of social reproduction in capital at precisely the same time reproduction was in the process of being conjured as an experimental core of the economization of life.

In this account, I have not used economy as an analytical wrench that simply explains the emergence of population problems, nor do I want to portray the economy as an *a priori* juggernaut that spreads insidiously into more and more facets of life. Instead the economy is that which must be explained, not that which does the explaining. I want to keep in mind the anti-Malthusian insight that dispossessions, disposable excesses, and devaluations are *produced* and rendered legible, or invisible, in historically specific ways. The economization of life can also be situated among an array of interlinked recursive measures that designated avertable and disposable future life. As Melissa Wright's work reveals, to render raced and gendered workers devalued to the point of being killable is not the limit point of value, but a desirable potential of labor (Wright 2006). Devalued future lives-yet-lived, with time, became present lives subjected to the fantastical ruler of low GDP per capita, and later uninvestable lives with less future.

It is thus fully within the logic of the economization of life that intensive family planning projects of 'continuous motivation' were so often accompanied by high rates of infant and maternal death, or other forms of letting die. While economy continues to be reiteratively generated in a cacophony of transnational practice, the economization of life names a regime of value-making in which what it means to live an abundant life, a life worth living, and by extension what it means to live a life to be averted, or a life unworthy of investment, has been transformed and instrumentalized in the formula of a calculus.

Abundant life was both the good life of capital accumulation and ignorable, excess life. In this sense, economization operates doubly: to economize is to make productive while avoiding excess. Excess is not outside these calculative infrastructures, but rather is constitutive: a designation relied upon to underwrite both accumulation and aversion, futures and the end of future.

Note

1   This chapter is based on a larger book project on the economization of life in the late twentieth century.

Bibliography

Ahmed, S. (2004) 'Affective economies', *Social Text*, 22: 118–39.

Becker, G.S. (1974) 'On the relevance of the new economics of the family', *The American Economic Review*, 64: 317–19.

Becker, G.S. and Tomes, N. (1976) 'Child endowments and the quantity and quality of children', *The Journal of Political Economy*, 84: S143–62.

Bergeron, S. (2004) *Fragments of Development: Nation, Gender, and the Space of Modernity*, Ann Arbor: University of Michigan Press.

Bhandari, L.P.R. (1976) 'Communication for social marketing: a methodology for developing communication appeals for family planning programs', PhD Thesis Business Administration, New York: Columbia University.

Coale, A. and Hoover, E.M. (1958) *Population Growth and Economic Development: A Case Study of India's Prospects*, Princeton, NJ: Princeton University Press.

Cohen, L. (2001) 'The other kidney: biopolitics beyond recognition', *Body and Society*, 7: 9–29.

Davies, J., Mitra, S.N. and Schellstede, W.P. (1987) 'Oral contraception in Bangladesh: social marketing and the importance of husbands', *Studies in Family Planning*, 18: 157–68.

Demographic Division of the Population Council (1970) *A Manual for Surveys of Fertility and Family Planning: Knowledge, Attitudes, and Practice*, New York: Population Council.

East, E.M. (1927) 'Food and population', in M. Sanger (ed.) *Proceedings of the World Population Conference, Geneva*, London: Edward Arnold.

Engerman, D., Latham, M., Gilman, N. and Haefele, M. (eds) (2003) *Staging Growth: Modernization, Development, and the Global Cold War*, Amherst: University of Massachusetts Press.

Enke, S. (1966) 'The economic aspects of slowing population growth', *The Economic Journal*, 76: 44–56.

Fairchild, H.P. (1927) 'Optimum population', in M. Sanger (ed.) *Proceedings of the World Population Conference, Geneva*, London: Edward Arnold.

Foucault, M. (2003) *Society Must Be Defended: Lectures at the Colleges de France, 1975–1976*, New York: Picador.

— (2008) *The Birth of Biopolitics: Lectures at the College De France, 1978–1979*, New York: Palgrave Macmillan.

Gilman, N. (2004) *Mandarins of the Future: Modernization Theory in Cold War America*, Baltimore, MD: Johns Hopkins Press.

Goswami, M. (2004) *Producing India: From Colonial Economy to National Space*, Chicago: Chicago University Press.

Lawson, S. (2007) 'Women hold up half the sky', *GS Global Economic Paper*, New York: Goldman Sachs.

Lury, C. and Lash, S. (2007) *The Global Culture Industry: The Mediation of Things*, Cambridge: Polity.

Mackinnon, A. (1995) 'Were women present at the demographic transition? Questions from a feminist historian to historical demographers', *Gender and History*, 7: 222–40.

McCann, C. (2009) 'Malthusian men and demographic transitions: a case study of hegemonic masculinity in mid-twentieth-century population theory', *Frontiers*, 30: 142–71.

Mitchell, T. (2005) 'The work of economics: how a discipline makes its world', *European Journal of Sociology*, 47: 297–320.

New York Times (1959) 'Making foreign aid work', *New York Times*, July 24, 1959.

Notestein, F. (1960) 'Abundant life', in M.L. Qureshi (ed.) *Population Growth and Economic Development with Special Reference to Pakistan: Summary Report of a Seminar September 8–13, 1959*, Karachi: Institute of Development Economics.

Patel, G. (2006) 'Risky subjects: insurance, sexuality, and capital', *Social Text*, 24: 25–65.

Pearl, R. (1927a) 'Biology of population growth', in M. Sanger (ed.) *Proceedings of the World Population Conference, Geneva*, London: Edward Arnold.

— (1927b) 'Differential fertility', *Quarterly Review of Biology*, 2: 102–18.

— (1930) *The Biology of Population Growth*, New York: Alfred A. Knopf.

President's Committee (1959) *Composite Report of the President's Committee to Study the United States Military Assistance Program*, Washington, DC: Government Printing Office.

Ravenholt, R. and Gillespie, D.G. (1976) 'Maximizing availability of contraception through household utilization', in J. Gardner, R. Wolff, D. Gillespie and G. Duncan (eds) *Village and Household Availability of Contraceptives: Southeast Asia*, Seattle: Battelle Human Affairs Research Centers.

Schultz, T.W. ([1979] 1992) 'The economics of being poor: Noble Prize Lecture', in A. Lindbeck (ed.) *Nobel Lectures, Economics 1969–1980*, Singapore: World Scientific Publishing.

Speich, D. (2007) 'The world of GDP: historicizing the epistemic space of postcolonial development', *Borders and Boundaries – Grenzüberschreitungen – Geschichte – globale Gleichzeitigkeit*, Centro Stefano Franscini, Ascona.

Sretzer, S. (1993) 'The idea of demographic transition and the study of fertility: a critical intellectual history', *Population and Development Review*, 19: 659–701.

Stycos, J.M. (1964) 'Survey research and population control in Latin America', *The Public Opinion Quarterly*, 28: 367–72.

Summers, L. (1992a) 'Investing in *all* the people', *Policy Research Working Papers*, World Bank.

— (1992b) 'The most influential investment', *Scientific American*, 267: 132.

Thomas, V., Dailami, M., Dhareshwar, A., Lopez, R.E., Wang, Y. and Kishor, N. (2000) *The Quality of Growth*, Oxford: Oxford University Press.

Walle, E.V.D. (1992) 'Fertility transition, conscious choice, and numeracy', *Demography*, 29: 487–502.

Warwick, D. (1993) 'The KAP Survey: dictates of mission versus demands of science', in M. Bulmer and D. Warwick (eds) *Social Research in Developing Countries: Survey and Censuses in the Third World*, New York: John Wiley and Sons.

Wright, M. (2006) *Disposable Women and Other Myths of Global Capitalism*, New York: Routledge.

Chapter 9

The ecology, economy and politics of the 'one' in food culture

Gail Schwab

Luce Irigaray has sought to expose the dangers that are inherent in the modern western relationship to the Earth and to Nature. Resulting from relationships based on appropriation, extraction, and exploitation, these are dangers for shared community existence, dangers for the future of the planet, and dangers for the very survival of the human species (Irigaray 2000: 49–50). She has always maintained that vis-à-vis Nature and Being we are handicapped by oblivion and by blindness, or our utter inability to see that both Nature and Being are at least Two, and that their continuing existence is predicated on the flourishing of difference and diversity, and ultimately on the endless invention and creativity of sexual difference. Irigaray has unceasingly sounded the warning of the perils of the One. Her entire *oeuvre* is in many ways an extended deconstruction of the One, universal, gender-, race-, ethnic-, and generation-neutral Truth; of unilateral, univocal, and unisexuate social institutions and structures; and of reasoning based on minimal, discrete, countable, interchangeable units of one + one + one. What follows is an attempt to show that the hegemony of the One and of the one + one + one permeates not only our western modes of thought from philosophy to science to economics, but also our most concrete and empirical economies, such as food production, and our most personal and intimate activities, such as eating.

Epistemological foundations

In *The Death of Nature: Women, Ecology, and the Scientific Revolution* (1983), Carolyn Merchant has written what might be called the philosophical narrative of the discrete, interchangeable, countable, 1 + 1 + 1 unit in western thought, tracing its pervasiveness back to seventeenth-century mathematics, philosophy, physics, and mechanics, and carefully demonstrating how it became the basic building-block of both western reality and western knowledge. The framework and methodology of seventeenth-century science and philosophy were heavily influenced both literally and metaphorically by the fragmented modularity and repetitive motion of the machine. The examples developed at length in Merchant's book are drawn in large part from the work of Francis Bacon, but her argument and analyses are entirely appropriate to much of western epistemological thinking from Descartes on. Descartes's scientific method – in particular, his decisions to accept as true only that which could be conceived of and understood clearly and distinctly, and to solve problems by breaking them down into their simplest constitutive elements – posits that we can *know* only through an operation that begins with the fragmentation of that which we would know into parts that can stand alone as clearly framed discrete units. Subsequent to the fragmentation, the work of philosophical and/or mathematical reasoning reassembles the units into linked logical chains leading ultimately to conclusions that constitute the one universally valid Truth, transparent and self-evident to the universal rational mind. Merchant underlines the continuing relevance to contemporary thought of these ontological and epistemological assumptions, which now serve as 'guidelines for decision-making in technology, industry, and government' (Merchant 1983: 228).

Irigaray has repeatedly criticized this scientific paradigm of fragmentation. In 'A Chance for Life,' she characterizes the traditional western scientific way of knowing as 'entropic,' interested in exploring and creating 'disintegration, fission, explosions' (Irigaray 1993: 204–5), and insufficiently concerned with or even aware of wholeness, or with exploring or creating integration. Irigaray advocates new ways of knowing and of relating to nature and to the earth that assume both the fundamental integration of the knowers and the would be known – Nature – and the inseparability of nature and culture, thus rejecting the traditional binary opposition between them. Irigaray argues for what she calls the 'cultivation of nature,' a way of both coming to know and to relate to nature that would evolve a new way of thinking about and doing science.

> Culture is a refinement or perfection of living nature, an accomplishment rooted in natural capacities … And then what is nature? It is the way we refer to the materiality of our existence and that of the natural world, the

Gail Schwab

elements of earth, air, fire, and water upon which our physical survival
depends, and a part of which is studied by science. It is the set of possibilities that we do not create but can develop.

(Burke, in Irigaray 2008a: 199)

All culture, and this includes science, is part of nature, or 'rooted in natural
capacities,' as Irigaray writes. It is inappropriate to conceive science and
technology as cultural tools to be manipulated by the active human subject for
the purpose of first knowing, and then changing at will, the object – nature –
outside itself. Science and technology as cultivation of nature grow organically
out of the 'elements of earth, air, fire, and water upon which our physical survival
depends'; they are not superimposed from above.

Lorraine Code's philosophical project as developed in *Ecological
Thinking: The Politics of Epistemic Location* (2006), also constitutes an effort
to reconceive knowing in general, and specifically knowing nature, as the
re-establishment of integration and of connections. Ecological thinking seeks to
understand the relationships and connections 'among the physical, biological,
and chemical and the social, ethical, and political' (Deleuze and Guattari 1994,
cited in Code 2006: 27) – or precisely that integration of nature and culture
Irigaray refers to. The complexity and interconnectedness of ecological thinking
also leads, not to the illusion of the One, totalizing, universally valid Truth,
but rather results in positioned, local, and relational knowledges of 'diverse,
complex, multiply interconnected milieux' (Code 2006: 27). Since it conceives
of scientific knowledge as inextricably bound up with 'the social, the ethical,
and the political,' ecological thinking constitutes a powerful epistemological tool
for analyzing the liberal, free-market democracies' propensity to 'perpetuate
a mythology of the instrumental innocence and neutral expertise of scientific
knowledge, and [to] generate illusions of benign equations between power and
knowledge' (Code 2006: 31).

Food, politics, power, and knowledge

American social, ethical, and political values lie at the foundation of the American
industrial food system, and are precisely that which has allowed it to dominate
the agricultural and culinary/nutritional landscape. In the early 1970s, protests
and boycotts against rising food prices in the United States threatened to
create a level of political unrest that was of serious concern to then President
Richard Nixon, who had just lived through the turmoil of the Vietnam years and
was well aware of what political unrest could bring about. To keep things quiet,
Nixon delegated his Secretary of Agriculture, Earl Butz, to confront the political
problem by bringing food prices down. The rise in prices in the supermarket was

closely correlated with the rising energy costs of the 1970s. The failure of the wheat crop in the Soviet Union, and the subsequent political decision to sell millions of bushels of American wheat to the USSR also had a major role to play: as did the demographics of the growing world population in general, and specifically in the US, the coming to adulthood of the very large post-World-War-II baby boom generation. But rather than acknowledge the demographics or tackle the energy problem – a much thornier political issue involving not farmers but oil companies – Butz told American farmers to 'plant fencerow to fencerow' and to 'get big or get out,' which they were in large part forced to attempt to do (Pollan 2006: 51–2).

It would be difficult to find a clearer example than Earl Butz of a non-benign 'equation of power and knowledge,' or of the perpetration of the 'mythology of the instrumental innocence and neutral expertise of scientific knowledge. Butz, 'when dean of agriculture at Purdue University, [also simultaneously] sat on the boards of directors' of: 1. the Ralston-Purina Company (back in the 1970s a manufacturer of both animal feeds and products for human consumption such as boxed cereals); 2. the J. I. Case Company (at the time a manufacturer of heavy construction and agricultural equipment); 3. the International Minerals and Chemical Corporation (miners of the fertilizer phosphate); and 4. the Stokely-Van Camp Company (originally Van Camp, a processor of canned fruits and vegetables since the late nineteenth century, subsequently merged with tomato-processor Stokely) (Berry 2002: 286).[1] Thus, a former academic officer at a prominent and highly respected institution of higher learning, turned government administrator, stood to gain a great deal for himself and for his powerful corporate friends by solving Nixon's political problem through ensuring that agribusinesses got an inexhaustible supply of cheap commodities from American farmers, who themselves in most cases profited little or not at all, and ended up 'getting out' of agriculture because they were unable successfully to 'get big' enough without collapsing under a mountain of debt.

Examples of the promiscuous relationship between politicians, scientists, agribusinesses, and the mega-food industries far more recent than those of President Nixon and Earl Butz are the subject of Marion Nestle's minutely researched book, *Food Politics: How the Food Industry Influences Nutrition and Health* (2007). Nestle formerly held a position in the US Food and Drug Administration (FDA), and *Food Politics* can in some ways be read as the tale of the adventures of the FDA as hero. This unlikely hero is the endlessly beleaguered (and shamefully underfunded) solitary defender of the public good and last bastion of uncorrupted Science who struggles endlessly with the combined dark forces of politicians and scientists corrupted by and in thrall to corporate power – politicians whose election campaigns and scientists whose research corporate money so generously funds. Nestle shows, often in excruciating detail, how agribusinesses and the food industry managed to: 1. obfuscate, shielded under the banner of 'personal responsibility for food choices,' all efforts to educate the American public on proper nutrition with the clear and simple message to eat less, and to select fruits, vegetables, and whole grains in preference to meat, dairy, and sugar- and salt-laden snacks and desserts (Nestle 2007: 51–66); 2. corrupt local school boards and administrators with the promise of desperately needed funds to run their educational programs in return for maintaining vending machines in schools, in order to sell soft drinks and snacks to children in the name of 'freedom of choice' (Nestle 2007: 173–218); and 3. promote what Nestle has labeled their 'techno-foods' – so-called nutrient-enriched, reduced-fat, -sugar, -salt alternatives to Cocoa Pebbles, Fruit Loops, Oreos, and so on – as healthful, disease-preventing products (Nestle 2007: 295–357).

Although it is certainly troubling, it is not at all unprecedented that American food science, food supplies, and food and agriculture regulatory policy (or lack thereof) have been inextricably bound up with the political system. Indeed, historically, all complex political systems have been founded upon food systems. As Evan Fraser, a UK academic, and American journalist Andre Rimas have shown in *Empires of Food: Feast, Famine, and the Rise and Fall of Civilizations* (2010), political power is only as stable as the (literally meteorological) climate surrounding it is stable, and is only as functional as its agriculture, markets, and food-commodities-transport logistics are functional. Fraser and Rimas demonstrate clearly that the successes (and the failures) of several Mesopotamian empires, of Minoan Crete, of the Myceanean Greeks, of the Zhou, Qin, and Han dynasties in China, of the western Roman Empire, of Byzantium, of Europe of the High Middle Ages, and of many other great urbanized civilizations closer to us in space and time, were all closely linked to food surpluses (and shortages), and that political power, population growth, and civilization itself are dependent upon climate, soil and water, agriculture, and food supplies (Fraser and Rimas 2010).

Thus, it could be said that Nixon and Butz were just 'food emperors' like so many others throughout history, attempting to make some needed adjustments to their food empire in order to bring it in line with the realities of a growing population that needed to eat, and that was furthermore expected to spend its days, and often its nights too, as well as its energy, producing not the wherewithal for its own sustenance, but rather goods and services for the military-industrial complex – that is, for both a massive war machine and an awe-inspiring (or a horrifying) quantity of consumer products the likes of neither of which the world had ever seen before. Americans were once willing to dedicate a far larger percentage of their income to nourishing themselves, and were also once able to put a lot more time and effort into doing so. 'Fast, cheap, and convenient' was not always the sacred mantra of nutritional values it became from the middle through to the end of the twentieth century. Americans' sense of entitlement to cheap food, and to the right to live the consumer lifestyle, spending their money on anything and everything but food, was the result of a series of political and social choices, and the foundations of their industrial agriculture were not so much scientific,[2] or inspired by the professed obligation to 'feed the world,' as they were driven by the culture of the marketplace.

Accounting, agriculture, and the 'real' costs of resource use

Industrial agriculture is one of the clearest instances ever devised of the scientific and economic hegemony of the One, and its products some of the clearest instances of the proliferation of the one + one + one in the world today. Enormous monocultures are the foundation of the system. Cultivated on huge properties, comprising thousands of acres of rice or corn or soy, managed by ever-decreasing numbers of farmers growing (what were in the past, but are no longer guaranteed) ever-increasing yields, or ever-increasing numbers of units of one single output, monocultures appear to be the completely rational and efficient use of land and resources. World populations need grains, and monocultures can produce – at least for a limited time – more of them per acre of land than other more traditional and diversified agricultural methods. Fraser and Rimas lay out the history of the monoculture, tracing it back to the initial efforts of the American Norman Borlaug, who won the Nobel prize for having developed dwarf varieties of wheat and rice that increased yields per hectare from 4,500 kilos to as much as 9,000 kilos (Fraser and Rimas 2010: 215). As Fraser and Rimas write, although 'Borlaug had seemingly solved the problem of world hunger,' one of the inevitable results of the Green Revolution he was so instrumental in starting was a sharp decline in biodiversity, a decline often termed 'genetic erosion.' They observe that 'China is now a vast sea of monocultures dotted with little islands of native rice. Virtually every indigenous wheat cultivar disappeared from Greece between 1930 and 1960' (Fraser and Rimas 2010: 215). In an impassioned defense of biodiversity, ecofeminist Vandana Shiva has exposed the flawed logic of the agricultural One, along with some of the more practical consequences of genetic erosion.

> Local knowledge ... focuses on multiple-use diversity. Rice is not just grain; it provides straw for thatching and mat-making, fodder for livestock, bran for fish ponds, husk for fuel. ... The so-called high-yield varieties increase grain production, by decreasing all other outputs, increasing external inputs, and introducing ecologically destructive impacts ... Ironically, breeding for a reduction in usefulness has been viewed as important in agriculture,

because uses outside those that serve the market are not perceived and taken into account.

(Shiva 1993: 48–9)

Industrial food production ultimately constitutes an epistemological problem; it's about what passes for knowledge, and about for whom and by whom that knowledge is produced and disseminated. What Vandana Shiva or Lorraine Code would call 'local knowledges' are trumped by a superimposed marketplace logic. Shiva demonstrates that this marketplace model is able to show a profit on the bottom line only through what it would not be totally unrealistic to call fraudulent accounting – that is, by carefully ignoring all the external costs, and focusing only on the marketable product. On paper, in spreadsheets and accounting ledgers, it looks very like efficiency to plant one crop fence-row to fence-row in order to maximize yield, because yield is fungible; it is the discrete, interchangeable, countable units you can sell. Everything else – the non-fungible – must be eliminated to maximize yield, and that includes other species traditionally cultivated in tandem, or in rotation, with the cash crop, species that might have co-evolved with the cash crop and functioned as a natural brake on pests, or as a means of restoring soil fertility. Biomass that was once highly useful, and was in fact crucial for the lifestyle, if not indeed the survival, of rural populations, and thus distinctly had value, ends up being discounted as of no value; it's off the spreadsheet.

Also off the spreadsheet are the external inputs – that is, the water for the intense irrigation monocultures require, in addition to the chemical pesticides and fertilizers, chemicals that have to be purchased mostly on credit, increasing the indebtedness and financial dependence of smaller cultivators on agribusinesses and petrochemical manufacturers, nowadays mostly one and the same entities. These fertilizers and pesticides also pollute water resources and aquifers and damage soil fertility; however, monocultures, which are notoriously water parched, soil depleting, and susceptible to insects and diseases, will not yield anything at all without them. And finally, also off the spreadsheet are any of the fossil fuel energy costs required to transport and spread the chemicals and ultimately move the cash crop to market, industrial agriculture being entirely predicated and utterly dependent upon the ready and ubiquitous availability of cheap petroleum, which will soon disappear as we move into the era of peak oil production, when supply levels or even drops off as demand continues to rise in both developed and developing nations (Gilding 2011: 80–1). It is clear that, as Fraser and Rimas have phrased it, 'the maths is skewed.'[3]

In the groundbreaking anthology, *Ecology, Economics, Ethics: The Broken Circle* (1991), editors F. Herbert Bormann and Stephen R. Kellert and their contributing authors analyzed the economic paradox as far back as the early 1990s, although they did not focus specifically on agriculture, but more generally on ecology. In the chapter entitled 'Economics, Ecology, and Ethics: Mending the Broken Circle for Tropical Forests,' Malcolm Gillis observes:

> although the depreciation of man-made capital equipment and infra-structure is recognized in the national income accounts, the depletion of soils, minerals, hydrocarbons, and forests is not. The result is a perilous asymmetry in the way we measure, and therefore the way we think about, the value of natural resources. This asymmetry gives rise to patently anomalous, and uneconomic, practices. ... Although there is nothing inherently wrong in drawing upon natural resource assets to finance economic growth, there is something wrong in using systems of information that ignore the real economic costs of such actions.
>
> (Gillis 1991: 177–8)

In *The Real Wealth of Nations* (2007), American sociologist Riane Eisler takes the discipline of economics to task for being a system of information that perpetuates this 'perilous asymmetry.' Eisler criticizes academic economics for being 'market-centered,' for perpetrating pseudo-knowledge that is not only inaccurate, but manifestly harmful to both nature and to world populations (Eisler 2007: 153), and for focusing on short-term profits for the few while ignoring 'social and ecological costs' (Eisler 2007: 125). Many economists and political activists critical of free-market capitalism and its thoughtless and unquestioned exploitation of the planet's resources have begun to address the blind spots in this economic epistemological void; for example, in *The Great Disruption* (2011), Paul Gilding emphasizes the economic value of ecosystem services to the global economy. Referencing a seminal study that appeared in the journal *Nature* in 1997, Gilding notes that, 'the total value of ecosystem services was between $16 trillion and $54 trillion annually, with an average of $33 trillion,' while 'total global gross national product in 1997 was around half that at $19 trillion ... What we get from nature is fundamental to our economy, and without these inputs we would in fact produce nothing' (Gilding 2011: 43). Without ecosystem services, there would be no economy, much less economic growth, and yet they remain off the spreadsheet.

And it is not only academic economics departments, businesses, government agencies, and whole nations that indulge in these fantastical accounting practices. Each of us, as we add up our grocery bill, is individually guilty of, and each of us profits from, calculating our budget using this same 'skewed maths.' In the words of Fraser and Rimas:

> when people buy a loaf of bread for $2.99, they're not calculating the additional monetary cost in water contamination, deforestation, global warming, and social ruin. ... If the market worked as it's supposed to, then

it would transfer those costs to the consumer instead of tricking them into thinking that food is, in fact, cheap. But it doesn't, and it isn't. We just think we're getting a free lunch.

(Fraser and Rimas 2010: 160)

Jared Diamond concludes that in reality it is not that we just naïvely think we're getting a free lunch. His monumental book *Collapse* (2005) has demonstrated, through historical narratives rich with material archaeological detail, that our economic model of sustained (although clearly unsustainable) growth will lead to severe environmental devastation unless we adjust our ecological thinking and policies. Many of us – specifically those who profit the most from the current economy – are what Diamond calls 'rational actors,' deemed rational because they/we 'reason correctly that they/we can advance their/our own interests by behavior harmful to other people' (Diamond 2005: 427), to the environment, and to society. I would relate this pseudo-rational behavior to what Lorraine Code has called the 'perversion of autonomy' in white affluent western societies. In the perversion of autonomy, social cohesiveness and interconnectedness, or, as Code writes, 'forms of interdependence, [are cast] as marks of weakness, immaturity, as falling beneath the threshold of rational respectability' (Code 2006: 169). The rational actor 'in his [or her] radical self-making is free to sidestep the constraints of materiality and the hegemony of instituted social-political structures' (Code 2006: 168), and to maximize profits whatever the costs to Nature and to the human species. In other words, the rules – or even the laws of nature – do not apply to rational actors; nor can they/we, in their/our socially disconnected, self-aggrandizing autonomy, be affected by the future realities of ecological and environmental catastrophe.

Products of the agricultural 'one'

Food culture has received a great deal of attention recently in the American public media.[4] Americans are gradually being forced into awareness of the unhealthful and anti-ecological nature of their industrial food, which is not so much grown or raised, as assembled on the factory line, where the agricultural One is transformed into the supermarket proliferation of one + one + one. In the United States, for example, most of the millions of tons of corn and soy that are grown (and, it should be noted, heavily subsidized by the federal government) are not harvested for direct consumption by humans or even animals, but are sold as commodities to agribusinesses. They are then fragmented into various starches, sugars, and chemicals and sold to giant food processors to be tested and experi-mented on in laboratories by 'food engineers,' who combine and recombine them with salt and sugars (also subsidized by the federal government), along with fabricated odors, flavors, and texturizers, in order to create food products to be sold in supermarkets. Consumers finally purchase them as commercial cereals, cereal bars, pop tarts, corn chips, tortilla chips, soft drinks, or packaged microwaveable 'nutritious' meals fortified with more components – that is, with all sorts of vitamins, supplements, and other substances difficult for the non-chemist to identify. Doctors, nutritionists, and bio- and medical ethicists are now expressing serious concerns about these processed foods and the role they are most likely playing in the epidemics of childhood obesity and diabetes currently developing.[5]

The animal food chain is even more troubling than the vegetable, and raises many questions among environmentalists because of the extreme risks industrial animal wastes pose to nature; among ethicists and animal rights groups because of the ways food animals are both raised and slaughtered; and among human rights groups because of the exploitative labor practices of the meat-packing industry. In slaughterhouses and butchering facilities, (mostly) immigrants, many of them undocumented, are forced to work long hours without rest, at speeds that endanger their health and even their lives, and very often result in unhygienic conditions in meat production, and in the spread of dangerous bacteria such as salmonella or *e.coli*. The chickens sold in super-markets are not raised in farmyards, pecking at worms, bugs, and seeds out in the air, but are actually manufactured in grotesquely overcrowded poultry sheds where they are forced to struggle all their short, unhappy lives for daylight, space to move about in, or air to breathe (Singer and Mason 2006: Chapters 2–3). Nor are cattle out bucolically roaming the prairies of the west, except only briefly; as soon as a calf's weight reaches a minimal critical mass it is sent to a confined animal-feeding operation, or CAFO, to gain as much weight as possible eating mostly corn, which provides many more calories per pound than the pasture grasses which, over the course of millennia, natural selection designed ruminants to consume. CAFO steers are also fed beef fat and undefined animal protein, which transform these cattle into cannibals susceptible to bovine spongiform encephalopathy, or mad cow disease.

Life for a steer in a CAFO is in some ways a race against time; the animal must be slaughtered – that is, turned into its component units of steaks, roasts, and chopped sirloin – before it succumbs to liver failure or to any of the other diseases of the stomach or intestinal tract CAFO steers are prone to develop, diseases that are caused in large part by over-crowding and by inappro-priate CAFO feeds. Massive doses of antibiotics keep these animals alive until slaughter time (Pollan 2006: Chapter 4). The ubiquitous presence of antibiotics in beef and chicken then goes on to cause another whole set of problems, since as humans ingest the drugs the animals were treated with it encourages the evolution of highly resistant strains of bacteria the currently available antibiotics cannot touch. Farmed fish like salmon are also treated with antibiotics, along with pesticides, to attempt to control the diseases and parasites they tend to host. And it is worth noting that the salmon labeled 'wild' in the supermarket has a fairly good chance of being one of the millions of farmed salmon that escape their farms each year, mixing with whatever remnants are left of wild populations, infecting them with the parasites and diseases the farmed fish are susceptible to, and modifying their genetic stock through interbreeding.

Genetics and the 'one + one + one'

Although many geneticists are convinced that the problems of industrial food production can be solved, or at least greatly ameliorated, by genetic modifi-cation techniques, a great deal of uncertainty and controversy remains among scientists, environmental activists, farmers (both conventional and organic), nutritionists, and consumers – with some groups vigorously opposed to the presence of genetically modified organisms (GMOs) in the food supply, and others hailing GMOs as the potential next Green Revolution. GMOs are even a serious point of legal contention between traditional allies like the US, Canada, and Argentina, on the one side, and the European Union on the other. Europeans have generally resisted GMOs in the food supply for both environmental and nutritional reasons, despite enormous pressure both from their allies and from the World Trade Organization, while US consumers are far less sensitive to potential environmental and health issues relative to GMOs and more focused on the supermarket sticker-prices.[6]

GMOs are difficult to characterize. On the one hand, the genetic science that produces them can be conceived as yet another advanced technology based on the disintegration/fragmentation scientific model of the one + one + one, since the genome, like a collection of building blocks, is treated as an aggregation of modular components that can be taken apart and reassembled at will. On the other hand, the results of this fragmentation and manipulation of the genetic basis of life appear to escape the logic of the One, since it seems they can actually add to biodiversity through the creation of new forms of life, including forms that can be beneficial to ecosystems and world populations. Pamela C. Ronald, a geneticist from the University of California Davis, and Raoul W. Adamchuk, the gardener supplying California Davis's organic market, report in their book *Tomorrow's Table* that (as of winter 2008–9) a billion acres of genetically engineered crops had been cultivated and eaten by hundreds of millions of people for more than a decade (Ronald and Adamchuk, 2008: 52). By far the largest GMO-planted acreage is in North America, but such crops are not unique to this area, and they will increasingly be grown around the world – wherever agribusinesses can find a market for their expensive patented seeds, and, as Ronald and Adamchuk point out, wherever nonprofits can prevail over private patent-holders and make beneficial GM products 'available free of charge, via national and international public research institutions' (Ronald and Adamchuk 2008: 140).

GMOs may help prevent or even repair harm to the environment caused by over-use of chemical pesticides and fertilizers. American journalist and essayist Michael Pollan tells the story of Monsanto's ill-fated NewLeaf potato, whose genome contained a gene borrowed from a common bacterium naturally occurring in the soil, *bacillus thuringiensis*, also known as Bt, a gene that allowed the potato plant to manufacture internally an insecticide it needed to protect itself against the Colorado potato beetle (Pollan 2002: 191). I describe the NewLeaf as 'ill-fated' because the product line was discontinued by Monsanto after McDonald's, under pressure from its customers, refused to purchase the potato to make its French fries, and in fact stopped using all GM products in its restaurants. McDonald's marketing decisions notwithstanding, Bt toxin is actually the preferred insecticide used by organic farmers, and it had been used as a topical spray, without any observed toxic harm to humans or to the environment, for over twenty years before the Environmental Protection Agency and the FDA authorized Bt-bioengineered corn for commercial use (Ronald and Adamchuk 2008: 72). Bt bioengineering is now used on many crops, with positive results that can be documented; for example, in China the Bt gene spliced into the cotton genome eliminated the use of 78,000 tons of insecticides in 2001 alone. Seventy-eight thousand tons is the approximate equivalent of all the insecticide that is used for all crops in the state of California over the course of an entire year (Ronald and Adamchuk 2008: 71). In another illustration, Michael Pollan describes an industrial Idaho potato field he once visited as a 'bright green circle of plants that have been doused with so much pesticide that their leaves wear a dull white chemical bloom and the soil they're rooted in is a lifeless gray powder. Farmers call this a clean field, since, ideally, it has been cleansed of all weeds and insects and disease – of all life, that is, with the sole exception of the potato plant' (Pollan 2002: 217). There is something to be said for avoiding agriculture that ends in this type of chemical sterility; indeed, soil that is a lifeless gray powder may be the next Dust Bowl waiting to happen. And would it be reasonable to prefer the 78,000 tons of insecticide, the 'dull white chemical bloom,' and the lifeless gray powder to genetic modification?

Many of those who are seriously concerned about soil degradation and chemical contamination of aquifers and water supplies argue that GMO research and cultivation are not the answers, and that only organic agriculture or a return to a system of small local cultivators à la Vandana Shiva will help to mitigate some of the environmental harms industrial agriculture has inflicted on the planet. If it were only a question of environmental harms, I might have agreed with them without hesitation; there is, however, an additional concern that cannot be ignored. According to the data amassed in *The Coming Famine:*

The Global Food Crisis and What We Can Do to Avoid It (2010) by British journalist and science writer Julian Cribb, global population is expected to reach 9.2 billion by 2050, and demand for food to be 70–100 percent greater than it is today. As Cribb writes, 'population and demand are together rising at about 2 per cent a year, whereas food output is now increasing at only about 1 per cent a year' (Cribb 2010: 10). Cribb makes a number of reasonable recommendations regarding the wiser and more productive use of the agricultural resources we currently have available,[7] and goes on to conclude that we cannot afford to limit our food production methods for ideological reasons – however ethical.

> The truth is that the world will need both schools of agricultural thought in order to feed us through the mid-century peak in food demand. … To forcibly return the world to a condition of small-scale, low-input farming would be a prescription for mass starvation. And to turn global agriculture over wholesale to intensive modern broadacre farming would throw a billion subsistence farmers off their land, as well as expose the entire food supply to shortages of nutrients or fossil fuels. Proponents of both forms of agriculture need to join forces.
>
> (Cribb 2010: 65–6)

Cribb's position is in fundamental agreement with that of Ronald and Adamchuk, who find the conflict between organic agriculture and genetic engineering technology a specious one, since they are convinced both by the science and by their own experience as organic growers that what they call the 'judicious incorporation of two important strands of agriculture' – that is, genetic engineering and organic farming – 'is key to helping feed the growing population in an ecologically balanced manner' (Ronald and Adamchuk 2008: xi).

Conclusion

Even as we acknowledge the importance of marshalling all those technologies we currently possess in order equitably to supply the growing world population with food resources, we must also be acutely aware of the dangers of the agricultural One.[8] The fundamental problem in industrial agriculture – in industrial meat and fish production methods, as well as in plant monocultures, and, of course, in bioengineering technologies – is the creation of an unbalanced uniformity, the unnatural crowding of thousands of units of one and the same organism into limited space and within a limited time period. Nature does not work in discrete, interchangeable, countable units of one + one + one. Nature requires diversity for health; ecosystems are groups of diverse organisms that have evolved together over geological time within the soil, water, and climatological conditions particular to a specific location. The organisms in the ecosystem have programmed into their genetic codes the information they need to survive together. The One and the one + one + one are always at a disadvantage in nature, even as they disadvantage all that surrounds them. On the one hand, the One is harmful because it is ill-equipped to survive on its own, and for survival requires either a modification to its genome, or various chemical aids that are harmful to the soil, the water, and all other life that surrounds it. And on the other hand, the One is harmful when it is randomly, or intentionally, introduced into an ecosystem whose elements have not evolved to protect themselves against it; it can destroy native plants and animals and turn once-thriving ecosystems of many thousands of organisms into what looks like a monoculture. Difference and diversity are life creating; they are the very basis of life, where sameness and the One are death and destruction. At the foundation of Luce Irigaray's thought is her insistence on the primacy of difference, notably sexual difference. For a detailed development of the concept of sexual difference as the engine of nature and of life itself, I refer the reader to Elizabeth Grosz's chapter in this volume.

In *Sharing the World*, even as she emphasizes the unbridgeable existential gap that alienates all of us from each other,[9] Irigaray insists that one dimension of human life that all humans can share and together cultivate is our relationship to nature. Nature is ultimately that which we *must* share for our survival on the planet. When humans face natural phenomena we cannot control that pose problems we cannot easily solve alone as individuals, or as isolated societies – hurricanes, tsunamis, earthquakes, volcanoes, droughts, famines, evolution, the mutation of pathogens, and so on – some kind of collective effort is necessary to ensure our survival, ideally and pragmatically an effort that is not gender-, race-, ethnic-, or culture-specific, but reaches beyond these divisions. Irigaray writes that 'nature is a universal that is shareable by all. … The same does not apply for already constructed worlds and cultures. They are neither universal nor easily shareable. And one of them cannot act as mediation between the others' (Irigaray 2008b: 67). Irigaray also envisions nature's mediating role between individuals, genders, races, cultures, and so on, as consisting at least partially of common efforts undertaken on behalf of the cultivation of nature, in which all humans together have an important stake and can together play an important shared role. Nature thus constitutes a middle space – an 'inter-world' between two human beings, or two cultures, that is neither the one nor the other and that can, therefore, be shared by both, provided that 'it be subject by, or to, none' (Irigaray 2008b: 66). Karen Burke has noted that humanity's common obligation to care for nature extends beyond what we tend to call 'environmentalism' to encompass the cultivation of the body (and this is one of the areas where food culture is of vital importance) and to the cultivation of gender and sexual difference as well (Burke 2008). In some ways, we might think of care of nature, of the human body, and of sexual difference as our common human project, upon the success or failure of which our survival as a species depends. Furthermore, if we do not, as a species, take it upon ourselves to share this project, we will inevitably share in the hastening of our own destruction.

Notes

1 Loren Soth discusses Earl Butz's corporate board positions in the *Nation*, quoted in *The Art of the Commonplace* (Berry 2002: 286).
2 Marion Nestle's book makes this point very clearly (Nestle 2007). See also Michele Simon's *Appetite for Profit: How the Food Industry Undermines Our Health and How to Fight Back* (Simon 2006) for a discussion of the power of corporate boards, lobbyists, and pusillanimous politicians to determine our food horizon and prevent change.
3 See discussion of Japanese rice production from the 1950s to the present in Fraser and Rimas (2010: 216).
4 This attention has come from all levels and sectors of the media – from the daily press and popular magazines like *Ms.*, which ran an article in the summer of 2010 proclaiming that women are 'taking back food'; from popular cinematic documentaries like Morgan Spurlock's *Supersize Me* (2004), or Richard Linklater and Eric Schlosser's *Fast Food Nation* (2006), or Robert Kenner's *Food, Inc.* (2008); and from best-selling journalistic writers such as Michael Pollan (see Pollan 2002 and 2006) and Eric Schlosser (see Schlosser 2002), as well as from more traditionally academic scientific (see Nestle 2007), social-scientific, and political writers, and from animal and human rights philosophers, bioethicists, and activists (see Simon 2006).
5 Nestle (2007) and Simon (2006) demonstrate how difficult it is, in the face of corporate resistance, to make any changes in a system that is harming large numbers of individuals, including ever-growing numbers of children, and costing society millions of dollars in health-care expenses.
6 For some background on this GMO conflict and measured views of some of the risks involved, see, for example, *BioCycle World* (2010), Carlarne (2007), Davidson (2004), and Lee (2008).
7 For example, Cribb logically argues that a shift in global diet away from meat and protein consumption would help avert the 'coming famine' (Cribb 2010: 163–4).
8 Technology has always produced very 'mixed' results, solving certain problems while creating new, often more serious, problems along the way. Irigaray, who has consistently criticized the endless cycle of technological problem-solving/problem-creating, writes that 'science contributes to destruction, then repairs things as best it may' (Irigaray 1993: 187). Jared Diamond, a scientist who can hardly be accused of being a luddite, also warns us against the argument made by the optimistic, or the merely naïve, that there is no need to change our behavior or lifestyle in order to remediate and/or prevent environmental harms, because technology will solve our problems. Diamond writes that:

> new technologies, whether or not they succeed in solving the problem that they were designed to solve, regularly create unanticipated new problems. ... Most of all, advances in technology just increase our ability to do things, which may be either for the better or for the worse. All of our current problems are unintended negative consequences of our existing technology.
>
> (Diamond 2005: 504–5)

The economics of Diamond's argument is developed in detail in Tim Jackson's *Prosperity Without Growth: Economics for a Finite Planet* (2009). In his critique of our addiction to economic growth, Jackson writes that 'technological efficiency is both an outcome from and a fundamental driver of economic growth. ... Rebound effects from technological change push consumption even higher' (Jackson 2009: 121–2), which leads in turn to further exploitation of the planet's limited resources.

9 I originally wrote much of the discussion of nature that follows (Schwab 2011) for a review of Luce Irigaray's three books, *Sharing the World* (Irigaray 2008b), *Teaching* (Irigaray 2008a), and *Conversations* (Irigaray 2008c) that appears in *Metaphilosophy*.

Bibliography

Berry, W. (2002) *The Art of the Commonplace*, Emeryville, CA: Shoemaker and Hoard.

BioCycle World (2010) 'GMO Canola discovered in the wild', *BioCycle* 51, 8 (August): 6. Online: http://biocycle.net/2010-08/biocycle-world-82/ (accessed 10 July 2012).

Bormann, F.H. and Kellert, S.R. (eds) (1991) *Ecology, Economics, Ethics: The Broken Circle*, New Haven, CT: Yale University Press.

Burke, K. (2008) 'Masculine and feminine approaches to nature,' in L. Irigaray (ed.) *Teaching*, London: Continuum.

Carlarne, C. (2007) 'From the USA with love: sharing home-grown hormones, GMOs, and clones with a reluctant Europe', *Environmental Law*, 37 (Spring): 301.

Code, L. (2006) *Ecological Thinking: The Politics of Epistemic Location*, Oxford: Oxford University Press.

Cribb, J. (2010) *The Coming Famine: The Global Food Crisis and What We Can Do to Avoid It*, Berkeley: University of California Press.

Davidson, S. (2004) 'Improving the weak assessment of GMO risk', *ECOS*, 122, Nov–Dec, 34. Online: http://ecosmagazine.com/?act=view_file&file_id=EC122p34.pdf (accessed 10 July 2012).

Deleuze, G. and Guattari, F. (1994) *What is Philosophy?*, trans. G. Burchell and H. Tomlinson, London: Verso.

Diamond, J. (2005) *Collapse: How Societies Choose to Fail or Succeed*, New York: Viking.

Eisler, R. (2007) *The Real Wealth of Nations*, San Francisco, CA: Berrett-Koehler.

Fraser, E.D.G. and Rimas, A. (2010) *Empires of Food: Feast, Famine, and the Rise and Fall of Civilizations*, New York: Simon and Schuster.

Gilding, P. (2011) *The Great Disruption: Why the Climate Crisis Will Bring on the End of Shopping and the Birth of a New World*, New York: Bloomsbury Press.

Gillis, M. (1991) 'Economy, ecology, and ethics: mending the broken circle for tropical forests', in F.H. Bormann and S.R. Kellert (eds) *Ecology, Economics, Ethics: The Broken Circle*, New Haven, CT: Yale University Press.

Irigaray, L. (1993) *Sexes and Genealogies*, trans. G. Gill, New York: Columbia University Press.

— (2000) *Democracy Begins Between Two*, trans. K. Anderson, London: Athlone.

— (ed.) (2008a) *Teaching*, London: Continuum.

— (2008b) *Sharing the World*, London: Continuum.

— (ed.) (2008c) *Conversations*, London: Continuum.

Jackson, T. (2009) *Prosperity Without Growth: Economics for a Finite Planet*, London: Earthscan.

Lee, M. (2008) 'The governance of coexistence between GMOs and other forms of agriculture: a purely economic issue?', *Journal of Environmental Law*, 20, 2: 193–212.

Merchant, C. (1983) *The Death of Nature: Women, Ecology, and the Scientific Revolution*, New York: Harper and Row.

Nestle, M. (2007) *Food Politics: How the Food Industry Influences Nutrition and Health*, Berkeley: University of California Press.

Pollan, M. (2002) *The Botany of Desire*, New York: Random House.

— (2006) *The Omnivore's Dilemma*, New York: Penguin.

Ronald, P.C. and Adamchuk, R.W. (2008) *Tomorrow's Table*, New York: Oxford University Press.

Schlosser, E. (2002) *Fast Food Nation*, New York: Harper Perennial.

Schwab, G. (2011) 'Review of L. Irigaray's *Sharing the World*, *Teaching*, and *Conversations*', in *Metaphilosophy*, 42, 3 (April): 328–40.

Shiva, V. (1993) *Monocultures of the Mind*, London: Zed Books.

Simon, M. (2006) *Appetite for Profit: How the Food Industry Undermines Our Health and How to Fight Back*, New York: Nation Books.

Singer, P. and Mason, J. (2006) *The Way We Eat: Why Our Food Choices Matter*, New York: Rodale.

Part IV

Biological and medical architectural ecologies

Chapter 10

Sexual difference as sexual selection

Irigarayan reflections on Darwin[1]

Elizabeth Grosz

I want to begin with a bold conjecture: perhaps Irigaray's work on sexual difference might find unexpected confirmation from Darwin's account of sexual selection. Ironically, it may turn out that Irigaray finds the greatest philosophical confirmation of her claims regarding sexual difference from Darwin's understanding of the power and force of sexual selection. And, with equal irony, Darwin's work may be interpreted not only as a systematic account of the forces that compose and transform natural existence but also as the first theoretical framework that makes the amorphous forces of sexual attraction and sexual differentiation productive of the richness and complexity of life. If Irigaray sees sexual difference as the motor of cultural life, Darwin sees it as the motor of natural existence. Can Irigaray's concept find resonance in biological theory? Can biology provide feminist thought with the conceptual resources by which to understand sexual difference?

I propose to use Irigaray and Darwin to confront each other's concepts of sexual difference, to open Darwinian interpretation up to feminist readings whose objectives, unlike those of Darwin's feminist contemporaries, are not the equality of the two sexes but a more adequate recognition of their differences; as well as to open up Irigaray's work, which has primarily focused on cultural, political and linguistic differences, to new questions about nature and the animal that she has not addressed but which may enable a richer concept of sexual difference to be elaborated. I want to produce a kind of cross-mutation, an unexpected evolutionary effect of the coupling of the two, Darwin and

Elizabeth Grosz

Irigaray. I will address sexual difference not as imaginary (as a relation of self and other) or symbolic (a social, linguistic and legal relation) but as real, as part of the forces of the real that pre-exist both the human individual and the social order and that exceed the social order insofar as they imply problems, provocations that every form of symbolic order must address.

Irigaray and the concept of sexual difference

Irigaray has argued that sexual difference is the threshold concept of our age, the singular philosophical issue that defines the present (Irigaray 1993: 5). Sexual difference is not only a concept of interest to women, to feminists, to activists involved in women's struggles: rather, Irigaray's claim is stronger – that sexual difference is the most significant *philosophical* concept, the most significant thought, issue, idea, of our age. Through its entwinement with all the other concepts it is bound up with and affects – all those concepts related to all lived differences, among them, differences in sexual orientation, in race and ethnicity, religious, economic, geographic and political difference, through differences generally inassimilable within the forms of democracy that we currently recognize – sexual difference marks the threshold of a new way of understanding ourselves, the world, and conceptuality itself. It is a defining concept, a concept that opens up conceptuality itself, a *philosophical* concept *par excellence*, which makes it also a concept that affects life and the social that it generates, but also the natural, as well as, for her, the divine. For Irigaray, sexual difference, as that which has been repressed by patriarchal cultures, is the concept whose elaboration has the potential to transform our relations to ourselves, to our world and to our future. Along with the concept of difference itself, which I believe is the constitutive concept of twentieth century philosophy, sexual difference is the engine of all living difference, the concept whose elaboration has helped to specify the research paradigms and forms of conceptuality that mark the present.

    I will briefly outline Irigaray's account of sexual difference, recapitulating many of her main claims regarding the concept, claims that have been elaborated in considerable detail in the primary texts of Irigaray, as well as through her most astute readers (for example, Whitford or Mortensen):

1   Sexual difference is the most basic, irreducible, non-reciprocal difference between the sexes, the incapacity of one sex to step into the body, role and position of the other sex (Irigaray 1994: ix);
2   Sexual difference is morphological difference, the difference in the significance and meaning of the body, and in the perceptual and qualitative immersion in the world that is developed through the body. Irigaray has

insisted that bodily difference is lived, is never a raw nature but is always mediated by cultural and psychic significance. The bodies of men and women are never lived merely anatomically, but only ever in terms of their psycho-social value and meaning. Sexual difference is the concept that differentiates bodies, not in terms of their nature but in terms of their value and use;[2]

3 Sexual difference is not only irreducible, it is also immeasurable, incalculable, a relation between terms that have no third term, no outside measure by which to judge this relation or its constituents (Irigaray 2004a: 77);

4 Thus, sexual difference is not a comparative relation between two entities that are independently given: it is not a comparison or contrast of two autonomous entities but is a relation that is constitutive of the two sexes, which do not pre-exist their differentiation;

5 Sexual difference does not exist in its own terms, or in terms adequate to its conceptual and political expression. It has been reduced to forms of opposition, in which man and his associated masculinized qualities are regarded as positive and woman and her associated feminized qualities are regarded as the negation of these positive terms; to sexual complementarity, in which the feminine is only ever regarded as that which complements the masculine rather than that which itself required complementing; or to sexual equality, in which women and the feminine are regarded as versions of, or formally the same as, men and masculinity;

6 Thus, sexual difference, which is not based on existing qualities of the two sexes, which at best reflect the social constraints of patriarchy imposed on one sex for the interests of the other, but is indeterminable, does not yet exist, but nevertheless has the right to exist and elaborate itself. Sexual difference is indeterminable difference, the difference between two beings who do not yet exist, who are in the process of becoming. It is a difference that is always in the process of differentiating itself, a project that requires the future to produce it;

7 Sexual difference is also a form of sexuality, a mode of erotic encounter that links different bodies in specific if open-ended modes of intensity that may result in reproduction but is not directed to it. Sexual difference, as bodily difference, is not reducible to genital differences but does include such differences and the practices they enable;

8 Sexual difference is a universal. It is that which marks all of natural as well as all of cultural life; and moreover, it marks two modes of transition in the movement from nature to culture. It is a lived universal that is the condition for the emergence of other natural and cultural differences;

9 Sexual difference cannot be reduced to reproduction, which is its indirect product but never its *telos* or goal. Sexual difference enables the existence of two radically different beings to create a third being, irreducible to either

but the product of both. This third cannot be identified with the child, who is usually one of these two. This third is the creation of something new in the relation between the two, an object, quality or relation – perhaps even a work of art – that can mediate between the two;

10 Sexual difference is not simply the existence of two irreducibly different types of subject, but at least two irreducibly different perspectives, frameworks, experiences, modes of conceptualization, forms of knowledge, techniques of existence, at least two ways of undertaking any activity. The ontology of sexual difference entails sexually different epistemologies and forms of pragmatics, different ways of thinking, acting and creating, that is, different relations to subjects, objects and the world itself;

11 Sexual difference is the condition for the existence of multiple worlds, not just a single shared world. Sexual difference entails that each subject not only occupies its own morphological, perceptual and associative relation to the world but that it can indirectly access other morphological, perceptual and associative relations through their capacity to address, engage with and co-occupy a shared world, a world other than the one immediately available to the subject, through its relation to the other. The one who is sexually other than me is the one who offers me a world other than the one I occupy, who opens up new worlds to me; and

12 Arguably Irigaray's most contentious claim: sexual difference is the engine or force involved in the production of all other differences, and thus has an ontological status that is radically different from that of racial, ethnic, religious, class and other differences, for sexual difference is both the universal accompaniment of all other lived differences and is one of the means for their transmission and propagation. None of these other differences has the same relation to the transition from nature to culture – all these other differences are social and cultural – and none of these other forms of social discrimination can propagate themselves without the cooperation of sexual difference.

While this outline has no doubt reduced Irigaray's conception to its most elementary formulation, the various components may help to explain Irigaray's hostility to those egalitarian projects that have marked much of feminist theory and practice. Any egalitarian project, whether directed to the equalization of relations between the sexes, or between races, classes or ethnicities, is, for Irigaray, antagonistic to the project of specification of differences. Egalitarian projects entail a neutral measure for the attainment of equality, a measure that invariably reflects the value of the dominant position. Egalitarianism entails becoming equal to a given term, ideal or value. Irigaray's work on sexual difference, along with the writings of other feminists and anti-racists focused on the work of specifying non-reducible differences, problematizes any given norm by which sexes or races can be measured independent of the sexes and races thus measured, problematizing the belief that there are independent variables by which equality can be charted. It is her anti-egalitarianism, her anti-essentialism and her refusal to privilege the present and the actual over the future and the virtual that marks Irigaray's unique and ongoing contribution to philosophy, and that are key elements of her understanding of sexual difference.[3]

Another nature

Though Irigaray never refers to Darwin's work or to a conception of nature that is dynamized and fully compatible with and inseparable from culture (at least in the case of social animals) she nonetheless approximates many of his concepts. For example, she distinguishes between something like natural and sexual selection, natural necessities for life, and sexual requirements:

> Two natural necessities dominate societies. One of them may appear to be neuter, unmarked by the sexual: we all have to breathe, feed, clothe and house ourselves. Our societies are controlled by this need, which, rightful as it is, accords money a power that is totally disproportionate … In addition to need, there is another dimension in the person, that of desire, which is linked to energy, particularly sexual energy. This dimension of the person as sexed is important for social production and reproduction: without it, there is no society. Yet the dignity and necessity of sexual difference goes unrecognized.
>
> (Irigaray 1996: 50)

Although she does not use his language, this distinction between two natural necessities is the distinction between natural selection and sexual selection, a distinction between the struggle for existence against natural elements and chance itself, and the struggle to attract sexual partners that characterizes sexual selection. These two forces, Irigaray recognizes, are what nature bequeaths to all forms of social organization: the necessity to provide for conditions which sustain life; and the necessity of addressing sexual energy and attraction. Cultures may vary immensely in how they address these two necessities, but each must find some way in which they are adequately addressed. Patriarchy is one such attempt, but by no means the only one possible.

A philosophical exploration of the concept of sexual selection in Darwin's writings, directed by a commitment to a feminism of irreducible difference, would enable a new non-reductionist understanding of sexual selection as a principle vital to natural selection. Feminism, to the extent that it is implicated in egalitarianism, tends to resist Darwin's understanding of

Elizabeth Grosz

sexual selection which has privileged maleness and attributed activity to it while affirming the relatively passive position of femaleness; yet even though Darwin provides us with a theory of the centrality of sexual dimorphism (or polymorphism!) to the production of greater and greater variation, his work has been understood in largely essentialist, biologistic or invariable terms by the vast majority of feminists, who either affirm this essentialism,[4] or in some way want to challenge it.[5] Those feminists who are committed to the concept of the irreducible difference between the sexes may find in Darwin's writings surprising confirmation of their claims, as well as a deeper understanding of the nature/culture relation.

Darwin carefully distinguishes sexual from natural selection. While natural selection privileges sexual reproduction over the forms of asexual repro-duction that characterize some forms of life (bacterial, viral, protozoan), sexual selection is a principle irreducible to natural selection. Natural selection is always ultimately directed by the struggle for existence, the struggle to survive. It is oriented to factors regulating life and death. Sexual selection, by contrast, is directed to the struggle to attain desirable sexual partners and thus the stakes are much less severe and dire.[6] While it is in some sense subordinated to the forces of natural selection, which remains the final arbiter in the assessment of the value of any characteristics, sexual selection is a principle separate from natural selection. This is perhaps the most major distinction between Darwin's own writings and those of contemporary sociobiology, for whom sexual selection is in fact a subtle form of natural selection, and attractiveness is an index for fitness. But for Darwin, sexual selection is not only a separate principle from natural selection, for it could have never been deduced from a knowledge of natural selection; sexual selection attenuates and problematizes the criteria by which natural selection operates and substitutes its own, sometimes contrary, principles of taste, attractiveness or desire. Sexual selection not only complicates natural selection; it has the potential to imperil life, to render various activities or qualities more noticeable, more obvious and as vulnerable to attracting prey as potential sexual partners.

Sexual selection heightens and intensifies the manifest differences between the sexes. Paradoxically, sexual selection regulates many of the perceptible differences between the sexes but it does not direct itself to those sexual differences that lead directly to reproduction! The reproductive capacities of living bodies are regulated by natural selection and are part of the struggle for existence to the extent that they determine questions of life (and death). Thus sexual selection can only refer to those characteristics and activities that surround reproduction but fall short of fertilization. All those organs and activities that are directed to reproduction and to the care and nourishment of the young are considered to be the products of natural selection (Darwin 1872: 256). Thus, both the existence of differently sized gametes – sperm and ova – and of some so-called secondary sexual characteristics, such the existence and operation of breasts or abdominal sacks, are the result of natural selection: their presence has proved advantageous in sustaining life. All other sexual characteristics, those not directly related to the reproduction and care of the young but rather to attracting sexual partners, are forms of sexual selection, even if these may also serve in some way as forms of advantage in the struggle for existence (Darwin 1872: 254).

Sexual selection explains the manifest differences between the sexes in those species where they differ in appearance (other than in sexual or reproductive organs). To the extent that the two sexes of a species face the same exigencies of life and death, when they are perceptually differentiated (either visually, sonorously, through smell or in any other discernible way), especially in secondary sexual characteristics or in other manifest differences, this is the result of sexual rather than natural selection:

> Thus it is, as I believe, that when the males and females of any animal have the same general habits of life, but differ in structure, colour, or ornament, such differences have been mainly caused by sexual selection; that is, individual males have had, in successive generations, some slight advantage over other males, in their weapons, means of defence, or charms; and have transmitted these advantages to their male offspring.
>
> (Darwin 1859: 118)

Sexual selection tends to differentiate the sexes more and more from each other in appearance. That these are forms of sexual selection rather than natural selection is clear from the fact that both males and females survive equally well though they look and act in increasingly divergent ways over the passage of time. And the less attractive members of either sex would continue to reproduce in lieu of the presence of more attractive members. Sexual selection produces characteristics and activities that are linked to both appeal and attraction and to spectacle and display (Darwin 1872: 256–8).

Sexual selection generally takes two forms. On the one hand, it consists in various battles or forms of competition between members of the same sex, usually males (or more rarely, females) for the right to select the sexual partner who appeals most to them. These various forms of competition between males – whether they are contests of strength and prowess, singing competitions, the creation of the most appealing nest, arriving well before one's rivals at a mating location, or forms of strutting and display, produce a productive spiral of intensification of appealing characteristics (for not only are these characteristics heritable, so too is the finding of these characteristics attractive). The most successful males competing with other males are not always the most successful males in attracting female interest, but commonly they are. Male

competition intensifies and stimulates the creation of erotically desirable characteristics, whether these are linked to strength and agility, pugnacity and vigour,
singing abilities, beauty of plumage or scales, upright stance, or the elegance of
their built structures. In competing with each other, there is a struggle among
various forms of strength and attractiveness, that intensifies and proliferates the
successful bodily forms and forces, actively transforming the appearance and
capacities of such competing individuals (and their offspring):

> the advantages which favoured males have derived from conquering other
> males in battle or courtship, and thus leaving a numerous progeny, have
> been in the long run greater than those derived from rather more perfect
> adaptation to the external conditions of life.
>
> (Darwin 1872: 279)

Sexual selection also entails forms of female discernment, in which females
select from a number of possible partners those which most appeal to them.
This distinction between as it were active male competition and passive
forms of female discernment has, not surprisingly, been the object of much
(egalitarian) feminist criticism, for it seems to reproduce precisely the most
stereotyped images of male and female as oppositional, active or positive and
passive or negative, terms. In fact, however, Darwin devotes considerable detail
to the analysis of female competition and male discernment, which seems more
common in insects, fish and some species of birds than in higher mammals
(Darwin 1872: 272). For him, this is an empirical question, a question determined by the observation of the activities of various species rather than an *a
priori* assumption. In any case, for those patriarchs contemporary with Darwin,
the very idea of female discernment was disturbing, for it assumes a degree of
intelligence, preference and choice that was at odds with the assumption that
it is males who are the primary force of sexual encounters and female preferences are of little consequence (such too are the current forms of sociobiological
justification of rape as evolutionary tool: they assume that the only sexual forces
are active forces and that these are male). Darwin makes a strong argument in
favor of female selection: only female discernment can explain the increasingly
different bodily forms of males relative to females, only the advantages on males
imposed by their attractiveness to females can intensify and exaggerate these
qualities in successive generations. Only female taste can explain the ongoing
existence of extravagant, sometimes even endangering, ornaments. Females
are generally both less eager and more discerning in their sexual encounters
than males of the same species. They function to consider sexual encounters
rather than to immediately enact them.

Darwin argues that if male competition intensifies the physical
capacities, strength, energy, agility and war-like activities of males, it is female

discernment that intensifies male appearance, the production and extension of ornaments, forms of charm and beauty. Female discernment intensifies male beauty and attractiveness, sometimes even at the cost of male survival. He evinces a number of arguments for the distinctness of sexual selection from natural selection. The attributes produced as a result of sexual selection generally:

1   are much more marked in adults than in the young; particularly the qualities of adult maleness are often attenuated or difficult to observe in the young and only emerge after sexual maturity (this is what enables Darwin to suggest that human male hairiness, and especially the beard, are consequences of sexual selection, and thus exert an appeal for human females);

2   tend to be inherited by offspring of the same sex and are thus heritable: males tend to inherit those characteristics that mark their successful male progenitors; females, the same with their female progenitors. Without their tendency to be inherited, sexual selection would not accumulate characteristics but would function only for the current generation;

3   become increasingly intensified as time progresses, that is, the sexes are less and less alike with the passage of time (this forms the basis of Darwin's assumption that sexual dimorphism emerges as a powerful evolutionary strategy to supercede or surpass hermaphroditic or single-sexed reproduction – an issue we will discuss in more detail soon);

4   not only characterizes many perceptible qualities of the body, but also character traits, forms of personality and modes of activity, that is, it functions with both the products of body and those of mind; and

5   function primarily through subjective qualities, taste, appeal, what is attractive, alluring for its own sake. This may coincide with a discernment of fitness, as much of contemporary gene-centered evolutionary theory claims, but it may not. Sexual selection elevates the artistic, the gratuitous, the ornamental, for its own sake, for the sake of pleasure or beauty, even to the point of imperiling the more beautiful and noticeable individuals over their less beautiful competitors. Sexual selection both augments and problematizes natural selection.

Sexual selection is primarily creative: it enhances and exaggerates individual differences, to make them as appealing as possible. It intensifies attractive individual differences. Sexual selection relies on altogether other criteria than those regulating natural selection, not the impersonal criteria of random chance, but the personal criteria of attractiveness, 'sexiness' in its full range. Darwin suggests that if natural selection directs those qualities, those differences that privilege survival, it is sexual selection that maximizes difference, that generates individual variation and that guarantees that offspring will be more different than their parents, even as they share certain inherited qualities with them. Sexual selection is the engine for the creation of those differences that natural selection evaluates: it is the generator of individual variations which are then assessed by natural selection.

The origin of sexual selection

As is well known, Darwin held off publication of both *On The Origin of Species by Means of Transmutation, or Preservation of Favoured Races in the Struggle for Life* (1859) and *The Descent of Man, and Selection in Relation to Sex* (1872) for a number of years.[7] After he had drafted an early version of *Origin* but before he published it, and well before the publication of *Descent*, he devoted a mystifyingly long time, eight years, to the thorough analysis of a lowly creature, the barnacle. Rather than seeing this as a distraction from the anxieties surrounding the publication of what he understood would be the profoundly contentious claims of the transmutation of species, his work in this area, which admittedly took a good deal longer than Darwin had expected, was in part directed to major revisions in the taxonomy and categorization of barnacles, but was largely directed to an analysis of the origins of sexual selection and the very peculiar forms of sexuality that emerged from his laborious observation, dissection and analysis of the vast range of living and fossil barnacles. In this process, he became the world authority on barnacles and his four monographs on the topic remain even today an 'indispensable reference' for those interested in it (Ghiselin 2003: 104). While I don't want to delve into this rather technical but fascinating material in too much depth, it is important for us to explore his hypothesis about the origin and descent of sexual difference which is perhaps more developed in his work on barnacles than in his analysis of sexual selection elsewhere.

Darwin discusses the possible origins of sexual bifurcation briefly in *Descent* where he speculates on the origin of certain vestigial or rudimentary organs of the one sex being found in the other sex. This is quite striking in the case of the embryos of many species, but there are also clearly traces of the other sex, such as nipples in males, that occur in the mature individuals.[8] The existence of such organs attests to 'some extremely remote progenitor of the whole vertebrate kingdom [that] appears to have been hermaphrodite or androgynous' (Darwin 1872: 207). The earliest ancestors of sexually bifurcated species, he speculates, may have included the reproductive organs of both sexes within a single form. Mammalian life may have descended from earlier forms that were organically bisexual. The sexes divided well before mammals as a category were distinguished from their progenitors (Darwin 1872: 208) and each sex still carries the rudiments of its preceding pre-mammalian androgynous state. It is perhaps his fascination with this question of the origins of sexual difference, raised so briefly in *Descent*, that directed him to the laborious investigation, by no means a detour, of the evolutionary history of the barnacle.

Barnacles have many peculiarities – their anatomy and morphology, certainly their variety and scope, and their amazing success in surviving in a wide range of environments, virtually on every shoreline – which were largely unknown when Darwin began his researches. He believed that barnacles were insensibly differentiated from crustaceans over vast periods of time, and hypothesized that their capacity to secrete a glue-like substance which enables them to cement themselves onto various surfaces derives from the presence of a substance, seen in crustaceans, that lines the female tract. Darwin suggested that the contemporary barnacle has descended from a hermaphroditic ancestor, which may explain how barnacles acquired their cementing capacities, but would not explain how male barnacles could attach themselves either to objects, as do the females, or, most importantly, to females in order to facilitate reproduction. He needed to hypothesize an intermediary hermaphroditic stage between the existence of the female crustacean progenitor and present day male and female barnacles.

Darwin's detailed research provided intermediate examples, drawn from fossilized barnacles, that could explain the sequences of anatomical transmutation of an hermaphroditic ancestor into two sexes. Many of the oldest barnacle fossils exhibit an hermaphroditic anatomy, but, more peculiarly and surprisingly, this is also true of some quite rare contemporary forms of barnacle, which appear to be hermaphrodites, though with the male organs in a process of atrophy becoming 'microscopically small.' These largely female hermaphrodites have various small parasites attached to them that are seen to be, after microscopic inspection, dwarf or complemental males, males in the processes of emerging as a separate sex but which are still little more than primitive modes of insemination.[9] In one and the same species, then, there are hermaphrodites, hermaphroditic females with atrophying male organs, as well as tiny self-contained males. Although hermaphrodites (both in the plant kingdom as well as among various sea creatures) have the possibility of self-fertilization, Darwin argued that this rarely occurs; hermaphrodites generally cross-fertilize. They require the close proximity of these hermaphrodites/females and males.

Sessile or immovable animals, such as the barnacle (or Darwin's other favorite, coral) grow their shells directly onto a fixed place and after this attachment, they are not able to move. Thus barnacles can only exchange sperm with their nearest neighbors. If their nearest neighbor is one of two sexes, then there is only a 50 percent chance that a male and female will be in proximity with each other. With two hermaphroditic individuals, the possibilities for cross-fertilization are greatly enhanced for any two individuals in proximity. And the emergence of complemental or parasitic males, males which attach themselves to the female/hermaphrodite to live parasitically, are also much more likely to result in cross-fertilization. In addition, male barnacles, even those of dwarf stature, are known to have extraordinarily long penises (the largest penis size to body ratio of any animal, Stott 2003: 85) to maximize the chances of fertilization. Having both types of morphologies only further guarantees the likelihood of reproduction. This indeed may explain the remarkable evolutionary stability of barnacles, which, while they have well over 1,200 different species that differ widely in their anatomical structure and in their reproductive relations, all still bear a striking resemblance to their most primitive ancestors.

In his exploration of the stalked barnacle *Ibla*, common in the Philippines, Darwin discovered only females in all of his dissections but no males. It was only when he turned his attention to the tiny parasites on the body of the female *Ibla*, that he understood that these parasites were tiny males, very primitive creatures with no mouth, no digestive system, little more than living tubes of sperm, burrowed into the female's body. When he dissected an Australian *Ibla*, he discovered, along with females, some hermaphroditic specimens which had complemental males burrowed into their bodies, males which in no way resembled either female or hermaphrodite morphologies. These resembled no other animal forms, though they did resemble species 'in the Vegetable Kingdom' (Darwin, quoted in Stott 2003: 100). The *Ibla* provided a concrete illustration of the sequence of evolutionary elaboration: first, are the ancient progenitors of today's range of barnacles and barnacle forms, hermaphroditic barnacles. Then emerged barnacles like the *Ibla* which represent a transitional stage: here hermaphrodites incorporate male organs that are clearly in the process of atrophy, as well as robust female organs, for their function can now be assured fertilization with the emergence of the complemental males. Eventually these hermaphroditic male organs will either disappear or become vestigial (much like the atrophied stamen and pistils of hermaphroditic plants). Through gradual, imperceptible changes come separately sexed barnacles, the females resulting from the hermaphroditic forms, and the males emerging as complemental. These complemental males are perhaps not truly autonomous, for they usually have no modes of sustenance, ingestion or digestion. They are neither autonomous, nor entirely submerged in and part of the female/hermaphroditic body.[10] These species are currently in the slow process of transforming from hermaphroditic to bisexual and then to two separate sexes.

Barnacles are very much like the earliest forms of life to appear after the emergence of animals from plants (and their bisexual structure attests to this). Yet barnacles are also pervasive, along every coastline and tidal location across the globe. Some barnacle fossils are as old as 500 million years, while many have stable forms that can be dated back 20 million years. Darwin hypothesizes a genealogy of contemporary barnacle forms from an originally hermaphroditic ancestor, an ancestor that emerged by slow degrees of change from the crustaceans as distinctively and uniquely hermaphroditic. The question was: how does this hermaphroditic creature become a sexually differentiated creature? What emerges from Darwin's analysis of barnacles is the story of the half-emergence of maleness, not femaleness, whose reproductive capacity must be marked somewhere in the living being. The significant question is less, how do living beings (plants and animals) reproduce themselves, for in order for life to emerge at all, the (female) capacity for generation must be assumed. The question is really, why is there a second force of generation? Why is there maleness? What advantages does the emergence of a separate form of maleness create? Why, in other words, does sexual selection erupt? What advantage does sexual selection bring such that it generates more than one body type, more than one form of inheritance?

Sexual bifurcation, the eruption of more than one (by default, female) sex is a strategy to maximize the potential for variation, to maximize the forms of living beings, to maximize difference itself. Natural selection selected the strategy of dividing the sexes into (at least) two bodies rather than a single morphological type – not for all forms of life especially those invested in evolutionarily stable environments, but for those involved in changing situations. Sexual selection is the most reliable form of reproductive strategy in a large number of contexts, for plants and for animals, because it provides the conditions under which the greatest variety of living beings can be produced from which the fittest, or the most contextually embedded, can produce the next generation in greater numbers than their less fit or embedded counterparts. Sexual bifurcation is privileged by natural selection as a means for maximizing survival of some if not all the members of a particular species, that is, as a mode of differentiation that guarantees the maximization of differences between individuals. And in turn, sexual selection then functions to deflect natural selection through its excessive pleasures, its inventions and intensifications of new relations, forms of attraction and modes of artfulness. Sexual selection is arguably the greatest invention of natural selection; it ties life to taste, pleasure, the artistic.

Darwin claims that it is responsible for the vast range of variations of life on earth, but also for the creation of a kind of arms war that intensifies the value of certain qualities, those that are sexually alluring and attractive, and gives them a disproportionate value over other qualities that may not be warranted in terms of natural selection alone. It is responsible for the intensification of beauty over generations and for the proliferation of colors, sounds, forms that are pleasing to members of one's own species. Darwin even suggests that sexual selection has played a powerful role in the creation of the human, which has its present form not only as a result of biological fitness, but through forms of appeal and pleasure that account for many of the perceptible features we still find appealing today, those linked to racial differences, to degrees of hairiness, to the timbre of the voice, to height, strength, grace and other tangible qualities.

Sexual difference as sexual selection

Darwin is in fact the first theorist of sexual difference! Although clearly for him sexual difference is not irreducible insofar as it is derived in a slow movement from anterior forms of existence, nevertheless once sexual difference, di- or polymorphism, erupts as a random invention of life, it comes to characterize most of life. Once hermaphroditic or female forms elaborate the possibility of other morphologies of the same species as their forms of variation, sexual difference is increasingly marked, and each sex is sent on its own specific trajectory, never to be reconciled in a single entity again. Sexual difference is the random acquisition that alters the course of life as we know it, deflecting all other forms of evaluation and selection through the inexplicable, incalculable vagaries of taste, desire, appeal.

Sexual bifurcation generates a problem for all forms of life: How to engender life, given that life is no longer self-perpetuating, that life now requires (at least) two? How to engender sexual attraction, sexual selection and the production, with variation, of new generations? Darwin addressed these questions very carefully because it is not only in the world of animal existence that they are relevant: these are of course also the most basic questions for human life. Irigaray has no such hesitation: the domain of human relations, and especially the relations, sexual, domestic, economic, linguistic, between the sexes are the objects of her analysis throughout her writings. Although she does occasionally mention animal and plant relations, she addresses them only in passing and only in relation to how they illuminate or alleviate the position of woman in phallocentric cultures.[11] There can be no direct reconciliation between Irigaray and Darwin to the extent that each is implicated in quite different projects, Irigaray in philosophy, and addressing only the human, Darwin in biology and addressing primarily the animal. Yet it may be that by cross-fertilizing their quite different contributions, the work of each can be sharpened, made more conceptually incisive, more broadly relevant.

Darwin's work can be understood as a profound mode of analysis of the proliferation of differences, differences without any hierarchical order, without fixed identities or biological archetypes, generated for their own sake and evaluated only through social and natural contingency. Darwin's work seems to be readily understood through the concept of radical difference more directly than through the creation of a norm that measures the possibilities of equality. Darwin's understanding of the production of variation is fundamentally embedded in his understanding of sexual selection. Sexual selection proliferates differences as asexual reproduction cannot.

Moreover, Darwin's work on the world of nature is not drastically divisible from his analysis of culture. Nature and culture are not two separate domains, the cultural growing out of the seeds of the natural or somehow moving beyond the natural, superseding it. Rather, the cultural is always already natural, that which the natural enables and that which at least some of the forces of the natural confirm and validate. Darwin has demonstrated that culture resides within rather than beyond nature: that the most elaborate and complex creatures – ranging from the highly socially stratified insects to various social collectives of primates – complexify nature to create social networks and interrelations that are regulated by natural and sexual selection, by necessity and preference. As is all life on earth, from the most humble and elementary protozoa to the most complex forms of social organization. Darwin has shown that difference is the engine of the natural and its smaller subset, the cultural.

And if Irigaray's work can be understood in terms of the biology of lived bodies, an open-ended and dynamic sense of sexually differentiated bodies that are always in the process of transmutation, then she would not need to account for a transition between nature and culture which figures so centrally in her more recent writings. Culture is not the movement away from nature, its supersession or transformation, but the complication of nature, the functioning of the same broad principles to regulate social and cultural relations as structure natural relations. Irigaray's account of sexual difference as that which has been elided by patriarchal cultures but is nevertheless their unacknowledged condition and which must have its day is only confirmed and strengthened through Darwin's understanding of the pervasive and productive role of sexual selection in the proliferation of differences in nature. It is the force of the natural that insists on sexual difference, and that is a kind of assurance of its return in culture in spite of any forces for its repression (the promise of feminism itself).

Sexual difference is ineliminable, the force that proliferates all social as well as natural relations. Sexual selection refers to the possible erotic relations and encounters between sexes (whether within one sex, between two, or across a number of sexes), sexes themselves separated by difference. Sexual difference is made more and more visible and perceptible over time as the sexes diverge further from each other through the operations of sexual selection. Sexual selection is how sexual difference transforms itself, intensifies itself, selects the most attractive, noticeably forming new ideals, new types of body, qualities and activities. Sexual selection enhances sexual difference; sexual difference proliferates and varies itself through sexual selection. While different, they operate hand in hand to complexify social and natural life and to divide and increasingly differentiate populations. Irigaray and Darwin have each, in separation from the other, come to a point of commonness in which different bodies, divided along the lines of sex, become the means for new natural and cultural relations, the road to new forms of politics and new forms of life.

Notes

1 A different version of this chapter has been published in E. Grosz (2011) *Becoming Undone. Darwinian Reflections on Life, Politics and Art,* Durham, NC: Duke University Press.

2

> Obviously I do not agree with the expression used by Freud in reference to the feminine condition, 'Anatomy is destiny'. The use made of it is at once authoritarian, final and devalorizing for woman. But what has served to exploit women is a biology interpreted in terms more masculine than feminine.
>
> (Irigaray 2008: 5)

3 'to become equal is to be unfaithful to the task of incarnating our happiness as living women and men. Equality neutralizes that dimension of the negative which opens up an access to the alliance between the genders' (Irigaray 1996: 15).

4 Helena Cronin asserts that biology provides or should provide an account of human nature, one that is of relevance in the work of policy- and law-makers who address this given nature in a variety of forms to transform behavior enacted on its basis: 'All policy-making should incorporate an understanding of human nature, and that means both female and male nature' (Cronin 2003: 61).

5 In, for example, the writings of Anne Fausto-Sterling in her more postmodern understanding of the problem of essentialism (see Gowaty 1997: 47).

6 Darwin's first published reference to sexual selection occurs in *Origin* (Darwin 1859: 117).

7 He did this in part in fear of the likely reception of these works and in the belief that they needed to demonstrate his empirical and observational credentials before presenting his quite wild and clearly philosophically oriented understanding of the movements that constitute evolution.

8

> The mammary glands and nipples, as they exist in male mammals, can indeed hardly be called rudimentary; they are simply not fully developed and not functionally active. They are sympathetically affected under the influence of certain diseases, like the same organs in the female. At birth they often secrete a few drops of milk; and they have been known occasionally in man and other mammals to become well developed, and to yield a fair supply of milk.
>
> (Darwin 1872: 210–11)

9 In a letter to his friend Hooker, Darwin explains his discovery of the emergence of maleness in a particular barnacle species:

> I have lately got a bisexual cirripede, the male being microscopically small and parasitic within the sack of the female. I tell you of this to boast of my species theory, for the nearest closely allied genus to it is, as usual, hermaphrodite, but I had observed some minute parasites adhering to it, and these parasites I now can show are supplemental males, the male organs in the hermaphrodite being unusually small, though perfect and containing zoosperms: so we have almost a polygamous animal, simple females alone being wanting. I never should have made this out, had not my species theory convinced me, that an hermaphrodite species must pass into a bisexual species by insensibly small stages; and here we have it, for the male organs in the hermaphrodite are beginning to fail, and independent males ready formed.
>
> (Darwin, quoted in Ghiselin 2003: 115)

10

> The whole [male] animal is reduced to an envelope ... containing the testes, vesicula, & penis. In male *Ibla*, we have hardly any cirri or thorax; in some male Scalpellums no mouth ... I believe that males occur on every female; in one case I found 12 males & two pupae on point of metamorphosis permanently attached by cement to one female!
>
> (Darwin, letter to Hancock, in Stott 2003: 213)

11 In, for example, 'Introducing: Love Between Us', from *I Love to You*, where she discusses plants and flowers (Irigaray 1996: 34, 38), as well as in 'Animal Compassion' (2004b).

Bibliography

Cronin, H. (2003) 'Getting human nature right', in J. Brockman (ed.) *The New Humanist: Science at the Edge*, New York: Barnes & Noble Books.

Darwin, C. ([1859] 1998) *On the Origin of Species by Means of Transmutation, or Preservation of Favoured Races in the Struggle for Life*, New York: The Modern Library.

— ([1872] 1981) *The Descent of Man, and Selection in Relation to Sex*, Princeton, NJ: Princeton University Press.

Darwin, C. and Wallace, A.R. (1958) *Evolution by Natural Selection*, Cambridge: Cambridge University Press.

Ghiselin, M.T. (2003) *The Triumph of the Darwinian Method*, Mineola, NY: Dover Publications.

Gowaty, P.A. (ed.) (1997) *Feminism and Evolutionary Biology: Boundaries, Intersections and Frontiers*, New York: Chapman and Hall.

Grosz, E. (2011) *Becoming Undone: Darwinian Reflections on Life, Politics and Art*, Durham, NC: Duke University Press.

Gruber, H. and Barrett, P.H. (1974) *Darwin on Man: A Psychological Study of Scientific Creativity, Together with Darwin's Early and Unpublished Notebooks*, New York: EP Dutton.

Irigaray, L. (1993) *An Ethics of Sexual Difference*, trans. C. Burke and G.C. Gill, Ithaca, NY: Cornell University Press.

— (1994) *Thinking the Difference: For a Peaceful Revolution*, trans. K. Montin, London: Routledge.

— (1996) *I Love to You: Sketch of a Possible Felicity in History*, trans. A. Martin, London: Routledge.

— (2004a) *Key Writings*, London: Continuum.

— (2004b) 'Animal compassion' in P. Atterton and M. Calarco (eds) *Animal Philosophy: Ethics and Identity*, London: Continuum.

— (2008) *Conversations*, London: Continuum.

Lenoir, T. ([1982] 2003) *The Strategy of Life: Teleology and Mechanics in Nineteenth Century German Biology*, Chicago: University of Chicago Press.

Mortensen, E. (2003) *Touching Thought: Ontology and Sexual Difference*, Lanham, MD: Lexington Books.

Stott, R. (2003) *Darwin and the Barnacle*, New York: W.W. Norton.

Vandermassen, G. (2005) *Who's Afraid of Charles Darwin? Debating Feminism and Evolutionary Theory*, Lanham, MD: Rowman and Littlefield.

Whitford, M. (1990) *Luce Irigaray: Philosophy in the Feminine*, London: Routledge.

Wilson, E.O. (1975) *Sociobiology: The New Synthesis*, Cambridge, MA: Harvard University Press.

Chapter 11

'Between the womb and the world'

Building matrixial relations in the NICU

Katie Lloyd Thomas

When a baby is born very prematurely and looked after in the Neonatal Intensive Care Unit (NICU) a vast assemblage of medical kit and practices takes over the baby's care from its mother. This includes hi-tech equipment such as the incubator, monitors, syringe drivers and breathing apparatus, but also everyday and handmade objects such as towels, nappies, tiny hats made up by nurses and blankets crocheted by volunteers. There are also the artefacts and practices of countless mundane procedures, the bottles, tubes and litmus papers of syringe feeds, the needles, notes and heel pricks that test blood gases, the soaps, gels and towels of handwashing and infection control, the 'gentle stimu-lations' or hand pats 'reminding' a baby to breathe, and the touches of nurses, parents and others that clean, oil, soothe and hold. It was through and alongside this constellation of objects and practices that I came to know my son in the NICU environment when he was born early at 26 weeks. And when it came to developing an art project for the mother and baby unit where he was cared for at Homerton Hospital in Hackney, East London, I looked back at the things I had kept from his stay and realised the extent to which this socio-technological matrix was ever present in all my notes, photographs and keepsakes from this time. It was the kit and procedures, despite and through which mothers make relationships with their child, that became the focus of the project I developed, 'This Is For You'.

At the time of writing This Is For You is almost complete, or at least ready to be handed over to NICU staff who will continue its curation. Together with five other artworks in the delivery suite and postnatal ward at Homerton made by other artists and architects in the feminist collection **taking place**, it is part of long-term participatory project, 'The Other Side of Waiting', that involved many groups of staff and users within the mother and baby unit (Lloyd Thomas with **taking place** 2009).[1] The outcome of This Is For You is a softly lit bespoke cabinet made out of timber from a London plane tree felled to make way for the new extension, and set into the wall outside the milk-expressing room at the heart of the NICU. Inside is an intimate display of texts, photographs and objects drawn from my own documentations and from interviews and workshops with a small group of mothers of preterm babies about the ways they found to make relationships with their babies through and despite the kit. Some of these were made by the 'mums'[2] themselves, a diary written on hospital issue paper towels, a pair of syringes and tubes knitted in pastel blue, lilac and milky cream wool, a gold talismanic matriarch fashioned out of toys and detritus from the unit. The illustrations and the words you read here of the participating mums, who asked to be named only by an initial, are also on display in the cabinet. This chapter offers another mode in which to think them through.[3]

This Is For You proceeded by making relationships – bringing me into contact with staff and mothers, and them into contact with each other – and finally through the cabinet bringing us all into future contact with new unknown parents in the unit, but this chapter explores, in particular, the relations made between humans and non-humans in the context of the NICU where technologies, kit and routines of clinical care do not simply supplement or mediate the maternal role but instead can be seen to replace it. In the early days of a preterm infant's care it is the womb, placenta and protective envelope of the mother's gestating body that is replaced by hi-tech intensive care equipment and medical routines. As the baby gets stronger, however, it is the more ordinary routines of early postnatal maternal care – such as breast feeding or the constant observation of the baby's health and level of comfort – that are at least in part substituted by technological procedures such as syringe feeding and electronic monitoring of oxygen levels, heart rate and so on. There is a tendency in much feminist literature about new reproductive technologies to see substitutions such as these as the replacement of the mother (whether as pregnant body, or as primary care giver after birth) by the machine. At best, medical technologies and practices are understood as intruding on, or rupturing a naturalised mother/ infant dyad most clearly represented by the image of skin to skin contact or 'bonding' between mother and new baby immediately after birth[4] that is, of course, impossible in very premature birth.

This chapter argues that it is reductive to see the constellation of kit and practices that take care of a very premature baby in the NICU (that I shall for ease of reference term the 'NICUbator') as a simple replacement of mother by machine. In the first place this assemblage of equipment and practices is also made up of a multitude of actors – nurses, cleaners, doctors, technicians, administrators and, of course, parents, family and friends. Turning to Bracha Ettinger's psychoanalytic work on the intrauterine relationship between mother and foetus, and its importance in subject formation (neglected in conventional psychoanalytic accounts), we should recall that the womb is not simply an interior, a container for the gestating infant but it has an 'outside' – the mother. Ettinger calls the intrauterine two-way exchange 'matrixial borderlinking' and I use her term 'matrixial' here because it suggests the importance of the prenatal relationship that in the case of gestation in the NICUbator might also be extended to interpolate other subjects involved in the care of the infant. Rather than overstate the technological nature of the NICU environment we might ask instead about the range of social or matrixial connections that it also makes available.

In the second place, I want to challenge whether the mother/infant relationship (both within the womb and without) is ever constructed prior to material and relational practices. This is perhaps easy to see in early infant care, which involves a full range of paraphernalia from wipes to buggies, to teddies, and so on, and less obviously, also in the prenatal relationship. To catch sight of this I turn to Luce Irigaray's accounts of the intrauterine scene. She described the 'gap' between mother and foetus as materially constituted. Amniotic fluid, the tubes and networks of the placenta both connect mother and baby and hold them apart. Their relationship is constituted through and because of the fluid and fleshy exchanges between them. Might we not consider the material exchanges in the NICU as also constituting specific kinds of relationship, albeit different and differently to the intrauterine condition? If relationships are not just abstract connections between hitherto unconnected individuals, but always-at-once material processes, as the philosopher Gilbert Simondon has argued, then we might not only ask how the maternal relationship is ruptured in the NICU, but also how it is constituted anew.

Simondon's ideas about technical objects and systems are important here in two ways. First, and contra the relational ontologies of philosophers such as Bruno Latour and Alfred North Whitehead, he does not see relations in terms of a generalised connectivity. Rather he understands relationality as itself a process, whose possibility is always prepared just as a material such as clay is always made ready for the possibility of its encounter with a mould. It is through relation that individuals come into being, and those relations must themselves be seen as constructed and specific. Second, Simondon sees some technical objects as inserting a new reality into the world that is neither simply the trans-lation of human thought (or 'abstract' in his terminology) nor the same as nature:

> The technical object, thought and constructed by man, isn't only restricted
> to creating a mediation between man and nature; it is a stable mixture of

the human and the natural, it contains the human and the natural; it gives to its human content a structure similar to natural objects and allows the insertion of this human reality in the world of natural causes and effects.

(Simondon 1989: 245)

It is common in feminist work on reproductive technologies to find them described as intruding upon or replacing another preferable and natural condition that has been lost. The anthropologist Robin Davis-Floyd, for example, has described the 'persistent intrusion of procedures, technologies, and nursery care' as preventing an otherwise natural bonding between mother and child (Davis-Floyd 1998: 272). Barbara Duden considers foetal imaging as leading to 'a highly consequential *loss* of embodied connection and a diminution of earlier kinds of relations between pregnant women and their potential children' (Duden 1993: 53).[5] Might we not see the NICU situation instead as a radically new situation that is neither exclusively artificial (or 'human') nor natural? This is a point made by Kyra Maria Landzelius with great clarity and prescience:

A preterm infant is not simply a patient of high-tech healing, it is acutely a product / byproduct of technoscientific parentage and modes of knowing and doing. By making life possible for a human who 'ought' to have been as yet unborn or fated to a near certain death, the technology 'at our disposal' introduces a taxonomic puzzle. The 'preterm' infant – a being who, by another name, could well be called a 'post-corporeal foetus' – begins life betwixt and between the womb and the world.

(Landzelius 2001: 326)

If this life 'betwixt and between the womb and the world' is not reducible to either, then we might also ask what kind of maternal role and relations it engenders in the strange and unnatural world of the NICU?

'Mother the machine'?: an 'unnatural world'

S__: *Then Alice being born prematurely – not my idea of wonderland – but a weird place. The connection seems very right. That whole idea of Alice falling down a rabbit hole. It does feel like Alice dropped into this strange unnatural world.*

With its eerie bluish lighting, endless beeps and alarms, its banks of equipment, machines and tubes, and the tiny bodies that should not yet be born, barely visible behind all the paraphernalia, the NICU is for most parents an alien and

Katie Lloyd Thomas

unfamiliar place. Many accounts of the NICU environment stress the entry into this 'strange unnatural world'. Landzelius describes the 'ritual' or 'initiation' of scrubbing hands and forearm and donning a sanitary mask and gown, rubber gloves and paper shoe covers in an American NICU in the 1990s. This scrubbing, she suggests, marks the entry into this medical and institutional space, but it also demarcates 'the multiplicity of a mother's separations from her newborn' (Landzelius 2003: 1–3). For Margaret Cohen, the security doors at the entrance to the London NICU where she worked as a psychotherapist for 12 years perform an alternative protective enclosure to the womb:

> One enters the neonatal intensive care unit through a locked door. From the very beginning one has strong thoughts: this is a world apart – some privileged people have cards that open the door, others have to wait until they have identified themselves. It is a world to which one has to gain entry. There is a sense that what is inside is fragile and that what is outside may be dangerous. ... I have often thought that there is something womb-like about the unit: it is apart from the rest of the hospital, hard to gain entry to, and very enclosed.
>
> (Cohen 2003: 1)

Figures 11.1–2 High-Dependency Kit in the NICU, Katie Lloyd Thomas, 'This Is For You'.

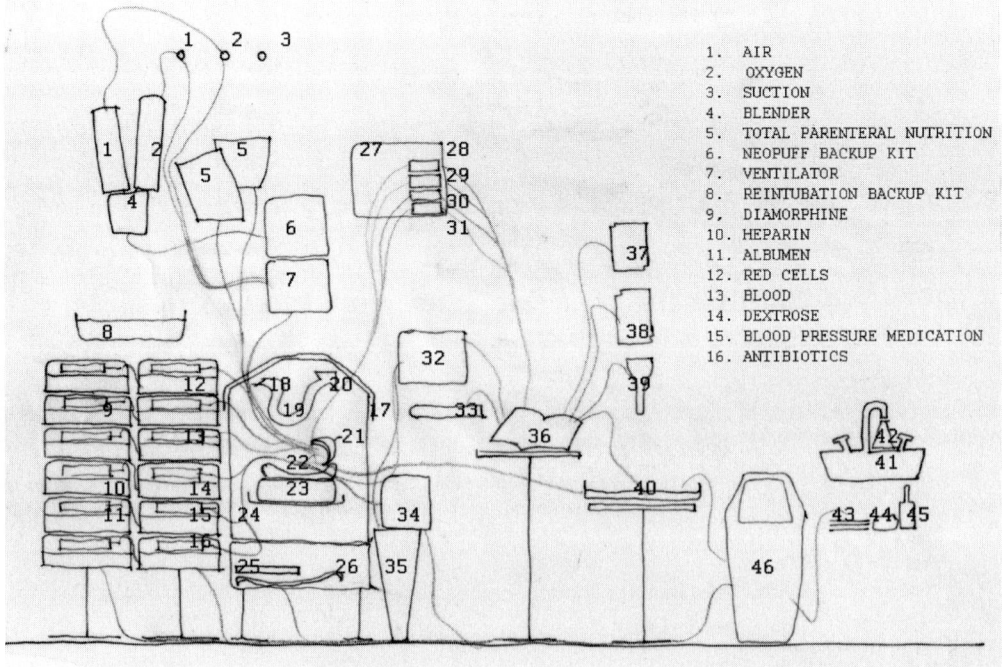

1. AIR
2. OXYGEN
3. SUCTION
4. BLENDER
5. TOTAL PARENTERAL NUTRITION
6. NEOPUFF BACKUP KIT
7. VENTILATOR
8. REINTUBATION BACKUP KIT
9. DIAMORPHINE
10. HEPARIN
11. ALBUMEN
12. RED CELLS
13. BLOOD
14. DEXTROSE
15. BLOOD PRESSURE MEDICATION
16. ANTIBIOTICS

196

During my observations for This Is For You, I made a drawing of the nexus of kit that supports a very early baby in the highest dependency room of the unit and was also struck by its womblike nature (Figure 11.1). Later, I mapped some parts of the kit on to an image of the placenta – the syringe drivers that give the infant nutrition, fluids, drugs and blood transfusions; the ventilator that delivers oxygen; and the monitors and daily tests that regulate these flows. On to an image of the womb, I mapped the parts of the kit that replaces its containment: the incubator, the bedding, the practices of making, remaking and cleaning them, and the constant hygiene and security procedures. I represented the kit as if it replaced the maternal gestating body (Figure 11.2). Landzelius goes as far as naming the incubator the 'cyborg womb'. In the NICU, she suggests, the mother–child dyad has been replaced by machine–child hybrid.

The idea of a cyborg womb has its own history within feminism. Famously, Shulamith Firestone's radical polemic The Dialectic of Sex, published in 1970, put forward the notion of the artificial womb (or 'ectogenesis') as a means to liberate women. It would be a 'technology capable of freeing women from the tyranny of their sexual-reproductive roles', and provided an opportunity that feminism should not ignore (Firestone 1970: 31). Following Firestone, Marge Piercy's 1976 feminist science fiction novel, Woman on the Edge of Time, imagined just such a utopian future. There, foetuses are grown and gestated in the 'brooder' – a yellow windowless building that hums gently and disinfects

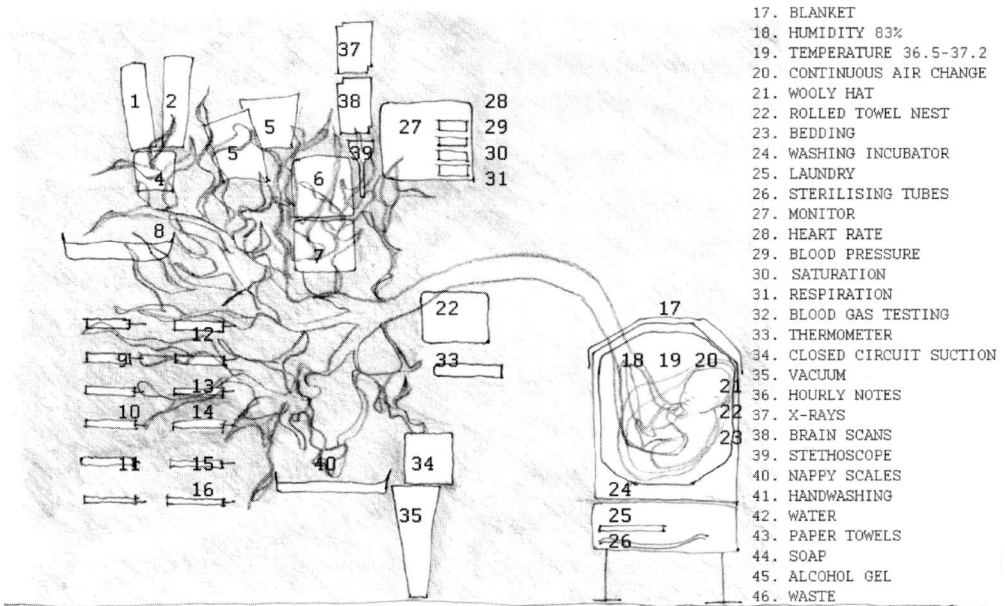

17. BLANKET
18. HUMIDITY 83%
19. TEMPERATURE 36.5-37.2
20. CONTINUOUS AIR CHANGE
21. WOOLY HAT
22. ROLLED TOWEL NEST
23. BEDDING
24. WASHING INCUBATOR
25. LAUNDRY
26. STERILISING TUBES
27. MONITOR
28. HEART RATE
29. BLOOD PRESSURE
30. SATURATION
31. RESPIRATION
32. BLOOD GAS TESTING
33. THERMOMETER
34. CLOSED CIRCUIT SUCTION
35. VACUUM
36. HOURLY NOTES
37. X-RAYS
38. BRAIN SCANS
39. STETHOSCOPE
40. NAPPY SCALES
41. HANDWASHING
42. WATER
43. PAPER TOWELS
44. SOAP
45. ALCOHOL GEL
46. WASTE

visitors on arrival. A single attendant keeps watch over the infants' receptacles and he has no interaction with them:

> A door slid aside, revealing seven human babies, joggling slowly upside down, each in a sac of its own inside a larger fluid receptacle. ... All in a sluggish row, babies bobbed. Mother the machine. Like fish in the aquarium at Coney Island.
>
> (Piercy 1976: 102)[6]

In the 'brooder' the machine has replaced the mother's body, it is 'mother the machine'. For Firestone and Piercy the advantage of ectogenesis is precisely that it severs the relation between mother and foetus. The corporeal mother/foetus dyad seems to them to set in motion inescapable gendered social structures unless it is literally and physically interrupted. Certainly mothers in the NICU experience relations with their babies as ruptured:

> L__: *I knew they were mine but I couldn't connect to them at all. If anything had happened to them I would have been absolutely distraught like any parent. I remember saying to M__ 'If one of these dies I think they'd have to sedate me and take me off the unit'. But when I was there and I wanted to put my hand on T__ or put my hand on B__ just to comfort her, I felt like I was doing something wrong, like they weren't mine and I shouldn't have been doing it. They belonged to the hospital. It's really strange.*

This rupture can be seen as doubled. First the baby is no longer inside the mother's body and second, normal maternal care – holding, comforting, feeding and washing – is also carried out by kit, machines and staff. As professor of nursing Jean Lancaster puts it: 'The long-awaited physical contact with a newborn, the anticipated interaction, and the provision of nurturing care to their offspring are all fantasies of parents-to-be and are all abruptly terminated by the birth of a sick, premature infant' (Lancaster 1986: 409). Few NICUs have the capacity for the mother to stay in hospital with the baby. She must go home overnight and is literally removed from her child – a rupture that is repeated with the end of every visit:

> Cherríe Moraga: It was harder than ever to leave Rafael in the hospital yesterday, to be parted from him. Each leave-taking a violent rupture. ... I am not inside this writing at all in my heart. I am across the city, my face pressed to the steaming plastic glass of Rafaelito's isolette.
>
> (Moraga 1997: 70)

Certainly, then, there are ruptures in relations and endless separations between mother and infant. But, at least in contemporary neonatal care in the UK and in the US, it is not at all the case that the mother is reduced to the role the attendant has in Piercy's imagined 'brooder'. It is through a great range of practices, some symbolic, some more physical and material that mothers make relations with their preterm babies, despite and with the technology. And in fact the NICUbator can also be seen to make possible the insertion of the mother into the apparent machine–child dyad.

'She's listening, we have a connection': matrixial relations in the NICU

> S__: *It's weird to think your child is in this little box being looked after by a lot of machines. Somehow I didn't feel that distance. I used to talk to her a lot. ... R__ and I both did this – we used to tell her what she needed to do... As the days went by and I started to understand what the monitors meant then we would tell A__ that she needed to bring her blood pressure up or down, or her heart rate down or up. This is magical thinking but it seemed like she did it. I know that's mad but it did feel like: 'she's listening, we have a connection'.*

Landzelius's ethnographic research into mothers' decoration of their baby's incubator with toys, pictures and teddy bears has much in common with my own in its concern with maternal practices in the NICU. However, she paints a stark picture of the potential for the mother's involvement. In the hospital context, she writes, she 'is a visitor, a spectator, a satellite figure'. Her role is 'at risk of becoming secondary at best, superfluous at worst'. According to her, when mothers place toys and other symbolic objects in the incubator it is a 'gesture to concretize maternal presence in the cyborg womb'. Clearly, it is not done for the baby who can't interact with these toys, but rather it is 'through these mediating actions, a mother *symbolically* brings the incubator into the moral economy of "home" and enculturates it into familiar cultural logic and everyday grammars' (Landzelius 2003: 7). Landzelius sees it as the mother's attempt to locate herself within the machine–child hybrid, as if it already necessarily excluded her. This Is For You revealed the invention and imagination of mums in establishing these symbolising practices. In addition to the 'ornamental practices' with cuddly toys that Landzelius looked at, mums also described placing a whole range of texts, images and objects in the incubator:

> J__: *I had a little airplane. It was the first thing I put in because I was so terrified about bacteria that at the beginning I didn't want to put any cuddly toy in so I bought these toys you put in the bath for children. So I put in a*

little airplane that was orange. I put it in because of the colour and because at some point he would fly away out of the unit.

They also recounted other practices such as 'magical thinking', story telling and singing through which they made connections with their babies.

S__: *I have a song that I sang to her before she was born ... it was my variant of the L- L song. ... I sang it to her to try to keep her going. ... In fact K__'s mom swears that L__ recognized it. She quieted when I would sing it to her.*

Others said that they would have felt self-conscious speaking or singing to an unresponsive child in a plastic box, or that they wanted to stay with the harsh reality of the situation rather than transform it.

There are two points we might make here. The first is that the picture Landzelius paints is of a mother who can only resort to symbolisation to make a connection with her baby. But there are also – as we will see – many practical and material ways that mothers get involved in the care of their child, that offer other conduits for making relations with them. The second is that the very fact that the mother is there at all, next to her infant and able to look into the incubator, is the result of a particular set of medical beliefs and technological developments.

As Jeffrey Baker explains in his marvellous history of the incubator, *The Machine in the Nursery* (1996), it could well have been otherwise. Baker differentiates between two lines of incubator development – first, incubators that were intended to be fully automated and second, those that interpolated the care of nurses and mothers. The emergence of these, he suggests, in part depended on the prevailing attitude to mothers and who was believed to care best for the infant: for example, in the United States in the early twentieth century the mother was seen as unreliable or as 'nervy' – whereas science was understood to 'imitate and improve on nature ... and save the infant from the harmful influences of its own mother' (Baker 1996: 73). So incubators were developed to be as fully automated as possible. 'Minimal stimulation' was encouraged and formula milk was preferred because it did not vary on account of 'emotional causes'. A photograph of the American Chapple Bed of 1933 shows a nurse standing peering down through a small vision panel, her hands entering an otherwise entirely closed, flush-metal box through two holes to minister to the infant (Marx 1968: 72). But in France, two obstetricians recognised that the involvement of the mother could improve survival rates. Pierre Budin realised that rising infection rates among infants were caused by using wet nurses to supply milk. Adolphe Pinard's research suggested that infants survived better once they went home if breastfeeding had already been established. So mothers were encouraged to 'lie-in' with their sick babies and feed them, and incubators became transparent on all sides to allow them to watch over their babies and tend them. A journalist described the change in rather flowery terms:

> The glass cover permits the mother to watch every moment of the poor fragile little being. And thus by watching him, almost minute by minute, the mother becomes attached to her baby; she trembles for him during the weeks she remains at the Clinique.
>
> (Belmin 1905–7; cited in Baker 1996: 60)

These developments reduced premature infant mortality rates but they also produced a technology that allowed for a relationship between mother and child, particularly by involving her in feeding, by allowing the maternal gaze, and enabling proximity.

> A__: *You know it was a life and death thing. I just wanted to know whether she was going to survive and I felt that it was so primitive, the only things I could do was have skin to skin contact, touching, and looking into her eyes. Nothing else.*

So, in contrast to Piercy's vision of babies growing in a self-regulating environment free of human involvement, the contemporary incubator is transparent. It opens at the side and allows for the baby to be held by nurses and by others. We might acknowledge that while some socio-technological constellations would leave very little place for the mother, others are designed to involve her, even if at a remove from her infant.

This interpolation of the mother into the technology of the NICU might recall Ettinger's acknowledgement that the womb is not simply a container or machine. It has an outside – the mother – who is reinserted into her account of intrauterine subjectivisation:

> I also want to focus attention on the bodily specificity of the female in the Real. Here 'matrix' means womb outside as well as inside, not only as the infant's originary container. At the same time I wish to create a hiatus ... by spinning the usual connotation of the uterus itself – considered as a basic passive space, an imaginary 'only interior' locus – towards that of a dynamic borderspace of active/passive co-emergence *with*-in and *with*out the unknown other.
>
> (Ettinger 2001: 91)

Whereas conventional psychoanalytic models propose, in various ways, that we become subjects by separating from our mothers (or the maternal object) – and so demarcating what is 'not-me' – Ettinger considers the more ambiguous condition of baby in the womb instead. The matrixial 'dynamic borderspace', she suggests, provides a model for a '*shareable dimension of subjectivity*' (Ettinger 2001: 92) that is very different to the 'not-me' model. This 'matrixial time and space' provides the conditions for both 'the *becoming*-mother (the mother-to-be) and the becoming-subject (baby-to-be)' to 'turn into partial subjects' or '*I(s)* and *non-I(s)*' (93). Although Ettinger's account of the intrauterine relation is entirely naturalised,[7] might we not consider the NICUbator as more than a container, even as a 'dynamic borderspace of active/passive co-emergence' for babies *and* the many actors involved in their care, and as one that may alter the kinds of subjectivities and relationships that emerge?

One of the peculiarities of the NICU matrix is that, by its inclusion of the mother, it also opens this role to others, even if in only the most partial of ways. At the furthest remove of community, these may be blood donors or milk donors. At Homerton there are volunteers who knit blankets and clothing. There are staff who clean, maintain supplies and make the bespoke hats for the tiniest babies to wear so that breathing kit is kept close to their heads. There are technicians, doctors, administrators and nurses. And yet closer, there are families, friends, parents – whether women or men – for whom this social matrix transforms the gendered exclusivity of some aspects of infant care:

> S__: *It [the situation in NICU] really equalized things. There was really nothing I could do that he couldn't do except for the milk expressing, and in some senses that was a disadvantage because it meant that I had to leave L__. [laughs] It got him more contact time with L__. I still think it was incredibly good for their relationship and created a bond that he might not have ... there would still have been a bond but I don't know if it would have been as strong.*

We might detect ambivalence in this mum's words. The opening the situation provides for her daughter's father is also marked by a loss for her. It is not so much the point to valorise the productive potentials of this socio-technological matrix, as to acknowledge that there are specific material constitutions of the relations it engenders that may also alter boundaries between identities, bodies, artefacts and technologies.

Material matrixial practices: building relations in the NICU

In her chapter 'Maternal stuff', Lisa Baraitser reminds us that 'there is no such thing as a mother–infant dyad' (Baraitser 2009: 125). The early post-birth relationship between mother and infant, she points out, is always accompanied by 'stuff' – the inescapable plethora of child-rearing paraphernalia. Might there be, she asks, 'something worth charting of the materialist-maternal feminine, something of what it is like to be "tied" to a child through more than emotional bonds?' (124). In the NICU the 'stuff' is omnipresent and impossible to ignore. It intervenes in every mother/infant interaction:

> S__: *You got permission to take her out of the incubator. You couldn't even do it yourself. Someone else had to help you, manipulate the wires and everything. You couldn't put her back yourself. So it made everything mediated, even more mediated.*

But manipulating the 'stuff' also becomes one of the primary ways mothers make relations with their babies in the NICU. Indeed, from the very start, they are encouraged to take part in what at Homerton was sometimes referred to as 'the cares' – oiling the babies' skin, changing their tiny nappies, laying hands gently on them to provide comfort, cleaning out their mouths and so on. A chapter from a guide to neonatal care advises nurses that parents should be encouraged:

> to participate in selected caretaking activities for their infant soon after birth. ... However menial this task appears to the health professional, it is of great significance to parents because it lessens their feelings of helplessness and facilitates the development of the maternal role.
>
> (Lancaster 1986: 411)

Even the process of syringe-feeding a baby (as I discovered) can facilitate a certain tenderness and sense of connection, despite the sterile packaging, the medical procedures and the literal distance of your hands high above the incubator:

> L__: *When they were very small there were rare occasions when somebody would say, 'Do you want to do the tube feed?' and they'd let me, when she was still on the ventilator, and they'd let me hold it, and it felt like I was actually doing something, I was taking care of her. I think it does make a difference no matter what way you're feeding them, whether it's a tube feed or a bottle or whatever. It gives you more of a connection to their care and to getting to know them.*

While Baraitser writes only about the material constitution of the postnatal maternal relation Irigaray has written powerfully about the material connections and exchanges that characterise the prenatal relation and grants a special significance to the 'placental relation'. In 'On the Maternal Order', following biologist Hélène Rouch's work on the placenta, Irigaray suggests that the placental economy represents a condition that is neither (psychic) fusion nor separation and 'respects the one and the other' (Irigaray and Rouch 2007: 35).[8] In Irigaray's philosophy this is a model of relation in the feminine that we should aspire to – a relation without fusion that retains difference. In the intrauterine situation this means acknowledging that there is both gap and connection between foetus and mother, that is made possible through the particular material conditions within the womb: 'In gestation, there will always be a gap, an interval between the body that is in the envelope and the envelope itself which will more or less fit that body, and the amniotic fluid which separates the two' (Irigaray 2004: 42).

Irigaray's description of the placental network as 'a whole world with its layers, its circuits, its vessels, its nourishing pathways, etc., a whole world of invisible relations', brings to mind the technological matrix of the NICUbator (Irigaray 1993: 33). Like the other figures Irigaray uses in her work for this material spacing – breath, mucus, touch, skin, the gaze and so on – amnion and placenta are corporeal and 'natural', but her account reminds us that a gap is there even in the intrauterine condition, and already traversed by material and flows. We might also consider the NICUbator in her terms – as a material thickness which holds apart and, at the same time, connects.

What is striking in the NICU is that these connections are no longer 'invisible' and can themselves be intentionally performed by mothers and by other carers. Some parents become expert in a range of activities that are usually carried out by nurses, from inserting the naso-gastric tube to rolling towels to form 'nests' that contain the baby:

> J__: [The baby's father and I] were experts in building nests. We always wanted him to have a nest and if there was no nest we would build a nest with towels. ... At the beginning the nurses did it, but I knew how to build a nest with some towels so I just got some new towels and wrapped them and put them in. ... We could feel that he liked to have boundaries especially because he loved his feet, he liked to kick against something, so we felt 'he is lost without anything', so ... [we would] do it at the sides, so they would surround him.

Here, containment – that would have been provided by the mother's womb – becomes a practice that is endlessly re-enacted by *both* parents in the remaking of the bedding. A material connection to the baby that would have been hidden in the womb is recast visibly as a process of relation.

It is here that Simondon's model of relations seems particularly pertinent. Where relational ontologies such as actor-network theory describe a kind of generalised connectivity between entities, Simondon sees relating (or in his terms 'communication between different orders of magnitude') as what brings individuals into being within discrete systems of individuation. Before individuation, there is only the 'preindividual' or 'metastable' state, rife with tensions that are, as yet, unresolved and not yet in relation. Individuation itself arises when those previously compatible orders come into communication. We can think of a snow-covered slope just before an avalanche forms. Only a few slopes are in a state which might produce an avalanche. They have the potential for avalanche-forming – or are 'metastable' – but whether or not, or how the avalanche will form is not yet determined, and this potential, in Simondon's terms, marks them out from other slopes. The process of the avalanche forming (individuation) is the point at which what was previously incompatible comes into relation.

Simondon distinguishes between physical or 'natural' systems, such as the avalanche (his best known example is the formation of a crystal), and technical systems (famously the taking form of wet clay in a brick mould), where the metastable state is prepared through what he calls 'preliminary operations' with some degree of 'form-intention'. With respect to the clay brick, he traces all the processes – extraction of the clay, drying, grinding, wetting, kneading and so on – that prepare the clay for the possibility of its encounter with the mould. The actual 'communication' is a set of dynamic processes within the mould as molecules transmit forces, one to the next, in a release of energy that is limited by the mould. This taking form is not accomplished by the worker, it is accomplished by the system itself. Rather, it is the conditions for mediation that are created or prepared:

> It is the *system* constituted by the mould and the pressed clay which is the condition of the taking of form; it is the clay which takes form according to the mould, not the worker who gives it form. The man who works prepares the mediation, but he doesn't accomplish it, it is the mediation which accomplishes itself by itself after the conditions have been created.
>
> (Simondon 1989: 243)

Importantly, for Simondon, 'relation does not spring up between two terms that are already separate individuals' (Simondon 1964: 11). It is a mistake to consider relations merely as concepts that link individuals. Instead we need to consider:

> any veritable relation as something existing in its own right' and understand it as 'belonging to the being [or system of individuation], that is, a way of being and not a simple connection between two terms that could be adequately comprehended using concepts.
>
> (Simondon 1964: 17)

Relations are themselves processes, made possible within specific conditions that may have been prepared through technical work. And furthermore it is only through relation that individuals can be said to come into being.

Simondon's schema draws our attention to the *processes* through which relations between infant and carer are constituted in the NICU. We might also think of the intrauterine relation between mother and infant as constituted through material processes, although like the snowy slope they have not been prepared through any technical activity. In the case of different 'systems' of gestation – from incubator technologies that have tended towards automation to those that have to some extent interpolated the mother in the infant's care – each establishes specific conditions with the potential for specific kinds of relation to arise. We cannot simply consider the relations specific to the NICU assemblage as equivalent or inadequate to the relations that arise in other infant/mother systems. They are instead constituted through material processes that are particular to this system that is human, non-human and collective.

In *Waiting in the Wings* (1997) – the book that remains for me the most thoughtful and nuanced single account of the experience of becoming a mother in the NICU – Cherríe Moraga describes how having a son born early in an American NICU brought her into new relations with people and with things. As a Chicana feminist, in a same-sex couple whose son was conceived using artificial insemination, Moraga is deeply struck not only by the building of her relationship with her son in the Unit, but also by how her time there transformed her relations with heterosexual families, medical practices and staff and with the technologies involved in her son's care. Particularly striking is the link she made between her own 'milk-hard-breasted body' and the 'incubator walls' in the midst of the Unit routines, of sitting, watching, pumping, expressing and feeding:

> Cherríe Moraga: In that place [my heart] resides a seamless connection between my baby's essence beating inside those incubator walls and my milk-hard-breasted body.
>
> (Moraga 1997: 57)

As Suzanne Bost has written, Moraga's experience also challenges the social norms of maternity: 'This intimacy of life with the machine further queers the "queer motherhood" Moraga narrates, unmooring maternity from female essence, "natural" reproduction, heterosexual intercourse, and mother-father families' (Bost 2008: 354).

We can, I think, accept that the situation in the NICU, where there is no non-medical unmediated relation to return to, provides openings and potentials for new kinds of relation between infants and their carers, even between humans and non-humans, and for new ways of considering them, particularly insofar as it extends care to a community of others and at the same time makes this clearly visible. But the situation in the NICU is painful and fraught for all concerned. Its outcomes are often not without ongoing difficulties and it uses vast resources that might be better spent, and this chapter is not intended to universally promote ectogenesis. It would be more accurate to say that, perhaps, in these altered material conditions, and as a result of these altered processes, where life begins 'betwixt and between the womb and the world', we are not seeing obstructions and impediments to the building of *maternal* relations, but rather, temporarily, and for as long as this condition lasts, the building of other relations – *matrixial*, perhaps – that are necessarily institutional, technological, material, social and, importantly and, very visibly, collective.

Notes

1 For more on 'The Other Side of Waiting' see www.takingplace.org.uk; and Lloyd Thomas with **taking place** 2009.
2 At Homerton staff called all of us 'mum' and in this chapter I use this term to refer to the mothers who participated in This Is For You.
3 I am grateful to Lisa Baraitser, Chrysanthi Nigianni and Peg Rawes for encouraging me to write about TIFY.
4 For a rigorous and convincing account of how mother–infant bonding immediately after birth came to have such significant popular influence and to affect hospital procedures despite its foundation in problematic scientific research, see Eyer 1993.
5 Also see Roberts' discussion of Duden (Roberts 2008: 78).
6 Piercy's reference to Coney Island recalls one of the many displays of incubators with 'live' preterm babies inside that appeared as futuristic exhibits in amusement parks and international expositions at the turn of the century, and are usually photographed without medical staff or carers in attendance (Piercy 1976: 102). For details on the resident incubators exhibit in 1903 at Luna Park, Coney Island, see Baker 1996: 93–9.
7 During an interview, Craigie Horsfall suggests to Ettinger that this shareable dimension (that will, according to her, persist in later life in analysis, in art practice and perhaps in conversations between two, three or four people) must open her account into the communal – and the 'large and complex societies of which we are a part'. Ettinger acknowledges that although there may be political implications of the matrixial borderspace, they remain unexplored in her own work, and she states clearly that 'the matrixial is not the social' (Ettinger 2001: 61).
8 Rouch uses the term 'the materiality of this relationship to the maternal body' to describe what is overlooked in masculine accounts of the placental relation and explains that the placenta is literally discarded after birth (Irigaray and Rouch 2007: 38).

Bibliography

Baker, J. (1996) *The Machine in the Nursery: Incubator Technology and the Origins of Newborn Intensive Care*, Baltimore, MD: Johns Hopkins University Press.

Baraitser, L. (2009) *Maternal Encounters: The Ethics of Interruption*, London: Routledge.

Belmin, A. (1905–7) 'Visites de la societé internationale: la Clinique Tarnier et le Dr. Budin', *Revue Philanthropique*, 18: 490.

Bost, S. (2008) 'From race/sex/etc. to glucose, feeding tube, and mourning', in S. Alaimo and S. Hekman (eds) *Material Feminisms*, Bloomington: Indiana University Press.

Katie Lloyd Thomas

Cohen, M. (2003) *Sent Before My Time: A Child Psychotherapist's View of Life on an Intensive Care Unit*, London: Karnac.

Davis-Floyd, R. (1998) 'From technobirth to cyborg babies', in R. Davis-Floyd and J. Dumit (eds) *Cyborg Babies: From Techno-Sex to Techno-Tots*, New York: Routledge.

Duden, B. (1993) *Disembodying Women: Perspectives on Pregnancy and the Unborn*, trans. L. Hoinacki, Cambridge, MA: Harvard University Press.

Ettinger, B. (2001) 'The matrixial gaze' in C. de Zegher and B. Massumi (eds) *Bracha Lichtenberg Ettinger: The Eurydice Series' Drawing Papers No.24*, New York: The Drawing Centre.

Eyer, D.E. (1993) *Mother–Infant Bonding: A Scientific Fiction*, New Haven, CT: Yale University Press.

Firestone, S. (1970) *The Dialectic of Sex: The Case For Feminist Revolution*, New York: Bantam Books.

Irigaray, L. (1993) 'Belief itself', in *Sexes and Genealogies*, trans. G.C. Gill, New York: Columbia University Press.

— (2004) 'Place, interval', in *An Ethics of Sexual Difference*, trans. C. Burke and G.C. Gill, London: Continuum.

Irigaray, L. and Rouch, H. (2007) 'On the maternal order', in *Je, Tu, Nous*, trans. A. Martin, London: Routledge.

Lancaster, J. (1986) 'Impact of intensive care on the parent–infant relationship' in S.B. Korones (ed.) *High-risk Newborn Infants: The Basis for Intensive Nursing Care*, St Louis, MI: C.V. Mosby Company.

Landzelius, K.M. (2001) 'Charged artifacts and the detonation of liminality: teddy-bear diplomacy in the newborn incubator machine', *Journal of Material Culture*, 6, 3: 323–44.

— (2003) 'Humanizing the impostor: object relations and illness equations in the neonatal intensive care unit', *Culture, Medicine and Psychiatry*, 27, 1: 1–28.

Lloyd Thomas, K. (with **taking place**) (2009) 'The other side of waiting', *Feminist Review*, 93, 1: 122–7.

Marx, F. (1968) *Die Entwicklung der Säuglings Inkubatoren*, Bonn: Verlag Siering KG.

Moraga, C. (1997) *Waiting in the Wings: Portrait of a Queer Motherhood*, New York: Firebrand Books.

Piercy, M. (1976) *Woman on the Edge of Time*, New York: Ballantine Books.

Roberts, C. (2008) 'Relating simply? Feminist encounters with technoscience in the early twenty-first century', *Australian Feminist Studies*, 23, 55: 75–86.

Simondon, G. (1964) *L'individu et sa Genèse Physico-Biologique*, Paris: Press Universitaires de France.

— (1989) *Du Mode d'Existence des Objets techniques*, Paris: Aubier.

Toscano, A. (2007) 'Technical culture and the limits of interaction', in J. Brouwer and A. Mulder (eds) *Interact or Die!*, Rotterdam: V2_Publishing/NAi Publishers.

Chapter 12

The global healthcare biome and building the ecological medical school

Anita Berlin

Introduction

A biome is a large ecosystem, extending over a wide geographic region transcending frontiers, characterised by dominant life forms and communities (biota) of interdependent organisms. The largest biome on earth is the Taiga – stretching around the world across the forests of Canada, Siberia, northern Russia and Scandinavia – a space dominated by coniferous trees coexisting with, and sustaining, fauna and flora which vary from region to region.

The idea that healthcare[1] can be understood as a global biome – albeit man-made – is both descriptive and idealistic. I use it as a metaphor for the growing interconnectedness of local and global health needs and threats across the world, and the interdependence of healthcare provision required to address these for individuals and populations. Once we could imagine that the functioning of one healthcare system has little to do with the provision or absence of healthcare on the other side of the globe (save for the exceptional global pandemics such as Spanish flu in 1919). Now we see a range of trans-national phenomena leading to a global coalescence of healthcare provision. Despite marked and persisting inequities in health between regions the phenomena *affecting* healthcare are global. This chapter focuses on healthcare and its manifestation within spaces and places – both global and local. The notion of the biome has spatial and ecological connotations, evoking ideas of natural equilibrium, sustainability and holism. It also implies vulnerability to preventable man-made threats and 'natural' disasters.

I write as an inner-city family doctor. My clinical practice is made up of thousands of personal stories, some as short as a haiku and others volumes running over a life-course with supporting characters on and off stage. My door is open in the sense that patients choose to see me when they want (appointment system allowing), bringing the problems they deem as needing attention. I apply an eclectic mix of clinical and intrapersonal know-how. I have also been a university educator for twenty years. The chapter contains stories. All but one are fictitious – they are inspired by, rather than based on, real people. The last story, which illustrates the section on the ecological medical school, is true and I have the consent of the patient and the student to include it here.

What follows are my current responses to the questions: what space does healthcare occupy in the twenty-first century? How do we best prepare today's healthcare students to take their place in tomorrow's world? Guattari's three ecologies provide the broad frame for examining the healthcare biome (Guattari 2000).[2] Seeking to understand our globalised world and 'the impossibility of locating its source of power', Guattari offers a taxonomy with three 'registers': the environment or physical ecology; the ecology of social relations; and the ecology of human subjectivity. He suggests that we use this to illuminate new ethico-political articulations in a delocalised and unbound-aried world. This framework incorporates a moral dimension and effortlessly embraces the internal and the external, the local and the global, even the male and the female – and the many links between.

An examination of the healthcare biome draws attention to gender: first, in the literal sense, to gender differences in health and healthcare; and second, through the sexed phenomena of dyads. In general dividing the world into dyads facilitates our recognition of power relationships, how a single (masculine) discourse or structure tends to dominate the 'other' (female). Take for example: north/south; rich/poor; hospital/community; specialist/generalist; cure/care. It is not hard to see, regardless of the biological genders involved, these constructs as sexed. Healthcare and medical education occupy a sexed world where the good, healthy, rational 'male' doctor/teacher treats/instructs the weak, compliant 'female' patient/student. Such a feminist evaluation of medicine is not new, it is only striking because it is still so true decades after early critiques (see, for example, Daly 1978). This grossly gendered dynamic, which no longer reflects societal expectations (and maybe never did) or the actual gender balance in the workforce is still practised and promoted extensively by western medical men (and women).

Although Guattari acknowledges that the global homogenisation of structure and subjectivities tends to lead to a 'return to old hierarchies' and his heterogeneous tri-ecology is an explicit break with dualism, he is virtually silent on the issue of gender so relevant in my biome. The first half of the chapter applies Guattari's first register to an extended discussion of the healthcare environment. I set the scene across two dimensions. First, the shared factors that shape contemporary healthcare and connect healthcare systems, regardless of country or continent; and second, the transnational threats to global health that, at its best, global healthcare might address. The application of the environmental register continues with an examination of local healthcare ecologies and the morphology of health systems dominated by the hospital/community dyad. As such this is an examination of place and space – actual and virtual – and a changing ecology. I consider the solid, contained structure of the hospital as a place of highly technical episodic care and contrast this with the less homogenised and unbounded nature of community practice, where care is diffuse across space and time, often embodied in the care worker, and truth is co-constructed. To what extent is the old adage taught to medical students still true? 'In hospitals diseases stay and people come and go; in general practice people stay and diseases come and go.'

I then use Guattari's second register to explore social relationships within and between healthcare places, exposing the fundamental challenge of a central dyad – doctor/patient. This section flows into the third register, multiple human subjectivities. The second and third registers are linked together in this way to illustrate how the key social relationships in healthcare and education are shaped by the manifold subjectivities of groups and of the unique individual: patient, health-worker or student.

Finally,[3] drawing on my experience as a teacher I imagine the 'ecological medical' school to offer a new stable, but flexible, solution based on the rethinking oriented to the practice of global health across the three ecological registers. The ecological curriculum would be enacted through the synthesis of a wide range of disciplines leading students and their teachers to engage in new ways with patients and healthcare settings. An 'ecological medical school' manifests a *feasible utopia* (Barnett 2010),[4] an *imaginary* that nurtures and prepares doctors-to-be for the uncertain local and global challenges facing contemporary healthcare.

The viability of any biome is its ability to withstand, accommodate or adapt to threats and challenges. The healthcare biome requires alternative thinking to achieve this allostasis where traditional hierarchical relations are dissolved and new, multiple bonds are formed across time and space. Guattari proposes an interconnecting tool, 'transversality', which links and transects the personal, local and global. Thinking transversally refocuses the way we construct relations between nation states, health systems, the inner and outer world of communities and individuals. Healthcare within the biome is thus a therapeutic endeavour of cure plus care, in the broadest sense, for the environment, social relations and mental wellbeing. Focusing on the education of those who will need to forge this ecological praxis of 'ecosophy' is as good a place to start as any.

The ecology of the healthcare environment

In spite of local variation, healthcare across the globe functions as a single biome which is increasingly unaware of borders, interdependent and open to common environmental financial and political phenomena. The principal shared transnational threats to human health are global environmental changes undermining food and energy security leading to drought, crop failures and famine, exacerbated by numerous areas of conflict and civil unrest. These in turn produce a growing number of desperate people displaced within and between countries – with the highest health needs – as well as novel patterns of migration. Increasing global human mobility facilitates the rapid spread of new infections with pandemic potential.

> D, a 16-year-old unaccompanied refugee, spoke little English. He had pain all over his body. He was living in a bed and breakfast hostel, looking for work but he wanted to study. Physical examination was (as expected) normal. Before running some bloods tests I asked how was he surviving? For two weeks he had eaten only breakfast – two slices of toast. He was hungry. I remember a tale a colleague had told me: how her grandmother had been a doctor in California during the depression. She kept dollar bills in her desk drawer, which she dispensed instead of prescriptions. I gave D £10. A fortnight later he came just to return the money; he had work as a labourer. I saw him on and off over the next six years – minor health concerns, social advice and chats. When last seen he was finishing a radiography degree and came to ask me whether it was the right time to marry his girlfriend.

The healthcare biome has evolved as part of a changing global ecology where the previously longstanding taken-for-granted differences in the provision of healthcare and vital statistics have become more complex and uncertain. A set of mobilities criss-cross the globe. Some represent threats, such as the mobility of microbes mentioned above. Others, such as the mobility of people, ideas and innovation, bind us with the biome. The emptying of a bedpan in New York or Stockholm pays for an education in Sri Lanka or the Philippines.

Despite dramatic advances in health sciences there are still glaring inequities in health outcomes. However, there are increasingly, interconnected patterns emerging: differences no longer cleave along a line between the global North and the global South. The world's poor (those with a GDP of < $10) share dreadful outcomes regardless of region. The greatest number now live in intermediate-income countries.

Within regions there are also huge variations outside the poorest. Health gains in terms of life expectancy at birth are not directly correlated to GDP per capita; the USA has similar outcomes to Cuba, which has a quarter the per capita GDP. In some countries life expectancy is worsening, mostly those wracked by civil wars, although some of the greatest declines in health outcomes in the last two decades are seen in parts of Russia.

Functioning planned health systems that integrate hospital services, primary care and public health, have been shown repeatedly to provide the most cost-effective and equitable healthcare (Starfield *et al.* 2005). And while many intermediate economies are now moving towards comprehensive systems, simultaneously, wealthier nations are unable to establish or sustain a system. Thus it is possible, albeit for ostensibly different reasons, both in sub-Saharan Africa and the United States for a single major health event within a close social unit, such as the death or permanent disability of a breadwinner, to provoke an economic crisis from which an extended family may take a generation to recover. Failures of healthcare affect women more greatly and maternal and infant survival are directly correlated with the quality and scope of health services. Health systems are vulnerable to the economic power of a market ideology and multinational industry that frames all healthcare as a commodity rather than a human right. In the UK, the NHS – arguably the largest public project in Europe – is vulnerable to political interventions justified as economic imperatives, leading to a shrinking provision. Inevitably the 'Inverse Care Law' (Hart 1971) applies most to those in greatest need of healthcare locally and globally least likely to receive it. Global threats to human health and wellbeing are manifest in a single life story. When once conflict or hardship was the cause, now the threat is the sustainability of a healthcare system in a hostile economic and political environment.

Further challenges to the provision of healthcare ensue when societies rise out of absolute poverty in the shifts from endemic communicable diseases to global 'epidemics' of non-communicable conditions in aging populations, such as heart disease, diabetes and dementia, which blur the boundaries between health, social and personal care. As women receive education, control their own fertility, increase their income and have access to healthcare, demographic charts change from youth-full pyramids, into funnels top-heavy with older people with a wide range of needs.

The ties that bind

Mrs T is a Mauritian nurse in an NHS hospital who was coughing up blood. She is now starting treatment for TB and is worried about her family at home: they need her remittances to pay the bills.

Worldwide, we are facing increasing demands on healthcare, yet many systems offer relatively unattractive working conditions (Action for Global Health 2011), a combination that stimulates a global market for health professionals, for example, leading to British midwives working in Australia, Senegalese nurses in France. The Philippine economy depends on this market with the remittances of migrant healthcare workers forming the single largest stream of income to the national economy. Many European health systems have depended on this human flow for decades. In the UK 30 per cent of doctors are not home trained, which represents a considerable saving on training costs and a tragic brain drain for many countries (Pang *et al.* 2002). Figures are not available for the proportion of migrant ancillary staff from the global South that mop and scrub European and North American healthcare facilities. Overall 80 per cent of the global healthcare workforce is female (Kuptsch 2006). Millions of women are displaced so that it is not just the 'brains' that are drained by economic migration but whole women – daughters and mothers – working away from their communities, families and children, in a vicious cycle.

These shared phenomena provoke transnational interventions from formal international agencies, aid organisations and unaligned NGOs in a combination of monitoring, funding and campaigning. The 2000 Millennium Development Goals (MDGs) are aimed at global poverty eradication, representing probably the largest exercise in transnational co-ordination to date.

Three of the eight MDGs are health related (maternal health; infant mortality; communicable diseases, especially HIV/AIDs and malaria) and when added to those promoting universal primary education and women's equality and empowerment the MDGs can, at least in theory, highlight the starkly gendered challenges facing healthcare. Over a decade on there is evidence of progress in all MDGs. Some excellent, such as maternal health in Latin America and South East Asia, but few will be fully achieved by 2015. Why? Essentially the approach replicates the existing dualisms: north/south; rich/poor; donor/recipient; germ/system. The MDGs are for the poor, not the rich; they are donor-driven not system-building; aggregate nation and region together without taking into account local subtleties; are not supported by a plan or good data, and key donor countries have rescinded on commitments. And in the background increasingly dominant market forces undermine such noble global intentions driven by the growing deregulation and internationalisation of the 'health industry'. This includes local and multinational pharmaceutical manufacturers and for-profit healthcare organisations operating outside national governance, particularly in the emerging economies of the BRIC[5] countries.

The deregulation and industrialisation of healthcare is reflected in education systems. For-profit medical schools have led to overproduction of professionals and a distortion of provision. In North America student debt also drives graduates into profitable surgical specialities. At the same time universities in the resource-rich countries are internationalising and globalising their enterprises, often with the objective of increasing fee-paying overseas students, institutional status through offshore campuses and exchange via educational networks and partnerships.

Most countries in sub-Saharan Africa have one or no medical school; similar deficiencies apply to nurse education (Frenk *et al.* 2010). Moving away from aid models funders now support university partnerships. The largest are the Nursing and the Medical Education Partnership Initiatives (NEPI and MEPI), the latter with thirty African partners linked to twenty North American collaborators to the tune of $130 million from the US government, as part of America's response to the MDGs. Such programmes have huge potential for good but are fraught with concerns regarding lack of mutuality, paternalism and neo-colonialism (McCoy *et al.* 2008). Staff exchanges and elective placements for students can be transformative experiences but lead to legitimate accusations of one-way 'edu-tourism' without sustainable investment in the university infrastructure for hosts (Crane 2011).

The Internet and mobile technologies facilitate educational traffic across the biome. Between countries students and staff can collaborate directly and international publications and course materials can be freely shared. Within countries mobile technologies increasingly supply immediate support in remote locations (Valk *et al.* 2010).

This combination of closer institutional links and rapid knowledge exchange draws current and future healthcare workers together in an instant, but begs questions of relevance, empowerment, moral authority and power gradients.

A group of young people in the USA are looking at a screen on which appear a small group of young women in Malaysia (wearing traditional tudung headscarves). They are animatedly discussing a paper on childbirth. This is a virtual seminar between medical students in an offshore medical school and their parent institution. A male student in the US asks, 'we know that female genital mutilation can interfere with childbirth. What is your opinion?' Silence. Then the Malaysian students talk among themselves for a while and glance off screen at an invisible tutor, 'This is a difficult topic, but yes we think it can be a big problem, and not just when a baby is born.'[6]

A century after its publication, the Flexner report on medical education can be seen as a foundation stone in the globalisation of healthcare by establishing a science-based university-led model with worldwide reach (Flexner 1910). While raising standards it also ensured a colonial approach to content, assessment and regulation with no regard to local health need or system relevance. Now, programmes such as MEPI, which were ostensibly intended to do the opposite, may well be replicating this approach.

One response to the challenges posed by the health impact of environmental change, health industrialisation, international interventions and partnerships is 'stewardship' through transnational monitoring, governance and regulation. International agencies assume or are given responsibilities previously located in nation states. Here the sustainability of both local ecosystems and the wider healthcare biome coincide and at once are most stretched between global solutions and the need for local adaptability and self-determination (see WHO 2010; Anonymous 2010). Many are only voluntary. They highlight consensus on complex scientific, practical and ethical challenges. The offshore students want a US or UK medical degree and regulators ask themselves: how do we licence a medical school when students visit mental hospitals where homosexuals receive compulsory treatment? These are, as Guattari says, the ethico-political problems of the global ecology.

What therefore counts as the local and global scope and responsibilities of healthcare are difficult moral questions. Healthcare and the training of health professionals in one continent impacts on the health system in another, and then ricochets back home again, interconnected across an enormous space.

Local spaces

> Everyone who is born holds dual citizenship, in the kingdom of the well and in the kingdom of the sick. Although we all prefer to use only the good passport, sooner or later each of us is obliged, at least for a spell, to identify ourselves as citizens of that other place.
>
> (Sontag 1978: 3)

I now consider Guattari's first register in relation to the local spaces and places of healthcare – the hospitals and community services within the health system and the manifestation of the body within these. Following Sontag's 'dual' term, hospitals might represent the palaces in the kingdom of the sick – safe places where cures are available, malfunctioning parts removed or repaired. By contrast, healthcare provided outside hospitals is less constrained. Primary or community care is not focused on a single cure-orientation but aspires to an integrated practice that addresses uncertain and diffuse problems of prevention, care and cure. Here, healthcare is more embodied in the mobile person of healthcare professionals than in the defined architectural spaces of a hospital. A national healthcare system can be seen as a local ecosystem within the global biome – those that have thrived depend on the synergy between the hospital and community components. Very simply, regardless of context, the most equitable, clinically, and cost-effective systems are those where generalist, multidisciplinary community-based primary care works in synergy with a specialised hospital service (Starfield *et al.* 2005). We are all susceptible to the common challenges of the wider healthcare biome, but many countries have no functioning health system. They rely on aid directed at a small number of diseases which is now delivering diminishing returns (Lancet Editorial 2012). More comprehensive, sustainable, ecological healthcare systems are needed across the biome (Starfield 2011).

There are many examples of such systems in high- and middle-income economies (including Costa Rica, Cuba and Thailand). However, in considering the ecology of health systems and their link to medical education, I refer mostly to Europe and, in particular, the British system. First, because I am most familiar with the British NHS and second, warts and all, it is still regarded globally as one of the better and most influential models (Berwick 2008).

Hospital healthcare – bounded space

Hospitals have evolved as places of containment, bounded spaces where the sick can benefit from the growing possibilities of science and technology. Money and power are concentrated in the hospitals (especially the teaching hospitals) as well as the rationality of science. Historically, they made possible 'the setting aside of the extrinsic' (Foucault 1984: 17), initially, the miasmas, humours and curses; latterly, the subjective psychosocial causal factors in suffering.

Under this 'gaze' the body and its diseases are relocated from the subjective 'sick room' in the community to be read as cryptograms of objective spaces in the clinic. This recontextualisation has allowed science to enter medicine and, at once, represents progress and loss. The growth of the hospital has also increased the steep knowledge and power gradients between patient and professional and fixed views of truth.

Many initiatives have been developed to render the hospital more human, for patients and for staff. Nonetheless hospitals are increasingly specialised caregivers that continue to depersonalise and dissect the whole person. Technical advances mean that, for example, it is now possible to spend days being carefully monitored through remote telemetry by medical staff who never see or touch the patient. This machinery sustains a sanitised space where objectification is facilitated and the subjective subordinated.

Given the choice, patients may opt to objectify their own bodies and health problems and abdicate involvement in decisions, but hospital cultures assume this is the default position despite much rhetoric regarding autonomy and consent. Even in extremis we seek signs of trust and care. These are enacted through relationships – not just the social relations between people but a more fundamental, subtle, atavistic dynamic – between our bodies and our environment.

Community healthcare

As the result of a nineteenth-century border skirmish in the UK GPs were excluded from hospitals (and, for nearly a century, medical schools), but by agreement, they filtered the referral of patients to specialists (Stevens 1966). GPs are therefore defined by their proximity to their patients and communities over time, not by a specific place in which the tools of their trade were located. They conduct these longitudinal relationships in 'sick rooms', the place where the patient is, be that home or health centre. The proximity and continuity affords GPs a 'rich understanding of the inconsistent relationship between symptomatic illness and biomedical disease, between suffering and pathology' (Heath 2011). Contact over time has a therapeutic value separate from the relationship itself. This has allowed GPs to emerge as influential clinical epidemiologists and importantly exposes the benefits of medicine and also its harms. Up to 20 per cent of patient problems have no explanation, most resolving alone in time. Managing uncertainly and knowing when not to label, investigate and refer is key. The regime of truth (Foucault 1984) – the apparatus for the generation and diffusion of truth statements – in community settings is a range of perspectives less routed in the dominant scientific discourses that characterise hospital practice. This is the place for 'and/both/many' interpretations of suffering (Launer 1996). And because of a presence in place and time the GP can be 'dispenser of cures and the repositories of memories' (Berger and Mohr 1967).

> One of those bright April days, blossom on all the trees. M, a man in his fifties, sits down holding his brow with both hands. 'I've never had a headache like it.' We met once before. His notes are sparse – an infected cut, an episode of bronchitis and nine years ago, to the very day, I had written the following: 'Soldier son killed by sniper in Bosnia this a.m. Asking for tranquilisers for wife.' I asked quietly, 'Do you know what the date is today?' He raised his head, glanced out of the window, stood up: 'Thanks', and left.

Community practice provides a window into work lives and living conditions which are, in turn, invitations to acts of social justice: advocacy, for example, on behalf of the man in wheelchair, but no ramp to leave his home; the single mother of a bedwetting child who has one set of sheets and no washing machine.

Once again there is a gendered and sexed dimension at play. General practice in the UK and elsewhere has benefited from more women graduates. Usual explanations include negative experiences and lack of role models in hospital practice, and more flexible working conditions. But general practice and hospital specialisation have become 'gender marked': their practice associated with 'femininities' or 'masculinities'. Specialists are strongly associated with positive, masculine attributes such as efficiency, technical skill, focus or control. GPs were notoriously described as 'having fallen off the specialist ladder' (Curwen 1964), and are therefore seen as weaker, softer, dumber, emotional or domestic. The focus on care as well as cure, the use of talk over tools, doctor-as-treatment, emphasise a feminine/masculine dualism which is manifest in statistics. As a prominent (woman) hospital physician observed, female professions are weak and lack influence: the rising proportion of women in medicine is perceived to undermine the profession's status in society (Black 2004).[7]

These views of general practice may be romantic[8] and certainly the notion of healthcare 'embodied' by the GP, when and where needed along a life-course, is currently being replaced by a more fixed location. The privilege of home-visiting now falls mainly to a network of community nurses whose role in sustaining individuals, and in fact the entire NHS (by reducing the need for hospital admissions *inter alia*), I cannot do justice to here.

The GP's work is increasingly hitched to an intrusive technicism: paper-free records on computers that avert the attention and use objectified classifications; pop-up reminders for screening with its associated hazards of false results and politically motivated health promotion of sometimes dubious effectiveness and relevance. Machines that measure blood pressure and pulses, but which stop us hearing the beating human heart. Clinical checklists which generate payments; consulting rooms in Tesco and Walmart. Not all is bad, of course, for example: accurate monitoring and safer prescribing; instant links to test results and correspondence; access to research evidence; opportunities to share information, images and personal records with patients in real time and remotely; a foetal monitor that allows a mother to hear her baby's heartbeat too.

General practice is susceptible to all the threats and challenges that circulate within the healthcare biome. Creeping mechanisation, marketisation, and education dominated by a performative paradigm are leading to a convergence with the more bounded, technical hospital practice. They remain inextricably linked. For the sick or the not yet sick (that is, as Sontag says, all of us), a health system that offers prevention, care and cure, science and humanity in home, health centre or hospital, is still within the possibility of the NHS and similar health systems. The turbulence in our global healthcare biome highlights the need to create the ecological conditions which retain the principles of a single, comprehensive service that resists the domination of one (more masculine) model in favour of a heterogeneous, pluralistic environment that supports new praxes through attention to social and human relations. It is to the ecology of such intricate connected social relations that I turn next.

The ecologies of social relations and subjectivities

Healthcare is a vast and varied enterprise shaped by the ecology of its environment. The place of medical practice within it is predicated on a simple and universally recognised dyad – the doctor and the patient.

The real work of a doctor is not an affair of health centres, or laboratories, or hospital beds. Techniques have their place in medicine, but they are not medicine. The essential unit of medical practice is 'the occasion when, in the intimacy of the consulting room or sick room, a person who is ill, or believes himself to be ill, seeks the advice of a doctor whom he trusts. This is a consultation, and all else in the practice of medicine derives from it' (Spence 1960).

Taking Guattari's second register to consider the ecology of social relations in healthcare I now focus on the consultation, the 'essential unit' of doctor–patient relations. This is a story of a shifting dynamic between inner/ outer worlds, between subject/object, and person/population. As such, it also overlaps, inevitably, with Guattari's third register – the ecology of subjectivities.

There is a vast literature on the doctor–patient relationship from sociology, psychology and ethics. Its clinical locus is almost exclusively general practice, with notable exceptions from oncology and palliative care (for example, Fallowfield 2005). This literature, largely originating from the UK, and later Canada, clearly shows an Anglophone publication bias, but may also suggest that the accident of history that separated GPs from specialists in UK medical history has created a particular ecology of social relations.[9]

Writing about professionals in general, Schön suggests that many remain impatient with anything other than the 'high ground' of technical rationality. However, 'Some ... choose to work in the "swampy lowlands" immersing themselves in confusing but crucially important situations' (Schön 2001: 55).

In the swamps of general practice the concept of patient-centred practice emerged, in part an attempt to give voice to the subjective experience of the sick rather than merely the objective vessel of their pathology. During the twentieth century the patient's contribution to the consultation increased as part of a ritualised medical history determined by medical semiology and taxonomies, stage-managed entirely by the enquiries of the doctor who typically determined all the solutions. Although many strove to incorporate what they knew – from experience, to be important – into the doctor–patient encounter, the patient's subjective, social, psychosocial perspectives remained supplementary to core medical business (Tuckett et al. 1985).

From the 1950s onwards we find explorations of the inner and outer worlds of the patient. Freudian approaches permeate re-examinations of medical practice and discourse (as opposed to psychiatric) primarily through the work of Balint (1957). He sought to help reunite body and mind in mainstream practice as well as to help doctors appreciate the complexity of the conscious and unconscious – in their patients and in themselves – to connect with their patients' and their own subjectivity. Balint brought together aspects of illness and disease in general practice that continued to be silenced in the hospital clinic, resetting the dialectic between the social and the biological, and psyche and soma, and inviting a revised praxis for the consultation (Armstrong 2004).

The idea of 'patient-centredness' now dominates the consultation and doctor–patient communication. It is strongly associated with 'client-centred therapy' (Rogers 1951) and 'student-centred education' (Rogers 1969), themselves responses to the excesses of behaviourism in psychology and teaching. The wide appeal of person-centredness captures concerns regarding professionals in western society, the impact of education and the media on assumed trust and hidden knowledge, and societal expectations, particularly those of women.

Stewart *et al.* (1995) presented patient-centredness as both a humanistic and communicative way of being with patients, a moral project and a hermeneutic method for integrating and interpreting the patient and her experience. Stewart is associated with a diagrammatic model emphasising two (equal) sides to the every encounter – the patient's (the illness) and the doctor's (the disease). This disease/illness dyad arises from a linguistic quirk in English. Although the words are usually used interchangeably they have assumed subtly different meanings. 'Disease' denotes a medical view of ill-health based on eliciting symptom and signs and assigning labels. 'Illness' encompasses the subjective, unique patient experience of being unwell. The two sides are finally brought together in a process of shared problem definition and decision-making.

At its best, the dual patient-centred approach establishes the therapeutic value of interactional work through which the patient's subjectivity may be both understood and engaged (May *et al.* 2006). The ubiquitous reach of the term, out of individual encounters into all aspects of healthcare, may give the impression of 'job done', a successful rebalancing of the ecology of the key social relationship in medicine and the re-territorialisation of the subjective patient within it.

But there are a number of complexities. To legitimise the approach it needed to be researched and assessed: here was a new space between individuals which 'could be safely examined' (Gothill and Armstrong 1999). To evaluate the impact of the patient-centred approach and credentialise its application in teaching programmes and examinations, patient-centrednesss has been broken into constitutive behaviours.[10] These render it with considerable utility for research, teaching and patient satisfaction surveys which can capture measurable outcomes.

D, a popular and knowledgeable trainee, was surprised to fail her communication assessment. The examiner's checklist indicated she had not asked any patients directly about their ideas and expectations. In preparation for a reassessment she began, rather mechanically, to ask all patients, 'what were you expecting from this appointment?' Critiquing her responses, she commented: 'I was amazed how often people wanted something other than my prescription and reassurance.'

The research community uses a wide array of interpretative approaches, but overall, especially in education and service governance, the integrative, humanistic project is drawn towards the positivist paradigm, translated (or reduced) into a list of defined and observable behaviours homogenising the doctor–patient ecology into a technology applied in a sequence of structured episodes, rather than a caring relationship which might extend over time and place. So, despite the nominal centrality of the patient, checklists subordinate holistic endeavours (that lie in spaces between the items in the list) such as the integration of knowledge to solve problems, trustworthiness, care and kindness. This is compounded by a question of place: the locus of learning is not the locus of practice. Patient-centred communication was born and raised in general practice and GPs became its proud (pushy) parents. It became, in part, their ticket of admission into the academy. Its teaching has flourished in medical schools, however what is taught in the classroom is often dissonant with what is seen in the 'wild' of practice as the majority of medical teachers remain hospital doctors unattuned to the approach.

The binary disease/illness distinction does not allow for the flux between the scientifically reified and the unlabelled, nor does it accommodate the uncertain spaces in between: who decides which of Sontag's passports is needed and when.

Perhaps the greatest insight Guattari's registers offer is the way in which patient-centredness has become a space governed by a dogma of a single subjectivity – that of the individual patient. This has served to some extent to help reunite body with mind into one person. The doctor, however, is still gazing out from a separate objective side of this space, a dualism where asymmetric power relationships are sustained and other subjectivities excluded.

> the genie of medical subjectivity was not to be released, but rather installed into a larger and better-furnished bottle, designed to keep the professional and the personal hygienically separate. The boundaries which had been established to protect the patient ... and the doctor ... effectively delin-eated a new social space.
>
> (Gothill and Armstrong 1999: 10)

Guattari's third ecosophical perspective is that of subjectivities. For him, this is neither an isolated place of the individual's essential, innate 'identity' and unique lived experience, nor is it a passive subject, constructed by her physical, social or political environment. The body-self is not a pragmatic amalgam of the essentialised identity or the socially constructed, but a confluence of multiple components, influenced by multidirectional, intersubjective dynamics. Narratives are co-constructed between practitioner and patient (Launer 1996), both oscillating between objective and subjective, influenced by individual and collective imperatives (Heath 2011).

The subjective patient has multiplying incarnations: the 'expert patient' a sequestered agent of doctors helping themselves, other patients and students; the critic–consumer of commoditised healthcare (May *et al.* 2006); or the 'resisting consumer', whose health identity centres on lay models and non-allopathic remedies (Fox and Ward, 2006). The practitioner's subjectivity is encouraged in parallel, reflexive 'inner consultations' (Neighbour 2004). But while GPs physically embody the care they provide, they do not have an elaborated embodied self – organs and all – but are a vulnerable 'Dr no-body', without, as yet, a healthy place for a full subjective self (Gothill and Armstrong 1999). Vital for healthcare is that Guattari's 'subjectivities' can be individual and collective, linking 'transversally' practitioner/team/institution and person/family/community/population. Patients are not homogenous subjects and future doctors are not homogeneous products: they are all active parts of the hetero-geneous ecosophere.

The imaginary of the ecological medical school

We clinicians can love our patients and the population they are a part of only when we can comprehend the needs of both in emotional as well as clinical and epidemiological terms (Sabin 1998: 1003).

You have an idea of how you want your doctor to be – knowledgeable, skilful, trustworthy, caring, able to inform and involve you; a socially responsible advocate for individuals and populations and a collaborative member of a team, prepared to practise in the healthcare biome – whether in Luton or Luanda. The changing ecologies of the teacher–student and doctor–patient relationships, and the position of the 'patient' in broader, diverse collective and individual subjec-tivities, invite us to imagine the potential of a tri-ecological curriculum.

Ostensibly the job of a medical school, although large, appears relatively simple – to transmit the prerequisite body of knowledge and skills so that the graduate can fulfil his side of a traditional social bargain, the application of this knowledge in exchange for a degree of autonomy and social status. This deal binds together the two elements of the doctor–patient dyad. Medical schools have striven to modernise and reflect the changing nature of the social contract. They aim to ensure graduates can bring the stunning advances in science to patients while recognising the limitations of decontextualisation. Greater interdisciplinarity includes sociology, psychology, ethics and communication skills as core subjects. The principal goal of the medical curriculum is now a humanist project, to produce patient-centred doctors through a learner-centred programme (GMC 2009). There is much emphasis on a clear, homogenous professionalism through self-conscious, reflective identity formation as part of a community of practice. Despite this, medical education, in general, has rightly been accused of decades of 'reform without change' (Hafferty 1998) and 'failing to keep pace due to fragmented, out of date and stale curricula … producing ill equipped graduates' (Frenk *et al.* 2010: 1925).

There is an inexorable and persistent tendency to support sexed power gradients in the key relationships. It is the primacy of facts and labels, faith in isolated positivistic enquiry, unease with uncertainty and heterogeneous messy realities that remains at issue. The dominance of the hi-tech hospital locus creates a dissonance in which social (or moral) context and the patient's (and student's) unique experience sits awkwardly, as lesser realities. Students learn all this within a week of starting medical school. This is the powerful influence of the 'hidden curriculum' (Hafferty 1998), a socialising phenomenon which impacts upon students as they engage more with doctors in the workplace and 'can serve to increase distance between students and patients' (Bleakley and Bligh, 2006: 92); a gap that widens as students progress through their course (Haidet *et al.* 2002).

The emphasis on developing the students' reflective inner-doctor may suggest a feminine influence. Nonetheless the broader feminist concerns for achieving equality of opportunity and understanding difference have not followed the feminisation of the workforce. Neither women, nor the very significant numbers of ethnic minority students see themselves reflected in senior role models. The importance of a homogenous professional identity setting clear boundaries for personal development and licensing purposes simultaneously obliterates the multiple subjectivities of the students and the wider world of real practice.

So the ecological medical school can consider a number of options. What happens when we disrupt the traditional dyads? What if we teach uncertainty and complexity before we teach scientific method? Or encourage students to use their own subjectivity and agency for patients and population benefits; or ensure they are critically aware of the ethico-political dimensions of their overseas elective placements; or we remove the clinical teachers and ask the patients to teach the students? Or we engineer patient contact along new spatio-temporal pathways (varying both in time and place)?

To reshape how students learn about cancer an oncologist and I introduced a 'cancer patient project'. Each third-year student is matched with a patient who is receiving treatment. After gaining consent, the student is responsible for following the patient (at the patient's convenience) over the next few months and accompanying him or her to appointments. Students regularly meet peers to be briefed; cover core topics on cancer medicine; receive support and advice from tutors and peers; and share experiences. Such a longitudinal project is not new to medical education (Maughan *et al.* 2001). The underlying ethos is to give patients their own voice through which they effectively act as a teacher. The clinical teacher is removed from the stage and waits in the wings; the dialogue between the student and the patient is direct and personal, not mediated and controlled by an experienced third party. Students observe from the patient's side, not the doctor's side, of the proceedings. They submit a written report relating the patient's narrative with a commentary on the medical and scientific aspects. They are asked to synthesise these different dimensions in a reflective coda. Attention was paid to preparation, guidelines and safety netting. The project has challenges – some patients withdraw, and some die. But, despite a range of struggles, students feel more confident, intensely aware of the patients' experience and often optimistic about their future. Every student has submitted a project, many both erudite and moving. I kept in touch with one student (J) from my first tutor group who later joined me on a research project. She proved to be full of joy and energy. I accepted an invitation to J's graduation dinner and J introduced me to DD: 'this is the person that I met through my cancer patient project.' She greeted me warmly and I was a little taken aback. After dinner J's mother asked DD to say a few words. In short, she described how, three years earlier, J had been allocated to her in an oncology out-patient clinic and then accompanied her to all her chemotherapy sessions. After the third or fourth session she was so sick that she insisted the treatment was stopped, she was never coming back. J gently encouraged and then cajoled her into continuing treatment. 'Without this young doctor I don't think I would be standing here today.'

Increased exposure to general practice helps (Howe 2001). It can provide an ecological practicum, with individual, community and, in the inner city, international dimensions, where theory and practice, illness and disease co-exist, biographies are co-constructed. Students acknowledge the value of primary care, but do not accord it the same status as hospital practice – it is a swamp after all.

Including 'global health' as core content in high-income countries increases curriculum relevance, reduces the dominance of a local, parochial monoculture and provides bi-directional opportunities for staff and students. Although globalised curricula may be institutional responses to pressure to demonstrate social accountability such initiatives can also contribute to a medical school and its graduates being more transversally connected to and prepared for the global healthcare biome.

Conclusions

Guattari holds that traditional environmentalist perspectives obscure the complexity of the relationship between humans and their natural environment by maintaining a dualistic separation of human (cultural) and non-human (natural) systems; he envisions ecosophy as a new field with both a monistic and pluralistic approach to practice. Ecology in Guattari's sense, then, links complex phenomena, including human subjectivity, the environment and social relations.

This 'tri-ecology' has provided a productive approach for reviewing the place of healthcare in the world, despite Guattari's neologisms and rejection of metaphors, which make his text challenging, as well as his tendency to a sweeping anti-science perspective. An ecological solution does not seek to eliminate difference or change but allows for a process of positive allostasis – responding and changing rather than merely adapting to ebb and flow.

This chapter articulates a biome where the rich but messy reality of multiple, simultaneous relationships and (eco)systems can be theorised, learned and practised, based on a dynamic interconnected ethic. It imagines an ecological medical school in which new doctors integrate, rather than subordinate, uncertainty, social and personal differences and values with increasingly precise clinical sciences. Dealing with human health my focus is inevitably anthropocentric. I have however also highlighted how healthcare and medical education are androcentric – globally women bear the greatest burden of care and preventable ill health. I have focused on this and the implications of the dyads that dominate healthcare discourse.

Guattari's thinking suggests a praxis, a revised interdisciplinary practice based on a cohesive theory which draws on experience and empirical observation as well as an ethico-political position cognisant of relevance and context in the broadest sense. It is this praxis I have attempted to apply to the ecological medical school and its role in preparing the doctors of the twenty-first century to care for individuals and populations in the healthcare biome of our increasingly vulnerable planet.

Notes

1 Throughout, I refer to 'healthcare' to include public health practice.
2 Guattari has a specific aversion to metaphors.
3 I do not have the space to consider the specifics of mental health care and its history, the roles of the wider healthcare team or the medical built environment.

4   Some of this is informed by Ron Barnett's chapter 'The ecological university' in Barnett (2010), itself drawing on Guattari's work. *Feasible utopia* is the phrase used by Barnett in his analysis of the possibilities of the university.

5   BRIC stands for Brazil, Russia, India and China.

6   It is estimated that 140 million women have undergone some form of female genital mutilation (see Forward 2010).

7   Carol Black was the President of the Royal College of Physicians. Her point was that the more women in a profession the lower its perceived status and influence. Her response was that women should work harder and give up aspirations of work–life balance and even abandon family life. In contrast, Maureen Baker's response, from the Royal College of General Practitioners, was 'this is society's problem'.

8   As in any profession there are money grabbers, incompetents and plain criminals. The murders of Harold Shipman, a psychopath, not by all accounts an incompetent doctor, exposed the perils of isolated practice, and poor governance.

9   Each day in the UK there are one million GP consultations, accounting for over 80 per cent of all doctor–patient contacts in the NHS.

10 The process of 'creditentialising' professional practice through training and assessment is an important way of delineating entry criteria to a profession and reassuring clients that individual practitioners have reached the required standard (by earning the requisite credits). It is a form of *technology* that has some benefits but the 'checklist' approach may distort good practice in order to support professional self-interest through assessment.

Bibliography

Action for Global Health (2011) *Addressing the Global Health Workforce Crisis*, Brussels. Online: http://www.actionforglobalhealth.eu/fileadmin/AfGH_Intranet/AFGH/Publications/HRH_REPORT_-_SCOPE_WEB_LORES_.pdf (accessed 12 May 2012).

Anonymous (2010) *Global Consensus for Social Accountability of Medical Schools*. Online: http://healthsocialaccountability.sites.olt.ubc.ca/files/2011/01/GCSA-Consensus-Document-English.pdf (accessed 3 March 2012).

Armstrong, D. (2004) 'Time and space in the consultation: a history of the doctor–patient encounter in general practice'. *The Cardiff Lecture*. Online: http://www.cf.ac.uk/encap/research/hcrc/publications/index.html (accessed 2 June 2012).

Balint, M. (1957) *The Doctor, the Patient and their Illness,* London: Churchill Livingstone.

Barnett, R. (2010) *Being a University*, Abingdon: Routledge.

Berger, J. and Mohr, J. (1967) *A Fortunate Man*, New York: Vintage.

Berwick, D.M. (2008) 'A transatlantic review of the NHS at 60', *British Medical Journal*, 337: a838.

Black, C. (2004) 'Women docs "weakening" medicine', *BBC News*. Online: http://news.bbc.co.uk/1/hi/health/3527184.stm (accessed 17 June 2012).

Bleakley, A. and Bligh, J. (2006) 'Students learning from patients: let's get real in medical education', *Advances in Health Sciences Education*, 13, 1: 89–107.

Crane, J. (2011) 'Scrambling for Africa? Universities and global health', *The Lancet*, 377: 1113.

Curwen, M. (1964) 'Lord Moran's ladder', *Journal of the College of General Practitioners*, 7: 38–43.

Daly, M. ([1978] 1990) *Gyn/Ecology*, Boston: Beacon Press.

Fallowfield, L. (2005) 'Learning how to communicate in cancer settings', *Supportive Care in Cancer*, 13, 60: 340–50.

Flexner, A. (1910) *Medical Education in the United States and Canada: a Report to the Carnegie Foundation for the Advancement of Teaching*, New York: The Carnegie Foundation for the Advancement of Teaching.

Forward (2010) Female Genital Mutilation (FGM). Online: http://www.forwarduk.org.uk/key-issues/fgm (accessed 4 May 2012).

Foucault, M. (1984) *The Birth of the Clinic: An Archaeology of Medical Perception*, trans. A. Sheridan, London: Routledge.

Fox, N. and Ward, K. (2006) 'Health identities: from expert patient to resisting consumer', *Health* 10, 4: 461–79.

Frenk, J., Chen, L., Bhutta, Z., Cohen, J., Crisp, N., Evans, T., Fineberg, H., Garcia, P., Ke, Y., Kelley, P., Kistnasamy, B., Meleis, A., Naylor, D., Pablos-Mendez, A., Reddy, S., Scrimshaw, S., Sepulveda, J., Serwadda, D. and Zurayk, H. (2010) 'Health professionals for a new century: transforming education to strengthen health systems in an interdependent world', *The Lancet*, 376: 1923–58.

General Medical Council (GMC) (2009) *Tomorrow's Doctors*, London: General Medical Council.

Gothill, M. and Armstrong, D. (1999) 'Dr No-body', *Sociology of Health and Illness*, 21, 1: 1–12.

Guattari, F. (2000) *The Three Ecologies*, trans. I. Pindar and P. Sutton, London: Continuum.

Hafferty, F.W. (1998) 'Beyond curriculum reform: confronting medicine's hidden curriculum', *Academic Medicine*, 73: 403–7.

Haidet, P., Dains, J., Paterniti, D., Hechtel, L., Chang, T., Tseng, E., and Rogers, J. (2002) 'Medical student attitudes toward the doctor–patient relationship', *Medical Education*, 36, 6: 568–74.

Hart, J.T. (1971) 'The Inverse Care Law', *The Lancet*, 297: 405–12.

Heath, I. (2011) *Divided We Fail: The Harveian Oration*, London: Royal College of Physicans.

Howe, A. (2001) 'Patient-centred medicine through student-centred teaching: a student perspective on the key impacts of community-based learning in undergraduate medical education', *Medical Education*, 35: 666–72.

Kuptsch, C. (ed.) (2006) *Merchants of Labour*, Geneva: International Labour Office.

Lancet Editorial (2012) 'Global health in 2012: development to sustainability', *The Lancet*, 379: 9812.

Launer, J. (1996) '"You're the doctor, Doctor!": is social constructionism a helpful stance in general practice consultations?', *Journal of Family Therapy*, 18: 255–67.

Maughan, T.S., Finlay, I.G. and Webster, D.J. (2001) 'Portfolio learning with cancer patients: an integrated module in undergraduate medical education', *Clinical Oncology*, 13: 44–9.

May, C., Rapley, T., Moreira, T., Finch, T. and Heaven, B. (2006) 'Technogovernance: evidence, subjectivity, and the clinical encounter in primary care medicine', *Social Science and Medicine*, 62: 1022–30.

McCoy, D., Mwansambo, C., Costello, A. and Khan, A. (2008) 'Academic partnerships between rich and poor countries', *The Lancet*, 371: 1055–7.

Neighbour, R. (2004) *The Inner Consultation: How to Develop an Effective and Intuitive Consulting Style*, Milton Keynes: Radcliffe Medical Press.

Pang, T., Lansang, M. and Haines, A. (2002) 'Brain drain and health professionals', *British Medical Journal*, 324: 499–500.

Rogers, C. (1951) *Client Centered Therapy*, Boston: Houghton Miffin Company.

— (1969) *Freedom to Learn*, Columbus, OH: Charles E. Merrill Publishing Company.

Sabin, J. (1998) 'Fairness as a problem of love and the heart: a clinician's perspective on priority setting', *British Medical Journal*, 317: 1002–4.

Schön, D. (2001) 'The crisis of professional knowledge and the pursuit of an epistemology of practice', in J. Raven and J. Stephenson (eds) *Competence in the Learning Society*, New York: Peter Lang.

Sontag, S. (1978) *Illness As Metaphor*, New York: Farrar, Straus and Giroux.

Spence, J. (1960) *The Purpose and Practice of Medicine*, Oxford: Oxford University Press.

Starfield, B. (2011) 'Politics, primary healthcare and health: was Virchow right?' *Journal of Epidemiology Community Health*, 65: 653–65.

Starfield, B., Shi. L. and Macinko, J. (2005) 'Contribution of primary care to health systems and health', *Milbank Quarterly*, 83, 3: 457–502.

Stevens, R. (1966) *Medical Practice in Modern England*, New Haven, CT: Yale University Press.

Stewart, M., Brown, J., Weston, W., McWhinney, I., McWilliam, C. and Freeman, T. (1995) *Patient-Centered Medicine: Transforming the Clinical Method*, Thousand Oaks, CA: Sage.

Tuckett, D., Boulton, M., Olson, C. and Williams, A. (1985) *Meetings between Experts. An Approach to Sharing Ideas in Medical Consultations*, London: Tavistock Publications.

Valk, J., Rashid, A. and Elder, L. (2010) 'Using mobile phones to improve educational outcomes: an analysis of evidence from Asia', *The International Review of Research in Open and Distance Learning*. Online: http://www.irrodl.org/index.php/irrodl/article/view/794/1487 (accessed 2 June 2012).

WHO (2010) *Global Code of Practice on the International Recruitment of Health Personnel.* Online: http://www.who.int/hrh/resources/Code_implementation_strategy.pdf (accessed 17 June 2012).

Part V

Communal ecologies and architectures

Chapter 13

The social handprint

Decentring the politics of sustainability after an urban disaster[1]

Bronwyn Hayward

This chapter reflects on the ecological handprint, a metaphor for citizen agency which has emerged spontaneously in discourses of sustainability as various attempts are made to rally citizens to '*reduce* their ecological footprint and *increase* their handprint', that is to take action to restore degraded environments, reduce carbon emissions or address ecological and social injustice. This reflection is set in the immediate context of the 8,000 earthquakes and aftershocks which have devastated my home city of Christchurch New Zealand in the months since 4 September 2010. From within our urban disaster, I explore the possibilities for citizens to take action to re-imagine and recreate alternative futures. In discussion I draw on Arendt's concept of 'natality', Honig's vision of 'emergence', and Iris Young's ideas of 'decentering', to offer an alternative vision of a *social* handprint as the imprint of an embedded struggle for ecological citizenship and social justice.

Introduction: a 'shaky' start

I begin my discussion by acknowledging that I am currently standing on very shaky ground. Earthquakes are part of the childhood geography of New Zealanders; they form a shared physical backdrop of life lived on the interface between the Indian-Australian and Pacific plates. A major 7.1 magnitude earthquake struck Christchurch, the largest city of the South Island of New Zealand, in the early hours of the morning of 4 September 2010. The quake had a devastating impact on the buildings of the central city, particularly the Victorian stone and brick buildings of English settler heritage. Yet a combination of the timing of the disaster (4.35am when most people were home asleep) and earthquake building codes for residential homes, contributed to the absence of fatalities.

However a few months later on 22 February 2011, Rūaumoko, the Māori god of earthquakes, unleashed his terrible energy again in a series of shallow and therefore devastating aftershocks almost immediately below the city. Over 184 people were killed in that February event; the majority of fatalities occurred in downtown central city areas, and included significant numbers of women and international students working or studying in two office buildings now the subject of an official government inquiry. The New Zealand head of the Reserve Bank, Dr Alan Bollard, has described the impact of the Christchurch quake events as 'one of the biggest natural disasters in relative terms to befall an OECD country since World War II' (Bollard cited in Brett 2011).[2] In our state of shared grief and collective exhaustion, Christchurch residents learned the news a few weeks later of Japan's own devastating cascade of events.

In the months that followed the February 2011 quake, Christchurch has been wracked by further earthquakes, over 50 at magnitude 5 or more. For many communities each event brings more invasive mud or liquefaction into homes; heightens uncertainty of land and home tenure; increases fear for physical safety; and underscores a sense of loss of loved ones and loved places including public spaces – galleries, museums, schools – and loss of ease of getting around our city, as traffic snarls along redirected road routes. Re-establishing any community after a disaster is a daunting challenge, made

13.1
The earthquake impact in a central city area of Christchurch after February 2011.

more difficult not only because of the physical landscape (with much land prone to liquefaction) but because of our underlying economic and social vulnerability.

A political quake

Natural disasters have a way of exposing much more than geological fault lines. Whenever a disaster threatens a community it tests more than our physical infrastructure, it tears at the fabric of our cities, their social economies and their local democracies. How we respond to a disaster is affected by what has gone before, our relationships, our experiences, and even our cultural and spiritual norms and assumptions (Hayward 2011; Leichenko and O'Brien 2008). However with the grief of disasters comes opportunity for new insights. Amid the turmoil of the earth cracking, and the rubble of the stone buildings of central Christchurch (an English delusion we probably should never have built, but which we loved anyway), there have been some significant opportunities to rethink some basic principles.

To use novelist, Fiona Farrell's evocative phrase, Christchurch also faced a 'political quake', one which exposed the wider cracks in our democratic, social and urban landscape (Farrell 2011). The earthquakes struck Christchurch at a time of political, social and economic vulnerability. As a nation, New Zealand had experienced some of the most rapid growth of income inequality in the OECD in twenty years (Hayward 2012). The earthquakes also struck after two decades of town planning which had moved away from planning for the future, in favour of leaving the urban landscape to social and economic 'entrepreneurs'. It had become fashionable to restrict the role of elected councils to managing the negative impacts of the bright ideas of investors, and monitoring community outcomes, rather than detailed planning for our city. The earthquakes also struck a community with the most deregulated insurance industry in the world, and one which was fully exposed to a global trade economy, reliant on international exports, and international tourism.

These problems are not exclusive to Christchurch. Governments in all English-speaking nations have experienced both rising inequality, and a move away from long-term planning and regulation in the public interest toward market-led development of global cities, aimed at attracting and retaining globally mobile capital in an international market. The aftermath of the Christchurch earthquakes has forced us to confront the limits of the market as a tool for recreating a new collective vision for the future. Eighteen months after the quake, thousands of residents remain in inadequate, 'munted' (damaged) housing. While homeowners await the outcome of land-use zoning decisions, city and central government leaders are distracted by a '100-day plan' to rebuild the city centre to re-attract 'global entrepreneurs' and international investment in a shaky provincial economy (Oram 2012). As demand for social housing rises, so does the cost of rental accommodation. In the wake of our disaster, the invisible hand of the market appears unable to support community recovery.

Despite its faith in the market, the government's immediate response to the problems of rebuilding a city has been to impose a 'command and control' style of centralised decision-making in planning, retaining wide ranging decision-making powers under their auspices. Critics argue however that the government is failing to address the wider issues that confront Christchurch, including the difficulty of obtaining reinsurance, lack of transparency in land use decision-making, a shortage of warm, affordable housing, and the absence of a wider vision for medium- to long-term economic and social recovery (Oram 2012).

From footprints to handprints: rediscovering human agency

The experience of the earthquakes and our responses to the problems these quakes caused or exacerbated has coincided with a significant, complex shift in the imagery and language of sustainability politics from ecological footprints, to ecological handprints. A new language heralds a shift in policy emphasis from impact assessment (represented by ecological footprints), towards deregulated action, depicted in a plethora of handprint models – a metaphor for citizen agency which has emerged spontaneously in discourses of sustainability as various attempts are made to rally citizens to '*reduce* their ecological footprint and *increase* their handprint', that is to take primarily individual actions to restore degraded environments or reduce carbon emissions (Hayward 2010). Elsewhere I have discussed the wider political implications of ecological handprint metaphors at length (Hayward 2010, 2012, 2013). Here I want to briefly review the implications of this shift in policy language before recasting citizen agency as compassionate, collaborative and tentative social action in urban environments.

In 1996 Wackernagel and Rees published their ground-breaking Ecological Footprint model, a tool that graphically represented the physical space required for meeting the needs of a given population through manufacturing, distribution, consumption and waste (Wackernagel and Rees 1996: 51–2). The model sparked other ways of measuring human consumption and impact on the environment, including carbon footprints (Druckman and Jackson 2009; Wiedman and Minx 2007), or water foot-printing (Hoekstra and Chapagain 2007).

Handprint images have also emerged in environmental education programmes, in campaigns of social movements and in the green economy. Each appearance, implicitly or explicitly, suggests it is possible and morally imperative for individuals to take action to address environmental degradation. For example, the 'Your positive handprint campaign' aimed to 'commit 1 million people globally to look beyond reducing their carbon footprint, ... to take positive action ... to restore the great ecosystems around the planet; forests, oceans, freshwater, tundra, corals and the soils' (Restore the Earth 2009). The Catholic charity CAFOD organised a hands for climate change protest in 2009 (CAFOD 2009) while handprint metaphors are also used in discussion of the green economy. In the latter case for example, the company Carbon Handprint UK argues, 'Your carbon footprint is your effect on our planet, your handprint is what you do about it', from carbon offsetting Christmas shopping to developing pro-environmental technology (Carbon Handprint UK 2010).

As I have argued in other contexts, these handprint metaphors are ambivalent. On one 'hand' they represent an Aristotelian return to active citizenship (Hayward 2012, 2013). On the other 'hand' they can also reinforce unexamined notions of self-help citizenship in which disembodied individuals are urged to 'fix' environmental symptoms, in ways that often leave the underlying issues of justice and economic growth unchallenged. The use of the handprint metaphor also raises a variety of questions: Whose handprint is it? Under what conditions can we, and should we, use our hands to effect change? Who should and can act? Why and how?

The metaphor of the ecological handprint also underscores the current limitations of our thinking about human agency in neoliberal democ- racies. We can define citizen agency here as the capability of citizens to freely develop independent thoughts (will formation) and exercise autonomy (choosing to act or refrain from acting) (Barber 1984). In the Aristotelian vision wellbeing is achieved by participation, by doing or being (Barry 1999: 180–1). At one level the emerging ecological handprint models resonate with powerful symbolism of agency as citizen activism and resistance that has inspired environmental, civil rights and indigenous people's movements. As Barry notes, for example, this approach differs from the dominant ideas of human wellbeing expressed through consuming.

Yet, viewed in other lights, an emphasis on the value of individual agency seems less a reflection of active citizenship and resistance and more an extension of years of neoliberal emphasis on the centrality of the individual. Neoliberalism is used in a variety of ways, but here I refer to a policy project which aims to extend free-market values including values of efficiency, competition and choice to citizenship and the state (Larner 2000; Ong 2004). Neoliberalism has equated good citizenship with the individual citizen-entre- preneur, or citizen-consumer behaviour at the expense of social citizenship or engagement in collective decision-making about the common good (Dobson 2010a). Psychologist Albert Bandura illustrated the underlying limitations of consumer-citizenship, in particular when he argued:

As long as consumers' daily needs are met, they have little incentive to examine the humaneness of the working conditions, the level of pollution by the production processes, and the costs exacted on the environment to produce, ship, and market the profusion of goods and dispose of the wastes. Under these modernised conditions, lifestyle practices are disconnected in time and place from the very ecological systems that provide the basis for them.

(Bandura 2007: 14)

Bandura calls for citizens to reconnect lifestyle practice with the time and spatial consequences of their actions, a link he argues has been disconnected through globalisation and export economies which make it difficult for people to consider the indirect effects of their choices and everyday practices on countless distant others (Bandura 2007). Viewed in this light, can we begin to rethink handprint metaphors in a way to enable citizens to critically reflect on the potential and limits of our agency as the ability to make a difference 'for good' (Dobson 2003).

Yet even where citizens are highly motivated to effect change, the action of some individuals may be constrained or mediated by their context, including social institutions, norms, habits and the structures of the economy (Giddens 2009: Jackson 2009; Seyfang 2005). Despite their best efforts and intentions, citizens may find themselves wearing ill-fitting 'institutional shoes' that distort the size of their ecological footprint, or 'social gloves' that hamper their ability to effect change (Hayward 2013). Overwhelming urban disasters are a particularly obvious context for rethinking the potential of citizenship agency, away from individual action and toward action taken in collaboration with others. In the remainder of this chapter, I begin to rethink individual agency, offering the metaphor of the social handprint of citizens which is revealed in the struggles to rebuild Christchurch city in the wake of the earthquakes.

Natality of collective action: reflecting on the experience of a post-quake urban environment

Despite years of emphasis on individual agency under neoliberalism, many writers have noted that we do not always act with individualistic or selfish impulses; there are many times when citizens collaborate to effect change, particularly in response to large-scale disaster (Solnit 2009). What are some of those preconditions of citizenship that might enable us to exercise our capability for thoughtful, creative social agency, and to collaborate with compassion in the face of a collective challenge? When, as citizens, do we reach out to others with courage, or trust despite our fears? When do we act with hope as determination or with faith in an 'unrealised possibility' (Arendt 1958)? To begin to reflect on these questions I return to my experiences of the Christchurch earthquake.

In the immediate wake of the earthquakes a number of new, often youthful, leaders of the community emerged. In particular, university student Sam Johnston, and six others, organised 4,000 students to help volunteer to clean up the city in September 2010, via facebook. Building on what they learned in that experience, it took only a week after the February aftershocks before that small group of students were communicating with 24,000 people and co-ordinating 10,000 volunteers. The experience of the student volunteer 'army' inspired and energised a raft of similar spontaneous community projects in the wake of the earthquakes: baking armies, farming armies, community time banks, local gardening and landscaping projects, such as 'Greening the rubble' and street theatre, Gapfiller events, sprang up in the city (Brett 2011; Hayward 2012).

One of the first common features of these successful citizenship initiatives is that they built on existing organisations and networks, improving their communication and relationships within and between groups and across national boundaries (Hayward 2008). It wasn't just facebook and twitter that enabled this astonishing feat of political co-ordination and practical action. There was a raft of pre-existing relationships, friendship groups and community networks that enabled young citizens and many communities like them around Christchurch to co-ordinate to act in new ways (Brett 2011).

However Arendt (1958) also reminds us that while taking action is important, so too is taking time to pause and engage in dialogue before acting

13.2
Christchurch students volunteer to help clean up the city post-quake.

(Elliot 2009). Making room for dialogue and listening seems a prudent strategy if we wish to develop an idea of 'determinative morality', or a vision of what we ought to do, not just what we ought not to do (Dobson 2003). Making space for reflection before launching into action particularly matters in the urban context given the reach and grasp of some citizens. Aided by global communication, strengthened by financial investment and international infrastructure, the capability of some to define the problem, identify solutions and leave indelible handprints on the futures and pasts of distant others is inestimable and undesirable. In the wake of the quakes, many communities have enjoyed participating in large community action, but at the same time, expressed frustration at government's or powerful agents' attempts to impose solutions and plans, bulldoze iconic buildings and marginalise the values of the less powerful, women, minorities or indigenous communities (Hayward 2011).

In this light, and given the limits of our understanding, I suggest that in exercising our agency, perhaps our aim should be, not to always increase our handprint, but to ensure we act in ways that are reversible and humble, and our actions should be taken with the consent of those affected (Hayward 2012; Freeden 2009). Luce Irigaray puts this problem another way when she argues:

> Freedom must, at every moment, limit its expansion in order to respect other existing beings and, even more, to find ways of forming with them a world always in becoming where it is possible for each human or non-human living being to 'exist-or ex-ist'.
>
> (Irigaray 2008: xx)

Decentring political vision of a *social* handprint as the imprint of an embedded struggle for justice

Community struggles are often most animated by local experiences of injustice. Yet the danger of narrowing our vision and discussion of citizen agency to local action is that our enriched local conversations risk wider policy irrelevance and isolated conversations may simply continue local injustice as a result of insufficient scrutiny (Hayward 2008; Young 2006). Moreover, to think about human agency as the imprint of citizen action left at one local place, in one time, also overlooks the potential for citizens to connect empathetically with others across time and space. In this light individual handprint metaphors may also inhibit emerging understanding of citizenship as dependency rather than autonomy. Visualising our citizen agency through a handprint equates citizenship with individual autonomous action and overlooks the opportunity to think about citizenship as a quality of human connectedness, 'holding hands' in our mutual dependency and vulnerability with others to effect change.

Handprints are also often associated with incriminating evidence at the scene of a crime. Viewed in this light, centred approach to citizenship is also unhelpful where it encourages us to restrict our ideas of agency to focus on blaming others when things go wrong, that is to play ecological detective, identifying 'whodunnit' in environmental crimes (Hayward 2012, 2013). Accountability in decision-making is important, but centring blame for environmental and political problems shifts our focus away from the wider structural causes of ecological and social injustice (Young 2006). A centred symbol of a handprint, focused on understanding change in one place and one point in time, can leave systemic power unchallenged, especially where we narrow our ideas of agency and responsibility and ignore the wider responsibilities of others who benefit from a chain of human suffering and our ability to take action collectively to address systemic injustice (Dobson 2007: 174–5; Barry 1999).

In a thoughtful reflection on ecological citizenship, philosopher Andrew Dobson begins to recast citizenship as justice actions which are other oriented. He suggests that citizens should pursue ecological justice through actions that are other regarding but asymmetrical. By this he means we should not take action to address environmental degradation or human suffering in expectation that others will reciprocate, but because we think it's the right thing to do, 'I will even if you won't' (Dobson 2010b: 22–3). Yet acting in haste, without mechanisms to ensure our agency is thoughtful or consented to by others, can exacerbate injustice, as our experiences in Christchurch have shown.

Emergency and democratic 'emergence'

Rousseau reminded us two centuries ago that we should always be wary of those advocating significant reform in a crisis – however the New Zealand government did just that. In the aftermath of the urban emergency of Christchurch, the government passed the Canterbury Earthquake Recovery Act (CERA) 2011. This Act, and the calling of a National State of Emergency following the quake, was vital to securing national resources to help support the city in the immediate response to a full-scale disaster. Quickly however, the wide-ranging powers of the CERA legislation began to stand in the way of renewing local democratic leadership and supporting long-term community recovery.

The need to change our city management practices was evident to all. Witnessing the local city government's slow, bitterly divisive and confused attempts to respond to the earthquakes no one could be under the illusion that Christchurch's local councillors had performed well and disquiet was widely aired in local media. However, the CERA Act removed the powers of the local council, replacing an elected local council with a centralised model of recovery. The Minister responsible for CERA has been awarded far-reaching decision power, with few opportunities for national, let alone local scrutiny. The effect has been very disempowering for local residents. Despite the widespread surge of public energy and outpouring of compassionate, collaborative action, the more dominant government response has been a shock doctrine-style imposition of authoritarian decision-making (Klein 2007).

A wider climate of social inequality has also fuelled local frustration and exacerbated confusion about whose interests are being given priority in planning by CERA. As I write, the focus of government attention has largely remained on rebuilding the city centre, while thousands of homes waited uncertain futures, and the community struggles to recover from stress and hardship: a reported doubling in rates of domestic abuse, a shortage of housing and a 26 per cent increase in costs of rental accommodation are just three examples of wider social and economic stress on families. The gendered nature of the impact (with estimates of 70 per cent initial job losses being female) have rarely been discussed (MOWA 2012). The Minister of Local Government has also mooted plans to revise the Local Government Act in ways that may further limit the powers of local government on the grounds of reducing rates, and amalgamating local authorities to improve efficiency.

It has been difficult for anyone to exercise effective, ongoing civic leadership in a dynamic environment of aftershocks and confused economic planning arrangements, determined largely by the presence or absence of reinsurance funding. When faced with the frustration of poorly performing local politicians, a plethora of insurance agencies and a new, centralised government bureaucracy, it is easy to imagine that somehow appointing a team of highly paid expert managers might fix things. Yet our experience of a struggle to recover our community reminds us that good democracy delivers great economic and social prosperity by enabling scrutiny, transparency and local voices.

Before the earthquakes, the wider Christchurch hinterland of Canterbury was already facing some very tough planning decisions about how we manage our water and how we establish education and economic opportunities to support a new generation. These problems have not gone away; in many ways their resolution has become more acute. But the community also faces new problems. The impact of the quakes exacerbate an exodus of young citizens, particularly to Australia where wages are significantly higher (Gorman 2012). Many of those who remain are older people and those of limited economic means, many of whom are already struggling, facing a difficult second winter post-earthquake. The loss of many significant business offices foreshadows the challenge of rebuilding a new kind of local economy, one that is perhaps less reliant on international capital, yet still provides employment, public services and long-term social wellbeing. Not all of our young people can be builders, road engineers, painters or architects. To create meaningful long-term, local employment and training will require thoughtful, ongoing and public debate about new forms of social and ecological investment in a more sustainable economy (Jackson 2009).

Engaged listening, transparent debate and locally mandated leadership are vital to effective community recovery, but are remarkably absent in the months that have followed the earthquake. In a moment of hope in the aftermath of the February 2011 earthquakes, large numbers of citizens engaged in a rushed consultation plan led by the local council for the city rebuild, called 'share an idea', with thousands 'sharing their ideas' for a greener, more sustainable, city. However once the local plans were lodged with central government, disquiet immediately emerged as the plan to rebuild a lower level city appeared to raise the spectre of significant costs to landowners in the form of loss of insurance claims, and the government stepped in to take control of the planning process announcing a 100-day city rebuild which risks simply sweeping away much of the vision of a community of low-rise buildings, and a mix of green space and affordable homes.

Both Hannah Arendt and Bonnie Honig have portrayed the possibilities of alternative human action as uncertain and unknowable. In living through a grim period of uncertainty and civic tension I find Arendt's and Honig's validation of the importance of imaginative action, and the daily refounding of democracy, refreshing and inspiring. One difficulty with the way urban problems post-quake are framed is that they are characterised as ongoing emergencies, which require us to limit our opportunity for reflective democratic action and informed public decision-making (Honig 2009). Central government politicians for example have not released the details of land-use decisions which have evicted some residents from land deemed unsafe for occupation, but the grounds for these decisions are not open to scrutiny.

Honig's challenge is to remind us that we recreate our democracy in our daily actions. While we imagine our world views rest on ideas about rational unitary beginnings or places, in reality we take daily democratic actions and begin deliberation again from an indefinable place in time. She reminds us that it is 'what happens next' that legitimates subsequent action or decisions (Honig 2009). Irigaray also appears to intimate this when she argues that to begin to meet others you need to know the place you have started from (Irigaray 2008). In the situation of Christchurch city, as communities are being evicted in large-scale clearances of land, especially in low-income areas, many are beginning to express concern that their stories, and their rights to know the basis of the authority's decision-making, are being swept aside in attempts to create a fresh new beginning for a city, rather than continue a story of community located in places where people already live and have strong social networks (Coleman 2012).

The 'emergence' of democracy in new urban environments

Initially, in the months that followed the earthquake, I was frequently struck by the similarities of austerity-ravaged Europe and Christchurch, a city stripped to its barest services, a bleak landscape punctuated only by shopping malls and basic services. The planning impacts on a community ravaged by geological upheaval can be surprisingly similar to the effects of budget cuts imposed on communities in Europe in the wake of a financial economic crisis. In an environment of financial constraint it is not easy for any government to argue for more local services to enhance public life, particularly in the wake of a disaster, with limited finances. While most would agree that public bus services, parks, children's museums, libraries and small outdoor community pools are a good thing, they are highly vulnerable in difficult financial times.

However, public spaces and activities and services contribute significantly to community wellbeing (Sandel 2009). Yet finding ways to restore and maintain the public spaces and facilities that add much to quality of life of a comparatively low-income city is one of many questions that will be a real challenge for Christchurch. The situation has not been helped by city councillors, when they fail to make consistent decisions or open meetings to greater public scrutiny or where blueprint plans for the new city push local crafts and activities which have sprung up in new sites out of particular areas to make space for large commercial investment. Local media debate has questioned why commercial sensitivity is often used as an excuse for closed door council discussion. However despite these setbacks there are many small examples of community initiated co-operation to reclaim public space including a new civic trust, Life in Vacant Spaces, which teams up willing landowners with local artists, crafts people, food markets and gardeners to create temporary events and projects on empty properties.

These experiences in the aftermath of the Christchurch quakes underscore the value of citizen action at multiple levels to help ensure our proposed solutions are not simply displacing or obfuscating the problems. Moreover, effective citizen agency is rarely autonomous – as a result the Christchurch experience also underscores the limitations of the lone handprint image as a metaphor for citizen agency. In reality the most effective human agency is supported by interactions with others at multiple levels, not simply the impact of one person's efforts, no matter how heroic. Arendt decentres human agency and action, shifting the focus from the individual to the collective, when she reminds us that political action is action which is taken in concert with others (Arendt 1958: 189). Similarly, democratic theorist Iris Young, resists centred approaches to politics, arguing that while we attempt to give voice to the local community at one point in time and in one place, we risk overlooking the way power is increasingly concentrated globally, so that resistance needs to be decentred and targeted at all levels to be effective (Young 2006; Hayward 2008). While it is often at the level of the local that we come to know and experience our community, and want to make a difference, the challenge is to find ways to connect our local struggles at many levels, in ways which enable local communities to challenge regional and global power inequalities which limit or dominate their life experiences.

Honig helps us to decentre local citizen action by presenting an agonistic as well as a decentred view of politics, celebrating struggle as collective action taken in concert everywhere as a way to empower popular sovereignty. Like Young, Honig also suggests we should resist a focus in politics which privileges deliberation as rational argument and in the process to cede decision-making authority to external institutions who exercise external scrutiny of these deliberative processes (Honig 2009). She argues instead that we need to retain our focus on local communities and their struggles and at the same time decentre our thinking across space and time. The issues that matter are not only how we act and what we say in one community, at one point in time or in one place, but how our actions affect others, and how we might feel later over time.

Decentring struggle as well as dialogue enables us to take the long view, to better understand 'the struggle without end', as Māori author and legal scholar Ranganui Walker describes it (Walker 2004). In facing difficult challenges and thinking about how we will feel about the actions we take today, when we reflect on them over time, Honig argues we can deepen our human experience in very difficult situations. To extend Honig's argument, the imprint that matters may not be the social handprint on the urban environment, but the way those difficult experiences and environments change us. Similarly Pogge (2002) argues that the efficacy of our actions and our interactions with others need to be judged across space and time – often the impact can only be fully understood well beyond our lifetime, and in light of what went before, and what those who come after us do.

The views of decentring citizen agency as a social handprint I offer here are only suggestive. But scholars working on decentring citizenship remind us that it is when we interact and collaborate with others that extraordinary, new possibilities are created. One of the most powerful expressions of new possibilities of decentred human agency and connection has been articulated over many years by Vandana Shiva. Shiva, like Irigaray, calls for understanding the potential for human action as connection at multiple levels, and as action that is not presented as mastery or ownership but as connections of compassion and struggle. Shiva says the human agency that really matters is 'what we do in between' (Shiva 2005: 11) major events. This idea of seeing what we do, where we are women acting in-between major events, is picked up again and again by feminist philosophers and reflects the ongoing centuries of struggle below the surface of dominant politics to achieve new voice and new forms of agency.

Honig, Arendt and Young each suggest we could begin to see how our actions can be connected and ways we are mutually dependent as citizens in our daily life, including our suffering. Their discussion underscores the limits of a handprint as a metaphor for human agency – it implicitly reduces human agency to actions by an individual at a point in time. However, perhaps ultimately we also need some model other than a handprint to symbolise social struggle and resistance against illegitimate power, and creative collaborations to effect desired change. In sympathy with the latter project, and to extend it, I have drawn on Iris Young's ideas of 'decentring', which resonates with Arendt's concept of 'natality', and Honig's vision of 'emergence', to offer an alternative vision of citizen agency as embedded social struggle, holding hands in a vision of citizenship where we might draw strength from our mutual vulnerability and dependency acting in solidarity over space and time.

Conclusion: social handprints or holding hands?

In this chapter I have welcomed the return to Aristotelian concepts of active citizenship in the face of environmental change, symbolised in the emergence of social handprint thinking. However, I argue our agency should not be measured as individual actions, taken at one place and time, but should be thought of as 'decentred', collective efforts across time and space, taken with others and with consent. Implicitly, the ideas of Iris Young, Hannah Arendt and Bonnie Honig enable us to move beyond the traditional green mantra of 'thinking global, acting local' by suggesting effective agency in the face of global environmental change should also be global and regional, but taken in ways that are tentative, mindful of the limits of our knowledge and informed by local consent.

The alternative model of social handprints I sketch here is normative and partial. I offer an alternative vision of a *social* handprint as collective action, and 'decentred' resistance across generations, emphasising the time and space to imagine and create new or alternative futures. This contrasts with the dominant neoliberal interpretation of agency as disembodied individual and autonomous action. I suggest an emerging gendered perspective of social agency as shared imagining, care and collective action to effect change in ways that support human flourishing.

I suggest that handprints can be a valuable way of considering human agency, but our priority should be to make our handprints smaller and lighter. In limiting the heroism of our actions, I am not calling for a loss of courage to act. Rather, I have also argued that as we connect with others to enlarge our field of compassion, our concept of agency is enlarged and enriched by visions of holding hands to challenge injustice – with humility as well as courage, accepting we may not always know what is best to do in the face of global dangerous environmental change and the development of liveable human-scaled urban space.

Notes

1 Earlier or extended versions of this chapter have been presented at *Sexuate Subjects: Politics, Poetics and Ethics*, UCL, 2010, and in Hayward 2010, 2012 and (forthcoming) 2013. I am grateful to RESOLVE, University of Surrey and Earthscan/Routlege for permission to cite these works.
2 OECD stands for Organisation for Economic Co-operation and Development.

Bibliography

Arendt, H. ([1958] 1998) *The Human Condition*, 2nd edn, London: University of Chicago Press.

Bandura, A. (2007) 'Impeding ecological sustainability through selective moral disengagement', *International Journal of Innovation and Sustainable Development*, 2, 1: 8–35.

Barber, B. (1984) *Strong Democracy: Participatory Politics for a New Age*, Berkeley: University of California Press.

Barry. J. (1999) *Rethinking Green Politics: Nature, Virtue and Progress*, London: Sage.

Brett, C. (2011) 'Christchurch 3 months on'. *The Press*, 22 May. Online: http://www.stuff.co.nz/national/christchurch-earthquake/5037194/Christchurch-three-months-on (accessed 13 December 2011).

CAFOD (2009) 'Our climate is in our hands: Just one world'. Online: http://www.cafod.org.uk/news/uk-news/greenbelt-2009-04-09 (accessed 20 November 2010).

Carbon Handprint UK (2010) 'Your carbon footprint is your effect on our planet. Your handprint is what you do about it'. Online: http://www.carbonhandprint.co.uk/ (accessed 20 November 2010).

Coleman, M. (2012) 'The new land wars', *The Christchurch Press*, 10 June. Online: http://www.stuff.co.nz/the-press/opinion/7074743/The-new-New-Zealand-land-wars (accessed 10 June 2012).

Dobson, A. (2003) *Citizenship and the Environment*, Oxford: Oxford University Press.

— (2007) *Green Political Thought*, London: Routledge.

— (2010a) 'Democracy and nature: speaking and listening', *Political Studies*, 58, 4: 752–68.

— (2010b) *Environmental Citizenship and Pro-Environmental Behaviour: Rapid Research and Evidence Review*, London: Sustainable Development Research Network.

Druckman, A. and Jackson, T. (2009) 'The carbon footprint of UK households 1990–2004: a socio-economically disaggregated, quasi-multiregional input-output model', *Ecological Economics*, 68, 7: 2066–77.

Elliot, J. (2009) 'Building educational theory through action research', in S. Noffke and B. Somekh (eds) *The SAGE Handbook of Educational Action Research*, London: Sage.

Farrell, F. (2011) 'Free market turns citizens into assets', *The Press*, 28 July. Online: http://www.stuff.co.nz/the-press/opinion/perspective/5351237/Free-market-quake-turns-citizens-into-assets#comments (accessed 4 June 2012).

Freeden, M. (2009) 'Failures of political thinking', *Political Studies*, 57, 1: 141–64.

Giddens, A. (2009) *The Politics of Climate Change*, Cambridge: Polity.

Gorman, P. (2012) 'Survey picks exodus', *The Christchurch Press*, 1 June. Online: http://www.stuff.co.nz/national/christchurch-earthquake/7026937/Survey-picks-quake-exodus (accessed 4 June 2012).

Hayward, B. (2008) 'Let's talk about the weather: decentring democratic debate about climate change', *Hypatia*, 23, 3: 79–98.

— (2010) 'Decentring sustainability and the new consumer politics of UK Uncut', *RESOLVE Working Paper Series* 06-10, Guildford: University of Surrey.

— (2011) 'Addressing dangerous climate change: why citizenship matters more than behaviour change', in J. Lawrence, A. Cornforth and P. Barrett (eds) *Climate Futures: Pathways For Society*, Wellington: Victoria University.

— (2012) *Children, Citizenship and Environment: Nurturing a Democratic Imagination in a Changing World*, London: Earthscan/Routledge.

— (2013, forthcoming) 'The Social Handprint: towards and new politics of sustainability', in K. O'Brien, J. Wolf and L. Sygna (eds) *A Changing Environment for Human Security: New Agendas for Research, Policy and Action*, London: Earthscan/Routledge.

Hoekstra, A. and Chapagain, A. (2007) 'Water footprint of nations: water use by people as a function of their consumption pattern', *Water Resource Management*, 21: 35–48.

Honig, B. (2009) *Emergency Politics: Paradox, Law and Democracy*, Princeton, NJ: Princeton University Press.

Irigaray, L. (2008) *Sharing the World: From Intimate to Global Relations*, New York: Continuum Books.

Jackson, T. (2009) *Prosperity without Growth: Economics for a Finite Planet*, London: Earthscan.

Klein, N. (2007) *Shock Doctrine: The Rise of Disaster Capitalism*, New York: Picador.

Larner, W. (2000) 'Neoliberalism: policy, ideology, governmentality', *Studies in Political Economy*, 63: 5–25.

Leichenko, R. and O'Brien, K. (2008) *Environmental Change and Globalization: Double Exposure*, Oxford: Oxford University Press.

MOWA (2012) *Ministry of Women's Affairs Panui June–July*, Online: http://www.mwa.govt.nz/news-and-pubs/publications/panui/panui-june-july-2012#Updateon (accessed 10 August 2012).

Ong, A. (2004) *Neoliberalism as Exception: Mutations in Citizenship and Sovereignty*, Durham, NC: Duke University Press.

Oram, R. (2012) 'The right game for Christchurch to play', *Sunday Star Times*, 5 August. Online: http://www.facebook.com/notes/kiwiki/the-right-game-for-christchurch-to-play/10150975599036709 (accessed 10 August 2012).

Pogge, T. (2002) *World Poverty and Human Rights*, Cambridge: Polity Press.

Restore the Earth (2009) Online: http://www.restore-earth.org/ (accessed 20 November 2010).

Sandel, M. (2009) *Justice: What's the Right Thing to Do?* New York: Farrar, Straus and Giroux.

Seyfang, G. (2005) 'Shopping for sustainability: can sustainable consumption promote ecological citizenship?' *Environmental Politics*, 14, 2: 290–306.

Shiva, V. (2005) *Earth Democracy: Justice, Sustainability and Peace*, London: Zed Books.

Solnit, R. (2009) *Paradise Built in Hell: the Extraordinary Communities that Arise in Disaster*, New York: Viking.

Wackernagel, M. and Rees, W. (1996) *Our Ecological Footprint*, Gabriola Island, Canada: New Society Press.

Walker, R. (2004) *Ka Whawhai Tonu Matou: Struggle without End*, Auckland: Penguin Books.

Wiedmann, T. and Minx, J. (2007) 'A definition of "carbon footprint"', in C. Pertsova (ed.) *Ecological Economics: Research Trends*, Hauppauge NY: Nova Science Publishers.

Young, I. (2006) 'Too much blame, not enough responsibility', *Dissent Magazine* (Winter). Online: http://www.dissentmagazine.org/article/?article=158 (accessed 15 March 2009).

Chapter 14

Movement and stasis

Shifting subjectivities on the Mongolian border

Rebecca Empson

A few years ago I started the project of digitising my slides. Sometimes, an unexpected image emerged; when two pieces of film were caught in the machine, they recorded as a single picture. I start this chapter with one such image made from two photographs. In the first, children can be seen standing inside a house by a bed. In the second, the room is empty. Together, this layered image provides a starting point to explore the idea that in the households that I describe there is a prevailing sense that people are always present, even in their physical absence. Here, traces from different times and places live alongside people's physical presence in a variety of different forms.

Since 1999 I have carried out fieldwork among herding households along the Northeast Mongolian–Russian border. These people are composed of an ethnic minority called the Buriad. Their descendants migrated from Siberia to Mongolia in the early 1900s, fleeing war and disruption in their homeland at the advent of the Revolution. They now live as herders and hunters in subsistence-based household units, moving pasture up to four times a year. The way in which these people live is not to be viewed as archaic and somehow out of time. Yes, they source materials for their homes locally and live off their animals and produce from the surrounding forests. Their landscape is animated with various kinds of spiritual being whom they make offerings to, and shamans play a dominant role in bringing the past to life. But the turns of history have been crucial for shaping how these people are living.

While the Mongolian–Russian border might seem like a remote location, these people are not living on the periphery of central power. In many ways this area has been a site for the shattering and remaking of political

ideologies. People here are engaged in a dynamic process of making and remaking themselves in relation to national and global connections. They, like people everywhere, are subjects shaped by the politics of individual states and unions, and of people and communities. While seventy years of socialist rule in Mongolia structured people's lives in very particular ways, in the early 1990s the socialist state appeared to collapse almost over night, and the institutions and technologies that held its subjects in place seemed to disappear. In response, many local veterinarians, doctors, school teachers, accountants, and so on, turned to nomadic herding as a form of subsistence and outright survival. Their pastoral economies also rely on income and recourses from multiple kinds of activity which bind them to a web of obligations with friends and kin who live elsewhere. It is important to keep in mind that what we see in the following is an outcome of these various political and historical processes.

This border zone is comprised of lush open steppe with large rivers that rush noisily through the landscape and deep forests that reach up to craggy mountain peaks. Before the Buriad's arrival in the early 1900s the area was sparsely populated. Unlike the dominant nationality in Mongolia (called the Halh

Mongols), the Buriad have never had a state or country of their own. Instead, they may be viewed as a diaspora who inhabit areas that have been designated to them by the Mongolian, Chinese, or Russian states. The area that they currently inhabit is, quite literally, on the geopolitical border between Russia and Mongolia. This border also encompasses a topographical shift. It marks a transition from the dense central Eurasian taiga forest to the north, to the vast flat open steppe to the south that characterizes much of Mongolia. Living here, these people balance midway between two topological and political territories.

Throughout much of the twentieth century the Buriad have lived on the threshold of a violent state. They were forced to lower their heads to the country of Mongolia throughout much of the socialist period. This 'interstitial' position is reminiscent of the Buriad's uncertain relationship to the landscape. Separated from their homeland in Siberia, the history of the land in which they currently reside belongs to someone else's past, to a past over which they have little control and which sometimes appears out of nowhere to make certain claims on those who live here. While the landscape may look sparsely populated, underneath its surface are clustered areas of vast mineral resources, archaeological traces of previous settlements, burial chambers and forts. These hold memories of previous settlements and people. There are also the non-physical traces of past battles, executions, destruction of monasteries and relics. These activate certain locales in the landscape and bring a haunting sense of historical time to places that manifest themselves through their shamans. Who is able to successfully lay claim to these different resources and memories is sometimes a matter of contention and conflict.

A ubiquitous feature of this landscape is the cairn, or *ovoo* (meaning, simply, heap), situated on a mountain or hilltop, or on a rise with an auspicious configuration. The cairn's presence can be said to make the landscape into an inhabited territory or place. In the pre-socialist period, these features served to demarcate political borders. In the socialist period, they became a means to navigate passages, routes, and journeys according to movements between fixed sites. Cairns are often made of eclectic elements and offerings, such as stones, willow branches, batteries, sweet wrappers, prayer flags, blue ceremonial scarves, incense bowls, dried curds, pictures of Buddhist deities, monetary notes, biscuits, horse skulls, smashed or empty vodka bottles, and so on. These are gathered in the shape of a conical pile to form an assemblage or site made up of multiple people's offerings and can often be seen from a great distance. When focusing on each object in its singularity, they appear to contain the concentrated effort of innumerable journeys, but the structure as a whole provides a unity of form. It is a gathering point. The sum of innumerable objects, the cairn stands as a single feature.

For those who live in the vicinity of a cairn, it is a physical marker of their connection to the land in which they live. Daily milk libations are offered in the direction of these sites to different deities, such as the 'land masters' (*gazryn ezed*) and 'spirits' (*lus savdag*) who control the rains, or to 'shamanic ancestral spirits' (*ongon*) (Atwood 2004: 414). Some sites are the subject of large collective ceremonies or sacrifices (*tahilga*, lit to make an offering or sacrifice) where people gather annually, in the early summer, to ensure seasonal rainfall and fertile livestock. Worship at such cairns takes different forms according to the location of the cairn and the type of deities attended to. Some attract worship by men, others by local families or individuals, and some are places for the whole community.

While cairns remain in fixed locations and different people gather to them, houses move over the landscape throughout the year and the people attached to them remain the same. In the countryside, both single-roomed wooden cabins (*baishin*) and Mongolian felt tents (*ger*) are prevalent. Throughout the year people interchange kinds of residence. For example, a family may live in a wooden house at their summer pasture, but occupy a felt tent at their winter, spring, and autumn pastures, and both kinds of structure can move over the landscape. Indeed, parts of the wooden house, such as the door, the planks that

make up the roof, and the glass windowpanes, are physically removed and used to inhabit the shells of other houses at different seasonal locations.

It is not just the physical shell of a house that travels to different places. The people who inhabit a house also change seasonally. Throughout the year, people move from a house to different locations with different networks of people, in order to attend school, work, hunt, marry, or engage in seasonal work in towns and cities. While summer encampments gather together extended family members, winter encampments are often only inhabited by a few. During the autumn and spring, children attend school in district centres and younger family members may move away from the household to engage in temporary work, trade, or hunting. The point I wish to stress here is that throughout the

year different forms of sociality are enacted in different places as people move to different locations, activating different types of relation as they live with different people, while still being tied to a single household.

When fixed in a particular space, the house (be it a wooden house or a felt tent) becomes a container for storing valued possessions, meeting with visitors, sleeping, and eating, and for times when one needs to sit for long periods or to escape the extreme weather outside. From this perspective, the interior of the house appears in opposition to the movement that goes on outside it. As one-roomed, open-plan spaces, there are no direct personal areas inside these houses. Instead gender, hierarchy, and status define the interior. For example, the area from the door (which faces south) to the fireplace, in the centre, is the area assigned for juniors or people of low status. The area at the back (to the north), behind the fireplace, is the honorific section reserved for elders and for people and objects that are held in high regard. The spatial layout of the house is further divided by the male side of the house (to the west), from the left of the door towards the honorific section at the back, and the female side of the house which extends from the door, along the right-hand side (to the east), towards the rear of the house (Humphrey 1974). While people do move about the interior, they sit, eat, and sleep in their correct places. This demarcation of interior space allows for the incorporation of different configurations of people at any given moment. For example, a young female guest will know exactly where in the house to sit when she enters an unfamiliar house, or an elderly man will know where he may lie down for a rest after herding his horses.

During the socialist period in Mongolia (approximately 1924–90), Buddhist icons and shamanic implements were prohibited, but statues of Lenin and posters depicting, for example, strong industrious co-operative workers or joyful rosy-cheeked pioneers were encouraged and openly displayed. In the 1930s, however, officials from the Internal Ministry, locally referred to as the 'green caps', raided these families' household chests, confiscating valued possessions and burning their genealogical records and portraits going back seven or eight generations. Most of the male members of this community were brutally seized during this time by the secret police. A few were sent to labour camps but most were executed and accused of being counterrevolutionaries or Japanese spies. Differences, especially of an ethnic or class kind, were thought of as politically polluting and people were forced to use their father's name as a surname instead of their clan name, thereby limiting knowledge of a familial history to a single generation. Casting familial knowledge in new ways was one method by which the state could ensure that the Buriad ceased to use their own means of constructing the past as a working part of their present identity. Another way of breaking up familial networks was through the collectivization of private property in the 1950s and '60s. Here wealth was handed over to the state and only a small portion of animals could be owned for daily needs. People were placed in jobs located at a great distance from their relatives and could not easily visit family in other Provinces, let alone their relatives in Siberia. Given this destructive past it is no surprise that the Buriad have a vested interest in recalling family members and friends in spite of their physical absence.

* * *

People may be said to make aspects of themselves present in houses through the containment or display of different objects. These can be found in various displays across Mongolia, but my suggestion is that their presence has a particularly important role in addressing issues to do with forced and voluntary forms of separation for the Buriad. In the honoured rear section opposite the door as one enters a house, there often stands a painted wooden chest. This chest may be covered in embroideries or painted with interlocking patterns and never-ending knots. The chest forms part of a woman's dowry which, along with a mirror, beds, cooking utensils, and some animals, she takes with her when she moves to her in-law's and sets up a household with her husband. On receiving such a chest, a woman may find that it contains sheets, blankets, coats, and a sewing machine that she will be able to use throughout her life. Indeed, part of the marriage ceremony involves the bride's mother opening the chest and

making her daughter's bed with the sheets contained inside. But, while the chest contains some items at marriage, it should be able to carry much more as women gather things which they display on the chest's surface and store in its interior for their families.

Visible prized possessions that indicate wealth and prestige are often deliberately displayed on the chest's surface. These include objects such as radios, clocks, batteries, lipsticks, and perfume. Such objects are given as gifts at marriage, during New Year celebrations, or when people visit from the city and neighbouring districts. Displaying these items on the chest's surface is to invite people to comment, touch, and look at them. Behind these items, stands a large triptych mirror. On either side of the mirror, or attached to the wall above, are large frames containing a montage of three-quarter-length, portrait-style photographs (*jaaztai zurag*) of kin members on both the mother's and father's side. This montage creates a pile, or layering, of different images over time, as old photographs are concealed behind new ones. Above the mirror, religious icons and images can be found that comprise a small shrine on which religious books, consecrated images of animals, daily offerings of milk placed in small copper offering bowls, and the fortune vessel (or bag) are placed. Above this shrine, on the wall behind the chest, hang large painted portraits of deceased relatives (*jaaztai taliigaachiin hörög*), shrouded in ceremonial silk scarves (*hadag*). Like the cairns located on hilltops, this display forms a site that assembles different objects into a single form.

Young daughters-in-law and elderly female household members are in charge of maintaining this very visual display. They feed it with milk offerings, light candles and incense at the base of certain images, and attend to and change its form as they resurrect it in different seasonal places. In turn, visitors respond to it by looking at the display and commenting on some aspect of it. In doing so, they pay respect to their host by honouring the fact that they are part of a network of people who respect their elders and the land masters of particular localities (the term 'land masters' refers to the invisible spiritual 'owners', 'masters', or 'stewards' of the land). In addition, because the mirror is at the centre, when attending to or viewing this display a person may catch a glimpse of themselves at the centre of these relations.

Some time between the 1950s and 1960s, when photographs became more widely available, people began to embrace this medium and displayed images in the form of montages on the chest's surface. Having left behind their homeland in the 1900s, and losing so many of their relatives in the 1930s and '40s, for the Buriad, this technology was of particular importance. With images of family members placed next to each other, the montage provides a way for people to publically display a sense of temporal depth to their lives and a means by which they can build a narrative of themselves as embedded in relations with others, outside of those determined by technology of the socialist state.[1]

The montage element of this display is not arbitrary. It allows for different kinds of people such as school friends, grandparents, co-operative workers to be brought together in a single site. It also allows for flexibility over time. It is common for a single household to display very different images at different seasonal places, thereby displaying different subjectivities in different locations. In this sense, the montage is a flexible and changing site through which people craft very particular images of themselves for others. The images publicly display the shifting connections, alliances, and social networks available to the people of a household. For those who live under the gaze of the montage, however, the images trigger individual memories and remind one of obligations. In this sense, the photographs can be said to provide a 'pseudo-presence' of people in their absence (Sontag 1979).

There are other objects inside the house which also come to act as agents for people in their physical absence. Objects such as embroideries,

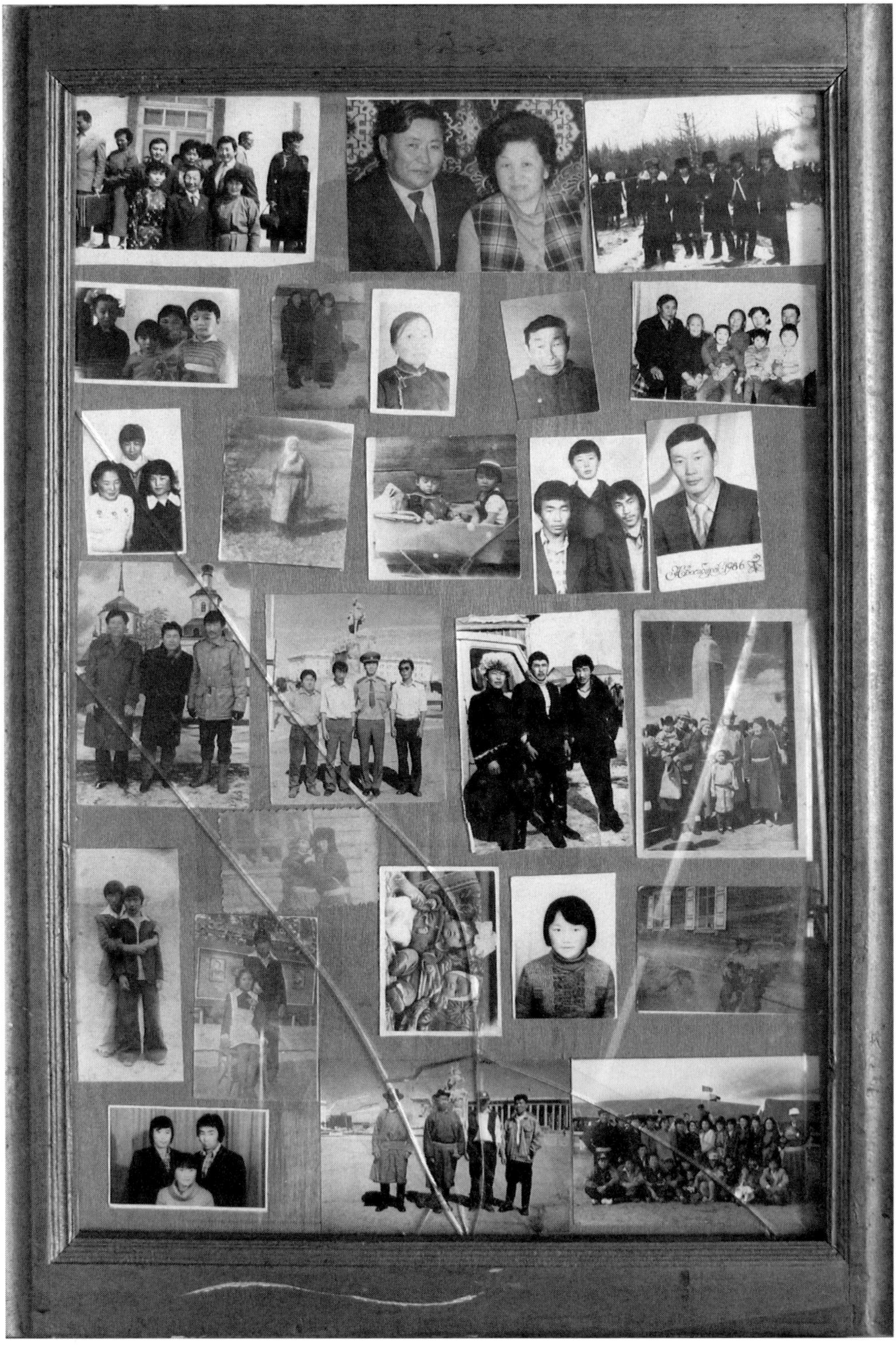
1986

which line the inside walls of people's homes, or memory books which can be found neatly bound in bundles of material inside the household chest. These media all point to alternative subjectivities and networks. They do not simply represent or evoke memories of people who are absent. In many cases, they are held to contain some capacity or force of these people that motivates those who live in their vicinity to respond to them in very particular ways.

In this short visual essay I have drawn attention to the way in which households contain multiple people, even in their physical absence. Due to experiences of migration, political persecution, and current seasonal forms of migration, people enact a host of different relationships with those whom they do not live in close proximity. Their physical absence is not felt so harshly. As long as some part or piece of them can be tended to inside the home their distance becomes manageable. Focusing on this constellation of human and non-human forms (such as houses, objects, and its inhabitants) we may say that they form a kind of mobile 'biodiversity' or 'ecology', an assemblage that moves through the landscape and is reconstituted in different places.

It is important to note the intense flexibility and malleability of this form. People foreground or hide images and objects in strategic ways to display very particular images of themselves to others. They play on this variability as the house is reconstituted in different physical places throughout the year. While this may be the case for households and their interiors, I also suggest that it is the case for individual people. They shift and change in their relations with others as they move to different locations, inhabiting different households and places. In this sense we may talk of a particular subject coming into being through movement (either seasonal migration or through separation experienced through forms of persecution).

People live and act and feel in relation to the different forms that populate this landscape and they appear, sometimes unexpectedly, through them, animate and vocal and full of vitality. Interacting with them in this way weaves together a shelter, a home, and a place that is familiar despite experiences of separation. Here persons are constituted through myriad social experiences. Through these experiences they are made and remade, forming, in turn, their own sites of memory, moral judgement, history, and action. This process is both disruptive and coherent. It may come together at one place and is erased in the next. In this movement, it gives rise to new subjects while leaving a path of different relations and encounters in its wake.

Note

1 I have argued elsewhere that photographic montages may be viewed as a modern take on Buriad genealogies (see Empson 2011).

Works cited and consulted

Atwood, C.P. (2004) *Encyclopedia of Mongolia and the Mongol Empire*, New York: Facts on File.

Biehl, J., Good, B. and Kleinman, A. (eds) (2007) *Subjectivity: Ethnographic Investigations*, London: University of California Press.

Empson, R. (2011) *Harnessing Fortune: Personhood, Memory and Place in Mongolia*, Oxford: Oxford University Press.

Humphrey, C. (1974) 'Inside a Mongolian tent', *New Society*, 31: 273–5.

Rawson, J. (2007) 'The agency of, and the agency for, the Wanli Emperor', in R. Osborne and J. Tanner (eds) *Art's Agency and Art History*, Oxford: Blackwell.

Sneath, D. (2000) *Changing Inner Mongolia: Pastoral Mongolian Society and the Chinese state*, Oxford: Oxford University Press.

Sontag, S. (1979) *On Photography*, Harmondsworth: Penguin.

Chapter 15

Gardeners of commons, *for the most part, women*

Doina Petrescu

The question of the *commons* is at the heart of current discussions about democracy.[1] In some of their recent texts, Michael Hardt and Antonio Negri define the commons as something which is not discovered but produced:

> We call 'biopolitical production' the current dominant model to underline the fact that it involves not only a material production in straight economic terms, but also it affects and contributes to produce all other aspects of social life: i.e. economic, cultural and political. This biopolitical production and the increased commons that it creates, support the possibility of democracy today.
>
> (Hardt and Negri 2004: 9–10)

A sustainable democracy should be based on a long-term politics of the commons but also on social solidarities understood as commons. 'Creating value today is about networking subjectivities and capturing, diverting, appropriating what they do with the commons that they began' (Negri and Ravel 2007: 7).

According to Negri, the contemporary revolutionary project is concerned with capturing, diverting, appropriating and reclaiming the commons is a constituent process. At the same time, it is a re-appropriation and a reinvention. This undertaking needs new categories and new institutions, new forms of management and governance, and new spaces and actors – an entire infrastructure that is both material and virtual. Setting up this infrastructure is a relational process: it is the creation of connections and links, a networking of concepts, tools and subjectivities. This networking should be itself a form of 'commons': accessible, fair, sustainable and so on. The reinvention of the commons needs space and time for sharing;[2] it needs continual and sustained 'commoning': that is, the production of social processes to reinvent, maintain and reproduce the commons.[3] It also needs specific agencies and the contribution of active subjects – agents – to instigate and carefully engineer this process. It is this re-appropriation and reinvention that interests me in this chapter together with its different agencies and agents. I would also like to add to the current discussion on the commons, a gendered perspective and a more situated and critical reframing, based on personal experience and practice of commoning. I will also bring the perspective of an architect and citizen involved in projects that instigate new forms of commons. Sustaining and designing commons is a challenge for architects today: designing as commoning, designing for sharing, designing collectively, accessibly in such a way that design is not perceived as a privilege and a commodity any more, it does not segregate and exclude but assemble, socialise and eventually politicise.

I'll take as example a few instances from my experience with the *atelier d'architecture autogérée* (aaa).[4] We have developed a collective practice that encourages local residents to participate in the reappropriation and self-managed use of space in the city. For us, as architects, the revival of the commons passes through a tactical reappropriation and a collective investment of immediately accessible spaces in order to invent new forms of property and shared living that are more ethical and more ecological. We have identified a particular type of space – urban interstices, leftovers and wastelands – as a possible common territory and as a new, specifically urban form of commons.[5] These are commons that are reclaimed and reinvented in fragments, through small abandoned or unused spaces that by their temporary and uncertain nature have, until now, resisted land speculation. These forms of spatial commons contribute to the reinvention of other social, cultural and environmental commons.

We have initiated self-managed spaces such as gardens or mobile facilities where those who take part can see and test the creation of their relationships with others, the effects of their actions, where they can use rather than possess, explore ways of sharing, and take responsibility towards what is shared. They are, as Félix Guattari puts it, 'local hotbeds of collective subjectification' (Guattari 1977: 56).

We have initiated processes – spatial, social or cultural approaches – that lead to other processes – political or emotional experiences – generated this time by the collectives that form around these spaces. These processes produce a new collective subjectivity that is local, relational and differential, at the same time as a common infrastructure. Our projects propose a wider understanding of architecture, above and beyond buildings and physical space, affirming its multiple forms based on social relationships and new forms of collaboration that develop the active participation and conduct of users to their gradual transformation into stakeholders.

For the most part, women

I have written about our practice on a number of occasions (Petcou and Petrescu 2005, 2007), and I will mention it again in this context to introduce the work of certain participants in our projects – *for the most part, women* – work I would not identify immediately as 'feminist', but rather as 'relational'. These actively involved participants, these agents – 'for the most part, women' – were essential to the creation of the collective subject within the process of reinventing the commons in our projects. These observations, based on the concrete evidence of experience, as well as data and facts related to our projects, support the hypothesis that a reinvention of the commons is a work of the relational and the 'differential' in which feminine subjectivity has an active role to play; that this work needs both specific spaces to take place – active spaces – as well as active people, agents, stakeholders of this reinvention.

The agents of this 'reinvention of the commons' who, in our projects, are *for the most part women* form a collective, elliptic subject, one that is indeterminate and unstable and does not belong to a single gender but is nevertheless defined by sexual difference, as long as it is constructed by reference to 'women'. To be considered, this subject needs a sort of 'realist essentialism' (Stone 2006),[6] an essentialism whose statements are based on unmediated experience and long-term observation. *For the most part, women*: a provisional, partial collective subject, not quite homogenous not quite heterogeneous, 'feminine' and possibly 'feminist' but without guarantee, evolving and changing continually.

As such, the imagining of a collective subjectivity that reinvents the commons requires the mobilisation of feminist knowledge, such as Luce Irigaray's work on *l'être-en-relation* (of women) and on sexual difference as a fundamental articulation of our relation with nature and culture (Irigaray 2004).[7] To link these feminist positions and the contemporary discussion on the 'relational', I am going to take the example of a certain type of agency in which the nature–culture relation is explicitly paralleled by a production of subjectivity and by processes of individual and collective becoming, which are necessarily gendered.

The 'relational'

The idea of the 'relational' took off in discussions in the late 1990s, notably in contemporary art after the publication of French art critic Nicolas Bourriaud's book on 'relational aesthetics' (Bourriaud 2002). Bourriaud used the term to speak about artworks in terms of the inter-human relations that they represent or create. He focused above all on the socialisation of the public by these works, while ignoring the spatial-temporal relations so created and the way that these relations can evolve, affect and be affected by space. He also ignored the ethical and political aspects of relationality and how a 'relational work' can transform its socio-spatial context.

We qualify our projects as 'relational' because they create connectivity; they stimulate desire and pleasure but also prompt political and civic responsibility on the local level, giving collectives of local residents the possibility of appropriating space in the city through daily activities (say, gardening, cooking, games or DIY). In fact, we understand spatial production as a collective process, which empowers architects and users alike. More than the spatial products themselves, we are interested in the processes they generate, in how they work and who they involve in their making and using. Rather than objects we design *agencies*.

Agency as activity

Sociologist Antony Giddens states first and foremost that agency 'presumes the capability of acting otherwise' (Giddens 1987: 216). In terms of architecture, this might involve that the architect and perhaps all other agents (i.e. users, clients or practitioners) have to engage *otherwise*, acting 'with intent and purpose' to create critical difference and take social responsibility (Schneider and Till 2009).

'Acting otherwise' translated for us into a way of getting engaged with the politics of the place in which we live and questioning the rules and regulations of current architectural and urban practice, introducing participatory approaches, promoting ways of working which are not, for example, 'service-led' or 'client-oriented'. If 'the potential of agency might first be understood as the power and freedom to act for oneself' and if, for an architect, this power usually means 'the power to act on behalf of others' (Schneider and Till 2009: 97–9) we have chosen instead to not act for ourselves or on behalf of others but to act *with* others, by empowering them to become agents themselves and to take collective responsibility. We valorise in this way the contribution of the *other* in this *otherwise* acting of our architectural agency.

In addition to definitions of agency as 'ends-oriented and means-oriented action', Scott Lash suggests also the notion of 'activity': 'Activity is much less goal-directed, it is much more situational. It's like Situationism in a way: you put yourself down anywhere, and see where it takes you' (Lash *et al.* 2009: 8).

The notion of activity is at the heart of our projects. Rather than an elitist profession-centred or a specialist conception of space, we have put architecture down to become an 'activity' shared with the users of our projects. We shared the knowledge necessary for the appropriation of space, the conception and management of architecture, a principle which conducts to what we call 'architecture autogérée' (self-managed architecture).[8] Instigating activities we consequently challenged the users of our projects to take active positions. The spatial transformation somehow generated transformations within the users themselves and changed their motivations and their engagement. We noticed that not all users were involved in the same way in the spatial transformation, nor they were ready for changing themselves in the same way.

'Gardening agency'

One of the most important activities that tactically drove this process was 'gardening', which started as a simple leisure activity and became a complex agency, involving other activities and networks: a 'gardening agency'. All our projects included, among other things, collective gardens understood as tools of a democratic agency of space: an agency by proximity, favourable to exchange, mobile and cyclical, anchored in the everyday and based on ethics of care (Petcou and Petrescu 2007). The 'gardening' attribute of this agency is both metaphoric and metonymic, qualifying all the processes and relations constructed though the project in a direct relation with nature and culture. The gardening agency involves large-scale environmental processes while also being adapted to small-scale, quotidian uses and practices. This way of acting through 'gardening agency' can produce, over time, a constituent space for collective modes of functioning and political action; it generates commoning practices.

We realised after a while that the most active 'gardening' agents in our projects were, as mentioned, *for the most part, women*. Not only because they were stakeholders in the gardening processes – that they were gardeners in the strict sense of the word – but also because they invested and maintained with care; they 'gardened' the infrastructure of the shared project and worked the project's shared space and time.

This is not because they have more time than others – for example, time for unpaid minor volunteer activities – but above all because they see an importance in these activities, as well as their political, ethical and environmental impact. We have realised that the kind of projects we do opens up a space in which feminine subjectivity finds its area of creativity and innovation:

projects that are cared for, engaged in and in which you see the results of your engagements with others, projects that teach patience, silence and attention. As Irigaray has noted in her recent work (Irigaray 2001, 2002, 2008), *women, for the most part*, have complex availability and motivations, both ontological and ecological, in developing 'sustainable' relations on a number of levels: with themselves and among themselves, between them and others, between them, others and the built and natural environment on local and global levels, between nature and culture in general, between spaces and ways of living.

Être-en-relation

Irigaray began talking about feminine subjectivity and its *être-en-relation*, its capacity to be-in-relation, in the 1970s. This idea of feminine subjectivity took a new twist in the 1990s with Rosi Braidotti's work on 'nomadic' subjectivity (Braidotti 1994) and Judith Butler's on 'performative' subjectivity (Butler 1990). Despite the large differences in position, all three have understood a particular capacity of the female subject to make herself 'available', to devote herself to and allow herself to be affected by different agencies at once (say, social, cultural, political, sexual and emotional) to create relations and be transformed by relations.

In our projects, most of the women came first to garden and after a number of years of activity began to take on responsibilities in the group, sometimes becoming engaged citizens and arriving on the 'edges of the political', to borrow Jacques Rancière's syntagm (Rancière 1988). Their personal transformation and their subjectivity re-construction was part of both the construction of the group and the processes that made up the project. These trajectories coming together led to gentle 're-territorializations' of the projects, generated 'lines of flight' heading towards certain types of activity and use that have become collective, towards moments of collective enunciation.

Most of the women were part of different micro-networks (friendship, shared time, self-building, production, dissemination and so on) and their involvement evolved over time. They became agents of different agencies, 'nodes' in the projects' branches of networks. Through this multiple and evolving affiliation, they created differentiations, relational shifts – and decisively influenced the future of the collective project.

Rancière has remarked that the collective allows a subject that thinks of itself in relation to others to appear: 'The formation of a one that is not a self, but the relation of a self to another' (Rancière 1988: 87). And, to follow Irigaray, I would say that even before the collective exists, these are subjects already in a position of opening towards others, in a relation with the other not yet there – 'beings-in-relation' who will initiate in the first place a collective *agency*. The gardener has this knowledge when she finds herself faced with a field that has not yet been tilled, or a garden that has not yet been planted. She knows how to open a shared space – a 'third space', as Irigaray would say – a space in which the other (person, plant or animal) can come with his or her own space. The gardener knows how to let herself be transformed by this relation, knows how to work the space she shares with others, the 'third space', criss-crossed by relations and networks.

It is a specific form of relationality that both de-territorialises and re-territorialises. Most women have taken part in the invention of new activities and processes in our projects, spaces and active processes, new objects of the commons (mobile facilities, such as a library, kitchen or a participatory urban laboratory, debates, flea markets and other forms of alternative economy in ECObox or ecological processes, such as dry toilets, water collectors and green roofing at Passage 56 in Saint-Blaise neighbourhood).

'Making a rhizome'

Our role as architects has been to develop, sometimes initiate, then support and prop up the networks that emerge around the different activities, spatial systems, processes and effects that allow both personal futures and collective futures, so as to seize the socio-spatial entity that arises, moves continuously, and forms new networks. In this process, our role as initiators and agents has to diminish progressively until its eventual disappearance, while at the same time the network's capacity to develop and reproduce grows. Others have then to take on the role of network gardeners. These networks of action and affection – mechanisms of democratic spatial construction – are necessarily rhizomatic, playing on proximity, the temporal and multiplicity.

ECObox, for example, has been moved and reinstalled several times by users, and the organisational and occupational systems have been reproduced in other independent initiatives (whether citizen-based or professional) in the neighbourhood and elsewhere. We call this a rhizomatic transmission – in which the prototype has the capacity to transmit all the information necessary for its reproduction, and where the product of this transmission – the reproduction of the prototype – becomes itself a new transmission source of the information, whether independently or in a chosen relation to the original prototype. These projects' existence in different sites may only be temporary, yet the accumulation of knowledge through experience is nevertheless passed on and is reproduced in new projects that, while being new and original, carry the torch and the continuation of the same model, a similar protocol and process.

'Making a rhizome' is a way of constructing the infrastructure of the commons, a way of commoning. And, once again, it is for the most part, women, who are involved in launching and maintaining these active lines, these rhizome stalks.

As Anne Querrien has pointed out in an article about Guattari's schizoanalytical mapping, 'the rhizome' – a central idea in Deleuze and Guattari's thinking – is an:

> idea that adds to that of the network – on top of those of horizontality and gradual construction – an underground dimension and a re-emergence that can be an illusion, a make-believe of a single stalk, while it is about a whole, an ensemble. Making a rhizome is about going towards the other, not as an enemy or a competitor with the idea of destruction, but in the perspective of an alliance and the construction of a temporary micro-territoriality that will soon after be shared with others, by the new offshoots of the rhizome.
>
> (Querrien 2008: 115)

In the process behind our projects, the role of rhizome gardener moves horizontally from one to another, from architects to users and users to other users.

Conviviality and resilience

So, in this *making a rhizome* of our projects, we have worked with those who were available and wanted to work in an invisible and underground alliance of 'little by little' propagation, who knew how to take into account time and cyclical nature, who had the patience to wait for it to grow and develop, who had both the knowledge of transmission and apprenticeship. Ivan Ilitch talks of conviviality as an alternative to capitalist production: 'Conviviality is opposed to productivity … productivity is conjugated with "to have"; conviviality with "to be"' (Ilitch 1973: 43).

A relational and co-operative practice, such as the one we have developed, has a different temporality and a different aim to those of a neo-liberal practice: rather than looking for a material value of profit, it creates the conditions for a liberating experience that changes both the space and the subjects.

Bruno Latour's analysis of the 'social' in his Actor Network Theory (ANT) mentions the active elements that human and non-human actors share and that take on the role of 'mediators': they transport, translate and transform the content and the nature of the network's links (Latour 2005: 204–5). Just like the 'gardeners', our socio-spatial and ecological devices have played the role of 'mediators' in the 'making a rhizome' of the project. For example, the mobile device for an urban kitchen was used very successfully by African women to open out into a functional kitchen space in chosen places and attract the most diverse cross section of users to the project, with their individual knowledge and motivations; it also connected the garden with other spaces in the neigh-bourhood and imagined spaces suggested by the recipes and ingredients that were used. Certain users, *for the most part, women*, also invented other 'mediators': a shared library, flea markets, artisan markets and so on. These mediators influenced and differentiated the nature of the project. We thus moved from gardening dominant activities and the free-use of time towards cultural, political and poetic production and distribution. These agent-users suggested new economic forms, which stressed personal exchange, reciprocity and giving (for example, 'honesty stalls', flea markets and 'feminine' knowledge exchanges at ECObox and communal picnics, teas and film projections at Passage 56).

Latour also mentions 'plug-ins' as tools that can help create and reveal agencies. He uses the analogy of these bits of software that, once installed in the system, make active what could not be seen before – plug-ins make visible what was before simply virtual. They can also make someone do something (Latour 2005: 207). Together with other tactical systems, we began mapping the project's relational processes that had acted like plug-ins; an activity that was added to the project to help us make visible to and discuss with others the facts and things that would have otherwise remained invisible and non-artic-ulated (for example, the evolving roles of a person or a system, the changes in the motivations of certain users, transformation in use and so on). By learning the importance of these aspects, we began to work with them and consider them active components of our projects. It was this mapping that revealed the structural role of *women, for the most part* in the project. This mapping also allowed us to understand the entirety of the relations as the project's social and political ecology.

The network of actors and general activities also forms ecological cycles in Guattari's sense: social, environmental and mental (Guattari 2000). These activities (such as gardening, DIY construction and recycling) were developed from daily cycles that link in time people, the things at stake and spaces through shared interests and friendships. The space was thus linked to a network of users by daily cycles, which transformed it and made it more dynamic and reactive to changes. Indeed, these networks are forms of resilience within the project. In this context, resilience is understood not only as adaption and thriving in changing circumstances, but as the opportunity for transformation and reinvention, knowing that this process has to take place at micro scale with each individual, each subjectivity in order to have effects at bigger scales.[9] Resilience takes a political dimension in our projects being related to practices of commoning. We believe that these processes are not possible without the active mediation of women.

These convivial agents, *women, for the most part*, are carriers of a soft and resilient revolution; they are 'those who make a rhizome' and

Figures 15.1–2
Self-organised organic food distribution at Passage 56, an urban eco-interstice initiated by *atelier d'architecture autogérée* and currently run by inhabitants of the St. Blaise area.

(re)conquer the city's territories by alliances and not by war, by transforming them into new forms of the commons, into shared spaces and temporalities. They are those who sometimes initiate and maintain – without any demands or need of gratitude – the infrastructure and ecological work of the commons. They are the humble gardeners of a rhizomatic reconstruction of democracy in times of change and resilience.

Notes

1 This text is a revised and extended version of a text published in French in the 'majeure' of the journal *Multitudes*, 42 (Petrescu 2010). The English translation of this text by Tom Ridgway has been amended and completed by the author.

2 See our discussion with Antonio Negri in *Multitudes* 31 (Negri *et al.* 2007).

3 In his definition of the commons, Massimo de Angelis underlines the importance of three elements: a non-commodified common pool of resources, a community to sustain and create commons, and the process of 'commoning' that binds the community and the resources together. This third term is almost the most important for understanding the commons, in Massimo's opinion (An Arkitektur 2010).

4 *atelier d'architecture autogérée* (*aaa*) was founded by Constantin Petcou and Doina Petrescu in 2001 as a collective platform to conduct explorations, actions and research concerning urban mutations and socio-political practices in the city. *aaa* acts through 'urban tactics' by encouraging inhabitants to occupy and manage disused urban spaces, engage in nomad and reversible projects and initiate collective practices (www.urbantactics.org).

5 The 'commons' traditionally defined common pool resources – usually forests, atmosphere, rivers or pastures – of which the management and use was shared by the members of a community. They were spaces that no one could own but everyone could use. The term has now been enlarged to include all resources (whether material or virtual) that are collectively shared by a population.

6 I echo here Peg Rawes's paper, 'Building sexuate architectures of sustainability', which considers Alison Stone's term 'realist essentialism' describing Luce Irigaray's approach in her later work. Stone writes:

> By 'realism', I mean the view that we can know about the world as it is independently of our practices and modes of representation. I therefore understand a realist form of essentialism to consist of the view that male and female bodies can be known to have essentially different characters, different characters which really exist, independently of how we represent and culturally inhabit these bodies. Realist essentialism, then, can equally be expressed as the view that natural differences exist, prior to our cultural activities.
>
> (Stone 2006: 18–19; cited in Rawes 2009)

7 Peg Rawes notes that the relationship between sex, nature and culture is one of ontological significance in Irigaray's work. 'Without working through this relation from the very beginning' – Irigaray argues – 'we cannot succeed in entering into relation with all kinds of other, not even with the same as ourselves' (Irigaray 2004: x; quoted in Rawes 2009). Rawes notes that for Irigaray, it is through sexuate difference that 'real sexed and ethical relations (i.e. relationships as "ecologies") can be actualized in cultural and natural environments'. She concludes that sexual difference should consequently mark all critical thinking of sustainable environments, management of natural resources and the development of space – a line that I will also follow in my chapter.

8 *Autogéstion* is a word that has a particular significance in French political history, referring directly to the ideological struggles and anti-statist social movements of the nineteenth

century, and to the idea of 'workers' control'. Following other thinkers like Lefebvre, Castoriadis, Gullierm, we were fully aware of this meaning, but in our case, the figure of the 'worker' is replaced by that of 'inhabitant' or 'user'. According to Negri, within the contemporary condition, the city has replaced the 'factory' as place of predilection for social production. *atelier d'architecture autogérée* promotes a kind of architecture in which the 'inhabitant', or the 'city user' plays a central role in the social production. For us, 'architecture autogérée' is an architecture which enables the 'users' to appropriate space in the city and take control of its organisation and management.

9   As Rob Hopkins puts it: 'Resilience is not just an outer process: it is also an inner one, of becoming more flexible, robust and skilled' (Hopkins 2010). Resilience includes processes of re-skilling, skills-sharing, building social networks, learning from others, learning from other experiences. These micro-social and micro-cultural practices are most of the time related to lifestyles and individual gestures; they prompt attention to details, to singularities, to the capacity of creativity and innovation that operates at the level of everyday life.

Bibliography

An Arkitektur (2010) 'On the commons: a public interview with Massimo de Angelis and Stavros Stavrides', in *e-flux* journal 17, June–August. Online: http://www.e-flux.com/journal/on-the-commons-a-public-interview-with-massimo-de-angelis-and-stavros-stavrides/ (accessed 15 October 2011).

Bourriaud, N. (2002) *Relational Aesthetics*, Dijon: Les presses du réel.

Braidotti, R. (1994) *Nomadic Subjects*, New York: Columbia University Press.

Butler, J. (1990) *Gender Trouble: Feminism and the Subversion of Identity*, London: Routledge.

Giddens, A. (1987) *Social Theory and Modern Sociology*, Cambridge: Polity.

Guattari, F. ([1977] 1980) *La Révolution Moléculaire*, Paris: Edition Recherches.

—— (2000) *The Three Ecologies*, trans. I. Pindar and P. Sutton, London: Continuum.

Hardt, M., and Negri, A. (2004) *Multitude, Guerre et Démocratie à l'Âge de l'Empire*, Paris: La Découverte.

Hopkins, R. (2010) 'Building resilience: what communities can do?' in R. Heinberg and D. Lerch (eds) *The Post Carbon Reader. Managing the 21st Century's Sustainability Crises*, Healdsburg, CA: Watershed Media and the Post Carbon Institute. Online: http://www.postcarbon.org/report/133875-building-resilience-what-can-communities-do (accessed 4 January 2012).

Ilitch, I. (1973) *La Convivialité*, Paris: Seuil.

Irigaray, L. (2001) *To Be Two*, New York: Routledge.

—— (2002) *The Way of Love*, New York: Continuum.

—— (2004) *Key Writings*, New York: Continuum.

—— (2008) *Sharing the World: From Intimate to Global Relations*, New York: Continuum.

Lash, S., Picon A., Cupers, K. and Doucet, I. (2009) 'Agency and architecture, how to be critical' in I. Doucet and K. Cupers (eds), *Beyond Discourse: Notes on Spatial Agency*, Footprint #4: Delft School of Design Journal, Spring, Delft.

Latour, B. (2005) *Reassembling the Social: an Introduction to Actor Network Theory*, Oxford: Oxford University Press.

Negri, A. and Ravel, J. (2007) 'Inventer le commun des hommes', in *Multitudes*, 31, Paris: Exils, 7–23.

Negri, A., Querrien A., Petcou C. and Petrescu D. (2007) 'Qu'est-ce qu'un espace biopolitique', in *Multitudes*, 31, Paris: Exils, 80–98.

Petcou, C. and Petrescu, D. (2005) 'Au rez de chaussee de la ville', in *Multitudes* 20, Paris: Exils, 75–82.

—— (2007) 'Agir l'espace: notes transversales, observations de terrain and questions concrètes pour chacun de nous', in *Multitudes*, 31, Paris: Exils, 100–24.

Petrescu, D. (2010) 'Jardinieres du commun', in *Multitudes* 42, Paris: Exils, 126–33.

Querrien, A. (2008) 'Les cartes et les ritournelles d'une panthère arc en ciel', in *Multitudes*, 34, Paris: Exils, 111–25.

Rancière, J. (1988) *Aux Bords du Politique*, Paris: La Fabrique.

Rawes, P. (2009) 'Building sexuate architectures of sustainability', paper at the Luce Irigaray Circle Conference, Hofstra, NY.

Schneider, T. and Till, J. (2009) 'Beyond discourse: notes on spatial agency', *Footprint #4: Delft School of Design Journal*, Spring, Delft, 97–111.

Stone, A. (2006) *Luce Irigaray and the Philosophy of Sexual Difference*, Cambridge: Cambridge University Press.

Chapter 16

The ecological relation

Verena Andermatt Conley

Ecology is often said to be a domain of study where technocrats take care of carbon dioxide emissions, turn ever-growing piles of garbage into sources of renewable energy, and devise means of reducing the growing acidification of the oceans. New technologies are awaited to remedy all ills independently of how humans choose to domesticate the earth. Others, such as Félix Guattari, the philosopher and psychiatrist of the generation of 1968, contend that we first have to change our ways of thinking and, in an engaging formulation of his own signature, of being in the singular or in a group in order to address problems of nature. I will take another retrospective (and, hopefully, prospective) look at Guattari's revolutionary essay, *The Three Ecologies* (2000; *Les Trois Écologies*, 1989) by bringing attention to singular and group subjects and, given the theme of this volume, to architecture both in a concrete and metaphorical sense.

Refining simplistic technocratic ways of addressing current dilemmas, Guattari urged his readers to distinguish between mental, social and natural ecologies. Critical not only of an ecology imposed by technocrats but also of another advocated by 'folkloristic nature lovers' whom he derided for calling for a return to simpler ways of living, Guattari argued that humans must analyse the world from today's conditions that include global markets, urban financial centres, intercontinental air travel, rapid transportation in cities, and innovations in the electronic sphere. In view of its accelerating transformation, they had, in turn, to reorient its inherited meaning. He used the term ecology in the sense of *oikos*, or house, that is, of exchanging, of inhabiting or organizing one's world. Written over two decades ago, his 'manifesto' advocated that with the waning of the East–West conflict, 'we' in the industrialized world are now free to turn toward problems that had been running along a North–South axis so as to address extreme economic imbalances still largely under the impact of colonialism. To correct current injustice Guattari began by decrying the lethal condition of Western subjects, under the influence of the media and consumerism, who are infantilized and reduced to largely immobile, 'molar' aggregates. The status of the subject, he declared, 'is not a straightforward matter' (Guattari 2000: 35). Structuralism and post-structuralism had habituated us to do without the individual subject in any concrete way. It now had to be rethought. Yet, he added, we cannot simply revert to phenomenology and to the idea of Sartre's full historical subject that would act unimpeded on an object.

Weary of the post-war communist adventure in France during which members held firm and unquestioned allegiance to a political party, Guattari was cautious about militantism. While he recognized that, at times, people must behave like 'good little soldiers', such militancy could only be temporary. People gathered to militate for specific causes – be it those of women, gays, other minorities or causes such as ecology – only to resingularize and become inventive along what he called an aesthetic dimension. Invention was vital for mental and social ecology. Yet, by quoting Gregory Bateson in an epigraph, 'There is an ecology of bad ideas just as there is an ecology of weeds' (19), Guattari reminded us that inventions can be both beneficial and nefarious. Inventions have to include an ethical component that calls for subjects assuming the responsibility of their thoughts and actions.

Unlike many of his French counterparts, in the wake of an essay by Martin Heidegger, who condemned advanced technologies, Guattari welcomed the latter for their creative potential that promises a freeing of humans from tedium and degradation. He did, however, criticize wholesale deployment of technologies in a market-driven society that acts without responsibility and for profit alone. In 1989, that is, before massification of outsourcing, Guattari noted that technologies in the industrialized world often only served to increase unemployment. People were either excluded from a market society or, if included, they were, for the most part, under the yoke of senseless consumerism. To replace capitalism's dictate of profit and consumption, Guattari proposed an *ecosophy*, a wisdom of the *oikos* that would enable humans to construct and inhabit the world in better ways, both for their own enjoyment and for that of others.

By way of what he called a generalized ecosophy, Guattari argued that it is only on condition of reconstructing the subject and improving social relations that one can begin to tackle natural ecology. Writing during the heyday of postmodernism and the apparent triumph of liberal democracy after the fall of the Iron Curtain, Guattari deplored the loss of the subject as well as the deterioration of other social links, from those of the family and friends to those of neighbourhoods. A generalized apathy toward others prevails, he said, be they human or non-human. To reconstruct the subject, or as he himself put it, to reinvent ways of engendering new subjectivities or *components of subjectification*, Guattari sought to be done with liberal democracy that, with help of the media, eradicated singularity and *dissensus* in favour of consensus and sameness, the agent of stifling molecular movement and change in every possible domain. A desire to consume had been imposed through ever more pervasive and, in Guattari's view, pernicious advertisement that invaded and controlled the very core of the self. When inoculated with massive doses of consumerism, he argued that humans lose their desire to create new maps of enquiry and to experiment with other ways of being in common in the world at large.

To counter this sorry state of affairs, he continued, we need to help humans unblock their exit roads and create *existential territories*. The latter, defined by consistency, intensity and a certain psychic depth, could be mental or physical. Guattari did not envisage going beyond a Freudian model of the psyche. Rather, he wished to refashion the latter. Historicizing the psychoanalytic project whose emphasis had been on sexuality, childhood and neuroses, he showed that other models of engendering subjectivity had existed – from Greek tragedy to courtly love – and others yet will follow it. Though he noted that we still operate within a distant Freudian paradigm, Guattari vigorously criticized any emphasis on pre-structuralist attachments – such as those underlying the Oedipal complex that continued to be cultivated by much institutional psychoanalysis. Long before, with Gilles Deleuze, he had argued in *Anti-Oedipus* that this type of psychoanalysis always finds in humans what its enthusiasts are looking for, that is, a reductive Oedipal fantasy. Institutional psychoanalysts were reinforcing the Oedipal scenario the way the French like to enclose their gardens in geometrical borders. For Guattari, such pre-traced forms prevented humans from inventing new forms of subjectivity. Ecological relations cannot be addressed without the creation of existential territories that humans can inhabit. Here Guattari was resolutely futuristic: condemning a psychoanalysis based on past events it retrieved for its own ends and invested in archaic fixation in all domains of the psyche, he felt that everything had to be begun anew over and again. An existential *tension* had to replace a phenomenological *intention*.

Brushing aside an older Marxist distinction between infrastructure and superstructure, Guattari claimed that today the world is composed mainly of four regimes of signs: economic, juridical, scientific and that of subjectification. They are all intertwined and interchangeable even if some – such as economics – are more prevalent in today's world. As a philosopher and a clinical psychoanalyst Guattari himself focused on the regime of subjectification – in the singular or a group – that also includes people working in related fields, such as education, architecture, urban planning, art, fashion, music, food or sports. All those who work in these fields are implicated directly or indirectly in the production of subjectivities: the psychoanalytical Guattari claimed that their discourse is never neutral and that with their interlocutors they always maintain a relation of transference. Therefore, they have an ethical responsibility toward themselves and others. There Guattari nodded to Bateson to remind his readers that one speaks and writes in and from a context based on an ecology of ideas that circulate much beyond the individual.

Were Guattari alive, he would say that we live in a world of molar aggregates in which dissident voices and differences have been reduced to a minimum; that traditionally subversive domains have been affected negatively; that under the spell of money, much art is no longer creative but has simply taken on the role of a 'vitaminic function' (Guattari 1992: 127). Those who work in the domain of subjectivity would have again to drive a wedge that would open, in Deleuze's parlance, a *vacuole* (Deleuze 1995: 176), a space for resistance from which new thoughts can be created. They would need to speak and act so that something *se met en travers* (begins to move crosswise) and at the same time opens a new space from which to think and make novel connections. On this point Guattari, critical of Bateson who reduced the circulation of ideas entirely to context, argued for an autopoiesis of the subject, for an apprehension both of the subject and the object and a *dis-positional mise-en-scène* (Guattari 2000: 37). While Guattari may have been overstating the autopoietic capacity of the subject in his striving toward invention that guarantees the smooth functioning of mental ecology, in today's context the claim need not be rejected. A spontaneous actualization of what is virtual (or, Guattari put the term in the plural nominative, *virtuals*) is always possible. Yet even more importantly for our purposes, the 'operators' in Guattari's terms who deal with regimes of subjectivity and subjectification have the responsibility of inventing new territories, of tracing new maps and diagrams while prodding their students and apprentices to do the same. The latter are called upon to imitate and, in turn, to deviate from the 'masters' – rather than oppose them in Oedipal fashion – so as to invent new territories (45).

We could follow Guattari's diagrams further to see how his findings translate today into social ecology in various domains such as sport, fashion or food. Nowhere is there seemingly more sameness than in today's sporting events where large crowds are made to behave in the same way. In fashion, consumers pay increasing sums of money to all 'shop this look'. Consumers must be made aware that in order to produce a stylish look, many people have to work knowingly in hazardous conditions – such as in China where workers dip their hands in deadly chemicals to dye blue jeans destined for the rest of the world. We must be made aware too that products, such as cotton, are often grown in unsuitable terrains that are artificially irrigated at high cost. The same can be said about food production where certain practices reduce diversity and create health and environmental problems for producers and consumers. Other examples abound. Given the theme of this volume, I will limit myself to education and architecture and its relation to urban planning.

Guattari worked at La Borde, a psychiatric clinic praised by the late Michel de Certeau for its affirmative techniques and therapies placing emphasis on invention and affirmation of life. Pedagogy was meant to show students how to invent a world rather than to reproduce it. Education would no longer be based on strictly utilitarian principles or on the regurgitation of existing knowledge. It would emphasize the creation of maps by way of an ecosophy that includes the arts as well as a science that recognizes its own narrative and temporal dimension. It would be both speculative *and* practical. Guattari made it clear: operators today have the obligation to help students reconstruct their own subjectivities so as to enable them to reorient a world that is headed in the wrong direction. They have to help rethink existing 'wrong' ideas and must urge students to take care of their *oikos*, their 'house' and even to find the world again (Deleuze 1995: 176). In *A Thousand Plateaus*, Deleuze and Guattari had argued that to think is to travel while to create is to resist and to open new spaces.

Today architects and urban planners have similar responsibilities. They have to engage theoretically and practically in an ecological urbanism that, while avoiding the narcissism that marks many postmodern architects, encourages reflection on how to inhabit a place by reconstructing the subject and its social bonds. These 'subjects' will hopefully reinvent the world in ways that are not purely utilitarian. Guattari's remarks about the responsibility of architects and urban planners are part of a standard critique of a certain modernist architecture and a failed urbanism emblematized by the *grands ensembles* in France that turned out to be dehumanizing for many inhabitants. People reside in these buildings without inhabiting them or being able to create existential territories.

Architects share the responsibility to create buildings and to reconstruct cities that will be habitable. They are enjoined to shift the emphasis from design to social practice. Before Guattari, Henri Lefebvre in *The Production of Space* (1991; *La Production de l'Espace*, 1974) and Michel de Certeau in *The Practice of Everyday Life* (1984; *L'Invention du Quotidien*, 1980) argued that architecture leads to spatial practices that control our subjectivities and ways of being in common. While Lefebvre called for reappropriating the city, Certeau, more poetically, pointed to the importance of alternative ways of creating habitable spaces, be they mental or physical. Guattari limited himself to telling architects that they have a responsibility toward their students and toward those who will live in the spaces they construct. He did not call for a return to the building of traditional (European) cities organized according to a centre and periphery. By coining the concept of the 'generic city' Rem Koolhaas (1995) has since shown, convincingly, that it is no longer necessary to construct spaces where, in the middle of an agglomeration, the church stands next to the Town Hall and market place, from which streets radiate to a distant and largely invisible periphery. This urban model established implicit and explicit social hierarchies and created a mental panopticon.

Yet the generic city cannot simply consist of *grands ensembles*, highways and shopping centres. The former foster isolation and crime while the latter produce mindless consumers. Guattari called upon architects to invent novel constructions that foster enjoyment and better ways of being in common. Today, visibly absent from his text is an emphasis on architecture in relation to natural ecologies, that is, to sustainability that was, when Guattari wrote the essay, most likely in its infancy. Though Slavoj Žižek (2008) and others have recently declared that 'sustainability' is part of a liberal ideology and corporatism, it can also be seen as necessary to help create habitable places in an ecological way in an urbanized world (Mostafavi and Doherty 2010). Cities are built in ways that no longer oppose aesthetics to social and natural ecological concerns. From an emphasis on more porous constructions to the increasingly popular greenways that offset pollution but also bring pleasure and enjoyment to everyday life while linking different and often socially diverse neighbourhoods. Examples can be drawn from Greenways in cities in China to reconverted former rail lines such as the elevated *La Promenade Plant*ée in Paris or The New York High Line but also to parks like the one reconfiguring a sensitive neighbourhood in Medellin, Colombia (Smith 2012: 24).

Guattari focused solely on questions of habitability by way of the 'opening' of new spaces from which to think and make novel connections.

He was adamant: operators, such as architects, cannot perpetuate existing conditions imposed by liberal democracies stifled by consensus. With reference to Sartre, in spite of his criticism of the philosopher's phenomenology elsewhere, Guattari urged for the reconstruction of the subject by denouncing an existing 'death-laden in itself'. He wanted to replace it with an unstable 'for itself', a fragile subject open both to itself and to the world at large. Such is the pre-condition that *The Three Ecologies* set in place for an optimal and desirable circulation of ideas and the making of connections. It was implied that the fragility of the subject can also be understood as the result of its contact with the natural environment: a subject is fragile because it is at risk from pollution, contamination and degradation. Guattari borrowed from Bateson only the notion of context and the circulation of ideas without touching upon another aspect in the anthropologist's reflections: that of the exchange between humans and environment. Bateson's 'eco-subjects' are in exchange with their environment, a dimension that is absent from Guattari's work.

The main question raised by the psychiatrist in 1989 is how to think creatively and to displace a residual East–West antagonism toward the erasure of injustices between North and South. He emphasized mental and social ecologies which he endowed with a philosophical inflection of his own. When discussing natural ecologies, Guattari mentioned an episode seen on French television. Alain Bombard, a presenter, put on display an octopus happily moving about in an aquarium filled with polluted water. The presenter then removed the octopus and plunged it in another basin filled with clean water. The octopus immediately folded up on itself and died. Guattari concluded somewhat hastily that the death of the octopus was symptomatic of the fact that the world has to be thought in and from its current state of pollution in which all creatures are supposed to thrive.

* * *

Since 1989, the world has declined further. How can we think mental, social and natural ecology today? How can we trace new diagrams? The world has witnessed an explosion of electronic technologies, social networks that have led to openings but also new closures. Advertising has been extended to include even ecological practices (Žižek 2010). The North–South conflict that Guattari wanted to see resolved has not abated. Former 'Third World' nations such as China, Brazil and others, including South Africa, are becoming nodal points. The economic crisis in the United States and in Europe has complicated Guattari's pronouncements. Fundamentalism is not quite so much the transient phenomenon as he had seen it. Terrorism has become widespread, while the impact of global warming and climate change has caused the number of eco-refugees to rise dramatically (Roy 1999).

To implement mental ecologies Guattari sought to open spaces that would enable new thoughts, alliances and connections. He joined an entire generation of French thinkers who focused on space at the very time when the traditional sense of the term became 'critical' and was put in question (Conley 2012). Technologies and acceleration introduced massive changes in the Western concept of space and time that had appeared to be stable for several hundred years. The 'cause' of the seeming compression (Harvey 1990) was first ascribed to the state before it became seen as part of an impending globalization. While Paul Virilio and others, in the wake of Heidegger, deplored the loss of more traditional spaces, others yet like Deleuze and Guattari and more recently, Bruno Latour and Étienne Balibar have looked for productive ways out of the gridlock. They all insist that we need to think from today's conditions, that is, those Paul Virilio described, but without the culture critic's negative turn. Guattari was sensitive to future computer-assisted subjectivities within the changes that he saw occurring through technologies many of which he was only anticipating. Though he cautioned about an information technology under the dictate of the binary digit, he also foresaw what he and Deleuze called new becomings. Avoiding binaries by way of an included middle, he strived to facilitate a generalized circulation of ideas and smoothing of space. He advocated ongoing de- and re-territorialization as well as the creation of existential territories that, as he made clear, do not have to be physical or be connected to a nation. In fact, for him, de-territorialization was to be practised where nationalism is rampant since, to follow his line of reasoning, the latter is always synonymous with molar aggregates and imperialism. Guattari's emphasis on de- and reterritorialization has not since been marshalled to address the necessity to create spaces in common between different nations, ethnic or religious groups and others defined by anthropological differences. He called for connections and alliances between heterogeneous subjects that could include people, things or partial components. Like Deleuze, he has now been criticized for creating a continuum that could too easily be associated with a 'capitalist hyper-space': in other words, not only circulation but also a certain 'situatedness' enters into every critical equation (Balibar 1998).

Through the making of connections, Guattari aimed to undo a Western universalism. Today, however, we can say that the world is made up of many different networks and universalities. The West's blind spot, as Bruno Latour argued, had been the emphasis on universal concepts such as nature that served as a backdrop to myriad cultures. By way of Isabelle Stengers (2010), Latour claims that humans live in different worlds that include many concepts of nature. In addition to the equation between natural, cultural and material goods decried by Guattari, another between democracy, technology, science and nature, can also be seen as part of a Western hegemony. Humans now live in many different worlds composed of nations but even more so of regions, cultures, religions or simply philosophies and ways of thinking.

If the twentieth century of Guattari's time had focused on the critique of universalism, the twenty-first of our own must come to terms with different universalities (Balibar 2010). In today's global era, people have to construct ways of being in common. Guattari urged subjects and group-subjects to construct 'equipment' aesthetically and ethically in order to undo the molar aggregates of nations and those under control of the media. If globalization is, at one level, the equivalent of homogenization, it has also, at another, brought to the fore an unsuspected diversity of singular and group constructions. Going beyond Guattari, we can now affirm that the latter more than ever have to engage in relations by way of translation and negotiation, the outcome of which is always uncertain. Nations themselves are composed of myriad networks – political parties, schools of thought of all kinds – that may or may not intersect. Even if humans aspire ultimately toward a borderless world, they are still defined by the state, by borders and travel with passports. They are not simply migrating masses; they ask for the right to move as well as to reside and to inhabit. An 'eco-subject' must also be a 'citizen-subject', to borrow a term coined by Étienne Balibar (1998), an individual who asks for a minimal existential territory that gives her or him the right to exist and without which it is difficult, even impossible, to invent new territories. Citizens do not have to be nationals to have the right to exist in a place whence to speak.

* * *

Where, in Guattari's ecosophy that tackles mental and social issues in transversal and relational terms, is natural ecology today? In *Steps to an Ecology of Mind* (1972) Bateson wrote that humans do not move and act against a 'natural' background. Rather, they are part of it. He reassessed nature that, far from that 'lifeworld' which Žižek (2008) justly condemns, is on the side of atomism and the *clinamen*, that is, ever-changing. Writing at the time of the discovery of cybernetics and complexity theories, Bateson strove to make humans part of their habitat. He developed the idea of feedback loops and argued that actions no matter how small can produce at times large, even delayed, effects often over a distance (his celebrated example being that of the butterfly that flaps its wings and produces a hurricane far away). Nature, ever in a dynamic equilibrium, reaches moments of bifurcation at which new orders emerge from chaos.

Guattari himself alluded to complexity theory of this stamp when he wrote that territories proliferate in conditions of disequilibrium. Applying the model to consumerism and the circulation of unmediated 'information', he advocated the creation of always unstable and uncertain existential territories that he deemed vital for creative thinking. Contrary to what happens in a world of information that suppresses any relation when speaking, writing or thinking from such territories, humans' narratives, he said, are part of their life. What interested Guattari were becomings, moments of bifurcation when a new order emerges in far from equilibrium conditions: a subjectivity in its nascent state, the social milieu in mutation and the environment in the process of being reinvented. However, when addressing natural ecology, he concurrently advocated massive recourse to technologies in order to deal with and even combat nature in disarray. For the reinvention of the environment, Guattari foresaw the necessity of huge investments into machines that would regulate the exchange of oxygen, ozone and carbon dioxide in the atmosphere. In his futuristic vision he urged readers to aim their war machines *against* nature so as to preserve human life. Arguing for the necessity of artificiality, Guattari declared that becomings are non-genealogical crossings over of sorts, on the side of the unnatural and even the monstrous. He wanted to replace natural ecology with 'machinic ecology', a technical science that would be responsible for helping life and for reversing the course that opposes nature to life. While Guattari thought the mastery over the mechanosphere to be transversal, in Bateson the connection 'Human + Human + Environment' was always relational.

In the domain of natural ecology, Guattari declared, anything is possible, from a supple evolution to the worst catastrophe. Yet, he added that because of demographics and techno-scientific 'progress' a *fuite en avant* (a flight forward) is necessary in order to *master* (emphasis mine) the mechano-sphere (Guattari 2000: 68). He saw it as necessary to change our position from a defence used by backward ecologists to an offensive against nature. This mastery that comes with the invention of new species would not only require the adoption of an ecosophical *ethics* adapted to this situation but a *politics* that focuses on the future of humanity. Guattari rarely mentions fauna and flora.

* * *

Guattari called for a new ecosophy, at once applied and theoretical, ethico-political and aesthetic, that would move away from the old forms of political, religious and associative commitment. Humans, he asserted, have to be analytically militant. 'We need new social and aesthetic practices, new practices of the Self in relation to the other, to the foreign, the strange – a whole program that seems far removed from current concerns' (2000: 68). Individuals live in solidarity yet they are different. The same re-singularization went for schools, architecture or urban planning. The reconquest of a degree of creative autonomy in one particular domain encouraged conquests in other domains – the catalyst for a gradual reforging and renewal of humanity's confidence in itself 'starting at the minuscule level' (69).

Almost fifteen years later we can say that the reconquest will at times be relational and, at others, in Guattari's own words, transversal. Yet, for Guattari, a relation is not simply a given. It was and is the task of operators in education or architecture to bring about new subjectivities and social mutations. The reconquest of nature, however, is always linked to the mastery of the mechanosphere, and it is only through the latter that humans can deal with 'nature'. While Guattari acknowledged the importance of relations in the domain of mental and social ecologies, he downplayed them whenever nature was concerned. Science and new technologies have shown, however, that it is impossible to simply dominate nature – even through the mechanosphere. Much of what had been done in this direction under wrong beliefs, beginning with the first scientific revolution of over three centuries ago, is now being undone. Simpler and more local technologies are used to restore wetlands, to bring back wildlife or to bring water to arid areas. The growing of ill-adapted crops such as cotton in arid areas is changed to more adaptable crops. One consequence of such relational thinking has enabled fish to return to the Aral Sea. Other felicitous examples abound.

* * *

To conclude, a review of Guattari's seminal essay shows how the author took salient account of how degradations in different areas – mental, social and natural – are interrelated. Today, in a fully urbanized and globalized world that is paradoxically less unified than in 1989, it remains to be seen how some of the psychiatrist's conclusions can be extended. First, Guattari's reconstruction of the subject was done from the standpoint of France and the First World: at the mental and social levels, it can be said that in a more globalized condition where many groups are living and moving, inherited models of domination no longer hold. If globalization is, at one level, the equivalent of homogenization, it has also, at another, brought to the fore an unsuspected diversity of singular and group constructions. Second, Guattari keenly remarked how one cannot simply go back to old political or associative ways of being. However, one cannot simply be done with them either. Today it is incumbent upon singular subjects or groups to engage more than ever in relations by way of translation and negotiation. They have to negotiate religious, symbolic and geopolitical issues as well as others pertaining to nature. The undoing of identitarian beliefs that Guattari had called urgent and necessary needs adumbration. Given that identity is always multiple, unstable and paradoxically enduring, in the midst of increasing numbers of relations and alliances in the contemporary world it is by nature plural and ungrounded. True cosmopolitanism is to be hoped for, but its advocates and practitioners who promote it still need a passport to peddle its virtues. In short, citizen-subjects have to complement eco-subjects.

At the same time, third, eco-subjects have to develop new sensibilities and other forms of intelligence by engaging in a direct relation with nature. While it is clear that few people today have a feeling of nature as they once did at the dawn of the nineteenth century, a relational mode of thinking, not that of mastery which Guattari had proposed, has the virtue of continually reassessing nature. Under the influence of the 1960s, Bateson and his fervent readers of the same generation had a somewhat utopian (and hence viably politicized) idea of nature. For that reason, as Sanford Kwinter recently argued, there is value in this decade to which Guattari also belonged (Mostafavi and Doherty 2010) because it favoured attention to the *oikos*. Although we can privilege the concept of transversality when dealing with the different registers of ecology as Guattari had outlined them, we must insist that humans' interaction with the world and nature continues to be relational in psychic and social senses alike. Awareness of fragility – which is relational where nature is concerned – raises consciousness of the interconnectedness of the world's components.

As in medicine, where more attention is given today to prevention and a holistic understanding of the body, so also in natural ecology, where its students look toward restoration of damage wrought by earlier excesses and prevention of their recurrence. Educators look for creative methods of coping with ecological dilemmas while architects work toward better-adapted constructions to minimize nefarious impacts on the ecosphere, such as, among many others, the urban greenways mentioned above. In this context, in being renewed and revived for our moment, Guattari's three ecologies will include eco-subjects and citizen-subjects who are in relation with each other and who take part in constructing a sustainable, ecological urbanism adapted to local and global ecologies in an entirely urbanized world.

Works cited and consulted

Balibar, É. (1998) *Droit de Cité*, Paris: Editions de l'Aube.
— (2010) *La Proposition de l'Égaliberté*, Paris: PUF.
Bateson, G. (1972) *Steps to an Ecology of Mind*, New York: Ballantine.
Certeau, M. de (1980) *L'Invention du Quotidien*, Paris: Bourgois.
— (1984) *The Practice of Everyday Life*, trans. S. Rendall, Minneapolis: University of Minnesota Press.
Conley, V.A. (1997) *Ecopolitics: the Environment in Poststructuralist Thought*, London: Routledge.
— (2012) *Spatial Ecologies: Urban Sites, State and World-Space in French Cultural Theory*, Liverpool: Liverpool University Press.
Deleuze, G. (1995) *Negotiations*, trans. M. Joughin, New York: Columbia University Press.
Deleuze, G. and Guattari, F. (1977) *Anti-Oedipus: Capitalism and Schizophrenia*, trans. R. Hurley, M. Seem and H.R. Lane, Minneapolis: University of Minnesota Press.
—(1987) *A Thousand Plateaus*, trans. B. Massumi, Minneapolis: University of Minnesota Press.
Guattari, F. (1989) *Les Trois Écologies*, Paris: Galilée.
— (1992) *Chaosmosis: an Ethico-Aesthetic Paradigm*, trans. P. Baine and J. Pefranis, Bloomington: Indiana University Press.
— (1993) 'Machinic heterogenesis', in V.A. Conley (ed.) *Rethinking Technologies*, Minneapolis: University of Minnesota Press.

— (2000) *The Three Ecologies*, trans. I. Pindar and P. Sutton, London: Athlone.

— (2008) 'Du postmoderne au postmédia', *Multitudes* 34: 128–33.

— (2011) *Lignes de Fuite: Pour un Autre Monde de Possible*s, La Tour d'Aigues: Aube.

Harvey, D. (1990) *The Condition of Postmodernity*, Cambridge, MA: Blackwell.

Herzogenrath, B. (ed.) (2009) *Deleuze/Guattari and Ecology*, New York: Palgrave Macmillan.

Koolhaas, R. and Mau, B. (1995) *S, M, L, XL*, New York: Monacelli Press.

Latour, B. (2002) *War of the Worlds: What About Peace*, trans. C. Bigg, Chicago: Prickly Paradigm Press.

— (2009) 'Spheres and networks: two ways to reinterpret globalization', *Harvard Design Magazine* 30 (Spring/Summer): 138–44.

Lefebvre, H. (1974) *La Production de l'Espace*, Paris: Anthropos.

— (1991) *The Production of Space*, trans. Donald Nicholson-Smith, Oxford: Blackwell.

Mostafavi, M. and Doherty, G. (eds) (2010) *Ecological Urbanism*, Baden, Switzerland: Lars Müller and Harvard University, Graduate School of Design.

Roy, A. (1999) *The Cost of Living*, New York: Modern Library.

Smith, P. (2012) 'A city rises along with its hopes', *The New York Times*, 18 May: 24.

Stengers, I. (2010) *Cosmopolitics*, Vol. 1, trans. R. Bonnono, Minneapolis: University of Minnesota Press.

Žižek, S. (2008) 'Nature and its discontents', *Substance* 117, 37, 3: 37–72.

— (2010) *Living in the End Times*, New York: Verso.

Illustration credits

Front Cover and Figures 2.1–3 copyright Agnes Denes, courtesy Leslie Tonkonow Artworks + Projects, New York.

Figure 3.1 Photograph: Nathan Moore.

Figure 6.1 Félix Trombe, Mont Louis, France, circa 1949. Photograph: Four Solaire Developpement.

Figure 6.2 Solar furnace at Vauban Fortress, Mont Louis, France. Photograph: David Cross 2011.

Figure 6.3 Self portrait with parabolic mirror, Mont Louis, France. Photograph: David Cross 2010.

Figure 6.4 Félix Trombe solar furnace, Odeillo-Font Romeu, France. Photograph: David Cross 2010.

Figure 6.5 Thémis solar power centre, Targassone, France. Photograph: David Cross 2010.

Figure 6.6 'Heliostat' mirrors and furnace, Thémis centre, Targassone, France. Photograph: David Cross 2010.

Figure 6.7 David Niven, Mylène Demongeot, Jean Seberg and Deborah Kerr in *Bonjour Tristesse*, directed by Otto Preminger. © 1958, Renewed 1986 Columbia Pictures Industries, Inc. All Rights Reserved. Courtesy of Columbia Pictures.

Figure 8.1 Raymond Pearl (1930) *The Biology of Population Growth*, New York: Alfred Knopf.

Figure 8.2 Raymond Pearl (1930) *The Biology of Population Growth*, New York: Alfred Knopf.

Figures 11.1–2 Katie Lloyd Thomas.

Figure 13.1 Photograph: Bronwyn Hayward.

Figure 13.2 University of Canterbury Student Volunteer Army, New Zealand.

Figures 14.1–7 All photographs from the northeast Mongolian–Russian border taken between 1999 and 2007 by Rebecca Empson. Copyright to the author.

Figures 15.1–2 Photographs: *atelier d'architecture autogérée*.

Figure 16.1 Photograph: Léa-Catherine Szacka.

Index

See individual chapter bibliographies for full author listings.